Framing Hijab in the Euroɪ

Ghufran Khir-Allah

Framing Hijab
in the European Mind

Press Discourse, Social Categorization
and Stereotypes

 Springer

Ghufran Khir-Allah
Faculty of Political Science and Sociology
Complutense University of Madrid
Madrid, Spain

Faculty of Languages and Education
Nebrija University of Madrid
Madrid, Spain

ISBN 978-981-16-1655-6   ISBN 978-981-16-1653-2   (eBook)
https://doi.org/10.1007/978-981-16-1653-2

This Springer imprint is published by the registered company Springer Nature Singapore Pte Ltd.
The registered company address is: 152 Beach Road, #21-01/04 Gateway East, Singapore 189721,
Singapore

Acknowledgments

I am full of gratitude to Allah who gave me the strength and patience throughout all the difficulties.

I would like to express my sincere gratitude to my advisor Dr. Mohamed El-Madkouri Maataoui for the unlimited support during my Ph.D. dissertation analysis which forms the basis of this book. I am deeply in depth to my advisor at then, and, currently, my colleague at Nebrija University, Dr. MariaCaterina La Barbera. This book would not see the light without her motivation and support.

A very special thanks to jury committee: Tomas Albaladejo, Ana Planet, Lasse Thomassen, Teun Van Dijk, and Margarita del Olmo whose arguments on the Ph.D. thesis were enlightening guidance in writing this book.

I am so grateful to my family in Siria, to my husband and to my daughters who passionately followed up the progress of the book, Thank you for cheering me up.

Finally, I thank Springer publishing team for all the work done to publish this book.

This book is not perfect because no human creation is. I finished this book in the COVID-19 pandemic which negatively affected the discussion of the content with experts in the fields. However, I consider this book a first step to multidisciplinary analysis in social studies.

Contents

Introduction

Introduction

Ethnic and cultural differences are somehow accepted by the European standards of diversity except for the rooted religious ones, precisely, the Islamic one.[1] The increasing secular dimension in the current European identity intensified the rejection of the European Muslim minority who are classified as "others" although they have been living in Europe for at least two generations.[2] Thirteen European countries do not recognize Islam as a religion, although it is the second-largest religion in 16 of 37 European countries.[3] Muslims are excluded from the minorities' rights of protection against religious discrimination because they do not fit the national definitions of minorities, which are based on ethnic and racial criteria. Governmental strategies wavered between marginalizing Muslim minorities from social, economic, and political rights and including them as a significant integral segment in the social structure. Robert Pauly explains that this hesitation is due to the Western's misconception of Islam as "a monolithic faith whose adherents possess a universal affinity for radical religious fundamentalism apart from their ethnic or national backgrounds."[4]

Only a few resources describe Islam in terms of legacy, philosophy, discipline, and worldview. The misconception of Islam as radical and of the Euro-Muslims as "others" justifies the academic and the social literature that pictures the European Muslim population as a domestic threat. The lack of a basic understanding of what Islam is creates an unbridged gap between rhetoric and reality. Stefano Allievi (2005) states that such unbalanced academic writing and confusing articles are incomplete academic work. They are done to offer needed reference to a phenomenon, a social reality that politicians cannot avoid and not easily accept.[5] Besides, these works are being best sellers.

---

[1] Modood (2016).

[2] Muslim generations are in their fourth or fifth generation in France and the United Kingdom. In, Spain, the Muslim generation is considered recent, Spain witness the third Muslim generation.

[3] Esposito (1999).

[4] Pauly (2016).

[5] Allievi (2005).

© Springer Nature Singapore Pte Ltd. 2021
G. Khir-Allah, *Framing Hijab in the European Mind*,
https://doi.org/10.1007/978-981-16-1653-2_1

As part of their rights, the European Muslim generations display their religious identity as a segment of (and not contrary to) the European identity. Yet, this visibility is used in the political and press discourse to promote Islam's incompatibility with the European national values. For example, the French political discourse used Muslim women's vestment in 2004 to promote the national identity *"Laïcité"* over Islam visibility. The political discourse announced the French ban law as the triumph of liberty and the equality principles of the Republic because the practice is stigmatized as "discriminative."[6] Although the law includes all the religious signs (the Christian, Islamic, Jewish), the ban law is referred to as the headscarf ban because veiling practices were the law's primary target, the hijab[7] and chador.[8] In 2010, France reasserted its national *Laïcité* identity, again, by controlling Muslim women's bodies. France passed a law that bans full-body covering: the burqa[9] and niqab[10] in the public sphere. However, this book's focus is limited to the hijab ban and the hijab debate.[11]

Although both the Universal Declaration of the Human Rights and the European Convention on Human Rights guarantee the liberty of faith and family life,[12] the two French bans were legitimized, as we will see in Chapter I. The Europeans' attitude toward the 2004 French ban law splits between those who rush to follow the French steps and legislate over the Muslim women's choice of vestment, and those who cheer the ban, but due to the social and the historical contexts, not ready to follow (yet). One of this book's objectives is to analyze the British and the Spanish reactions to the 2004 French ban law in the national press discourse. I also aim to analyze the Spanish and British press coverage of the national hijab exclusion cases and the debate on the hijab visibility in each national public sphere.

I choose to analyze the mainstream press discourse due to its capability to shape the public mind toward national and international experiences.[13] I also focused on articles written by national women journalists and writers because the book will analyze the dominant and Muslim discourse in the hijab debate. Barbie Zelizer (1992) explains that journalists use their interpretations of public events to shape themselves into an authoritative community. She calls it "cultural authority." Accordingly, journalists obtain the legitimacy to mold external events into preferred forms, to retell the story, and shape the European mind toward the national hijab visibility. The question is: How the British and Spanish (dominant and Muslim) women in the national press use their "cultural authority" in the national hijab debate?

---

[6]The ban law is referred to as "law 2004–228 of 15 March 2004". In this book I will refer to as the 2004 French ban law.

[7]The hijab covers the hair, ears and neck.

[8]The chador covers the body but not the face.

[9]The burqa is a full-body covering that includes a mesh over the face.

[10]The niqab is a full-face veil that leaves an opening only for the eyes.

[11]The hijab and the full-body veil visibilities have different impacts in the European public sphere. The articles that debate the full veil are not equal and can not be classified in the same category in the analysis.

[12]The articles that guarantee the faith right and the family life rights are going to be discussed in the first chapter of the book.

[13]Zelizer (1992).

This book is divided into two main sections: theoretical and analytical sections. The first section is a theoretical analysis of the hijab visibility in three European contexts (France, Spain, and the United Kingdom) across different disciplines: political, social, religious, and feminist studies. Although the French press discourse is not included in the analysis section, I included it in the theoretical section because I hypnotize that it is a "trigger" of exclusionary debate in the British and Spanish national press. This selection is interesting because it contains a Laïcité, confessional, and aconfessional European countries. In the first section, I also introduce the methodology I followed in the analysis section. I explain the Cognitive Linguistic approach, such as Mental Frames Theories MFT and Conceptual Metaphor Theories CMT and Critical Discourse Analysis CDA. I also introduce the innovative methodology of this book, the Cognitive Critical Discourse Analysis CCDA.

In chapter I in the first section, I analyze the fear-stimulus of Muslim visibility in Europe. I depended on Mohammad Abed Al Jabri and Tariq Modood's theories. Abed Al Jabri and Modood relate this fear to the colonial conflicts, such as the economic interests in the Muslim world and the resistance movements under the flag of Islam. In addition, there is a need for an enemy after the Soviet Union's collapse at the end of the twentieth century. The political discourse shaped this enemy depending on the cultural differences between the Western and the Occidental worlds. These cultural differences are also used as triggers for the Western superiority "we" over the Muslim "others" within the national borders. As an outcome of shaping the enemy, the construction of the European Muslim identity is rejected. It is labeled by "disloyalty" and treated with mistrust.

I also follow Lassen Thomassen's approach to identity construction. I agree with him that identities are contingent, on a constant change. I argue that there are no fixed standards for the European national identity to be considered a norm. Describing minorities as "different" "cultures" is an exclusive social attribute that perplexes social identification. "Different" "culture" labels a particular social pattern as the norm and stigmatizes all other cultural patterns as "the odd." Therefore, I use the term "diversity" instead because it provides an egalitarian framing of the social components. In this chapter, I also argue that secularism is not an approach for the European sphere's neutrality as announced. It is an instrument to promote secularity or Christianity as dominant (with un-conflictive signs) over the "other's" (conflictive) Islamic visibility. I include the ECtHR judgment on three cases on religious signs in the public sphere as evidence. One of these cases is related to hijab practice. The other two are related to a crucifix's visibility in a public classroom and at the workplace.

I briefly analyze the French political justification of the 2004 ban because I argue (in the hypothesis of this book) that it was an opening door for other European counties (the British and the Spanish contexts) to debate or/and legislate against the hijab practice. Since the analysis focuses on the British and Spanish contexts, I analyze the Muslim population and the Muslim public representation in these two contexts. I also summarize the relationship between the Church and the State as much as the religious visibility and religious education at the Spanish and British public schools.

In chapter II in the first section, I analyze the Muslim women's image from the past century to the current day. I went through the colonial feminist discourse which justified the political hegemony over Muslim women in the colonies. I analyze how the colonial "positionality" and the hegemonistic discourse were recycled at the end of the twentieth century to justify the Iraq and Afghanistan invasions. In both, gender equality was not the primary concern of the colonial agenda, but it was important rhetoric in justifying the occupation and the usurpation of "others" resources.

In this chapter, I follow Gunther Dietz's approach in analyzing the hijab practice.[14] First, I delineate the subject, which consists of two elements in this book: (1) European Muslim woman and (2) the hijab. Then, I analyze the reasons behind considering these two subjects as "problematic" in Europe. Finally, I propose Maria Caterina La Barbera's intersectional feminist approach as a potential solution for an inclusive feminist discourse.

The analysis of this section covers the dispute on faith and traditions among feminists. I followed Homa Hoodfar's criticism of the common assumption that take for granted "what is good for western women should be good for all."[15] She argues that individuals are social beings and understand the external world through their historical and social contexts. Thus, the vestment free choices are part of each woman's social identity (secular or religious), and it reflects her heritage as much as her personality.[16]

The confusion on the term Islamic feminism is also covered in this chapter. The political use of the term is one of the main triggers of miscaptions. Yet, Muslim feminists are, in a way or another, political agents because they call for a political change. The visibility of hijab-wearing activist Muslim women alarms the political authorities because these women can fight for their rights and ignite a social change through their religious frame of reference. Besides, they are well perceived by most Muslims.

In this chapter, I went through the legislative texts in the holy book, *Al-Quran*,[17] and in the *Sunnah*,[18] *Al-Hadith*,[19] that demand the veiling practice. The religious texts analysis guided me to find out the Islamic approach to gender relations in the public sphere. Secondly, the analysis compares the Islamic religious legislation and the UDHR on women's vestment. I managed to disclose the mist on the discrepancy in the hijab understanding between the Muslim feminist's claims that Islam is universal and supports human rights, equality, liberty, and the Occidental accusations that Islam is misogynic and submissive, announcing the hijab practice as evidence. The distinct understanding between the Islamic approach and the secular approach to sexuality and gender equality in the public sphere is the main trigger of dispute. As

---

[14] Dietz (2007).

[15] Hoodfar (1992).

[16] The right to vestment is included in the Universal Declaration of Human Rights, Art. 19 UDHR. https://www.un.org/en/universal-declaration-human-rights/.

[17] The Words of the God revealed to the prophet Mohamad ﷺ by the angel Gabriel.

[18] All the sayings and the doings of the prophet Mohamad ﷺ.

[19] The sayings of the prophet Mohamad ﷺ.

the religious framing stands still for more than 1400 years until today with clear reasonings on women's sexuality in the public sphere, the current secular approach went through historical and social changes that shaped the contemporary European reasoning on sexuality and gender equality. Each approach stands for a pattern of cultural values that deserve to be respected by the other. In this book, I use the term sexuality to refer to the sexual embodiment of women's bodies in the publich sphere.

Writing Chapter III in the first section was challenging because I introduced the hijab from two distant but related approaches. I joined multidisciplinary approaches altogether in the analysis of the hijab sign: social and feminist approaches, and Cognitive Linguistics, which consists of psychology, sociolinguistics, semiotics, conceptual metaphors, and discourse analysis.

As this book analyzes the hijab debate in the Spanish and British press discourse, it is essential to analyze the hijab sign system in the European mind. It is not a matter of how we individually understand a sign. It is how we, as embedded in a linguistic community, in a culture, and a historical context, understand that hijab sign.[20] I depended on Byron Kaldis (2013) and Anjuum Alvi (2013) arguments on signs (that has an embedded meaning) and symbols (an abstract concept which needs to be given a meaning) to argue that the hijab is a sign and not a symbol. It is a religious sign that stands for a specific criterion on gender relations in the public sphere. Treating the hijab as a symbol locates it in the populace's target zone to interpret it negatively or positively, attaching to it unrelated meanings without a former knowledge about the practice or any previous religious or cross-cultural formation.

In this chapter, I introduce the new Cognitive Critical Discourse Analysis CCDA Methodology. I followed Zoltan Kovecses' Conceptual Metaphor Theories CMT which indicates that humans depend on conceptual metaphors to understand the abstract concepts around us. Using conceptual metaphors, we project the abstract concepts into the physical, touchable world, so we become able to deal with them. I also followed Antonio Barcelona, George Lakoff, and Mark Johnson's theories on metaphors and mental frames. They argue that conceptual metaphors depend on already established mental frames that attribute meaning to the world. These mental frames control our understanding of the world, and it is not easy to think out of these frames. Finally, I depended on the literature of Tuen Van Dijk and Christopher Hart on Critical Discourse Analysis CDA. Van Dijk (2001) set CDA as a potent tool to analyze the ways discourse structures enact, confirm, legitimate, reproduce, or challenge relations of power and dominance in society.

Based on the literature of Chapter III, I introduce the innovative Cognitive Critical Discourse Analysis CCDA on the hijab debate in Spanish and British press. CCDA is the joint between the CDA and CMT. I aim to provide a coherent framework on the Spanish and British journalistic discursive strategies that control the national mental framing of the hijab and the hijab-wearing women's visibility in the public sphere. Despite the methodological differences, we conceive an enriching analysis tool by joining CMT and CDA. CMT insists that thoughts and embodied experiences shape our language and the metaphors we use. CDA asserts that the speaker chooses the

---

[20]Lindesmith et al. (1999).

language to convey specific thoughts (message) in mind.[21] CMT focuses on daily discourse, and CDA focuses on political and social discourse. Yet, is the political and press discourse on a minority capable of being a collective memory and a culturally shared mental frame reflected in the mainstream's daily language on that minority?

Discourse is never neutral. And the meaning of social signs does not mainly flow to the linguistic representation; it is the linguistic representation that imposes the meaning upon that physical or non-physical social signs.[22] Therefore, those who control public discourse control the public mind because they can dominate the public opinion toward social signs, especially those related to minorities.[23]ʻ This book analyzes the women journalists' cultural authority in their articles on the hijab and the hijab-wearing Muslim women. It also aims to observe the inclusion and exclusion processes of hijab-wearing women's mental frames in each press's mainstream discourse.

In the second section, the analysis section, I carry out the Cognitive Critical Discourse Analysis CCDA to analyze the cognitive process behind the European framing of the hijab and hijab-wearing women. The hypothesis of this book is multiple, as the research is multidisciplinary. I argue that the French ban is a trigger of (exclusive) (stereotypical) debate on the hijab and hijab-wearing women in the British and Spanish press. I argue that the CCDA on Spanish and British press discourse can capture the levels of social diversity and minority engagement in these public spheres. CCDA can also provide us with a cognitive framework on the abstract pivotal concepts in the hijab debate such as "public sphere" and "cultural integration."

The comparative analysis between Spain and the United Kingdom contexts is quite interesting because of the distinct Muslim communities' history, the integration models, and the perception of diversity. Such differences across these two European contexts are expected to be reflected in the press discourse on the national hijab and hijab-wearers. In the second section, I include an introduction in which I carry out primary comparative analysis on the selected data. This part analyzes the articles' general focus and the (inter)national trigger of the hijab debate in each context.

After this brief review of the data, I analyze the mental frames on the hijab in Chapter IV and the mental frames on the hijab-wearing women in Chapter V. In these two chapters, I divided the analysis into two levels: micro level and macro level. The micro-level analysis focuses on each social context separately. It is to say, the micro-level analysis studies the within-cultural variation between the hijab supporters and the hijab opposers in Spanish press discourse. It also studies the within-cultural variation between the hijab supporters and the hijab opposers in the British press discourse. The macro-level analysis studies the cross-cultural variation among the Spanish and British contexts.

Chapter IV and Chapter V answer multidisciplinary-focus questions on two levels. The first is a micro-level: How the press discourse introduces the 2004 French ban to national readers? Which mental frames are (de)activated to justify it? What mental

---

[21] Charteris-Black (2004).

[22] Francis and Hester (2004).

[23] Van Dijk (2001).

frames are (de)activated in the national debate on the hijab and the hijab-wearing women? Are the Spanish/British hijab-wearers included in the national debate on the hijab? How? What level of authority do they enjoy in the national press discourse? Is there a significant difference in the mental frames of the hijab between the secular participants or hijab opposers and the hijab-wearing women/or hijab supporters? The second is a macro level: Are there any unique mental frames activated in one social variety? What are the shared mental frames on the hijab and hijab-wearing women across the Spanish and British contexts? Do the discursive strategies that (de)activate, use, nourished, and/or demolish shared mental frames vary across two press discourses?

In chapter VI, I carried out an analysis of the conceptual metaphors on the pivot abstract concepts involved in the hijab debate, such as: "public sphere," "hijab," "ban law," and "cultural integration." Due to the limited findings, I joined the micro-level and the macro-level analysis. I took the risk to analyze the two levels together because the reader is already familiar with the metal frames on the hijab debate of each social diversity from the previous chapters. Reading chapter VI is enjoyable because it seems like putting the pieces together in the cognitive structures in the Spanish and British hijab debate.

Chapter VI answers the following questions: Can conceptual metaphors reflect the collective framing of the "public sphere" and "cultural integration" abstract concepts? Are there variations in the metaphorical structures on the hijab between hijab wearers and hijab opposers (and across cultures)? Can conceptual metaphors on the hijab provide an explanation of sexuality understanding in the public sphere? How do the founded conceptual metaphors correlate with the founded mental frames in previous chapters?

I conclude the volume with the conclusions that reflects on the multidisciplinary findings of the book. I sew through the diverse threads across the book chapters to reach comprehensive reasoning on framing hijab and hijab-wearing women in Spanish and British press discourse. The novel of this book is not limited to this innovative CCDA methodology. This book is novel because it analyzes the Spanish context that has not been covered in academia yet. The hijab visibility in Europe went through several social-political analyses (Salih, 2009; Scott, 2009; Thomassen, 2011), but the Spanish press discourse on the national hijab visibility has not been analyzed before.

References

Allievi, S. (2005). How the immigrant has become Muslim. *Revue Européenne Des Migrations Internationales, 21*(2), 7

Alvi, A. (2013). Concealment and Revealment. *Current Anthropology, 54*(2), 177–199

Charteris, J. (2004). *Corpus approaches to critical metaphor analysis.* Springer.

Dietz, G. (2007). Invisibilizing or ethnicizing religious diversity? In *Religion and education in Europe: Developments, contexts and debates* (pp. 103–132).

10 Introduction

Esposito, J. (1999). Clash of civilization? Contemporary images of Islam in the west. In G. M. Munoz (Ed.), *Islam, modernism and the West: Cultural and political relations at the end of the millennium*. IB Tauris.

Francis, D., & Hester, S. (2004). *An invitation to ethnomethodology: Language, society and interaction*. Sage.

Hoodfar, H. (1992). The veil in their minds and on our heads: The persistence of colonial images of Muslim women. *Resources for Feminist Research, 22*(3/4), 5

Kaldis, B. (Ed.). (2013). *Encyclopedia of philosophy and the social sciences*. Sage.

Lindesmith, A. R., Strauss, A. L., & Denzin, N. K. (1999). *Social psychology*. Sage.

Modood, T. (2016). Muslims, religious equality and secularism. Secularism, Religion and Multicultural Citizenship (p. 164). Cambridge, 2009.

Pauly, R. J. (2016). *Islam in Europe: integration or marginalization?* Routledge.

Salih, R. (2009). Muslim women, fragmented secularism and the construction of interconnected 'publics' in Italy. *Social Anthropology, 17*(4), 409–423

Scott, J. W. (2009). *The politics of the veil*. Princeton University Press.

Thomassen, L. (2011). (Not) Just a piece of cloth: Begum, recognition and the politics of representation. *Political Theory, 39*(3), 325–351

Van Dijk, T. (2001). 18 Critical discourse analyses. In *The handbook of discourse analysis* (pp. 349–371).

Zelizer, B. (1992). *Covering the body: The Kennedy assassination, the media, and the shaping of collective memory*. University of Chicago Press.

The Politics of the European Muslim Women's Identity: Challenging the Public Discourse and National Sign System

The Politics of Identity: Islam Visibility in the National Public Sphere

Introduction

The discussion of "Islam and Europe" is an asymmetric and irrational comparison because Europe is a fixed geographical space, in time and place. In contrast, Islam is a religion practiced worldwide and across history. The term "Islam and Europe" is derived from the historical conflict between Islam and Christendom. Indeed, religion (I refer here to Christianity) is not an essential element in the European identity as it was in the past. And the fear of Islam increases in the European political consciousness due to the historical conflicts since the Crusade. Today's European Muslim visibility is seen as an extension of the historical threat that comes from neighboring countries,[1] and secularity is perceived as an alternative to Christianity that stands effectively in opposition to Islam.

This section will provide state of the art on previous literature that diagnoses the asymmetrical unease relationship between Islam and Europe; considering the significant impact of politics in shaping that relationship in the public sphere. This chapter particularly pays attention to the political molding of the Muslim religious visibility in the European identity. I will focus on the French context as a referential model of *laïcité* and secularism for European countries.[2] It will analyze the British and Spanish Muslim communities as studied cases in this book. The analysis of the British and Spanish contexts includes an overview of the Muslim community in each context, the Muslim community's civic participation, and their governmental representation. It concludes with the Spanish and British governmental politics at public schools to manage diversity.

---

[1] Lewis (1994).

[2] I included the French secularism and laicism because I noticed that French secularism is always referred to in the hijab debate. The theoretical part intends to explain the basic notion of secularism with its historical use and to clarify the difference between secularism and laicism.

© Springer Nature Singapore Pte Ltd. 2021
G. Khir-Allah, *Framing Hijab in the European Mind*,
https://doi.org/10.1007/978-981-16-1653-2_2

The Need of an Enemy

There is common disapproval of the current understanding of "Europe" as a unified geographical or historical entity. Mohammad Abed Al Jabri explains that Europe needs to be understood in terms of three different civilizations. None of them coincides with the conventional borders of Europe these days: a Mediterranean civilization, an Atlantic civilization, and a continental civilization.[3] He critically analyzes the term "the clash of Europe and Islam." He detaches the conflict from the historical past and attributes this conflict to the colonial relationship between the West and the Muslim world in the last century. Indeed, most of the Muslim world was colonized by Western countries and overturned into underdeveloped "third world" countries after their independence. Abed Al Jabri refers that the imposed economic domination and exploitation of Westerns on the "third world" created a "conflict of interests" and not a "clash of civilizations."

From a related perspective, Rudolph Peters indicates that the local movements in the colonized countries gathered and organized under a political and a religious flag to call for *jihad* that resists the foreigner invasion and subordination.[4] Examples are presented in India's resistance movements against British Domination, in Somalia's against British and Italian, in Algeria's against French, Egypt against British, and in Libya's against Italian. The resistance movements had minimal economic and military resources. The main empowerment factor was the link between their legitimate causes, justice and liberty, and their religious beliefs in *shahada*[5] (to die in the cause of God and fear no one but Him). Shahada's impeded meaning irritated the Western (European) colonizer in the past and still irritating the European political agenda in the present. Muslim resisting believers were considered the colonizer's enemy. They are economic and political intimidators who threatened the natural, human, and economic resources. Current European devoted Muslims are not seen as less "threatening."

Gema Martin Muñoz provides a third explanation of the conflict between Europe and Islam.[6] Muñoz argues that the initial stages of the "West and Islam" clash had appeared right after the Cold War that divided the world into the East and the West between 1947 and 1991 when the Soviet Union collapsed. The destruction of the Berlin wall and the Soviet Union's collapse created an urgent need to find another

---

[3] Abed AL'Jabri (1999).

[4] Peters (2014).

[5] *Shahada* has double meaning in Islam. Shahada is the testimony of Islam. The first pillar out of five that declares the belief in the Oneness of God whose name is Allah *(tawhid)* and the acceptance of Mohammad as a God's prophet. Declaring the Shahada indicates that the one's life aims to live by it and belong solely to Him; to fear no one or nothing else. The second meaning of Shahada is to die for the cause of Allah; being killed defending the one's land and family is a prominent cause. The one who dies in this cause is called *Shaeed* (martyr) and he is promised with salvation in the Judgment Day, with a guaranteed place in paradise and with other more privileges. Both meanings of shahada contributed to empower the limited-en-resources resistance movements against the colonizers in the Muslim world.

[6] Martina Muñoz (2010).

enemy of the West. Since the late 1980s, the West confronted Islam using the cultural differences and the historical clashes as "triggers" of the conflict.

These three factors contributed to casting national Islam as the new enemy of the European nations. The clash between Europe and the Muslim cultures is repeated twice in recent history; First, when the European countries ignored Muslim cultural codes while colonizing their lands[7]; Second, and close in time, by misinterpreting the history of the resistance movements in colonized countries and not respecting the European Islamic cultural codes of Muslims in Europe as a markedly different context.[8]

One of the essential functions of politics is to determine the enemy. Displaying the enemy's horrible image and promising protection from a depicted danger is one of the most effective instrumental-use-of-fear strategies in electoral campaigns.[9] The political enemy has to look "morally evil" or "aesthetically ugly." There is no need to be an economic rival. Instead, fruitful economic relations can be established with the enemy. Yet, the enemy is the Other; he remains the different and the alien, so conflicts and abuses are justified and legitimized.[10] Within this approach, the Western political discourse (both European and American) presented Islam through inconspicuous Islamic terminologies with political arguments on identity and national security, over-generalizing the term "Muslims." The outcome is an irrational political discourse that casts Islam and all Muslims as potential enemies and promotes Islam's incompatibility with European values. The non-validity of this public discourse is evident if we apply it to the Jewish or Christian communities.[11] Can we argue on worldwide Christian or Jewish communities as one block? Is the argument "Judaism is incompatible with European values" acceptable?

The rapid growth of the Muslim population in Europe and the public visibility of Muslim diversity and instrumentally used to support the "enemy" propaganda. European Muslims are misrepresented as a worldwide monolithic block, and they are linked to backward cultures and underdeveloped economies. European Muslims attempt to refuse total assimilation in the European culture and to preserve their religious identity and the European one. Such new articulation of Euro-Muslim identity is perceived as an act of disloyalty and conspiracy against Europe because the political and social discourse fails to distinguish between the religious heritage and Muslim countries' cultural traditions. It is to say, the visibility of the religious identity in Europe, such as long beard, hijab, five prayers, or halal food, is understood as the devotion to outsider Muslim countries.

There is a conflictive duality in the European public discourse, which, on the one hand, has to be anti-racists and anti-discriminative. On the other hand, it stigmatizes national Islam as the "other" and the "enemy." Joselyne Cesari clarifies that political discourse has blinded many of us from the difference between religion and

---

[7] Martina Muñoz and Grosfoguel (2012).

[8] Ramadan (1999).

[9] Shally-Jensen et al. (2015).

[10] Schmitt (1996).

[11] Shryock (2010).

politics. They use religious vocabularies to express a new political context that "no longer could be expressed with the traditional words and concepts."[12] It is crucial to distinguish between extremism as a socio-cultural phenomenon that can exist in any society, whether it is religious or not, e.g., ETA in Spain, and the extremism that can control an entire population under one cause. According to Abed Al Jabri, the latter is stimulated by economic and social factors, e.g., Nazi in Germany under Adolfo Hitler's dictatorship between 1933 and 1945. Likewise, it is essential to highlight the difference between the political use of Islam and everyday religious practices. When Muslim's demands in the political sphere are restricted and limited to religious ones, this participation turns into a political Islam.

Muslims are citizens of the European countries they habitat in; they have their political opinions and objections; they have political responses and enjoy their civil rights provided in their countries. The Islamophobic exclusionary practices create a chasm between Euro-Muslims and the mainstream. Violent groups in Islam's name utilizes an excessive interpretation of *jihad* far away from its original and contextual interpretation to justify and legitimize violence.[13] These violent movements are not part of the Muslim cause because Islam calls for peace, and it sustains this meaning in its name; Islam means peace. These groups and movements do a favor to the European political discourse in framing, national or international, Islam as an enemy.

The political shaping of the West's enemy (in Europe and the United States) had been crowned by the 9 November 2001 twin towers attacks in the United States, the 11 March 2004 train bombings in Madrid, and the 7 July 2005 bombings in the United Kingdom. Right after the 9/11 attacks, the enemy was well defined in the United States. Europe made sure of the in-common enemy afterward.

When we are framing the enemy, there is no need to be fair. The progressive and liberal parties were the most zealous in their arguments. As Ramadan states, they are "hasty pronouncements" and lack social awareness or in-depth analysis. Muslims have been portrayed in many ways from many different perspectives; unfortunately, none was positive. Western discourse tags Islam and Muslims with negative stigmatizations by terms like Islamists, fundamentalists, fanatics, extremists, a rebirth of militancy, or radicalism. Such terms are repeatedly used in social and political discourse without a clear definition of their meanings or understandings of each different connotation. The arbitrary use of these stigmatizing terms confuses the understanding of Muslims, Islam, terrorism, and extremism. Western receptors of this manipulated discourse do not know if those who practice their daily five prayers are fundamentalists nor if those women who decide to adopt the veil are extremists, or if the kids who attend weekend Arabic classes are being prepared to be future terrorists. Muslims (even the second and third generations) are set to be an economic threat by taking over job opportunities, a threat to the national security (terrorist), a threat to the European identity, and finally, a religious threat as it becomes the second-largest religion in Europe. Islam is a threat to Christianity on the one hand and to secularism, on the other hand. The academic discourse is an important source of hostile terminologies

---

[12]Cesari (1999).

[13]Sherman and Nardin (2006).

against Islam in Europe, e.g., "Voices of Resurgent Islam,"[14] "Islamic fundamentalism gaining strength at Europe's door-step, notably in Algeria and Turkey,"[15] and "radical Islamic fundamentalism" and "the creation of an Islamic state in the heart of Europe."[16] Researchers include these terminologies in their studies without an empirical analysis of their credibility nor clear definitions of their connotations.

Europe has been through several stages in defining a common enemy for all its countries. The enemy is depicted through various "phobias" before the continent lately agrees on the consolidated enemy "Islamophobia."[17] Raymond Taras explains that right after the 9/11 attacks in 2001, the Islamic world was limited, both in Europe and the United States, to the Arab Middle East where the attackers came from. Madrid's Train attacks were carried out by Moroccans and Spanish nationals of Moroccan descent, which freshened the rationale of the historical fear of Moors "Maurophobia." Spanish "Maurophobia" is not exclusive but, rather, inclusive to all Muslim groups of different racial and ethnic backgrounds, even Iberian converts to Islam. However, "Arabophobia" is not applied in the United Kingdom because those who carried out the London attacks were non-Arab Muslims. These racialized scattered phobias were not a useful tool in the political agenda. The term Islamophobia triumphs because, as Taras argues, implementing religious cleavages is influential in the politics of fear in the West.

"Islamophobia" is used for the first time in the United Kingdom, in the late 1997s, as a tool to identify the discrimination against the Muslim community. Back in time, the term differentiated religious racism from biological racism. The Runnymede Trust was the first to use this term in his article titled: *"Islamophobia: A Challenge for Us All."* The article was a response to the anti-Muslim sentiment that increased in Great British after the 1989 Rushdie's Affair. Trust introduced the term as an "unfounded hostility towards Islam," which leads to unfair discrimination against Muslim individuals and communities and the exclusion of Muslims from mainstream political and social affairs. Both Taras and Abbas agree that although the article aimed at analyzing Islamophobia, it presented Muslims as monolithic and static "other" who do not share the values of the mainstream culture. They also indicate that the article highlighted Islam as a religion of a violent ideology that promotes intolerance and cultural clashes. These highlighted purports justified the discrimination against Muslims, and the term normalized the anti-Muslim hostility.

The term "Islamophobia" technically is perplexing because it confuses the criticism of religion with the stigmatization of religious people. Andrew Shryock indicates that campaigns against Islamophobia usually are challenging and hard for those activists who, in the majority, belongs to the secular intelligentsia.[18] In practice, "Islamophobia" is not only the act of rejecting religion. Nor it is a total refusal

---

[14]Esposito (1983).

[15]Wieland (2001).

[16]Sutton and Vertigans (2005).

[17]Taras (2012).

[18]Shryock (2010).

to include people whose skins and names are not "European."[19] Islamophobia is an extension of the colonial relationship between the West and the Muslims. It marks the line between autochthonous and Others (Muslims). It fulfills the political need to keep Europeans as "first-class" and Muslims as—not second but—third class, although the second and following generations are supposed to be autochthons.

The visibility of Islam in Europe is a political issue more than a social reality. Framing the term "Islamophobia" in the public sphere was part of the governmental electoral agenda that is cautious in defining the enemy to promise people protection. However, several politicians criticized Islamophobic practices to calm down an anti-racist public opinion or to guarantee the marginalized Muslim voters' support. This duality in political declarations is not limited to the interests in the votes. It is a needed discourse to keep the "self-image" of Western politics as inclusive and pluralistics.[20]

Constructing the Forbidden: European Muslim "Us"

"Identity" in social sciences defines a range of concepts and experiences related to individuals in a particular group and a particular context. Those ideas and experiences are shaped by social forces which assign identities to individuals.[21] Judith Howard (2000) highlights that individuals' struggles in any social identification have socio-political dimensions. Such struggles drive social movements to define the collective identity and motivate the group action. Constructing an identity requires, first, the perception of belonging to a group; second, the awareness of the group's ideologies and visible behavior.

In his recent book "British Multiculturalism and the politics of representation," Lasse Thomassen elaborates a comprehensive theory on identity. Thomassen, firstly, states that identities are contingent. Contingency does not mean a chance, an accident, or an absence of structure. In Thomassen's argument, contingency refers to the undecidability; it is to say, no identity can be fully constituted because it is continually evolving. Since identities are contingent, they are open to negotiation and articulation, so there is nothing natural or essential about identities.

Thomassen stresses three significant factors in identity constructions: contingency, hegemony, and discourse of representation and/or recognition. He concludes that there is no social inclusion without exclusion because any identity is constituted through specific exclusions of what it is not. "Inclusion and exclusion are intrinsically linked to identity" because "the universal is always articulated through the particular." He contributes that identity and inclusion "should be studied as the result of a hegemonic struggle over representations" because hegemonic (political) (Mass

---

[19]Godard (2007: 202).

[20]Mastnak (2008).

[21]Howard (2000).

Media) representation frames what is considered as true or false in national identities (2017: 10–13).

From a coinciding perspective, Floya Anthias (2013) stresses that identities should be understood mainly as a social outcome. She focuses on "positionality" in identity construction.[22] Positionality refers to location/dislocation placements (We/Others) with a set of relations and practices that identify each group. It can be spatial positionality or contextual positionality. "Positionality" can also be understood as "self-categorization," which means understanding the relationship between social identification and group's behavior, especially of minorities. An individual's self-perception as a group member might be affected by other's reactions. The significance of identity is mainly related to the mainstream recognition of that identity and to the desire to be recognized as a member of that group and not any other. Identities can be displayed strategically. It is to say, individuals of any group can adopt specific group attributes in a particular context to challenge the out-group stereotypes. More particularly, those who believe that their group belonging is questioned tend to practice and emphasize their "in-group relevant" elements.

Positionality and exclusion have an essential role in constructing European identity through history. The Europeans' consciousness of themselves has depended on defining the "Other." Historically, Europe always has kept the rival through which their identity is shaped and defined. In ancient times, Roman and Greek asserted their identities as "citizens" by the opposition to the slaves indoors and barbarians outdoors (positionality). In the middle age, Islam and Muslim empires significantly affected Europe's self-representation as a Christian. The end of the Reconquista in 1942 marked the exclusion of Muslims from the Peninsula as the opposite "others," including the Iberian Muslims. A similar exclusion of Muslims happened in Eastern Europe as well. Nowadays, such positionality and exclusion continue even though Christianity lost its effect.

The contemporary European "we" is still getting its recognition from the opposition of the Muslim "Others" to the secular "we" or Christian "we." Christianity and secularism are not seen as incompatible as both equally stand for the European "we" while Islam yes. This process enfolds inherent occidental superiority that has been accumulating since the long past of the Reconquista, throughout the colonial era all the way to the present. The European political discourse of representation depends on positionality between Islam and the West in defining the national identity (Western) "we" and the different (Muslim) "Others."[23] The Exclusion of Muslims from the European identity (self-categorization) is symmetrical to the exclusion of Islam from the European continental and restricts it to the Muslim countries (Spatial positionality).

The need to be recognized as European Muslims is getting a stringent requirement by the young Euro-Muslims. They display their identity in the public sphere through variable degrees of visibility according to their need to be recognized as such across Europe. Ingrained stereotypes and governmental attempts to control Muslim's visibility are potent stimuli for Euro-Muslims' need for recognition. For example,

----

[22] Anthias (2013).

[23] Adlbi (2016).

Jocelyne Cesari indicates that the hijab's visibility in France is higher than the hijab's visibility in German even though the hijab is banned in French public schools, and it is not in Germany. Besides, the number of Euro-Muslim hijab-wearers is increasing with a foreknowledge that it is the most controversial and misinterpreted symbol of Islam.[24] The determination to bring to the public this aspect of their identity is linked to their need to be recognized by the mainstream as Europeans, talking the native language, enjoying the native customs, and as Muslims.

Muslim identity in Europe has been through a lot of changes since WWI till today. The migratory dimension is still playing a crucial function in the out-group perception of the Euro-Muslim generations. The migratory dimension is significant because it is not limited to Muslims' migration from the last century. The migration from Muslim countries into Europe has not stopped since then. There have been years of flux and other years of restriction. Yet, the massive migration reached its peak at the begging of this century. The problematic issue is that the young generation of the previous-century migrants is in their third generation, and they identify themselves as European. The European public notion around Muslims does not differentiate between newcomers and the Euro-Muslim generation. Here we come back to the power of representation in the mass media whose discourse places all Muslims in Europe in one sack.

The mainstream representation of Muslims in Europe, firstly, points out the (visualized) stereotypical difference: "They" are patriarchal, misogynist, terrorist, and their women are veiled and oppressed, on the contrary of what "we" are. Secondly, these differences are condemned and Muslims are asked for total assimilation into European values. Thirdly, the public discourse calls for tolerance and respect for "Others." These strategies in the Western integrational system are another face of racism because they visualize the difference and indicate what the "Other" lacks instead of implementing "diversity."[25] Muslims who melt in the pot of the country's traditions by abandoning Islam or following a secularized version of Islam are called moderated, while those who practice Islam are stigmatized as *fundamentalists*. Yet, both are still perceived as "others" and treated with variable levels of "tolerance."

"Tolerance" invokes the "we" in opposition to the "Others" because it indicates that "we," the tolerators, are potent and supreme over the tolerated, "Others," who are typically marginalized minorities. Thomassen ensures that tolerance invokes "subjectivities and identities."[26] He states that people usually tolerate what they do not like. For that reason, using this term in public discourse assigns the "other" to this emotional state of being "in-need" to be tolerated, and it generates systematical behavior to deal with the tolerated difference. Due to the rapidly increased Muslim visibility in the public sphere, the public discourse on diversity failed to combine tolerance and rationality. Muslim's visible identity challenges the collective identity

---

[24]Cesari (1999).

[25]Alvi (2013).

[26]Thomassen (2011).

and national values. Debates on halal food, hijab at public school, Muslim burial rites, and women's rights often confuse tolerance with fueled Islamophobia.

This continuous exclusion of Muslims from the European "we" ends up pushing the Muslim youth out of the mainstream identity. Muslim autochthones (second or third generations and Muslim converts) across Europe feel marginalized and unwelcome in their home. In many European countries, Muslims do not even have a law that protects them from religious discrimination, such as other religious minorities, Jews and Sikhs, even though Islam is the second-largest religion in Europe.[27] In whatever way, Islam's recent visibility should not be understood as "the return of Islam" neither it means that Muslims turn to be more practitioners than their migrant ancestors. Simply, it is a civil need to change their passive position toward governments and stereotypes and to claim their civil rights: worship places, right to religious education at public schools, protective regulations from religious discrimination, or at least, liberty of visibility. Some European Muslims emphasize their religious identity to overcome their different ethnic origins or to avoid stereotypical social categorizations such as social class, migration, or suburb youth.

The notion of belonging to the one "Umma" is perceptible in constructing the European Muslim identity. "Umma" means the community of faithful, supra-national non-ethical universal community. It offers a self-pride of the diversity of the wide range of Muslim civilizations. Yet, mistakenly, the "Umma" concept affirms the monolith understanding of Muslim communities in the European mainstream consciousness. Muslims across the world belong to a wide variety of nations, cultures, ethnicities, languages, and social contexts. The practice of Islam varies significantly from one social structure to another. Yet, the religion, the Divine order, is the bond that unites them and puts them all equal in front of God. The allegiance to the unique Divinity draws the line of difference between occidental social structure, based on material interests and class ranking, and the Muslim social structure, in which individuals are all equal in front of God, the only source of authority, where gender and social classes disappear. Technically, the term "Ummah" is more theoretical than practical. It is to say, there are no social movements in Muslim countries to unite Muslims, across continents, under one religious' flag. We neither see that Muslims are putting physical and economic efforts or sufficient causes to support other Muslims who are going through server discrimination and religious persecution in other countries.[28] However, the embodied meaning of the term "Ummah" transcends Euro-Muslims's loyalties to the outdoors, especially in the discourse of national security and terrorism. The Muslim hybrid identity works effectively in two parallel directions. The first one is the "nostalgic affiliation" to the ancestors' origins and/or Islamic solidarity. The second level is the affiliation to the country they were born and raised in, their national belonging and traditions, and to Europe's

---

[27] Esposito and Kalin (2011).

[28] Movements in Muslim countries which provide support to Muslim causes are national foundations with limited resources. In Europe, we can find more cross-national causes such Islamic Relief for orphans and children in conflict areas. Yet, these movements, for example, provide limited contributions for Rohingya Muslims in Myanmar and for Syrian refugee crisis in the Neighboring countries such as Jordan and Lebanon.

religious-freedom framework guaranteed in the Universal Declaration of Human Rights, which theoretically warrantees them to practice their faith without fear.[29] Muslims can practice both loyalties homogeneously, which indicates that Islamic identity and European citizenship can be peacefully compatible. The conflict arises when the cultural differences are highlighted and mistakenly interpreted against the national values of democracy and equality.

Muslim third generation resists assimilation and secularism more than their antecedents did. The European young Muslim generation respects the European national values and constitutional norms. Yet, they fear total assimilation because it indicates the loss of their identity's religious features. Consequently, they insist on reconstructing a European identity that emphasizes religious differences. These differences are highlighted negatively by the mainstream. The challenging aspect of this diversity is that each party, the mainstream and Muslims, needs to redefine its identity, move toward the other, and be open to the other's perspectives. Muslims need to adapt the national norms and costumes in their identity, but the mainstream needs to broaden its diversity horizon, accepting hybrid Muslim identity. The mainstream should be aware of its assimilation patterns that refuse the accommodation or inclusion of specific diversities.

As I agree with Thomassen that identity is contingent, I argue that there is no fixed European identity model because it is in constant change. That is why I do not use the word difference to refer to the identity of minorities. "Difference" indicates the existence of a prime model of social identification, which is seen as the norm and casts other models of social identities as unusual, uncommon, and different. "Diversity," instead, puts all the identities in an equal position in the public sphere. All identities are accepted as normal, respected, and equally treated. "Difference" refers to exclusive patterns of framing minorities that restrict their social identification. For example, France set the hijab as "different" from the national values of equality to justify the ban law, which worsens the stumbling progress of Muslim women's construction of their French identity in the public sphere.

A Puzzled Battle in the Public Sphere: *Laïcité*, Secularism, and Religious Freedom

The European public sphere is built on a "cultural consensus" that restrains individual liberty.[30] The public sphere belongs to the social group, and the private sphere belongs to its members.[31] Individuals can bring into the public sphere only those issues which can be interesting to others. Public life is also understood as an opposition to State

---

[29]Peucker and Akbarzadeh (2014). It is important to annotate that after the increased Islamophobic attacks against Muslims in the United Kingdom and Germany, Muslim do not enjoy the liberal framework of Europe and they fear being attacked because of their religious visibility.

[30]Amiraux (2007).

[31]Arlettaz (2013).

"authority" and civil society.[32] Although the public sphere is outside the state's institutions, it is directly concerned with what occurs there.[33] It is the subordinate sphere between the government and the governed. However, religion in the European public sphere almost broke all of those theories because the religious sign's visibility has converted to a public issue that the State aims to regulate and legislate on.

Religion has always been a controversial issue since the eighteenth century when rationalists' and secularists' discussions emerged. Rationalists claim to depend on logic to understand the universe. They refuse to believe in the "unseen" and rest on the realm of visibility. From a different perspective, religious people assert that the interpretations of the universe—the realm of visibility—lead to the belief in God's existence—the realm of invisibility. Both approaches have been in a hostile relationship trying to dominate public opinion. Ashgar Ali Engineer contributes that each profoundly depends on the other.[34] He adds that religion is not limited to the "axis of faith," but it includes costumes and traditions. It is a fundamental issue to understand the difference between religion and faith, between what religion teaches and how the followers behave, and between religion practiced in different historical periods across distinctive contextual frames. Faith consists of a Divine definition of the world and Divine orders to be followed, while religion—as a practiced culture–is the set of unlimited human costumes and traditions that each social context adopts differently in the process of following the Divine orders. The confusion between Islam as a faith and Islam as a historical framework is one of the most common misconceptions. Today's terms "Islam and its Civilizations" or "Muslim Civilizations" which is used to enwrap worldwide Muslims from the past to the present is as inconsequent as the terms "Christianity and its Civilizations" or "Christian Civilizations" if used to refer to current Europe or South American Countries. The confusion between the faith and the Muslim cultures across history contributes to shaping the European's enemy image.

Laicism and Secularism are increasingly used in the European public discourse. Joan Wallach Scott, in her book *The Politics of the Veil*, refers that secularism marks the separation between the Church and the State through different historical meanings; for example, the separation in the United States was meant to protect religion from State undesired interventions. Yet, a century ago in France, secularism was meant to break the Church's political power, which was considered the enemy, in the attempt to demand undivided loyalty to the Republic. It also protects individuals from the claims of religion. Both versions of secularism, the American and the French, intended to keep politics free from religious influence.

Olivier Roy establishes a difference between Secularism and *Laïcité*. Secularism indicates a civil society's distance from the sacred realm, which does not necessarily include the denial of religion itself. *Laïcité* instead refers to an ideological denial of religion that is marginalized and limited to the private sphere by the State. The puzzling framework appears when the public discourse uses these terms (secularism

---

[32] Habermas (1991).

[33] Bhargava and Helmut (2005).

[34] Engineer (2007).

and *Laïcité*) synonymously across the different European contexts. Roy argues that the denial of religion in the public sphere through French *laïcité*, the most radical form of laicism, cannot be applied to the rest of the European countries because French *laïcité* is the result of a historical process in which the French class-system and the political system take part. Scott called "*laïcité*" a specific "French version" of laicism and a unique feature of the "French national character." According to her, *laïcité* indicates that an individual's consciousness is a private matter that should be separated from the public realm. A similar viewpoint is expressed by Ruba Salih, who stresses that the French *laïcité* resistance to accommodate the religious presence in the public sphere can never be the European norm. They all agree that *laïcité* is just a myth of consensus around the Republican values because France has been experiencing an identity crisis with Islam.

Secularism is perceived as an aspect of modernity, while religion belongs to the past and to the irrationality of traditions. Modernization is linked to "Westerniza-tion" and secularization of the institutional system. For this reason, privatization of religion and "individualization" of religious affiliation following the "do-it-by-yourself" approach are welcomed in the European public sphere. In Europe, secu-larism demands that political, social, and cultural moralities be maintained inde-pendently from religious influences because "European citizens are supposed to relate to societies as autonomous, responsible, reflective entities."[35] The visibility of Islam in the European secular public sphere initiates a fierce debate on religious freedom, tolerance, and the boundary of expressing faith and religion in public. Ramadan notes that when the religious visibility concerns small minority groups such as Yanomamis and Sioux, the discussion is seen as insignificant, and no fear is expressed. But when Islam is involved, the debate inflames the public with concerns and preoccupations. Ramadan explains this preoccupation mainly because of Islam's substantial influence, the increasing numbers of native Muslims and converts, the politics of international power balance, and the historical legacy mentioned above. Although the expressed concerns revolve around "extremism," Ramadan reveals that the problem's source is the "religious frame of reference." It intimidates the secular minds to speak about God and to confess faith publicly. The principle of *tawhid* (Monothelitism) creates social disorder by denying the social classes, and it "shakes the liberal universe to its roots" (1999: 147). Secular-minded governments, offi-cials, and politics make the immediate association between practicing Muslims and fundamentalists. In contrast to many other religions, Islam is not limited to a static personal system of beliefs restricted to individuals' private lives. Instead, Islam is a dynamic way of life that can be anything but restricted to a private sphere. Debates about Islam's compatibility in Europe nominate the "Islamic pious identity" as a "challenge" across all European contexts. Secularism across Europe does not mean denying religion. Indeed, the individual's right to religion is protected under secular constitutional law as much as in the Universal Declaration of Human Rights (UDHR) and the European Convention on Human Rights (ECHR) in article No. 18 in both. Yet, in France, *laïcité* denial of religion is justified.

---

[35] Amiraux (2007: 136).

Secularism's main objective is to keep the neutrality of the public sphere. However, such neutrality is nothing more than a needed discourse, an aspirational desire, to justify Muslims' religious discrimination. No measurement guarantees that religious groups are treated evenly in public or if the religious sings' visibility is accepted equally. For example, the European Convention on Human Rights guarantees freedom of thought, conscience, and religion. Article 9 states that everyone has the freedom "to manifest his religion or beliefs."[36] However, the European Court of Human Rights (ECtHR) ruled that France has not violated the ECHR in the 2010 full-veil ban law depending on articles 8 and 9, "the public safety" and "the protection of the rights of the rights and freedom to others." The European Court of Justice ruled in the case of Samira Achbita, an employee in a private sector G4S banned the right to practice the hijab, on 14 March 2017, that the ban of the Islamic hijab at the workplace "does not constitute direct discrimination based on religion or belief within the meaning of the directive." They argue that this prohibition is based on the internal rules of banning the visible wearing of any political, philosophical, or religious sign at work.[37] It aims at the protection of the staff members and the client from visible religious or political signs. The ECtHR, previously in 2013, ruled in favor of Nadia Eweida in a crucifix case at the workplace in British Airlines. The ECtHR declared defending the freedom of religion:

> The domestic authorities failed sufficiently to protect the first applicant's right to manifest her religion, in breach of the positive obligation under article 9 [of the European convention on human rights, which guarantees freedom of thought, conscience, and religion].[38]

The Prime Minister welcomed the ruling on Twitter; he tweeted: "Delighted that principle of wearing religious symbols at work has been upheld-ppl should not suffer discrimination due to religious beliefs."[39] Eweida was awarded 2000€ in compensation by the Court in Strasbourg after it ruled against the British company. In another inclusion of the Chrisitan religious sign, the ECtHR also rules in favor of the crucifix visibility in the *Lautsi v Italy* case in a state-school classroom. The Court decides that the Cross visibility is related to each European State decision, and there are no fixed rules about it:

> 70. The Court concludes in the present case that the decision of whether crucifixes should be present in State-school classrooms is, in principle, a matter falling within the margin of appreciation of the respondent State. Moreover, the fact that there is no European consensus on the question of the presence of religious symbols in State schools (see paragraphs 26-28 above) speaks in favor of that approach.[40]

The Court's final decision concludes that the cross's presence in the Italian public classroom does not violate "the protection of the rights and freedom to others" in

---

[36] See the full ECHR on: https://www.echr.coe.int/Documents/Convention_ENG.pdf.

[37] See the full case at: https://curia.europa.eu/jcms/upload/docs/application/pdf/2017-03/cp170030en.pdf.

[38] https://hudoc.echr.coe.int/eng#{%22itemid%22:[%22001-115881%22]}.

[39] https://www.theguardian.com/law/2013/jan/15/ba-rights-cross-european-court.

[40] See the full case on: https://hudoc.echr.coe.int/eng#{%22dmdocnumber%22:[%22883169%22],%22itemid%22:[%22001-104040%22]}.

Article 9 in the ECHR because "it was a religious symbol with which non-Christians did not identify. Moreover, by obliging schools to display it in State-school class-rooms, the State conferred a particular dimension on a given religion, to the detriment of pluralism" (p. 23). Among the justification of the decision of the ECtHR, I list the followings:

> 71. it is true that by prescribing the presence of crucifixes in State-school classrooms – a sign which, whether or not it is accorded in addition to a secular symbolic value, undoubtedly refers to Christianity – the regulations confer on the country's majority religion preponderant visibility in the school environment.

> 72. a crucifix on a wall is an essentially passive symbol, and this point is of importance in the Court's view, particularly having regard to the principle of neutrality (see paragraph 60 above). It cannot be deemed to have an influence on pupils comparable to that of didactic speech or participation in religious activities.

These justifications of the ECtHR, in this case, demonstrates that secularism is used to invisible the Islamic sings and exempt the Christian signs' visibility. It is worth saying that small crosses and other religious signs are not strictly controlled after the French 2004 ban at the public school, not even Muslim boys' beard. Secularism is a hegemonic approach to impose Western sovereignty over the European Muslim minority rather than a real separation between religion and the State. The term "Secular Europe" is no more than a myth that has been used to create an imagined community in opposition to the Muslim one.[41]

As secularism is used to justify the ban and the exclusion of the hijab across Europe, the practice is framed as troubling to the "public secular moralities." The inquietude of the hijab's visibility is related to the foe theory that stigmatizes the garment as the "enemy flag." The 2004 French ban was a law against the republic's enemy, relating it to colonial relations with Muslim countries and the resistance movements. The law excepts private, mainly Catholic schools from the law even though they receive economic support from the state. Also, hijab-wearing women who clean governmental departments are exempted. At the same time, the law is not applied fairly to all religious signs. Scott observes that the law is applied as an "afterthought" on Jewish boys' skullcaps, yet it is directly applied to the underage Muslim girls. The headscarf is targeted since it is a threat to the indivisible, secular French identity. President Jacques Chirac created the Stasi commission in July 2003 in the name of French unity. He wrote to Bernard Stasi that the republican community was in danger: "today is the headscarf and tomorrow?" (2009: 116).

Scott exposes the paradox of considering hijab minor girls as a national threat while cleaning hijab-wearing women are not. The debate of politicians, journalists, and public commentators turns the hijab into an alien flag that erodes the Republic's pillar. The left, who support the exclusion of the hijab from public schools, connected it to Islamic fundamentalism, portraying them as Nazis and pointing out the danger that underlies the practice. Stasi said that the law aims to counter "forces trying to destabilize the Republic" in an apparent reference to the "fundamentalism."[42] He

---

[41] Salih (2009) and Roy (2007).

[42] Henley (2003).

stresses that this law does not target the "moderate Muslims" in France. The ban's political justification had a worse impact on the French Muslim community than the ban itself. Muslim practitioners are stigmatized as the Republic's enemy who shakes the Republic values by the hijab practice, whereas those who quite their visible religious identity are seen as moderated. The French ban debate emphasizes the marginalization and exclusion of the Muslim community from the national identity. In contrast, the ban law's opposition considers it a continuation of French colonial politics denying Muslims' right to decide on their faith and identity in France. Scott states that the ban is a demonstration of "political hysteria" in which the "social anxieties" were replaced by a "phantasmatic enemy" and "phantasmatic solutions" were provided.

Critical social problems in France, such as Muslim exclusion, racism, and religious discrimination, are marginalized or even justified as a response to the Islamist threat. A threat extends from another continent, particularly from Saudi Arabia and Iran (Spatial positionality). In contrast, Secularism and *laïcité* are assigned as the core values of the French national identity (self-categorization). Scott draws a reference to a study of the French sociologist Francois Dubet (1996), who affirms that secularism's challenge depends on economic and social factors. He declares that after the 1970s, lower-class students increased in secondary and high schools, which caused a remarkable change in school mission, teachers' role, and school-society relations. According to Dubet, the heart of the problem lies in the class conflict, which is usually related to race and not religion. He asserts that the French attempt to neutralize public schools is converting schools to microcosm under siege. Relying on his interpretation, Scott argues that the headscarf ban is a "displacement of concern, a way to avoid facing a social and economic dilemma that facing the French schools" (2009: 108).

The British Muslim Community: An Overview

The critical reference in the United Kingdom's historical religious progress was around 1530–1540 when Henry VII broke with the Rome church because it would not approve his spouse's disposal plan. Afterward, there were series of Parliament acts that announced the church as a religious body accepted by the State, yet it was not a body part of the State. The transitional period was not easy, neither amicable. The conflicts on the religious principles, authorities, and domination caused three civil wars in England, and it took centuries to get the shape we recognize nowadays.[43] However, religion in the United Kingdom is still complex, ambiguous, and full of contradictions. The complexity of the United Kingdom contexts involves, apart from the religious minorities, a multi-national diversity: Wales, Scotland, and Ireland (Anglican Church, Catholic Church, Wales Church, and Ireland Church).[44]

---

[43] Bruce (2013).
[44] Hill et al. (2011).

Each national church developed in the past its religious frame. For example, the reformists, who were the primary motivators of the separation between religion and politics, were not welcome in Wales. On the contrary, they were trendy in Scotland and Ireland. The expansion of the franchise in the electoral arena, around 1832, motivated religion to be part of the political agenda and class identity. By the beginning of the nineteenth century, the number of diverse churches decreased. The Wales Church and the Ireland Church were disestablished. Still, the United Kingdom's religious conflict remains mainly between the Catholic Church and the Anglican Church. The Catholic Church persuades its power from its domination in Europe, even in France, the anticlerical republican. In the very late of the nineteenth century, the United Kingdom finally managed a homogenous coincidence of its churches and national identity.

The 1998 Human right act, enforced in the United Kingdom in 2000, had binary effects. The act accentuates religious freedom as a positive legal right rather than a negative accommodation, yet, it was inconsistent with some aspects of English constitutional heritage. This clash manifested in the political arena and caused several litigations. Anyhow, contemporary British politics is obsessed with the secular more than the sacred. Martin Steven recognizes two political approaches toward religion in the United Kingdom.[45] The first one represents the political scientists' approach, which opts to ignore religion and all aspects of its influences. This approach refers to churches' institutional failure, the decline of church attendance, and the absence of religious-social conflict. The second approach, which Steven calls "more rational," maintains that the church still enjoys its influence in voting processes. That is why political parties still include religious groups. Steven stresses that the religious heritage in the United Kingdom is more cultural than spiritual. Individuals might be motivated by their religious faith to help society and do good, but there is no need to talk publicly about it. Modood explains that religion's new political relevance in the United Kingdom has come out of the political mobilization of minorities who prioritized their religious identity over ethnicity and color.[46] Muslims were the last who attempt to overtake the rights already won by other racial and ethnic groups. It was somehow legal to discriminate against Muslims in the British context until December 2003 because, before that date, the court did not recognize Muslims as an ethnic group. Muslims did not manage that Muslim schools receive State subvention as the Catholic and Jewish schools. By 2007, only seven Muslim schools had succeeded in receiving state funding under strict criteria.[47] By 2014, twelve out of 140 Muslim schools were granted State funding.[48]

The British 2001 Census reveals that the membership of most Christian churches declined. The results indicate that the decline includes religious faith but not religious practices. The census reveals that in England and Wales, 71.75% of the population regard themselves as Christian, 2.97% Muslim, 0.50% Jewish, 0.29% Sikh,

---

[45]Steven (2010).
[46]Modood (2011).
[47]Rizvi (2014).
[48]Smith (2016).

and 7.71% did not respond.[49] Steve Bruce argues that Church attendance is more common in Scotland than in England or in Wales. Yet, the census showed a higher Christian population for England and Wales than in Scotland, which proves that religious practices are declined in the United Kingdom but not the faith. In the twentieth century, the increased religious minority population shifted the governmental concerns from a multi-Christian British identity to a multi-religious British identity. For example, the new African Pentecostalist churches in London altered the religious geography of the region.[50] These churches converted London to the most religious areas, even more than the countryside.

Minority groups are always more conscious of their religious identity. Their individual personal beliefs are not sufficient to perceive social recognition, but rather, the shared collective practices are. Remarkably, the salient controversial representation of religious minorities is the dress code. In contemporary Christianity, there is no need to dress or eat in a certain way to be recognized as a Christian in the public sphere, which converts the Sikh turban and the Muslim headscarf to the most prominent religious visibility in the British public school.

It is difficult to determine when exactly the first British Muslim generation appeared in the United Kingdom. The colonial relationship between England and Muslim countries, India in particular, allowed fluent movements of Muslim workers and professionals into the United Kingdom, even before WWI. The descendants of those workers formed the first British Muslim generation. They got no social recognition, and they were not involved actively in social life. They were few in number, and they were expected to go back "home" with their parents when they finish their work. Politically, this British generation was unseen nor considered as part of British society. The rapid growth of this minority is noteworthy due to the fertile nature of Muslim families. The first British Muslims were mistakenly seen through the intermittent waves of Muslim migrants after WWII, the 60s academic migrants, and post-European Union migrant-flows. In 2004, Savage indicated that the Muslim population rises 0.2% points in the United Kingdom per year: from 2.7% in 2001 to 4% in 2008.

Richard Kerbaj, in 2009 wrote in The Time Online: "Muslim population rising ten times faster than the rest of the society." He indicates that the Muslim population increased from 500.000 to 2.4 million in just four years. The 2011 Census[51] shows that the Muslim population increased from 3.0 to 4.8% of the total population, which ranks Islam as the second-largest religion in the United Kingdom after Christianity at 59.3%. The vast majority lives in England, then Scotland, and least are in Wales and Northern Ireland.

---

[49]Robinson and Gardee (2016).

[50]Modood (2015).

[51]See the full 2011 Census in: https://www.ons.gov.uk/peoplepopulationandcommunity/culturali dentity/religion/articles/religioninenglandandwales2011/2012-12-11.

Rushdie's Affair

The Muslim community's distinctive features in the United Kingdom are its ethnic diversity, social and educational various backgrounds, and language differences. Another salient attribute of the British Muslim community is the fact that it is a young community. The Muslim British collective identity had not been officially shaped till the British Kashmiri novelist and essayist Salman Rushdie published his conflictive novel, *"The Satanic Verse," in 1988.* The title refers to a legendary few verses recited by the prophet Muhammad as the words of God. The novel claims that those words were the devil's words who could deceive the prophet, so he thought they appertain to God. Those verses form an essential subplot in the novel. However, Muslim religious scholars proved that this legend is fabricated because it is not found in the authentic Islamic resources. The novel aroused the Muslim rage because it implies that the verses of the Quran, the authentic book and the source of the Divine faith and religious practices, were, or could be, the devil's work. On the international level, the conflict was politically used by Shiism In Iran. In 1989, Ruhollah Khomeini of Iran stated a fatwa that requires Muslims to kill Rushdie for his blasphemy. This fatwa generated numerous killings, killing, and bombing attempts against the publishing staff, translators, editors, and publishers. Finally, in 1998, Iranian president Mohammad Khatami declared that the government no longer supports this fatwa.[52]

On the British level, the Rushdie affair had a no-return impact. Tariq Modood, in his article "Multiculturalism, Britishness, and Muslims," published online in the Open Democracy website in 2011,[53] draws attention to five critical impacts of Rushdie's Affairs on the Muslim community in the United Kingdom. Firstly, Muslim politics, which appeared as a response to the Rushdie affair, were not created by a state's demand, as we will see in the Spanish context. Muslim political identity was a social need and a challenge for both minority–majority relations. Secondly, Muslim politics consists of a monocular minority mobilization and endeavor without any support from other British minorities. Thirdly, Rushdie's affair shifted Muslim minority's focus to the Muslim majority solidarity from the Atlantic to the orient. It marked the beginning of the internationalism of the minority in an unseen phenomenon ever. However, his transnational *"ummatic"* solidarity increased the Muslim suffering after the Khomeini fatwa. Fourthly, "radical and pragmatic" (or "moderate") leadership emerged among Muslims after Rushdie's affairs. Muslim leaders needed to adapt their public discourse on Rushdie's affair to the British's frame of reference on the issue. British Muslim representatives in the UK Action Committee on Islamic Affair campaign (UKACIA) changed their discourse keywords to fit the British public sphere standards. They first used the term "apostasy," then they replace it with a more British term "blasphemy" to achieve more comprehension and support. Yet, this second term also failed to capture the British interest. Later on,

---

[52]Garton (2007) and Jacobson (2006).

[53]See the full article in: https://www.opendemocracy.net/tariq-modood/multiculturalism-britis hness-and-muslims.

they used the "incitement to religious hatred" term that echoed the Northern Ireland term of "incitement of racial hatred." It is to say, the British Muslim political and social identity, in its initial stages, developed its criterion depending on their own experiences and scaling on their errors. Fifthly and lastly, the Rushdie affair drew Muslim leaders' attention that they are making more publicity criticizing the extremists, who are already popular in the media, instead of being unified in one central authority representing the actual Muslim community. Modood asserts that those five features are still present today. The most important consequence of the Rushdie affair is the Muslim Council of Britain (MCB), founded in 1998 as an outcome of the UKACIA collaboration. The government accepts the Council; it is a leading voice of the Muslim community in the United Kingdom. Add to this, Modood indicates that British Muslims, instead of limiting their cause by their own (religious) interests, cleverly used the already existing British arguments related to racial and multicultural equality. Accordingly, they could achieve active political adjustment, and they became part of the British political culture.

Multiculturalism, Britishness or Social Richness

Religious diversity in the United Kingdom has been through varied phases of recognition and control. First, the British framework implemented the term "multiculturalism" in social interactions and state-supported schools to challenge racism. "Multiculturalism," as a social structure, is seen as an exclusive approach to the UK social frame. After the 9/11 attacks, Muslim loyalty has been questioned. The Human Rights Act of 1998 was perceived as a terrorist's charter by "the law-abiding majority" rather than a set of values that ensure everybody's rights and responsibilities.

Modood indicates that the origin of "British multiculturalism," as an idea and a policy, relies on the Afro-American experience. It firstly appeared between the 1960s and 1970s as "race relations" with the young black men. When the diverse multi-origin youth became more numerous, assertive, and visible, the term "race" is replaced by terms as "ethnicity," "ethnic minorities," and "multiculturalism" to improve social negotiations. Modood defines multiculturalism as follows: "multiculturalism is where processes of integration are seen both two-way and as involving groups as well as individuals and as working differently for different groups" (2011: 6). It is to say, multiculturalism has different forms depending on the context and the timing. The term "multiculturalism" indicates the acknowledgment of the minority groups, all different minorities, not only Muslims, within the British frame. Although multiculturalism afforded respect for individual dignities and provided political accommodation for group identities, it could not fully obliterate exclusionary practices, especially those related to the Muslim community.

Multiculturalism became a target of criticism increasingly after 2010. The difference between the lived experience of multiculturalism and the multiculturalism policies is significant. Kenan Mallik indicates that the multiculturalism experience converts the British society to a "less insular, more vibrate and more cosmopolitan space which is positive."[54] She argues that multiculturalism policies aim to manage diversity by "putting people into ethnic boxes, defining individual needs and rights by virtues of the boxes into which people are put, and using these boxes to shape the public policy." Such a framework does not break stereotypes or open minds; it is created for "the policing of borders, whether physical, cultural or imaginative." The conflation between the lived experience and political policies ends up pointing at the minorities as the problem behind the social policy's failure. Malik attributes that multiculturalism "undermines" the valuable lived experiences of diversity. It does not empower minorities but the community leaders whose position and influence are in-debt relations with the State. Multiculturalism policies treat minorities as homogenous wholes. It ignores the class, religion, gender, and other differences and leaving those communities feeling misinterpreted and, indeed, disenfranchised. Such policies created conflicts within minorities instead of empowering them, and they transformed multiculturalism into a divisive force in British society. The distribution of political power and the financial resources according to ethnicity forced people to identify themselves in terms of these ethnicities even though these ethnicities recurrently set off one group against another.

The Media and political discourse tend to use the term integration as an "inclusive" framework of diversity. The term "integration" means the unification into the whole. Yet, it was used in public discourse to refer to migrants rather than the British Muslims. For that reason, "the unification into the whole" indicates learning the language and costumes and improving the economic and educational circumstances. The relation between the term and the collective of migrants conflate the discourse on the British Muslim generation and the discourse on the new migrant Muslims. In 2008, Derek Mcgheeassures, in his book *"End of Multiculturalism: Terrorism, Integration, and Human Rights,"*[55] states that the debate on the failure of multiculturalism should be based on the debate on human rights, citizenship, equality, and security in contemporary Britain. Mcghee points out that these debates frequently comprise concerns and accusations against the Muslim community as if they are central to "the merits and the demerits" of multiculturalism. Yet, Modood, in 2011, argues that multiculturalism is not dead nor ended or failed. He clarifies that multiculturalism aims at integration. The pro- and anti-multiculturalism arguments differ in the normative understanding of integration. Mcghee indicates that both Paul Gilroy and Tariq Modood, leader British academics, are pro-multiculturalism as a successful policy for managing diversity. Mcghee refers that Modood's vision of multiculturalism consists of praising multiculturalism as a guiding principle for integration strategies that prevent the falling in assimilation. While in fact, Modood sets the difference between multiculturalism, individualist integration, cosmopolitanism, and assimilation and indicates that each principle illuminates the other and intends to include what is thought to be missing.

---

[54]The article, titled "Multiculturalism undermines diversity", is published in *The Guardian*, 2010. https://www.theguardian.com/commentisfree/2010/mar/17/multiculturalism-diversity-political-policy.

[55]McGhee (2008).

British Public School

Religious education in British state schools is compulsory, but, contrary to the Spanish context mentioned later, there is no compulsory national curriculum. The Educational Reform Act in 1988 states that each local school authority should establish the Standing Advisory Council on Religious Education (SACRE). The council's role is to be a mediator between the authority and the school's religious needs. Religious education is set in accordance with the agreed syllabus of the authority and the religious diversity of that school. This does not include a compulsory national curriculum or specific religious education guidelines neither include a scientific approach to comparative religious studies. It is instead a pragmatic and well-disposed answer to the local diversity scope.[56] The Educational Reform Act aims to find a consensus that reflects the existing plurality of religions within the local community.

Nonetheless, the provided curriculum must reflect the religious tradition of the United Kingdom, Christianity, even in the daily act of collective worship. This emphasis is related to the close relationship between the state and the Anglican Church in Britain, which should not be loosened. This religious education pattern in the United Kingdom aims mainly to build up mutual recognition of the coexisting differences based on multi-faith teaching.[57]

An essential aspect of religious education in British public schools is that it constitutes an essential element in the anti-discrimination policies. They set an exclusive system of committees to protect equal opportunities in education. Yet, Muslim parents are concerned about the daily worship act, the content of religious education, and the unskilled teaching staff.[58] Sabina Mannitz indicates that teachers of religious education are not skilled in multi-faith subject management. They do not master the sufficient confidence or knowledge of other religions to balance their teaching performance in depth. This fact increases the non-Christian parents' worries, not only Muslims, that their faith will be presented in a distorted manner to their children in the class. For that reason, Muslims attempt to establish private independent Islamic schools or state-funded Islamic schools that cover secular, cultural, and religious subjects. Hence, many organizations have been established to address educational concerns, such as The Union of Muslim Organizations (UMO), the UK Islamic Mission, and the Muslim Educational Trust. They all intend to maintain the balance and to observe any presumed adverse effects. Muslim parents consider those schools as essentials not because of their religious instructions but because of their "cultural survival."[59] They introduce an innovative religious education pattern based on the British cultural norms combining both British and religious identities.

The accommodation and "tolerance" of other religious groups at British public schools are indirectly based on religion's general respect. It is to say, religious beliefs are agreed to be cultural and specific to ethnic groups. Accordingly, Muslim students

---

[56]Mannitz (2004).
[57]Hemming (2015).
[58]Khir-Allah (2015).
[59]Garbaye (2010).

are indirectly protected as they belong to specific ethnic communities but not as Muslims. From this perspective, headscarves are accepted in state schools, as long as it matches the uniform, as a cultural costume of certain ethnic groups but not as a religious sign.[60] The headscarf is accepted in British schools as part of the school uniform. There is no sign that this is going to change in the future.

Spanish Context

Spanish identity was firstly shaped in the late fifteenth century during the Muslim presence in Hispania. In 1492, Muslims, Arabs, Sephardic Jews, and Gypsy were all excluded from the peninsula, and Spain officially started the conquest of America. In the Reconquista, Muslim "Muladies," native Iberian origins who formed most of the Muslim population at then, were also excluded. When Islam had been historically excluded from the country equation, Spanish identity as Christian "Us" was built, and asserted, in opposition to Muslim "Others." The Spanish context did not witness the Catholic and Protestant clash as in France and the United Kingdom. Instead, the religious clash was between Christianity and Islam.

The term "la *hispanidad*" was revived after losing the colonies. It is used to stress the cultural and historical proximity with the previously colonized countries. It was reused again by Francisco Franco, a Spanish general, military dictator, who ruled over Spain from 1939 until he died in 1975. Franco used the term in the political discourse to accommodate the entire Spanish area. Under Franco's ruling, the Hispanidad included a sense of belonging to a linguistic "Spanish" component and a Catholic religious community. "*Hablo Chirsitano*" is a frequent term used in public discourse to delineate the included and excluded components of the Spanish identity during the Franco era.[61] Non-Spanish speakers, atheists, gypsies, and Muslims were officially excluded from the notion of "*la hispanidad*." After Franco's death, the democratic transition disestablished the Catholic Church's domination in politics, but the church continues enjoying economic, social, and cultural privileges. It receives about 250 million Euros a year from individual assignments and direct public subsidies. The State finances the Salaries of the bishops and priests, and Catholic schools receive considerable public funding. Catholic leaders are commonly invited to participate in national and traditional ceremonies. Catholic churches are exempted from following the municipal regulations and conditions.

In contemporary Spain, the Church-State relation, the Church's roles in public, and Catholic imposition in Spanish identity are triggers of political clashes between the progressive, liberal, and secularist Left from one side and the conservative pro-clerical Right, on the other.[62] Spanish governments extended the institutional privi-leges to an increasing number of religions to promote religious neutrality in front of

---

[60]Collet (2004).

[61]Zapata-Barrero and Diez-Nicolas (2012).

[62]Astor (2017) and Dietz (2007).

Catholic domination.[63] Spain ended up the post-Franco transition by joining the European Union. The new democratic state and national identification were built based on the myth of Europe. The political discourse of both socialists and Popular Party links the Spanish interests to European interests. This linkage is used to legitimize the brand-new domestic policies and justify the institutional regulations that aim to adjust to the European institutional frameworks. Since joining the European Union, Spain has started looking for its identity by imitating European neighbors.[64] Miguel Angel Moratinos points out that the Spanish imitation of the European frames attempts to forget its historical relation with the Muslim world. The current Spanish notion of "Westernization" is a false enjoyment because Spain is losing many defining aspects of its Spanish identity and Spanish heritage. Following the European approaches in defining "Islam" and "European Muslims" is incompatible with the Spanish national standards because the Spanish Muslim community is not similar to those European Muslim generations.

The current Muslim population in Spain has nothing to do with the ancient Islamic Kingdom (Al-Andalus). It is recent, started in the post-Franco period, and rapidly doubled in the last few decades. Numbers and statistics around the Muslim population in Spain vary according to the source of the study. Hussain Kettani (2010: 8) indicates that Spain's Muslim population increased from 1.75% in 2001 to 2.60% in 2009, with the lowest fertility rate. Rabasa and Benard in 2014 mention that Spanish official estimation of the Muslim population (permanent resident or Spanish Muslims) ranges up to one million, constituting 2.50% of the Spanish population. Rabasa and Benard's study indicates that from 2010 to 2014, the Muslim population has not increased; instead, it fell 0.10%. The Union of Muslim Communities in Spain (UCIDE) provides a higher result in 2014.[65] Muslims constitute 3.9% of the Spanish population. In 2017,[66] UCIDE published that the Muslim population reached 4% of the total population, of which 43% are Spanish Muslims, and 57% are migrants.

The research on the Muslim population in Spain reveals the contradiction of ratios and numbers provided by different national sources. Social estimations differ from the official governmental ratios and differ from the Muslim representative organization's estimations, which is labeled as unreliable. There is no official agreement between the governmental investigations and the religious entities on Spain's Muslim population, which kept the Muslim population in Spain ambiguous. The unclear official declarations on the Muslim population are not a coincidence. If the official data reveals the Muslim population's rapid increment, it will ignite inquietude and fears in the public discourse. These ratios will be a trigger for social and political demands for and by Muslims. It is part of Spain's public policy to hide the problem, deny it exists, and then profoundly believe in that denial and publicly defend it. As long as the Muslim population ratio is obscured, it is easier for the public discourse to ignore their religious rights and social demands.

---

[63] Álvarez-Junco (2013) and Townson (2015).

[64] Moratino (1999) and Casanova (2011).

[65] See the whole results on: http://ucide.org/sites/default/files/revistas/estademograf14.pdf.

[66] See the whole results on: http://observatorio.hispanomuslim.es/estademograf.pdf.

Muslim's Civil Participation

The problematic interrelation between the present and past Moors motivates the opposition to building new places for worship and increases the fear of seeing Islam's visibility in the neighborhoods.[67] The contemporary political discourse has not provided a much better impact. It narrates similarities between those who confess Christianity or have been born in this context, and it discerns the numerous "others," such as Muslims. The political discourse also tends to use Franco's theory in setting Christianity as a central pillar of Spanishness: la *Hispanidad.*[68] Post-Franco, the Spanish government is compelled to reorganize its relationship with the Catholic Church, reducing the growing Muslim community to Islamism, security, and terrorism. Besides, the Spanish government has difficulties negotiating with the Muslim community because of the structural variable representative figures.

One of the first institutional appearances of Muslims in Spain was the *Asociación Musulmana de España*, which appeared in 1971. The first president was Ray Al-Tatari of Syrian origin. This association participated actively in the preparation of the Organic Law of religious freedom signed in July 1989 when Spain recognized Islam as a deeply rooted religion *"de notario arraigado."* At then, the Religious Entity Registration in the Ministry of Justice registered 40 Muslim entities; in 2008, the number increased to 640 associations. Those multiple entities were united under an institutional umbrella *Federación Española de Entidades Religiosas Islámicas (FEERI)* with a Spanish convert's presidency. Later on, the *Unión de Comunidades Islámicas de España* (UCIDE) broke up from FEERI with the presidency of Riay El-Tatary. In 1992, the Religious Freedom Advisory asked for a unified representation of the Muslim community to sign an agreement of cooperation; thus, the *Comisión Islámica de España (CIE)* was born as a bicephalous institution. A few years ago, the Spanish government required the cancelation of the dual leadership and demanded a single commission president. El-Tatary was chosen. He became the only representative figure of Muslims in the Spanish state. After he died in 2020, Ayman Idlby, a retired Syrian doctor, was elected.

The 1992 agreement included religious education at schools, the registration of imams with the social security system, and the appointment of clergies in prisons. Since 1992, there has been no serious political well to carry out these rights. The inner conflicts between the two representative umbrellas and the lack of representational diversity contribute to the agreement's abandonment.[69] The *Fundación de Pluralismo y Convivencia* was created in 2005 to help faith minorities with grant subsidies. These grants are not dedicated to religious activities but are dedicated to maintaining the headquarters and official buildings. By 2007, a budget of €4.5 million was spent on all faith minorities in Spain. Since 1992, there has been no serious progress in

---

[67] De Madariaga (2015) and El-Madkouri (2011).

[68] Christianity is also attacked in the political discourse to promote secularism in an opposition to the Church power. See Cuevas (2016).

[69] Navarro (2009) and Cembrero (2016).

implementing the agreement. For example, the local administration obstacles the opening of new mosques much more than the neighbors' disagreement does, and Islamic religious education at public school has been introduced recently through only 35 teachers (the real demand is 314 teachers) assigned in the ministry of education to teach Islam with no straightforward program to be followed. The hijab's visibility in the classroom and the workplace is a trigger of a political debate in the shed of no clear State regulation about it. There have been difficulties in opening and maintaining mosques, which is the responsibility of municipalities. The collaboration between local Muslim entities and the municipality is affected by stereotypes, personal orientations, and obscured legislation. Besides, no new cemeteries have been opened, Muslim religious entities are not exempted from taxes, and clergies in prisons and hospitals are signed in very exceptional cases. Multiple attempts to opening a private Islamic school were obstructed; no attempt has seen the light yet. Add to this, the 1992 agreement involved Muslims in managing the Spanish-Muslim heritage; CIE indicates that it is excluded from the process.[70]

Spain has no clear social regulations to embrace The Spanish Muslim youth. The Islamization of migrants in Spain is practiced since the first generation of migrants in the last century.[71] The new Spanish Muslim generation, likewise, European Muslims, has not entirely abandoned its own religious culture. Instead, they became more visible than their parents with explicit religious and civic demands. They tend to identify themselves as "Spanish" more than their parents' origin country. At the same time, this generation stresses its "Muslim" identity and its religious rights more than their parents did. Like the British and French contexts, the self-categorization as "Muslim" is a response against multiple social stigmatizations practiced on them, such as migrants, Moorish, middle class, ethnic, or any other national categorization. As Muslims, they do not feel identified by their parents' country of origin because of the deep culture-Islamic overlapping practices. It is to say, the majority of those young Muslims learn pure Islam away from cultural influences. They can criticize and disapprove of the blend of Islamic practices and cultural or traditional practices, especially those related to women's rights. A fact that pushes them away from their parents' national identity. At the same time, they are not considered fellow citizens in Spanish society because they refuse to drop their religious identity. Despite their will to integrate, they reject the Spanish standards of integration that implies, similar to the French frames of integration, total immersion, and assimilation of the Spanish civic standards.

Spanish young Muslim generation insists on the compatibility between the Muslim identity and the Spanish identity. The constant refusal of losing the multi-identities establishes a gap that pushes Muslims aside. They are socially discriminated against, untrusted, and marginalized in the labor domain. Spanish Muslims are not seen as fellow citizens but as migrants or foreigners because they do not fit the (European) Spanish social standards. Even converts are considered to be betrayers to their mother culture. Spanish Muslims' new generation experiences a severe loss of

---

[70]Godard (2007: 129–194).

[71]Allievi (2005).

identity. As the mainstream exclusion forms the basis of the Spanish Muslims' identity crisis, the lack of elected representatives is the summit. There is a gap between the Muslim youth associations and the UCIDE, FEERI, and CIE.

One of the salient obstacles between Muslim associations is mistrust. The arguments of fundamentalism, Islamization, and the conspiracy control Muslim entities' relations, especially in the UCIDE. The inner conflict and the mistrust push the youth away and shift the UCIDE and FEERI's focus. There is considerable hesitation in collaboration with other Muslim entities, which ends in excluding some of them. The money dedicated to maintaining the mosques and Islamic centers is distributed according to the "trust" relationship the UCIDE holds with these centers' presidents. There has been no significant workshop or courses to introduce the rights signed in the agreement to the Muslim community. Finally, the young Spanish generation does not participate in the election of their leader and representative in the Spanish governmental and political sphere. In 2018, I interviewed Young Spanish Muslims for a project I participated in, called *"Civil Muslim society in Europe: Towards a new form of belonging and political participation?"*[72] The interviews revealed that the majority of Spanish Muslim youth do not feel identified with Riay El-Tatary, who had been the president of all the representative entities, except FEERI, since the 80s of the last centuries with no public elections ever. He managed to keep his position under the Spanish government's blessing. All of these inner challenges end up in a scattered and divided Muslim community. Despite the local attempts and the capacity of trained Spanish Muslim youth, the Muslim community is disoriented, weak, and underestimated. And that is precisely what the Spanish government needs to keep the national identity, fluctuated between Christianity and Secularity, defined and defended in opposition to the increasing Muslim population.

Ceuta and Melilla

A particular context of the Muslim population in Spain is Ceuta and Melilla. These two regions are officially Spanish territory, and they are expressed as such in the Organic Spanish ley in 1995.[73] In Spain, social science books teach that Ceuta and Melilla are Spanish territories as much as the Canary Islands and the Balearic Islands. Due to the historical origin and the high Muslim population in these two regions, the political and academic discourses deal with Ceuta and Melilla otherwise. The territory is Spanish, but the inhabitants are not. When Spain joined the European Union, it had to incorporate the Schengen acquis into the Spanish legal body (https://www.schengenvisainfo.com/schengen-acquis/). Within these new modifications, the Law of Immigration came into force. It limited the access to Spanish citizenship rights

---

[72]The project was founded by BBVA and carried out in the Complutense University of Madrid, IP: Cecilia Mayer.

[73]This law is available online on the following link: https://www.boe.es/buscar/pdf/1995/BOE-A-1995-6359-consolidado.pdf.

for Moroccan Muslims who lived for "centuries" in Ceuta and Melilla.[74] The law extended to mark their residency as illegal. The Muslim community received this new law by manifestations in both cities until this law was re-modified in 1987. In 2010, the Observatorio Andalusí published the demographic study[75] done by UCIDE, which reveals that the Muslim population in Ceuta is of 3.330 Muslim migrants and 30.631 Spanish Muslims, 83.517 total population.[76] In Melilla, there are 7.224 Muslim migrants and 30.222 Spanish Muslims, 81.323 total population. In the 2017 Census, the study indicates that the Muslim migrants' population in Ceuta is raised to 5.077 and the Spanish Muslims' to 31.726, 84.929 estimated total population. Whereas in Melilla, the Muslim migrants' raised to 12.014 and Spanish Muslims' to 32.729, 86.210 estimated total population. It is noticeable that the total population of 2017 is merely an estimation because the final results have not been published yet. These numbers reveal that almost half of the population of these two Spanish regions are Muslims, and they are in constant growth. They are called "nationalized Spanish," contrary to the catholic or secular inhabitants who are "Spanish citizens."

The exclusion of Ceuta and Melilla Muslims from the national identity has many faces. The most recurrent one is the academic work that stigmatizes them as the dark unwanted slop of the national identity. For example, The Real Institution El CANO published an investigation in 2014 coordinated by Felix Arteaga and titled "Spain looking at the South: From the Mediterranean to the Sahel." The analysis aims to investigate the zone problems that might affect Spanish security and defense. At the same time, it aims to analyze the interests and the opportunities of external exchange in the economy, energy, commercial, and investment. The study included Ceuta and Melilla contexts highlighting the Muslim population in these cities. The Spanish Muslim population was mainly referred to as the "Moroccan origin population" and "parents with Spanish nationality." The report reveals that the Muslim population lives in dire economic and housing conditions, mainly in poor neighborhoods. Their children suffer from school failure due to the "dialect Arabic mother tongue" and the "illiterate" mothers at home. Going through this report, it turns out that the Muslim population in Ceuta and Melilla is seen as merely recent migrants who can not speak Castellano. They are presented as the problem behind "*cisnes negros*," "illegal money transfer," and "poor welfare conditions." Such representation in academic studies takes away the Spanish government's responsibility to invest, seriously, in these regions to boost social and economic conditions. The report also draws a distinction between the Spanish Iberian and the Ceutanians and Melillan, who "hold Spanish identity."

The exclusion is framed in the public mind when media echoes such discourse. José Ángel Guti published a resume of the CANO study in *Hispanidad* titled: "*Ceuta y Melilla: cada vez menos españoles, Cada vez más Musulmanas. Y Rajoy no se*

---

[74]Gallardo (2008) and Dietz (2007).

[75]See results on: http://www.hazteoir.org/sites/default/files/upload/estademografico%20pobl acion%20musulmana%20HO%20febrero%202011.pdf.

[76]Ceuta and Melilla total population is detected in the City Population Portal of 2011 Census: http://www.citypopulation.de/Spain-Ceuta.html.

mueve"[77] (Ceuta and Melilla: less and less Spanish, more and more Muslim. And Rajoy does not move). The title itself sets clear the incompatibility between the Spanish identity and the Muslim identity; you either be a Spanish or a Muslim but never be both. The title arouses the readers' fear of the "Muslim growth" and asserts the need for political intervention to control the danger. Guti's article is almost a direct quotations of the exclusionary discourse of the El Cano study: "If this evolution continues," the Elcano Institute points out, "Melilla will be very soon, if it is not already, a Berber and Arab city, and Ceuta will follow in the footsteps later." The link between "Islam" as a religion and being an outsider "Arab" or "barber" is a constant falsified imposition over the Ceuta and Melilla Muslims. The term "morroquinización" is used in media to refer to the Muslim participation in the political arena in Ceuta and Melilla. Muslims in these two Spanish cities enjoy local parties that reclaim Muslim demands: The Collision of Melilla and The Movement of dignity and Citizenry of Ceuta.[78] Practitioner Muslims in Ceuta and Melilla can be found in all political parties, including the traditionally nativist conservative party. Muslim women run for office and have been elected and have reached positions of authority in those chambers. For example, Jadu Dris Mohamed Ben Abdallah was the first Muslim woman to become the second vice-president of the Melilla City assembly in 2006. A few years later, another member of Melilla's collision, Dunia Al-Mansouri Umpierrez, became the City Assembly's vice-president. Hijab-wearing women also are politically active and elected in the city assembly, such as Salima Abdul-Salam in 2005 and Fatima Hamade Hossain in 2007. The visibility of Muslims, especially the hijab-wearers, in the political sphere does not praise the accomplishment of women's rights or the "diversity" structure of these two cities. Instead, Muslims' visibility in the Ceuta and Melilla's political scene is interpreted as the "marroquinization" of the regions. It rings the alarm of the need for a political intervention from Madrid to limit it. The contemporary exclusion of Ceuta and Melilla Muslim from the Spanish mainstream identity is similar to the exclusion of Muladies in the Reconquista age: that land is Spanish, but the inhabitants who do not fit the national standards are not.

Spanish Public Schools

Multiculturalism in Spain is multifaced. Spain is built on multiple minority nations: the gypsies in the peninsula, the Islands and Ceuta and Melilla. In 1978, the Spanish constitution guaranteed political and demonstrative competences of the autonomous communities in Spain. The cultural diversity included the linguistic dimension in addition to traditional domestic practice. The Law of Linguistic Normalization in 1983 provided the regional authorities of Cataluña, El País Vasco, and Galicia the control over the educational system and the possibility to develop bilingual education programs and distinctive curricula. The regional languages are given equal official

---

[77] The *Hispanidad* is a Spanish Dairy of economy and Catholic actuality.
[78] Guia (2018).

status as the Castellano. Spain is already multi-national. These linguistic diversities are included in the Hispanidad except the Arabic language teaching at Ceuta and Melilla schools; it is taught as an extra scholar activity. It is perceived as a course for migrants' children.[79] The discourse of multiculturalism in Spain is not frequently used to signify the multi-national Spain. The term is used in the educational system to refer to migrants' integration and gypsies at public schools.

In Spanish schools, Migrants, Muslims, and Moroccan are synonymous with most Spanish mainstream teachers and school directors.[80] In 1994–1995, a new program was applied in state schools to teach the Moroccan language and culture to Moroccan origin and Spanish students. The objective of this program was to enforce intercultural education at schools. It was applied mainly in Madrid, Barcelona, and the South of Spain. The program generated many problems, most of which are the focus of the program itself. It increased the confusion between the terms "Muslims" and "Moroccan" in Spanish mainstream thoughts. The principles of intercultural education go against separating the students according to their origins, nationality, ethnicity, or language. Spanish students could not follow the program because of the advanced content, the academic overload in the curricular program, lack of materials and well-trained professors, etc.[81]

Contrary to the French educational model, and different from the British model, Catholic education at public school is still prominent. At primary school, Religious education is obligatory, and Catholic education used to be predominant. Lately, an option to opt the catholic education is provided, and an alternative subject is taught instead. The alternative subject was extra activities designed by the primary teacher of each class (extra readings, flashcards, and mental quiz) with one condition: It should not be related to the curriculum. Both Catholic education and the alternative subject were not valuable. In the 2014/2015 course, religious education is divided into two subjects: "Catholic values" or "social and civic values," which teaches ethics and values from a secular perspective. Primary students have to choose one of them. The educational system designs both of those signatures, and both of them are valuable. In secondary school, the alternative "the history of religion" is offered as a norm. Despite the signed agreement in 1992 and the numerous Muslim entities' attempts to have Islamic education at public school, the demand was not carried out seriously by the educational authorities, as I have mentioned above.

Jorgen Nielsen argues that public schools in Spain are going in the direction of a fully laïcité French model, and religious education would be limited to Catholic schools.[82] I argue that it is challenging to apply the French approach in Spanish public schools because laïcité is not only about religious education. As we have read above, laïcité is a systematic denial of the religion and its symbols and inferred meaning, such as Christmas celebrations, Saints vacations, and all different kinds of religious symbols or religious-rooted school activities. Even though a significant

---

[79]Maataoui (2015).

[80]Khir-Allah (2016).

[81]El-Madkouri (1995) and Abu-Shams (2006).

[82]Nieslen (1999).

number of Spanish citizens are not practitioners (they do not maintain the Christian faith), Christian celebrations and symbols are well rooted in the Spanish culture and Spanish national identity. Besides, the occult-rooted church-state relationship obstacles the development of a secular or *laïcité* approach.

The Practice of hijab at public school was not problematic in the past because it was not frequent. However, when the conflict occurs, opinions are divided between the right to education and religious freedom and between tendencies to prohibit all religious signs at public schools under the label of liberal values and gender equality. Generally, disallowing Muslim hijab-wearing students to access the classroom is related to the lack of clear state regulations on hijab visibility. The majority of Spanish public schools either prohibit covering the head or ban all signs of "discrimination." Hijab, according to the school, internal interpretation is a discriminative sign; it is a sign of discrimination between Muslims and non-Muslims and between girls and boys. In 2010, there was an attempt by the right-wing Popular Party to ban the hijab practice at public school. The attempt did not see the light because the Socialist Party, POSE, asserted the religious freedom and the right to education of the Muslim minority. Ricard Zapata-Barrero and Juan Diez-Nicolás state that the Spanish political conflict on the hijab is not between the righties and the lefties. It is between "dogmatic-intolerants" and "pluralist-tolerance." So far, and despite the multiple and successive exclusions, the Spanish educational authority, although it stresses the right to education, does not regulate the issue. The final decision is left to the school council and directors, where personal orientations and stereotypes interfere. There exist some schools which permit the hijab practice as long as it coincides with the school uniform. Yet, many others deal with the girl students and their hijab with conflictive procedures.

Conclusion

This chapter discussed how the European public discourse depends on the historical unfriendly colonial relationship with the Muslim worlds as much as on the cultural differences to promote Islam's incompatibility with the national values. It uses this argument to define the Nation's enemy and employs Islam as an instrument-of-fear in the political agenda. The giddy use of sensitive terms such as "fundamentalism," "terrorism," "radicalism," and "extremism" labels Muslim practitioners as such. Islamophobia feeds on national security discourse, which works successfully in fulfilling the political needs to stigmatize a whole minority across Europe, and in the United States, as "untrusted."

The European identity is facing a crisis due to the visibility of the Euro-Muslim population in the public sphere. The stigmatization of the European Muslim community as a community with a "different culture" evokes western superiority. Consequently, the European (secular or Chrisitan) identity is labeled as the norm, and other social and cultural norms are framed as the odd. As identities are contingents, there are no fixed standards for the (national) European identity. Indeed, it is continuously changing. The national identity reflects the Nation's inhabitants' identity. Trying to face the increasing visibility of Muslim's identity, the great majority of the European political discourse clings to a fixed secular European identity and imposes it on all the Nations' citizens. The hijab ban is one of these irrational impositions of the secular identity on European Muslims. Besides, there is a contradiction between the hijab ban and freedom of faith guaranteed in Europe.

The self-categorization of the European identity depends on spatial positionality that excludes the Euro-Muslims's origins from the continent. It also relies on the self-positionality that sets "us" in opposition to the "others," using cultural differences as triggers for supremacy and intolerance. The construction of a European Muslim identity is a taboo, especially in France. The visibility of the hijab is the straw that breaks the camelback. In French Laïcité, this piece of cloth is interpreted as a flag of resistance to the national values, a sign of militancy and women's oppression. This framing of the hijab in the French discourse merely recycles the colonial discourse in the twenty-first century. The French government associates the hijab with the colonies' religious resistance movements and projects it in the national arena.

Secularism is perceived as an approach of neutrality of the public sphere, but it is used to confront the increment of Muslim visibility in Europe. The unequal treatment of the religious signs at public schools and workplaces marginalizes the Muslim community in European countries. In France, the exclusion of hijab-wearing students from public schools is legitimized by the law, while in Spain, the opposite is true. However, the lack of clear laws on religious rights in Spain justified the hijab exclusion from public schools. In contrast to these two contexts, the United Kingdom normalized the hijab visibility in public schools as part of a multicultural social structure.

Framing the Muslim visibility in the European public sphere, especially hijab visibility, has passed through historical conflicts and colonial economic and social interests. In this chapter, I also covered the political utilization of European Muslim visibility to define the national identity in three European countries: France, the United Kingdom, and Spain. We have argued that the Muslim community differs across these three European contexts. The French Muslim community lives a challenging experience by shaping their religious identity through a laïcité national approach. In contrast, British Muslims enjoy a more diverse environment in which they work hard to combine their hybrid British identity across the multiculturalism pros and cons. Spanish Muslims live in a complex situation. They are torn between the lack of a fair election for a representative figure and the governmental blackout on implementing the agreements related to their religious rights.

References

Abed AL'Jabri, M. (1999). Clash of civilizations: The relations of the future. In G. M. Munoz (Ed.), *Islam, modernism and the West: Cultural and political relations at the end of the millennium*. IB Tauris.

Abu-Shams, L. (2006). Educación, lengua y cultura: la escolarización de los niños marroquíes en España. In *Actas Del Primer Congreso Árabe Marroquí: Estudio, Enseñanza Y Aprendizaje* (p. 1).

Adlbi, S. (2016). Narration of Spanish Muslim women on the Hijab as a tool to assert identity. In M. La Barbera (Ed.). *Identity and migration in Europe: Multidisciplinary perspectives* (pp. 251–268). Springer.

Allievi, S. (2005). How the immigrant has become Muslim. *Revue européenne des migrations internationales, 21*(2), 7.

Álvarez-Junco, J. (2013 [2011]). *Spanish identity in the age of nations.* Manchester University Press.

Alvi, A. (2013). Concealment and revealment. *Current Anthropology, 54*(2), 177–199.

Amiraux, V. (2007). The headscarf question: What is really the issue. In S. Amghar, A. Boubekeur & M. Emerson (Eds.), *European Islam: Challenges for public policy and society.* CEPS.

Anthias, F. (2013). Identity and belonging: Conceptualisations and political framings. *Nordic Journal of Migration Research, 2*(2), 102–110.

Arlettaz, F. (2013). Símbolos religiosos en la órbita del poder público: dos aproximaciones. *Revista de estudios políticos, 161,* 143–170.

Astor, A. (2017). *Rebuilding Islam in contemporary Spain: The politics of Mosques establishments 1976–2013.* Sussex Academic Press.

Bhargava, R., & Helmut, R. (Eds.). (2005). *Civil society, public sphere and citizenship: Dialogues and perceptions.* Sage.

Bruce, S. (2013). *Politics and religion in the United Kingdom.* Routledge.

Casanova, J. (2011). *Public religions in the modern world.* University of Chicago Press.

Cembrero I. (2016). La España de Ala: Cinco siglos después de la Reconquista los musulmanes han vuelto. Son Dos Millones y Siguen Creciendo. La Esfera.

Cesari, J. (1999). The re-Islamization of Muslim immigration in Europe. In G. M. Munoz (Ed.), *Islam, modernism and the West: Cultural and political relations at the end of the millennium* (p. 211). IB Tauris.

Collet, B. (2004). Muslim headscarves in four nation-states and schools. In *Civil enculturation. Nation-state, school and ethnic difference in the Netherlands* (pp. 119–146). Berghahn.

Cuevas, P. C. G. (2016). *Historia del pensamiento político español: del Renacimiento a nuestros días.* Universidad Nacional de Educación a Distancia, UNED.

De Madariaga, M. R. (2015). *Los moros que trajo Franco.* Alianza Editorial.

Dietz, G. (2007). Invisibilizing or ethnicizing religious diversity? In *Religion and education in Europe: Developments, contexts and debates* (pp. 103–132).

Dubet, F. (1996). La laicite dans les mutations de l'ecole, in Une societe fragmentee? In M. Wieviorka (Ed.), *Le multictilturalisme en debat* (pp. 85–170). La Decouverte.

El-Madkouri, M. (1995). La lengua española y el inmigrante marroquí. *Didáctica: (Lengua y Literatura), 7,* 355–362.

El-Madkouri, M. (2011). *La imagen del otro: lo árabe en la prensa española.* Editorial Académica española.

Engineer, A. (2007). *Islam in contemporary world.* Sterling Publishers Pvt. Ltd.

Esposito, J. (1983). *Voices of resurgent Islam.* Oxford University Press.

Esposito, J., & Kalin, I. (Eds.). (2011). *Islamophobia: The challenge of pluralism in the 21st century.* Oxford University Press.

Gallardo, F. X. (2008). Acrobacias fronterizas en Ceuta y Melilla. Explorando la gestión de los perímetros terrestres de la Unión Europea en el continente africano. *Documents d'anàlisi geogràfica, 51,* 129–149.

Garbaye, R. (2010). *Toward a European policy of integration? Divergence and convergence of immigrant integration policy in Britain and France* (pp. 165–177). Chebel d'Appollonia and Reich.

Garton T. A. (2007, June 22). No ifs and no buts. *The Guardian.* London. Retrieved 27 January 2012.

Godard B. (2007). Official recognition of Islam. In S. Amghar, A. Boubekeur, & M. Emerson (Eds.), *European Islam: Challenges for public policy and society.* CEPS.

Guia, A. (2018). Nativism, gendered Islamophobia and Muslim activism. In M. H. Davis, & T. Serres (Eds.), *North Africa and the making of Europe: Governance, institutions and culture* (pp. 133–154). Bloomsbury Publishing.

Habermas, J. (1991). *The structural transformation of the public sphere: An inquiry into a category of bourgeois society.* MIT Press.

Hemming, P. (2015). *Religion in the primary school: Ethos, diversity, citizenship.* Routledge.

Henley, J. (2003, December 13). France to ban pupils' religious dress. *The Guardian.* https://www.theguardian.com/world/2003/dec/12/france.schools.

Hill, M., Sandberg, R., & Doe, N. (2011). *Religion and law in the United Kingdom.* Kluwer Law International.

Howard, J. A. (2000). Social psychology of identities. *Annual Review of Sociology, 26,* 367–393.

Jacobson, J. (2006). *Islam in transition: Religion and identity among British Pakistani youth.* Routledge.

Kettani, H. (2010). Muslim population in Europe: 1950–2020. *International Journal of Environmental Science and Development, 1*(2), 154.

Khir-Allah, G. (2015). Veiling and revealing identity: The linguistic representation of the Hijab in the British Press. In *Identity and migration in Europe: Multidisciplinary perspectives* (pp. 229–249). Springer International Publishing.

Khir-Allah, G. (2016). Media discourse representation on adopting the Hijab in Spanish Public School: Islamic veiling and social inclusion and exclusion at Spanish classroom. In *Images of women in Hispanic culture* (pp. 173–187). Cambridge Scholar Publishing.

Lewis, B. (1994). *Islam and the West.* Oxford University Press.

Maataoui, M. E. M. (2015). El Árabe y el bereber en España: política lingüística y trasfondo cultural. *Nueva Revista del Pacífico, 63,* 23–58. file:///C:/Users/syria/OneDrive/Escritorio/El%20Árabe%20y%20el%20bereber%20en%20España%20política%20lingüística%20y%20trasfondo%20cultural.pdf.

Mannitz, S. (2004). The place of religion in four civil cultures. In *Civil enculturation. Nation-state, school and ethnic difference in the Netherlands* (p. 107). Berghahn Books.

Martina Muñoz, G. (2010). *Esto alimenta a la derecha islamófoba.* http://elpais.com/diario/2010/04/22/sociedad/1271887205_850215.html. 22 April 2010.

Martina Muñoz, G., & Grosfoguel, R. (Eds.). (2012). *La islamofobia a debate: La genealogía del miedo al Islam y la construcción de los discursos antiislámicos.* Casa Arabe.

Mastnak, T. (2008). Western hostility toward the Muslims: A history of the present. In *Forum Bosnae* (No. 44, pp. 235–301). Međunarodni forum Bosna.

McGhee, D. (2008). *End of multiculturalism: Terrorism, integration and human rights.* McGraw-Hill Education.

Modood, T. (2011). *Multiculturalism and integration: Struggling with confusions* (pp. 61–76). European University Institute.

Modood T. (2015). *Religion in Britain Today and tomorrow.* http://www.publicspirit.org.uk/religion-in-britain-today-and-tomorrow.

Moratino A. (1999). Europe and the Muslim world in international relations. In G. M. Munoz (Ed.), *Islam, modernism and the West: Cultural and political relations at the end of the millennium.* IB Tauris.

Navarro, B. Á. M. (2009). La acomodación del culto islámico en España. Comparación con Gran Bretaña, Alemania y Francia. In *Políticas y gobernabilidad de la inmigración en España* (pp. 185–206).

Nieslen, J. (1999). Muslim and European education systems. In G. M. Munoz (Ed.), *Islam, modernism and the West: Cultural and political relations at the end of the millennium.* IB Tauris.

Peters, R. (2014). *Islam and colonialism: The doctrine of jihad in modern history.* Walter de Gruyter GmbH & Co KG (original book published 1980).

Peucker, M., & Akbarzadeh, S. (2014). *Muslim active citizenship in the West.* Routledge.

Ramadan, T (1999). Relation between Europe and Islamists. In G. M. Munoz (Ed.), *Islam, modernism and the West: Cultural and political relations at the end of the millennium.* IB Tauris.

Rizvi, S. (2014). Use of Islamic, Islamicized and national curriculum in a Muslim faith school in England: Findings from an ethnographic study. In *International handbook of learning, teaching and leading in faith-based schools* (pp. 583–602). Springer Netherlands.

Robinson, L., & Gardee, M. R. (2016). Rapid appraisal in practice assessment: An example of work with Muslim youth in Scotland. In *Social work in a diverse society: transformative practice with Black and minority ethnic individuals and communities* (p. 75).

Roy, O. (2007) Islam terrorist radicalization in Europe. In S. Amghar, A. Boubekeur, & M. Emerson (Eds.), *European Islam: Challenges for public policy and society*. CEPS.

Salih, R. (2009). Muslim women, fragmented secularism and the construction of interconnected 'publics' in Italy. *Social Anthropology, 17*(4), 409–423.

Schmitt, C. (1996). *Roman Catholicism and political form* (No. 380, p. 27). Greenwood Publishing Group.

Scott, J. W. (2009). *The politics of the veil* (Vol. 7). Princeton University Press.

Shally-Jensen, M., Jelen, T., & Rozell, M. (Eds.). (2015). *American political culture: An encyclopedia [3 volumes]: An encyclopedia*. ABC-CLIO.

Sherman, D., & Nardin, T. (2006). *Terror, culture, politics: Rethinking 9/11* (Vol. 1). Indiana University Press.

Shryock, A. (Ed.). (2010). Introduction: Islam as an object of fear and affection. In *Islamophobia/Islamophilia: Beyond the politics of enemy and friend* (pp. 1–28). Indiana University Press.

Smith, J. T. (2016). *Key questions in education: Historical and contemporary perspectives*. Bloomsbury Publishing.

Steven, M. (2010). *Christianity and party politics: Keeping the faith*. Routledge.

Sutton, P. W., & Vertigans, S. (2005). *Resurgent Islam: A sociological approach*. Polity.

Taras, R. (2012). *Xenophobia and Islamophobia in Europe*. Edinburgh University Press.

Thomassen, L. (2011). (Not) just a piece of cloth: Begum, recognition and the politics of representation. *Political Theory, 39*(3), 325–351.

Thomassen, L. (2017). *British multiculturalism and the politics of representation*. Edinburgh University Press.

Townson, N. (2015). Anticlericalism and secularization: A European exception? In N. Townson (Ed.), *Is Spain different? A comparative look at the 19th and 20th centuries*. Sussex Academic Press.

Wieland, R. (2001). *Islam challenges the world*. Glad Tidings Publishers.

Zapata-Barrero, R., & Diez-Nicolas, J. (2012). Islamophobia in Spain? Political rhetoric rather than a social fact. In *Islamophobia in the West: Measuring and explaining individual attitudes* (pp. 83–97). Routledge.

Intersectional Euro-Muslim Women: Western Political and Feminist Responses

Introduction

Many different meanings and definitions have been given to the term *feminism* since it was coined for the first time in France, around the 1880s, by the journalist Hubertine Auclert. In her journal *La Citoyenne,* Auclert criticized male domination and claimed women's rights promised by the French revolution. Since then, similar critiques have been raised in different parts of the world. Feminism was widely spread in the first decade of the twentieth century, particularly in England and then in the United States. Yet, "feminism" varies across countries and cultures. We cannot assume that French feminism is identical to the American one, although both call for women's emancipation. Both are different from feminism that appeared in Egypt in the early 1920s when it was under the British colonial occupation.[1] Deborah Cameron (1992) asserted that feminism is a movement for "the full humanity of women" and not for the "equality of women." "Equality" proposes a standard (man) to which the other (woman) is equal. I agree with Cameron's view that defines feminism as a radical change, a world where one gender is not set as a standard for human values. Mary Diezt (2003) points out that over the past 20 years, Western feminism theory had been forced or encouraged to think through the limitations of previous North Atlantic and Anglo-American theories. Yet, the contemporary feminist theories are becoming less unthinkingly Western and more thoughtfully Western, more global, more comparative, and more democratic in their attempts to understand and contain the complicities of human cultures and women's role across the world.

Feminism is not a homogeneous theory nor a directional movement. Dietz indicated that feminism is a "historically constituted, local and global, social and political movement with emancipatory purpose and a normative content" (2003: 399). Accordingly, feminism is a movement that aims to eliminate stereotypes and prejudice imposed on women. As Dietz delineates, emancipation is done first, assuming a subject (women). Next, it identifies a problem (mainly related to women's subjection

---

[1] Badran (2002).

© Springer Nature Singapore Pte Ltd. 2021
G. Khir-Allah, *Framing Hijab in the European Mind*,
https://doi.org/10.1007/978-981-16-1653-2_3

and objectification through gendered relations). Thirdly, feminism declares various objectives to aim for specific principles such as overturning relations of domination, ending sex discrimination, securing female sexual liberation, raising consciousness, self-realization, dignity, justice, freedom, etc. Feminists' analytical debates are unavoidably political since it calls for political change and ethical transformation. This chapter follows Diezt's approach in analyzing the Muslim women's vestment: the hijab. I will first delineate the subject (which are two problems): (1) European Muslim woman. (2) the hijab. Then, I will analyze the reason behind considering these two subjects as "problematic." Finally, I will propose an intersectional feminist approach through which Euro-Muslim women's multi-realities can be anchored and the hijab Euro-visibility is interpreted.

Western Feminists' Framing of Muslim Women: From the Past to the Present

The representation of Muslim women half-naked behind barred windows with no hope is not an inspiration of the Thousand and One night. It is an output of the colonizer's mission to subjugate the colonized. The occidental feminist's superiority over Muslim women is related to historical racism and colonial power. By the end of the nineteenth century, Muslim women were used as a fundamental axis in building the new orientalist image. Hegemonic western imperialist countries, France and the United Kingdom, in particular, supported the representation of Muslims as "uncivilized" ignorant men and sexual slave women, promoted the binomial of Arab/Muslim as inferior/backward, and affirmed the urgent need to introduce them to progress and modernity, hence, justifying the colonialism.[2] Yvonne Haddad argues that the Occidental image of Muslim women is designed to serve the Western's interests.[3] Between 1800 and 1950, nine hundred movies featured Muslims as barbaric and irrational, while only three movies were found to portrait Arabs and Muslims away from the stereotypes. Besides, about 60,000 books were published whose content was to emphasize such stereotypes. Those publications not only introduced the fascinating image of Muslim Harem where Muslim men imprison their wives whose only mission in life is to beautify themselves and take care of their husbands' huge sexual appetites.[4] These movies and publications worked to build a stereotypical and hegemonic framing of Islam and Muslim women in the colonized countries. These frames are still controlling the perception of women in the Muslim world. The use of Islam in the political agenda as an instrument-of-fear maintains this negative and dominant discourse revived.

These stereotypical representations of the colonized Muslim women were accompanied by significant evolution of "feminisms" in the colonial countries, where

---

[2]Ang-Lygate (1996) and Said (2002).
[3]Haddad (2007).
[4]Hoodfar (1992).

women suffered from gender discrimination and subordination. However, Western critics focused on Muslim women's oppression even though those criticisms could be applied on a parallel scale to their societies. Both Muslim and Western women were taught to be obedient to their husbands, in need of male protection, and that their biological and intellectual destined dedication is the domestic domains. Men imperialists were known in their home societies for their opposition to feminism, contradictory, they attacked abroad to defend Muslim women's degradation. Their foremost liberation was the call for the unveiling.[5] According to many scholars, the western misrepresentation of Muslim women was as penning one's set of problems and attribute them to the "other" (Ahmed, 1982, 1986, 2000; Haddad, 2007; Hoodfar, 1992). Simon De Beauvoir pointed out that this is precise because the opposition with "Other" is needed to create a free, modern, and liberated self-image. He indicates that "otherness is a fundamental category of human thought. Thus, is it that no group ever sets itself up as the One without at once setting up the Other against itself" (1952, XIX–XX).[6] As we discussed in the previous chapter, Islam is used as an instrument-of-fear to justify the invasions. In the rhetoric of war, liberating the victim, the Muslim women, was a human endeavor. We have also seen that the "we" and "other" categorization is successively used to define the (colonial) (political) European identity (secular, modern, liberal, and democratic), to exclude the outsider (ethnic, religious 'non-Christian,' dark skin, etc.), and to define the Enemy. The same positionality is applied to (colonial) Western feminism to promote the occidental, colonizer, first-world, and liberated women's superiority over the oriental, colonized, third-world, and subordinated Muslim women's inferiority.

The West's increased obsession with the Islamic veil emerged in the XIX century when the Muslim world became more subordinated to the European countries. Although there were criticisms of the Muslim women's subordination in the colonies, there were no serious legislative or social intents to improve their situation. Gender equality was not the primary concern of the colonial agenda, but it was critical to justify the occupation and the usurpation of "others'" resources. Lila Abu-Lughod casts doubts on the colonial philosophy of "saving Muslim women." Saving someone entails protecting her from danger and providing her safety and integrity. The colonialism succeeded in expanding violence and nourishing their superiority in the name of this fanciful liberty. Haddad adds that the main enhancement the colonizers worked on hardly was unveiling Muslim women. She refers that both the British and the French conquests were politically presented as a generous endeavor for the Muslim world. British conquering the Muslim countries was overwhelmed by the "the white man's burden," and the French thought to be on a "civilizing mission." Although secularizing the Muslim world failed in the mid of 50s,[7] reformists and elite in the colonized countries were aware of the hijab's stereotypical image as a symbol of backwardness in the West. Therefore, they established a link between

---

[5]Muñoz (2010) and Haddad (2007).

[6]De Beauvoir (1952).

[7]Muñoz and Grosfoguel (2012).

formal education and unveiling, putting them in one inseparable package. Conservatives opposed the unveiling, but not the formal education of girls. Yet, this package had been applied for decades in many Muslim countries and was not changed until very recently.[8]

The term "women's freedom" was reused in the 90s to justify political and militant decisions.[9] A clear example was the rhetoric use of "freedom" when the United States invaded Afghanistan and Iraq at the end of the twentieth century. Women were portrayed as lacking the minimum perception of what "freedom" is; they were eager to throw their burqa off, and desperately wait for the Westerns to liberate them. Both Abu-Lughod and Haddad refer to the American amazement that Afghan women did not throw off their burqas after the invasion and after offering them the "freedom" they publicized in the political discourse. Abu-Lughod indicates that many women stopped using the burqa but not jumping to belly shirts and blue jeans. She stresses that vestment freedom is not limited to exposing the body, nor indicates an identical extension of the western style. The right to vestment indicates the free choice of the garments that reflect each woman's social identity and reflect her heritage as much as her personality.[10]

Faith and traditions are triggers of disagreements between feminists. Ayaan Hirsi, liberal feminist and public intellectual, and Elisabeth Badinter, French philosopher and public intellectual, both refer to the incompatibility of faith and traditions with two crucial European values: feminism and freedom. They propose that traditions and faith limit human freedom and promote women's subordination, while secularism and liberalism promote these values. This perspective promotes secularity as modernity in contemporary Europe and relates religion and cultural traditions to backwardness (see chapter "Introduction"). Serene Khader criticizes their "loose" and "non-technical" use of the term "freedom."[11] She states that the positive sense of self-freedom establishes a collective identity that humans, intuitively and socially, engage with and commit to. Throughout this process, behavioral and faith patterns are shaped and practiced. Discourses that coincide with Hirsi and Badinter's perspectives stigmatize the faith and the traditions of "other" women and not the European traditions and culture. Saba Mahmood argues that feminists who have difficulties respecting women from other cultures with different traditions rely on restricted "imaginary freedom," the liberal one.[12]

I agree with Mahmood, who uses the term "liberalism" and "feminism" interchangeably because when feminism views that women from other cultures are oppressed by cultural norms and need liberation, then it is the other side of the coin of

---

[8]For example, Syrian government, led by the only political party in the country, Al-Baèz; banned the hijab of the students but not teachers at the public schools until 1999, when the president, Bashar Al-Assad, the son; passed a Republican Decree that allowed veiling.

[9]Abu-Lughod (2002).

[10]The right to vestment is included in the Universal Declaration of Human Rights, Art. 19 UNDHR. https://www.un.org/en/universal-declaration-human-rights/.

[11]Khader (2016).

[12]Mahmood (2005).

liberalism. In the colonial and post-colonial political and feminist rhetoric, the hijab practice asserts the inferiority of Islam. It justifies every kind of undermining and marginalizing Muslim communities, even those in Europe.[13] Such debate increases the tension between anti-imperialists and feminists. Hoodfar states that such misconceptions are based on the assumption that what is good for western women should be good for all. Accordingly, western feminists are somehow authorized to underestimate and destroy the traditions of "others." This approach denies that humans are social beings, and their social and historical contexts are an essential part of their being and their understanding of the world. Their culture is part of their history, their legacy, and the booster of their self-esteem.

Although most Europeans admit their primitive knowledge of women's rights in Islam and women's current social situation in the Muslim world and Europe, the dominating image of Muslim women they hold in mind is still derived from the colonial era. They are convinced that Muslim women are oppressed without defining the specific content of that oppression; the hijab visibility supports the oppression theory. Patriarchy and subordination to male family members firmly embed the current European discourse on the European Muslim women stressing the mainstream's superiority over the Muslim minority: The West lectures the Muslim women, the "others," who are silent and covered.[14]

In her article, *Is Multiculturalism bad for women?*, Susan Okin highlights the tension between feminism and multiculturalism. She indicates that feminism needs to provide women with equal opportunities to choose their lives freely as men do. Multiculturalism needs to focus on the minority cultures as diverse groups, where gender has a significant impact, not as one block minority. She explains that religious groups are usually concerned with specific laws on personal issues such as marriage, divorce, child custody, the division of family property, and inheritance. These "personal laws" have a larger impact on women's and girls' lives than men's and boys'. To misinterpret these cultural practices (to criticize it or legislate against it) harms women who are practicing them. If governments turn their eyes away from this inner diversity of minority practices, it becomes complicated to regulate it later.

For example, the French government ignored for so long the polygamy problem that African, Arab, and/or Muslim women suffered from in the French contexts. Consequently, wives lived in poor conditions in overcrowded houses with no private space for wives or children. When the government finally decided to solve the problem because families of 30 or 40 members appeared in the Civil Registration, it recognized, under the cover of a feminist campaign against polygamy, only one wife and annulled the others, depriving others wives and children of their family rights and economic support. Such amputated accommodation masquerade with a feminist's cause reveals an unbridged gap between feminism and a multiculturalist's commitment to the group's rights of minority cultures.

Okin asserts that cultural practices are not limited to the domestic arrangement. Culture is the distribution of responsibilities and powers at home, which significantly

---

[13] Alexander (2006) and Volpp (2011).
[14] Said (2002), Amiraux (2007), and Jouili (2009).

impacts who can participate in and influence the public parts of cultural life. Gendered domestic and social roles differ from one culture to another. Accordingly, policies aiming to respond to the needs and claims of cultural minorities group must seriously consider the need for adequate representation of less powerful members of such groups and involve them in the negotiation. There is a lack of egalitarian dialogue between Western feminists and European Muslim women, a lack of transparent dialogue in which the elements that promote Muslim women's discrimination are examined and analyzed objectively by both sides, even these discriminations practiced by the European mainstream.

MariaCaterina La Barbera delineates that to reduce the tension between feminism and cultural diversity, there should be multi correct answers on gender inequality according to each social context.[15] She introduced the term "multicenter feminism"[16] to focus on several focus-centered approaches and overcome the inclusion and the exclusion of cultural diversity practices.[17] In the last twenty years, the "intersectionality" approach gained more and more attention because of its ability to deal with more complex forms of discrimination (social, political, economic, cultural, and ethical ones) in analyzing women's freedom equality.[18] The term has a multidimensional reference that focuses on the peculiarity of each women's context and the multiple discriminations women go through. It was firstly used in 1989 to refer to Afro-American women's feminism. Gender was grounded on the experiences of white women and middle-class family models and ignored how race, class, and sexual orientation pluralize and particularize the meaning of being women. Afro-American feminist women criticized the essentialism of gender. They exposed the need for feminist scholars to be self-reflexive, self-critical, and aware of their own positionality as a standpoint.[19]

Intersectionality is a significant contribution to contemporary feminist theories and praxis (McCall, 2005). It is at the core of gender studies and a keyword in the anglophone feminist scholarship (Davis, 2008). La Barbera argues that "intersectionality" can offer novel perspectives to the debate on democracy because it perplexes how we understand social inequality and design the tools to tackle and overcome them. "Intersectionality" allows addressing the situation of the most vulnerable and marginalized women that have been forgotten by mainstream feminism and convert feminism into "the very house of difference" where all diversity among women can find their place.

---

[15]La Barbera (2007).

[16]La Barbera uses this term as an alternative of "the multiracial feminism" to avoid the racial elements of the equation.

[17]La Barbera (2009).

[18]Sibai (2018).

[19]La barbera indicates that African women had been enforced to break down their experiences, to provide one fragment of it as a "meaningful whole" and give up all other constituent parts of themselves. By which, gender essentialism reduced multiple discrimination to a problem of arithmetical sum.

Islamic Feminism: Necessity and Sensibility

Islamic feminism appeared around the 90s mainly in Iran and Turkey, by Muslim women claiming their social and political rights. They were holding Islam as a significant component of their ethnic, cultural, or national identity.[20] Margot Badran was the first to define Islamic feminism as a "discourse of gender equality that derives its mandate from the Quran and seeks rights and justice for all human beings across the totality of the public–private continuum" (Badran, 2009: 4). Rather than locating the Quran within feminist discourses, Badran re-located feminism in the Quran. She indicates that Muslim women have been engaged in recuperating the egalitarian Quranic discourse much before the advent of full-fledged feminism as we know it today. Badran's definition of Islamic feminism is an essential contribution in the field because it de-secularizes the project of women's liberation. It is not exclusively Westernized secular humanism, but also a mode of God-consciousness that can lead Muslim women to emphasize justice and rights for all human beings by affirming human life's unity and equality. Islamic feminism is about analyzing the religious texts that arrange gender and social roles. Such interpretations of religious sources help Muslim women untangle patriarchy from religion and provide them with an Islamic perspective to understand gender equality and social power relations. The analysis of the religious texts empowers their role, potentials, and opportunities as Muslim women citizens. Such awareness is not only beneficial to Muslim women but also to the secular communities to which these women belong to.

Islamic feminism is fundamental in the sense that it depends on the fundamental and original holy text, the Quran, to recuperate the egalitarian message. That does not indicate that the Islamic feminism discourse consists of one school of thought. For example, Amina Wadud, in her focus on the interpretation of the Quran, combines classical Islamic methodologies with new social science tools and secular discourses of rights and justice while keeping a firm grounding in Islamic thoughts. Aziza Al-Hibri projects her reinterpretations of the Quran into the analysis of various cases in the Shari's. Fatima Mernissi and Hidayet Tuksal focus on the re-examination of the *hadith* (the narrations of the Prophet).

While Badran considers that the term Islamic feminism breaks down the polarities constructed between "religious" and "secular" and between "East" and "west," Asma Barlas is skeptical at using the term "feminism" because it self-defines the West in opposition to Islam. Barlas considers that the term "feminism" (in the West) aims at "reading oppression into Islam and reading liberation out of the West's imperialist depredations."

Asma Barlas' rereading of the Quranic texts aims at tracing back the patriarchalism and misogynistic texts in the holy book. Her research is based on two definitions of

---

[20]The term Islamic feminism appeared in Iran by Afsaneh Najmabadeh and Ziba Mir-Hosseini, and Turkia, Yesim Arat and Feride Acar, to express a new feminist paradigm by the mid of the 90s. The term is circulated by Muslims across the world.

patriarchy: (1) a tradition of father-rule,[21] (2) theories of sexual differentiation in the politics of gender inequality.[22] Her research proves that the Quran is not only egalitarian, "but that it is anti-patriarchal. Quran does not use categories of sex or gender to privilege males. In fact, it establishes ontic equality of human beings by locating their origin in the same self, *nafs*" (2006: 12). The Quranic text does not use men as a paradigm to define women neither uses the concept of gender to speak about humans; women in Islam have a direct relationship with God without a need of a male mediator or male authority. As for the Divine Speech to be responsive to Muslim women, they should be willing to engage critically by asking the right sorts of questions. This indicated the need for Muslim women's involvement in the reinterpretations and rereading the original religious texts.

One of Barlas' arguments is the restriction on the liberty of thoughts in the Western academic spaces. She argues that the West is now "everywhere, in structures and in minds," and refusing to speak "some common languages (the western feminists' discourse) […] shows how narrow the world grows daily for many of us, especially those who call ourselves Muslim."[23] Although there is an urgent need for critical research on the *Quran, hadiths,* and creative *ijtihad*, Muslim women practitioner-researchers who depend on the religious texts in their defense of women's rights are attacked by (secular) feminists who alleged that Islam is patriarchal, violent, and misogynistic. Such attacks are legitimized in the academic sphere where Muslim women's agency over their research is de-authenticated and repealed because of the religious frame of reference. Muslim feminists are perceived as oppressed because they are submissive to the Divine order, forgetting that the Divine text can be a successful approach for religious women empowerment. They (western feminists) also ignore the fact that their secular approach is, first and foremost, written by humans, mostly men (e.g., the Universal Declarations, International Convenient, laws, and Constitutions, etc.).

Ali Engineer indicates that religion is not limited to the "axis of faith," but it includes costumes and traditions. In the analysis of any religion, a fundamental issue is understanding the difference between religion and faith, between what religion teaches and how the followers behave, and between religion practiced in different historical periods across distinctive contextual frames. Faith is a Divine definition of the world and Divine orders to be followed. As a practiced culture, religion is the set of unlimited human costumes and traditions that each social context adapts differently. The confusion of Islam as faith and Islam as a historical framework is one of the most common misconceptions.[24] The term "Islamic feminism" generates

---

[21] Patriarchy is a historically specific mode of rule by fathers 42 that, in its religious and traditional forms, assumes a real as well as symbolic continuum between the "Father/fathers" that is, between a patriarchalized view of God as Father/male, and a theory of father-right, extending to the husband's claim to rule over his wife and children (Barlas 2006: 12).

[22] A broader definition of patriarchy is as a politics of sexual differentiation that privileges males by "transforming biological sex into politicized gender, which prioritizes the male while making the woman different (unequal), less than, or the 'Other'" (Barlas 2006: 12).

[23] Barlas (2006).

[24] Engineer (2007).

certain confusions when Islam is understood as a mere faith without considering the variety of religious practices. As Faith is transversal, the term confuses varied contextual frameworks of Muslim women. For example, Muslim women in Europe or Australia fight for different rights than those Muslim women in a Muslim country (Such as Arabic countries, Iran, Turkey, Malaysia).[25] Even in the same contexts, not all women share the same understanding of Islamic legislation nor practice their religion in identical behavior, rituals, and practices. Their ideas and understanding of Islam are influenced by their class, cultural background, neighborhood, education, and personal trajectory. It is to say, Muslim feminists defend women's rights through reinterpreting the Quranic texts, which is not necessarily analogical.

Another confusion that revolves around the term "Islamic feminism" is the political use of it. The fact that Muslim feminists (in national border, in the diaspora, or minority Muslim communities) activate an "opposition to social and gender discrimination" and call for social change.[26] This indicates that Muslim feminists are, in a way or another, political agents or, at least, call for a political change. In many Muslim or European countries, political authorities fear the visibility of intellectual activist practitioner Muslim women. Those activists claim for women's rights through the frame of reference of that society/community, which indicates a considerable positive impact on society/community members, which leads to a social and political change. For example, in Egypt, Heba Ra'uf, a writer and political activist who criticized corrupt politicians, was reported for "criticizing men in Muslim societies" (for not daring to face up to political authorities). There was an endless debate on women's *fitnah* and seductive dangers in Egyptian public debate as these are the only corruption to focus on.[27] In 2019, Hajar Raissouni, an active Moroccan journalist known for her opposition to the State and a Muslim practitioner of hijab, was sentenced to a year in prison for abortion, setting out abortion as the main social reform in the country.[28] However, abortion is not mentioned in her medical report, and the investigation revolved around her family, writings, and political orientation. Practitioner (hijab-wearing) Muslim women activists alarm the political authorities in the Arabic

---

[25] Amanda Keddie signifies that Muslim women voice is silent in Australia. And it is imperative to provide greater opportunities for listening to Muslim women and girls who are who are finding places of agency within the religious, gendered and racialized discourse that shape their identities, it is the voices in the current environment that tend to be silenced (Keddie, 2016).

[26] Tohidi draws a difference between the connotation of the term "Islamic feminism" and "Muslim feminism". She states: "I personally find the term 'Muslim feminist/m'(a Muslim who is feminist) less troubling and more pertinent to current realties than the term 'Islamic feminism.' The term 'Islamic feminism,'on the other hand, seems to be more appropriate to be used and conceived as an analytical concept in feminist research and feminist theology, or as a discourse. The definition of either term, however, is difficult since a Muslim feminist (believer) would probably define it differently from a laic social scientist like myself" (2003: 138). I use the "Islamic feminism2 to refer to the movement and "Muslim feminist" to refer to the individuals (see explanation in the introduction).

[27] Reported in Omaima Abu Baker "Islamic feminism? What's in a name?" (2001: 4).

[28] Abortion is not forbidden in Islam. It is restricted by specific conditions related to the mother's and the baby's situations. The court in Morroco did not assure if Ra'uf had an abortion or not. And if yes, no one questioned if it was carried out through the Islamic conditions.

Muslim countries as much as they alarm the European ones because they are capable, through their religious and academic knowledge and their activism, to conceive their rights and to ignite a social change, which is tagged as "social disorder" by political authorities.

Nayerh Tohidi, in her article "Islamic feminism: 'Perils and Promises'" (2003: 138–140), provides her perspective on the term "Islamic feminism." She indicates that the "politicized trend" in "Islamic feminism" appears as a response to three interrelated sets of domestic, national, and global pressures of new realities: **1) Responding to the patriarchy sanctioned by the religious authorities**: In which Tohidi classifies Muslim feminists into two categories: a. *"modernized educated upper-and middle-class activists"* who see Islam as a patriarchal and pre-modern religion. Hence, they maintain a secular or anti-religious attitude, b. *"(M)any others have not broken away from their faith and religious identity.* They have tried to resist and fight patriarchy within a religious framework. Tohidi refers that the second groups' claims (that religion does support the women's subordination) put "the norms of the society and norms of God are at odds." **2) Responding to modernity, modernization, and globalization**: Tohidi indicates that Muslim women negotiate with modernity, accept it, and create an alternative that looks different from Western modernism or feminism. A process in which globalization, transnational migration, the diasporaization, or de-territorialization of cultural identities contribute. **3) Responding to the recent surge of patriarchal Islamism:** It appears in the mechanisms that resist the sexist nature in the ongoing identity politics. To react, women need to be equipped with the tools (Arabic language, *Quran,* and *fiqh* knowledge) to reform democracy, pluralism, and civil rights. Tohidi asserts that modern liberal and gender-egalitarian reformation of Islam is a requirement for a broader societal and political reform toward democracy, liberalism, and civil and women's rights.

Tohidi's interpretations of the "politicized trends" of "Islamic feminism" negatively stigmatize Muslim practitioners through the opposition build between the secular approach of "educated and middle-upper-class" women and anonymous "many others" who live under siege of religion and they could not "break out." In the second stimulus, she refers to modernism as an imported strain into the Muslim culture (which Muslim women try to negotiate, etc.) as if the Islamic heritage and Islamic culture lack any aspect of modernity in its essentiality. In the third stimulus, she affirms modern liberalism as an essential element to reform Islam casting Islam as an oxymoron. Tohidi's discourse reveals the superiority of secular discourse over Muslim women's as much as undermining the women's liberation approach based on religion. Such academic discourse is an Islamization of post-colonial feminism. It uses the same hegemonic sovereignty discourse over Muslim practitioners to promote the secular Islamic approach that depends on the UDHR as a frame of reference instead of depending on the religious texts. The secular Muslim discourse aims at creating a counter-discourse to practitioner Muslim feminists' whose frame of reference is the religious texts and the Islamic jurisprudency. A secular Islamic approach on women's right creates a balance between the practitioner Muslims (who uses the religious texts to emphasize women's rights) and secular Muslim (who emphasize women's liberation under the name of Islam but not depending on its religious resources) in the Academia or the political sphere.

Women Vestment: Human Rights Vs. Religious Islamic Approach

The practice of veiling is mistakenly confined to Islam. Veiling and the concealment of women's bodies have been practiced throughout history in different social and political contexts and for different reasons, not necessarily religious, mainly for elite women in Greece, Rome, Byzantine, pre/Islamic Iran, and the Arabian Peninsula. When Islam first saw the light in Makkah in 610 AD, veiling was not the first thing Islam called for. The Divine revelation that demanded veiling had been realized after 17 years of the beginning of the Islamic journey. More precisely, it was in the fourth year after the pilgrimage to Yathrib[29]; it is to say, four years after the construction of the first Muslim community in Yathrib.

Since Muslim researchers and feminists indicate (as we saw above) that Islam can be universal and support Human equality and Human Rights, why, then, the Islamic dress codes are cast to be gender discriminative and to be incompatible with the universal standards of human rights? Are there contradictions between UDHR's important egalitarian principles and the Islamic dress codes?

The Universal Declaration of Human Rights UDHR signed by the European General Assembly on December 10, 1948 in Paris, boost up the debate of women's rights. Most Europeans think of the Universal Declaration of Human Rights as a product of occidental democracy that needs to be exported to other parts of the world. The European mind thinks over the UDHM as a privileged frame of reference for European women's freedom, stigmatizing "other" women (Asiatic, Arabic, African...) as submissive, discriminated against, lack personal and social freedom. Yet, in her recent research, Sonia Boulos highlights that the first draft of the UDHU was written based on an 8-page questionnaire sent to all parts of the world. Among those who responded were the pacific politician Mahatma Gandhi, the writer Aldous Huxley, and the thinker Quincy Wright.[30] The answers came from places as diverse as North America, Latin America, Europe, or Asia, with different religious traditions: Christian, Jewish, Hindu, Islamic, etc.

Despite these cultural and religious diversities, surprisingly, the different lists of human rights were approved as "basic" and shared among all. Sonia Boulos (2019a) indicates that it is thanks to the hard efforts of Charles Malik, a Lebanese diplomatic and philosopher, the final draft was signed first by the United Nations and then by the General Assembly.[31] Mary Ann Glendon (1997) delineates that the UDHD content was challenging because it offers equality, freedom, and solidarity to the

---

[29]Islamweb.net Fatwa number:30898. https://fatwa.islamweb.net/fatwa/index.php?page=showfa twa&lang=&Option=FatwaId&Id=%3Cspan%20style=%27color:red%27%20%3E30898%3C/ span%3E.

[30]Boulos (2019b).

[31]The Pakistani and Syrian representors in the drafting committee were form secular background. The Saudi Arabian representor was a Lebanese Christian. It is to say, the Islam thoughts in the UDHR was minimal. Boulos asserts on the importance of a cross culutral dialogue to over come the lack of Islamic perspective in the UDHR.

colonized countries. Boulos states that the colonial powers demanded an exemption clause for their colonies. They claimed that the human rights included in the UDHM require a high degree of civilization, and the colonies had not achieved that degree of development. For example, Rene Cassin claimed that the family's right is contextual and should not be applied in the colonies. The Iraqi woman delegate, Bedia Afnan, stood against Casin's position and the colonial exemption clause.[32]

In this part of the chapter, we will investigate the evidence if the hijab practice truly goes against the UDHR or not. To do so, we first need to go through the religious texts that demand the practice. And to understand the religious texts, the reader needs to go through basic terms and concepts related to the Islamic sources of legislation and advisory opinions (fatwa).

Islamic legislation is possessed from two main primary resources: The Divine Will and Words, which are limited to the Quranic text, and the *Sunnah* of the Prophet, narration *(hadith)* and acts, which are collected by trusted scholars in conserved books through serial documentation. Mainly, the *Sunnah* completes and explains the Quranic demands and legislations. For example, the Quranic texts demand Muslims do their prayers, but it does not specify how many times, the manner, or when. The narration, joint with the behavior of the Prophet, explains all the details about this practice.

There exist two secondary resources for the Islamic legislations: *Al-Qiyas* and *Al-ijmaá. Al-Qiyas* is the reasoning by analogy. Through *qiyas*, Islamic jurists combined revelations and *hadiths* with human reasoning to find similarities and relevance between the contemporary contexts and the revelation context. *Al-ijmaá* is the unanimous agreement of the *mujtahid*, doctors of Islamic law, on contemporary issues that did not exist in the revelation era. It depends mainly on human reasoning; it is considered legitimate because it relies on the Quran and Sunnah. It is important to differentiate between *Al-Qiyas* and *Al-ijmaá* (as juristic laws) and the Muslim community's common dominant tradition (local or national cultures). Finally, Islamic law includes some fixed and essential codes of creed and worship practices *(Ibadat)*. Due to the Prophet's various narrations and performances of the same practice, four leading Muslim schools of Sunnah Law *(fiqh)* appeared: Hanafi, Maliki, Shafi', and Hanbali. There are, as well, flexible Islamic rules related to social life covering all its aspects. These rules are dynamic and adapt to each social's actuality (called fatwahs) across time and space; Imams and fiqueh scholars manage these daily *fatwahs*.

The Quranic dress codes and gender communication in the public sphere appear in two different revelations with two different requirements for two different contexts. In the interpretation of the Quranic texts into English, I followed Mohammad Asad.[33]

---

[32] Boulos (2019a).

[33] It is important to point out that, from an Islamic perspective, the Quran can not be translated, since God's way of revelation in the Arabic language is not something incidental, but rather something essential to its meaning. Translating the Quranic text will decay the depth of its meanings. Therefore, we have to keep in mind that the verses that will be reproduced throughout the text are but an interpretation of the Koran.

After going through many interpretations, I made this decision because Asad's interpretation is nuanced and precise. He also includes the historical and contextual interpretation of the verses instead of being limited to a linguistic one.[34]

The first revelation that tackles the Muslim dress codes appears in surah Al-Noor in two verses (24: 30–31). Al-Noor's chapter includes numerous important legislations about women's rights, such as the protection of adultery false accusations, home privacy, and marriage. The first verse was directed to men to reduce their vision and guard their private body parts:

> TELL, the believing men to lower their gaze and to guard their private parts. That will be most conducive to their purity- [and,] verily, God is aware of all that they do. (Al-Noor: 30)

Muhammad Asad indicates that these two requirements (lowering the gaze and preserving the private body parts) could be understood in the literal sense of "covering the private parts"—being modest in dress—and in the metonymic sense of "containing sexual impulses," restricting them to what is lawful, that is, the marriage relationship. Both practices boost up physical and emotional modesty (2014: 737).

The second verse is directed to women to reduce their vision and guard their private body parts through precisely the same linguistic expressions. Yet, the second verse extends to ask women not to show their adornment, except those that inevitably appear:

> And tell the believing women to lower their gaze and to guard their private parts, and not to display their charms [in public] beyond that [decently] be apparent thereof; [...]. (Al-Noor: 31)

The revelation introduces a requirement of concealing women's adornment in the public sphere, yet; it does not indicate any specific dress code. "Charms" "*Zinah*" stands for the worn adornments and the act of making the women's charming prominent. The concealment exempts those adornments which are necessarily visible *"Illa ma Zahara minha."* The Islamic jurists set that *"Illa ma Zahara minha"* stands for also some body parts (e.g., hands, face, or foot) and not only accessories adornments. Asad indicates that the Muslim scholar Al-Qiffal determines what is necessarily visible as follows: "That which a human being may openly show in accordance with prevailing custom." The verse continues:

> "hence, let them draw their head-coverings over their bosoms" (Al-Noor: 31)

The Arabic word used in this verse is the word *"Khumur,"* in singular *"Khimar"* which means the headcovering customarily used by Arabian women before and after Islam. In the pre-Islamic costumes, it was worn loosely by free women. Women's tunic used to have a wide opening in the front, and their chest was exposed. This verse requires the concealment of excluding it from the category of "what necessarily visible."

The verse continues to list the categories of family male-members that women can feel free to expose their beauty in front of (step/fathers, step/brothers, step/sons, kids,

---

[34]The English translación is adopted from Mohammad Asad interpretation of the Holy Quran.

fathers in law, nephews, etc.). It is closed up with another reminder of adornment concealment, the hidden one not to be known. I will insert the entire verse to see the full sequence of Islamic dress codes:

> And tell the believing women to lower their gaze and to guard their private parts, and not to display their charms [in public] beyond that [decently] be apparent thereof; hence, let them draw their head-coverings over their bosoms. And let them not display [more of] their charms to any but their husbands, or their fathers, or their husband's fathers, or their sons, or their husbands' sons, or their brothers, or their brothers' sons, or their womenfolk, or those who they rightly possess, or such male attendants as are beyond all sexual desire, or children that are as yet unaware of women's nakedness; and let them not swing their legs [in walking] so as to draw attention to their hidden charms. And [always] O you believers- all of you- turn unto God in repentance, so that you might attain to a happy state! (Al-Noor: 31)

These two verses are not limited to dress codes. They introduce a code of (gender) public relations. Both verses ask men and women to lower the gaze when talking to the opposite gender and not to bother with uncomfortable looks. Islam does not favor one gender over another. It reduces humans to equal gender-less *nafs* in front of God. However, Islam recognizes the difference between the male and the female's physical bodies. Considering that women's body stimulates certain sexualities in the public sphere that the men's body don't, the Quran, in this verse, proposes to reduce women's sexual visibility in the public sphere through the concealment of some body parts (chest in particular). By reducing women's sexuality in the public sphere, Islam builds gender public relations away from sexual identities to avoid collateral consequences of such identification, such as sexual discrimination, sexual objectification of women, and the assessment of women's physical appearance over professionalism, etc.[35] It is noteworthy that none of these verses requires the full concealment of the hair with the *khimar*. These verses are about modesty codes in gender public relations that reduce the visibility of certain parts of the body (for both genders) and adornments that may arouse sexual impulses.

The second revelation on Islamic dress codes and gender communication is in surah Al-Ahzaab (33: 32, 33, 59). This chapter discusses a difficult time Muslims in Yathrib went through when all the Arabic tribes unified to attack them and eliminate the first Muslim community. The surah holds the name of the crises, and it discusses other social difficulties that appeared in the new Muslim community in Yathrib, hypocrisy in specific. Hypocrites are those who entered Islam not out of faith but to be part of the crowd.

In the first two verses (32–33), the women of the Prophet were directly spoken to. They are told their essential position and, then, they are asked not to display their charm in public as pre-Islamic practices. Those requirements come just after a couple of verses which reveal their awards if they accept these conditions as the

---

[35]These two verses also lead us to another social reality at the time of revelation. Muslim women lived with men in the time of the prophet, without limiting them to the domestic space, or being hidden behind an integral veil. Muslim received these verses to regulate existing (gender) public relations.

Prophet's wives with an option to a merciful release of the position if they do not feel relieved[36]:

> O wives of the Prophet, you are not like any of the [other] women, provided that you remain [truly] conscious to God. Hence, be not over-soft in your speech, lest any whose heart is diseased should be moved to desire [you]: but withal, speak in a kindly way (32) And abide quietly in your homes, and do not flaunt your charm as they used to flaunt them in the old days of pagan ignorance; and be constant in prayer and render the purifying dues, and par heed unto God and His Apostle: for God only ants to remove from you all that might be loathsome, O you members of the [Prophet's] household, and to purify you to utmost purity. (33)

In this narration, the Divine demands are directed straightway to the wives of the Prophet.[37] Due to their social position and their mission in narrating the hadith after the Prophet's death, they were informed by the criteria they need to follow as they were not allowed to remarry after the Prophet's death. Like the previous ones, this verse does not include any specific dress codes; it requires that the charming "Zinah" be concealed. Besides, it introduces a code on verbal communication that needs to be steady and firm. The social (sexual) disorder is not a constant phenomenon: it is limited to those who have a disease in their heart. Accordingly, the Quranic texts do not blame the women's voice; it is the listener's corrupted self. In the same chapter, the next verse focuses on the dress codes and gender communication (59), after four pages of somehow related narration. The verse is directed to the Prophet who has to tell his wives, daughters, and the Muslim wives that they should bring down their garments (the used word is the plural of *jilbab, jalabibihinna*) so they could not be known or abused:

> O Prophet, tell thy wives and thy daughters, as well as all [other] believing women, that they should draw over themselves some of their outer garments [when in pubic]: this will be more conducive to their being recognized [as decent women] and not annoyed. But [withal,] God is indeed much-forgiving, a dispenser of grace! (33: 59)

The abusers in this verse are the hypocrites who intentionally harmed and abused Muslim Muslims. Asad indicates that this verse is not meant to be an injunction (*hukum*) in the general, timeless sense of this term. It is rather a guidance that adapts to the social context of that time (2014: 884).[38] Accordingly, the Islamic full-covering requirement is required in war, social disorder, and lack of security when women are the first to be (sexually) harassed and abused.

Women dress codes in the narration of the Prophet, *Hadith,* appeared only once. The *Hadiths* on the modesty and dress code of men occupied more frequencies than

---

[36]The verse is the following: "But if any of you devoutly obeys God and his Apostle and does good deeds, on her shall We bestow her reward twice-over: for We shall have readied for her a most excellent sustance [in life to come] (Al-Noor: 31).

[37]Homa Hoodfar (1992: 40) opines that all the narrations of the hijab in the Quranic text are directed to the prophet's wives. Yet, the four Islamic shools indicates that not all of them are directed to the wives of the prophets. Only those which are referred to in this text. Hoodfar also cited the wrong verses in her article.

[38]When this verse was revealed, Muslim women immediately tore off their cloaks to cover. Muslim women met the criteria of this verse immediately.

of the women's.[39] The only prophetic narration on women's vestment is said when Asma (the daughter of the Prophet's best friend Abu Baker) came to the Prophet with thin see-through clothes. The Prophet turned his vision from her and told her: "Oh Asma, when a woman reaches the age of menstruation, it does not suit her that she displays her parts of the body except this and this, and he pointed to his face and hands" (Abi Dawud 4140, Al-Albani book 34, Hadith 85). Depending on this narration, the four schools of Sharia set that the necessarily visible physical parts *"Illa ma Zahara minha"* (Al-Noor: 31) are the face, the hand. Although the full covering is confined to a contextual time and place in the Quran, some highly conservative theologians use the literal linguistic meanings in chapter Al-Ahzaab (33:59) to announce the full-covering as an Islamic requirement to avoid sexual disorder in the public sphere *(fitnah).*

The international garment used to practice veiling nowadays is hijab, which is derived from the *hajaba,* which means to conceal from the view. *Hajaba* is used in the Quran in different verses to indicate the separation between two entities to preserve their purity.[40] Yet, the words *hijab* and *hajaba* do not appear in the verses analyzed above. The *khimar* (the headcover) was already part of women's dress code for elite women, and the *jilbab* is an outer garment like a cloak that both men and women wrapped around their bodies at that time. It is to say, the verses did not introduce a new dress code for Muslim women because it was already part of their needs in deserts and their costumes; the verses only regulated the use of these already existing garments. The verses introduce not a dress code but behavioral "modesty" codes for gender public relations in which concealing women's body is only part of it. The Islamic recognition of the physical difference between men's and women's bodies is used to cast Islam, as a whole, as discriminatory, misogynic, and patriarchal. These same feminists create causes and fight passionately for modifications in labor contracts that fit women's particularity, e.g., pregnancy, maternity, menstruation, and menopause. They also combat women's bodies' objectivation in media and struggle to end sexual exploitation, sexual harassments, rapes, and sex trafficking of women and girls. These causes are shared with Islam and can be legitimately defended by Muslim feminists within the religious frame of reference. When Islam argues that these problems occur because of the physical differences between men's and women's physical nature, these (secular) feminists get irritated. The Islamic gender public-relation codes (dress and behavior codes) let them lose their temper. Yet, supporting women's right and freedom is the concern in the hijab debate. In that case, these feminists need to be more open to other interpretations and understanding of sexuality in the public sphere. They need to accept that diverse frames of reference on sexuality can be applicable for those who do not share the secular mind. The Islamic dress code of the hijab stands for a model of gender-relation system that can be universally adopted even by non-Muslims.

It must be remembered that the Quran underlines the importance of freedom of decision in practicing Islam. For example, in Surah Al-Bakaraa, Allah says:

---

[39] Amer (2014).
[40] Gómez (2019).

THERE SHALL BE no coercion in the matter of faith. Distinct has now become the right way from [the way of] error. (Al-Bakaraa: 256)

Although Asad uses the word faith to interpret the Arabic word *Din,* he states that Din stands for religion as a whole: religion, faith, religious law, or moral law (2014: 99). The freedom of decision guaranteed in this verse and the non-judgmental principle established by its precepts because "God will judge" locate the vestment choice references in the casuistry (intention) of Muslim women, such as to practice or not hijab and the interpretation of "modesty" criteria. We can find women who opt for modesty but do not use hijab; others who wear clothes that mark the bodylines, use adornments and wear the hijab; those who, in addition to the hijab, wear baggy clothes; and other Muslims who do not consider vestments nor sexuality as a crucial element of their religious identity. In this way, Muslim women have the right in Islam to choose their dress codes according to their socio-cultural environments as well as their own desires, since these conform to their identity. Thus, the right to reduce the sexual effect that their bodies might generate in public space is just as legitimate as the right to make it visible.

These Islamic rights to vestment and body concealments are not incompatible with the freedom of faith guaranteed in Article 18 in the UDHR[41]:

Article 18

Everyone has the right to freedom of thought, conscience, and religion; this right includes freedom to change his religion or belief, and freedom, either alone or in community with others and in public or private, to manifest his religion or belief in teaching, practice, worship, and observance.

Religious coercion is not accepted in both. Women, and men, are guaranteed the freedom to choose their vestment, which manifests their identity, heritage, and religious (or secular) affiliation in the public sphere.

A Political Response

Talal Asad states that public spheres are dominated by powers that shape and constitute free speech, aspiration, fears, and hope of participants; it shapes their existence.[42] Rajeev Bhargava and Helmut Reifeld argue that the liberal public sphere is quite different from Asad's interpretation. They indicate that the liberal public sphere's debate aims to influence power but not to practice it directly on the participants.[43] Jurgen Habermas approves their perspective and adds that the public sphere is opposed to authorities that should not legislate on it: politicians can provide communication among members of the public but should not practice power on them.[44]

---

[41] Find the full text in https://www.un.org/en/universal-declaration-human-rights/.

[42] Asad (2003).

[43] Bhargava and Reifeld (2005).

[44] Habermas (1991).

Notwithstanding, the French government had not hesitated to legislate a national law that interferes with the individuals' freedom and limits religious visibility in the French public sphere. The 2004 law that bans the "ostentatious" religious symbols from public schools is forced on young Muslim girls, who are the main target of that law (see Chapter 1). After that, in 2010, France passed another law that bans the Islamic full covering, burqa, in public places. These polemic regulations were justified by the need to stabilize the secular nature of the Republic and to underpin the homogeneous public French sphere.[45] Moors and Salih (2009: 376) argue that the French law does not restrain "the public presence of religion"; it restrains "the public presence of non-native or alien religions." They point out that the French government uses women's bodies to indicate the national belonging and boundary-markers between French communities and social classes.

The hijab's visibility in the French public sphere is related to the colonial past: the resistance, where hijab-wearing women were active members as mothers, wives, and worriers. The visibility of the hijab in France is, as well, related to the refusal to accept the fact that some young female French citizens are Muslims and to the denial of other religious believes as part of the French public/national identity. The hijab's visibility and Islamic signs in general "blur(s) the border between what is public and what is private" (Cesari, 1999: 220) for the French politicians. Accordingly, the French version of confessional freedom can be understood as follows: the public sphere is a realm based on a cultural consensus that overrides individual liberty. It is based on the idea that behavioral practices can be reduced to preferences and choices.[46] In conclusion, people can believe in what they opt for in the private sphere, but they cannot confess it nor make it visible in public.

Joan Scott asserts that even though the 2004 French ban law is only applied to schoolgirls and allows the university students to express their religious identity, the university students were stigmatized. The vindicatory political discourse that preceded and followed the ban law motivated fears, increased the rejection, and asserted the practice's exclusion in the public school and at universities and workplaces.[47] Even Muslim men and boys, because of the ban, are more aware that adhering to Islam leads to integration obstacles. Chirac's ban law has macro-consequences on the French code of secularism and the European secular code in general. It developed a secular code of public employees and gave private companies the right to ban religious visibilities in their workplace. It paved the path for the European Court of Justice to give private companies the right to ban religious signs in 2017.[48] This law created confusion and increased discrimination against Muslims. The debate on which religious signs are allowed and which are not is not a neutral one. It depends on the art of justifying what is discriminative. In the previous chapter, we have seen that ECtHR ruled unequally for the visibility of the large crucifix in

[45] Savage (2004) and Joppke (2009).
[46] Amiraux (2007).
[47] Scott (2009).
[48] https://www.theguardian.com/law/2017/mar/14/employers-can-ban-staff-from-wearing-headsc arves-european-court-rules.

Italian public school and of Samira Achbita's hijab visibility at the Belgian work-place. Those macro-consequences of the French ban negatively affected religious minorities in all of Europe, not only in France, consequently, impede the healthy exercise of a pluralistic society in Europe.[49]

This liberal public sphere is not found in the same intensity in the British neither the Spanish contexts. Nevertheless, the presence of the headscarf inspires uneasiness in the Spanish context more than the British one. In the previous chapter, I mentioned that, in 2010, the right-wing (*Partido Popular*) proposed to ban the headscarf practice at public schools. The left-wing (*Socialists Party*) refused the proposal in favor of the young Muslim students' right to education. This political attempt, together with the municipal Catalonian law in 2009 that bans Islamic full-covering in the municipal buildings (although very few full-covering cases founded in Catalonia), was an enthusiastic inspiration of their neighbor's legislation on Muslim visibility.

Cloth decisions are based on our desire to behave in a particular manner or show our belonging to certain social classes or groups.[50] It can turn our bodies, the flesh, into a recognizable individual, communicating our identities. Besides, it determines the social categorization practiced upon us. As the strength of the identity and its performance is a mutual relationship between both,[51] the hijab plays twofold empow-erment for those who practice it: it is part of their public identity; without it, they feel incomplete. Simultaneously, the hijab is a negotiation technique with women's sexism and objectification found in daily public interaction. It provides its practi-tioners with strength, confidence, and comfort with the inner-selves. In the European contexts, Muslim women practice veiling to claim their religious and moral author-ities on their own decisions to conceive the recognition as Muslims despite their awareness of being an easy target of exclusion/discrimination.

The majority of hijab-wearers consider the hijab as a further step in their religious commitment; it is not a matter of being "less" or "more" Muslim. Donning the hijab initially starts with an embodied religious identity that shapes the mind and the heart; then, it turns to shape their body's visibility in public.[52] It is a reminder of a conduct code which Muslims should behave in accord with. According to the hijab-wearers, the hijab is a statement of the necessity to restrain women's sexuality and to assert the female-self in the public sphere. It is also a sign of refusal to be part of unconditioned sexual freedom. The practice also works as an identity definer. Positively or not, the hijab unifies all its Euro-wearers under one (gendered) identity, hijab-wearing Euro-Muslim women, overcoming the ethnical and racial categorization.

Muslim women across Europe, especially those who practice veiling, suffer from multi-dimensional, intersectional, discrimination because they are marked as members of ethnic or/and religious groups and as gendered social class. Even Muslim feminists and activists frequently go under such discrimination in feminist institu-tions when their frame of reference does not coincide with Western perspectives on

---

[49]Moore (2007).

[50]Entwistle (2015).

[51]Hopkins and Greenwood (2013).

[52]Marco (2008) and Dwyer (1999).

women's vestments and body. Muslim women are under pressure to fight racism from one side and to fight sexism from the other side.[53]

Euro-Muslim women's burden is structured on three dimensions: racism, accommodating their own Islamic culture within the mainstream culture, and, finally, challenging stereotypes and patriarchy within their community and in the wider society. Avtar Brah describes that racism against Muslim women is a "differential racialization" that indicates the biological racism and the superiority of a social group over others and the inability to exceed the cultural differences and the assertion on the incompatibility of these differences within the mainstream. This racism is a contemporary version of post-colonial racism. It is practiced on European Muslim citizens whose ancestors are from the colonies.

Euro-Muslim women have always been under the scope of the public debate. Gema Martin Muñoz states that Muslim women's problem is not religious, but it is a social issue. They feel pressure to perform a national belonging that claims to be secular.[54] Their visible religious public identity is questioned and rejected. The pressure to choose between religious commitments and secular social requirements creates multiple publics, in which religion and secularity are binary centers for Euro-Muslim women to engage with.[55] Oihana Macro asserts that Euro-Muslim female generation is in a continuous rediscovery of their multi-identities. It is not challenging for them to practice religion in the public sphere and maintain the secular approach in their civic participation. Wearing the hijab or praying is a private matter they need to practice in the public sphere. Yet, it does not indicate that they speak out or discuss their religious affiliation publicly.[56] Jeanette Jouili observes that Euro-Muslim women, even the most ordinary ones, turn to be political signifiers mainly because the political discourse sets them, especially practitioners, as a subject problem: subordinated, unwilling to assimilate the European values and can never be part of the nation.[57] Such political stigmatization pushes hijab-wearers to conform, compulsory, to the European political, cultural, and sexual expectations. The climax is when the hijab takes place in the political agenda to decide its legitimacy, or not, in public schools.[58]

After all, the Euro-Muslim women's struggle in Europe is a struggle of visibility, fighting stereotypes, and claiming respect for their Euro-religious, gendered identity. Levels of personalities, life conditions, self-esteem, and consistent ability are not the same among individuals. Many Euro-Muslim women opt out of their religious identity under the (secular) pressure and the need to get a job or academic formation. Even under the same social conditions, others hold on to the Islamic identity and, literary, fight for their religious freedom.

---

[53] Sibai (2010), Moghadam (2010), and KhirAllah (2015).

[54] I use the word "claim" because, as I mentioned in the previous chapter, the Secular dimension of the Euro-identity is nourished in an opposition to the Muslim visibility in the public sphere.

[55] Jouili (2009) and Moors and Salih (2009).

[56] Eseverri C.M., Khir-Allah G. (Working paper) Controlling Muslim Youth Association through Unique representation, Complutense University.

[57] Jouili (2009).

[58] Amiraux (2007).

Public Discourses on Hijab

Most of the contemporary writings about the hijab were actively published after the 2004 French law. Feminists, socialists, politicians, and religionists were all divided for or against such legislation in Europe. Each group has its evidence by which they defend their arguments. In the following, I try to list the pros and contra attitudes toward the 2004 French ban law of *hijab* through the two most used arguments in the discourse of hijab: (1) secularity vs. religious liberty and (2) gender discrimination vs. gender justice. In each, whether it supports or denies the ban law, we will discuss arguments from different approaches: western mainstream feminists, (Western) Muslim feminists, politicians, social activists, and religious figures.

Religious Liberty vs. Euro-Secularism: Inclusion vs. Exclusion

In this argumentation, interpreting the hijab visibility is tied to the exclusion and inclusion of the desired/undesired religious signs and those who practice them. For example, John Esposito,[59] whose perception of veiling is limited to Arabic traditions, uses the "Arab girls" expression to refer to French Muslim girls who chose to wear a chador (a headscarf integrated within a cloak) to school. He states that those "Arab girls" who insist on wearing chador are not French and do not want to be or feel European. Balibar, the French minister of education with ambiguous and contradictory reasoning on the headscarf, asserted that public schools are a place of integration. Therefore, the hijab practice, a sign of difference, should be excluded from the classroom.[60] Theoretically, integration includes the recognition and acceptance of cultural diversity (difference). How could the exclusion of those "different cultural signs" improve the "integration" at public school? Besides, President Jacques Chirac created the Stasi commission in the name of the French Unity because he considered the veil a dangerous (outsider) sign in the French secular identity. Those who opt for the secularity argument consider the hijab an external, irritating, and foreigner sign that encroach the national identity. They also depend on the post-colonial feminism that promotes secularity over the cultures of "others."

Evidence of excluding Islam is the fair judgment on the religious visibility discussed in the previous chapter. While the ECtHR ruled for the crucifix's visibility in the Lautsi case at public school and in Nadia Eweida's case at the workplace, the CHtHR ruled against the hijab visibility in Samira Achbita's case at the workplace. The former was justified by the visibility of pluralism and the uprising of the principle of religious visibility. In contrast, the latter is justified by the company's right to protect the staff members from any political, philosophical, or religious signs at work. It would be fair and neutrality-supportive to find equalitarian public or political discourse/attitude on a religious sign prohibition in Europe. Thomassen asserts

---

[59] Esposito (1999).

[60] Balibar (2004).

that the fair implementation of religious freedom can disassociate Islamic signs from political Islam. It will limit the rights to practice Islam to the civic sphere away from politics. The non-neutral political discourse asserts Islam's incompatibility, generates intolerance from both groups (minority and majority), and increases discrimination against the hijab-wearers. At the end of all, the "secularity" of the European public sphere seems to be a decent term to announce the "fanatic" and "intolerant" one.

Jocelyne Cesari considers that understanding the hijab visibility as "the return of religion" serves to expand the gap between religion and politics and affirm the East–West polarity. Cesari considers the legislation on the hijab as a religious-political movement that intends to desacralize public affairs to save the national identity.[61] Thus, the law claims to protect people's rights, but it is, in reality, depriving them of their religious rights. The political discourse, Stasi's Commission discourse, claims that the hijab is not compatible with secular French republic norms. Yet, many scholars respond that secularism has been fed and revived to limit the visibility of Muslims (Roy, 2007; Salih, 2009; Scott, 2009; Zapata-Barrero and Diez-Nicolás 2012). Joan Scott refers that those polarized views are just another way to say that French Muslims can never be European. Euro-debate on the hijab's visibility focuses on abstract (secular) principles and ignores important Human Rights such as children's right to education, religious freedom, and women's right to vestment. The ban law imposes a collective identity on the young French Muslim generation and takes away the autonomy of their personal identities, violates their personal space, and, more importantly, imposes an identity they did not ask for.[62]

Gender Equality vs. Gender Justice

One of the most frequent arguments used to justify the ban law was saving the young girls from the patriarchy they suffer from within their families. Remy Schwartz, a member of the French Council of State and member of Stasi Commission on Secularism, declares on a TV worldwide broadcast human right show "World in Trial" in 2011 that the ban law was not passed to discriminate against Muslim girls as many promote. The ban law is aimed to protect the young girls who came to them, asking for protection and expressing their desire to wear skirts and pants to school. Young girls dream of liberty and tranquility when they go to school. Remy Schwartz continues to consider the ban law as a victory of democratic French Islam against fundamentalists who want to impose their vision on others. He asserts that the law is a victory for "those immigrant women (who) wanted the protection by the state, they came to us and said: "thank you for allowing us to be free"" (cited in Beary 2012: 384). Schwartz used the "white man mission" to liberate the outsider migrant post-colonized women. He cast the hijab practice and the hijab-wearing women as an outsider and oppressing/oppressed, effectively.

[61] Cesari (1999).

[62] Alvi (2013).

Stasi (2004) considers the ban law a significant step in achieving the Republic's equality value. According to Stasi's argument, the law removes the sign of women's inequality from the classroom. It declares the equality between men and women, which, in its turn, matches with the republican *laïcité*. He highlights that anyone who pledge allegiance to the Republic must endorse that egalitarian principle, which casts Muslim practitioners, and hijab supporters, as potential un-loyal citizens.

The joyful exchange between sexes and the total accessibility to one another's sexual preferences are taken to be significant markers in French liberty and equality.[63] Sexuality is perceived as a positive influence on the free society and not as dangerous intercourse. Within this context, veiling, which points out the difference in the body structures between men and women, is an obstacle to the European "sameness" gender equation and to the abstract individualism of citizens (male and female). The new emphasis on sexual equality is a way of insisting on the immutability of the *republic's laïcité*.[64] Pro arguments of the ban law dispute that the hijab practice denies Muslim women's access to education, preventing them from using their rational faculty, which keeps Muslim women in the dark.

Scott indicates that the ban law does not challenge the structure of gender inequality of Muslim law because Islamic gender inequality is an imaginary colonial perspective. The "Islamic gender inequality" supposes that gender discrimination is limited only to the Muslim world and never found in European countries. Although the equality principle is dominant in France, it appears as an obstacle that takes no account of cultural and religious particularity. French policies, first, established centralized republic-traditional regulations of equality. Later, they introduce the possibility of recognizing individual choices but not those of Muslim women. The assumption of "what is good for western women must be good for all" could be the main logic behind the misconception of the Islamic gender perspective, which is based on gender "justice" and not gender "equality." It does not revolve around "sameness" and "equity"; instead, it stresses the "different" but "complementarily" roles of both genders in each life aspect.[65] It is complementary of need, function, and contribution in which each gender has his/her rights and responsibilities.

Islam affirms sexuality as a human good. It also confirms the potency of sexual desire, leading men and women to have inappropriate sexual contexts. The sexual connotation of the term *fitnah* in Islamic legislation refers to the exposure of the female's body in public, inevitably leading to sexual temptation, female sexual subjection, and political disorder. Accordingly, the goal of behavioral and vestment (modesty) codes for both gender is to prevent such social disorder. Scott points out that the French model of individualism and sexual differences involves denying the problem and the sexual difference between both genders and proclaims gender

---

[63]Ozouf (1995).

[64]Fassin (2005).

[65]The Muslim identity is above the gender identity, no difference in front of God between men or women. The preference standards is based on the good deeds of each. Although this is not well recognized in several Muslim countries because of the power of traditions, this self-identification dominates the construction of Euro-Muslims identity who learn "pure" Islam away from traditions.

equality by banning the Islamic headscarf. On the contrary, Islamic legislation recognizes the sexual difference as a potential political problem and puts veiling practice (modest dress code), reducing the vision, and sexes separation as suggested solutions. In her words, Scott says:

> Ironically, Islamic theory puts sex out there as a problem for all to see by conspicuously covering the body, while the French call for a conspicuous display of bodies in order to deny the problem that sex poses for republican political theory. (2007: 167–168)

Amiraux points out that the debate on the inappropriate dress of schoolgirls is not new. The "porno chic" is seen as an offense to decency, yet, decency is never mentioned when debating the headscarf because veiled schoolgirls are taken for granted to be oppressed. These debates do not explicitly mention the sexual practices that associate the inappropriate dress, yet, many public schools, especially elementary schools, ban the mini-skirt and very tight leggings.[66] Both seemingly separated but truly related debates, porno chic and the headscarf, aim to regulate women's sexuality to avoid a sexual disorder in the public sphere. Scott considers veiling a declaration of the need to curb the sexuality of women and men all together and a need to regulate the risks associated with our vital impulses.[67]

Conclusions

The hijab practice served well the western political agenda in the colonial and postcolonial policies. The Western political discourse on hijab recycled the same arguments used for describing Muslim women's situation in Iraq and Afghanistan and justify their invasions at the end of the last century. After these two invasions, such discourse needed renovation to convince the contemporary European public as much as to face the increasing visibility of the European hijab-wearing women. Thus, the (neo) colonial discourse promotes the western, colonizer, first-world, and liberated women's superiority over the oriental, colonized, third-world, and subordinated Muslim women's inferiority. This positionality is sustained within a new frame of reference that evolves around gender equality and concealing women's bodies.

The incompatibility between the hijab practice and human rights (included in UDHR) is used as a contemporary, easily sold, convincing argument that can effectively shape the current European public opinion. Although this incompatibility lacks a systematic analysis of the religious requirement of the hijab, it is well perceived by public opinion. The hijab incompatibility with the UDHR constitutes unquestionable evidence on the Euro-superiority because it is a continuum of what the European mind is used to since the colonial discourse.

We found out that only five verses (out of 6,236) of the Quran address gender public relations and women's vestment. Islam alleged for the free choice in practice,

---

[66] In the Spanish context, at least in Madrid, parents count a positive point for the elementary schools that ban the mini skirt and shorts.
[67] Hammoudi (2006).

no punishment is stipulated for unveiled women in the Quran, and the hijab practice is not one of the mandates or absolute duty, e.g., the five pillars of Islam. The analysis of the Quranic texts, the Sunnah, and the four Sharia schools summarizes Muslim women's dress code in two levels: (1) covering the hair and the body, (2) modesty. None of these sources determines a specific dress code for Muslim women, neither a shape nor a color. The door is left open to Muslim women to opt for the dress style that coincides with their cultural heritage and personal preferences. It is an aspect (among various) of personal progress in faith and spirituality. A fact that gives Muslim women the freedom to how they conceal (or not) their sexuality in the public sphere.

The alleged hijab incompatibility with human rights arises from the different understandings of sexuality in the public sphere across the secular and the Islamic approaches. While the secular approach calls for unconditional sexual liberty in the public sphere, the Islamic approach recognizes the differences between genders. It establishes behavioral and dress codes, for both men and women, to regulate gender relationships in the public sphere. As the analysis of this chapter argues, these codes aim at creating a neutral public sphere where individuals are evaluated by their inner values and professionality away from physical preferences. Although secular western feminists call for gender-specific legislation related to women and criticize the schoolgirls "porno chic" vestments, they attack the Islamic approach that puts out the physical difference between the two genders.

I do not claim that one way is better than the other. I suggest that the Islamic way of framing gendered public relations needs to be respected by non-Muslims or non-practitioner Muslims as much as Muslim practitioners should respect the secular way of framing gendered public relations. There is no justification for underestimating any of these approaches or setting one of them above the other, as it was perfect-for-all. Each woman has the right to a personal decision to display her body in the public sphere as much as to conceal it without being stigmatized because of any of these choices. After all, no individual is allowed, under any legislation in Europe, to determine a woman's choice of vestment and dictate what to wear and what not to wear.

The Euro-academia exclusion is not limited to the Islamic religious signs and the Holy texts that address gender relations in the public sphere. The academia exclusion also includes the academic and activist hijab-wearing feminist women who defend women's freedom to vestment from a religious perspective. Their religious-based frame is attacked and rejected by secular and liberal academics, although it is just another framing of gender relations in the public sphere. Academic and activist hijab-wearing feminists are problematic because their visibility in the European contexts ruffles the national (and secular) identity. Hijab-wearing feminists who study religious texts are perceived as "dangerous" because they have effective communication channels with Muslim women. Yet, their discourse is an engine for social change that lines up with the religious frame and is thus welcomed by the Muslim majority. Through this way, hijab-wearing feminists are able to claim their rights and achieve social change within Islam.

Hijab-wearing women in Europe use the veil to affirm their European religious identity, although they are aware of their stigmatization. The practice exceeds the religious realm and turns to be an intersectional tool to reaffirm their identity; an exercise of women's rights (to education, to equality, to work, and to vestment) guaranteed in international human rights treaties and claimed by feminists in European countries.

References

Abu-Lughod, L. (2002). Do Muslim women really need saving? *American Anthropologist, 104*(3), 783–790

Ahmed, L. (1982). Western ethnocentrism and perceptions of the harem. *Feminist Studies, 8*(3), 521–534

Ahmed, L. (1986). Women and the advent of Islam. *Signs: Journal of Women in Culture and Society, 11*(4), 665–691.

Ahmed, L. (2000). The women of Islam. *Transition, 83*, 78–97

Alexander, M. J. (2006). *Pedagogies of crossing: Meditations on feminism, sexual politics, memory, and the sacred*. Duke University Press.

Alvi, A. (2013). Concealment and revealment. *Current Anthropology, 54*(2), 177–199

Amer, S. (2014). *What is veiling?* UNC Press Books.

Amiraux, V. (2007). The headscarf question: What is Really the issue. In S. Amghar, A. Boubekeur, & M. Emerson (Eds.), *European Islam: Challenges for public policy and society*. CEPS

Ang-Lygate, M. (1996). Everywhere to go but home: On (re)(dis)(un) location. *Journal of Gender Studies, 5*(3), 375–388

Asad, T. (2003). *Formations of the secular: Christianity, Islam, modernity*. (p. 184). Stanford University Press.

Badran, M. (2002). Islamic feminism: What's in a name? *Al-Ahram Weekly Online, 569*(2002), 17–23

Badran, M. (2009). *Feminism in Islam: Secular and religious convergences*. Oneworld Publications.

Balibar, E. (2004). Dissonances dans la laïcité. *Mouvements, 3*, 148–161

Barlas, A. (2006). Four stages of Denial, or my on-again, off-again affair with feminism: Response to Margot Badran. *Ithaca College* (p. 4).

Bhargava, R., & Reifeld, H. (Eds.). (2005). *Civil society, public sphere and citizenship: Dialogues and perceptions*. Sage.

Boulos, S. (2019a). Integrating Muslim women within european societies: Muslim human rights discourse and the cross-cultural approach to human rights in Europe. In *Challenging the borders of justice in the age of migrations* (pp. 243–262). Springer, Cham.

Boulos, S. (2019b). Towards reconstructing the meaning of inhuman treatment or punishment: A human capability approach. *The Age of Human Rights Journal, 12*, 35–61

Cameron, D. (1992). *Feminism and linguistic theory*. Springer.

Cesari, J. (1999). The re-Islamization of Muslim immigration in Europe. In G. M. Munoz (Ed.), *Islam, modernism and the West: cultural and political relations at the end of the millennium*. IB Tauris.

Davis, K. (2008). Intersectionality as buzzword: A sociology of science perspective on what makes a feminist theory successful. *Feminist theory, 9*(1), 67–85.

De Beauvoir, S. (1952). *The second sex*. Bantam.

Dietz, M. G. (2003). Current controversies in feminist theory. *Annual review of political science, 6*(1), 399–431.

Dwyer, C. (1999). Veiled meanings: Young British Muslim Women and the negotiation of differences. *Gender, Place and Culture, 6*(1), 5–22

Engineer, A. A. (2007). *Islam in contemporary world*. Sterling Publishers Pvt.

Entwistle, J. (2015). *The fashioned body: Fashion, dress and social theory*. Wiley.

Esposito, J. L. (1999). Clash of civilization? Contemporary images of Islam in the west. In G. M. Munoz (Ed.), *Islam, modernism and the West: cultural and political relations at the end of the millennium*. IB Tauris.

Fassin, E. (2005). *L'inversion de la question homosexuelle*. Editions Amsterdam/Multitudes.

Glendon, M. A. (1997). Knowing the universal declaration of human rights. *Notre Dame Law Review, 73*, 1153

Gómez, L. (2019). *Diccionario de islam e islamismo*. Trotta.

Habermas, J. (1991). *The structural transformation of the public sphere: An inquiry into a category of bourgeois society*. MIT Press.

Haddad, Y. (2007). The post-9/11 hijab as icon. *Sociology of Religion, 68*(3), 253–267

Hammoudi, A. (2006). *A season in Mecca: Narrative of a pilgrimage*. Polity.

Hoodfar, H. (1992). The veil in their minds and on our heads: The persistence of colonial images of Muslim women. *Resources for Feminist Research, 22*(3/4), 5

Hopkins, N., & Greenwood, R. M. (2013). Hijab, visibility and the performance of identity. *European Journal of Social Psychology, 43*(5), 438–447

Joppke, C. (2009). *Veil*. Polity.

Jouili, J. (2009). Negotiating secular boundaries: Pious micro-practices of Muslim women in French and German public spheres. *Social Anthropology, 17*(4), 455–470

Khader, S. J. (2016). Do Muslim women need freedom? Traditionalist feminisms and transnational politics. *Politics & Gender*, 1–27.

KhirAllah, G. (2015). Veiling and revealing identity: The linguistic representation of the hijab in the British Press. In M. C. La Barbera (Ed.), *Identity and migration in Europe: Multidisciplinary perspectives* (pp. 229–249). Springer International Publishing.

La Barbera, M. C. (2007). Una reflexión crítica a través del pensamiento de Susan Okin sobre género y justicia. *Cuadernos Electrónicos De Filosofía Del Derecho, 16*, 1–15

La Barbera, M. C. (2009). *Multicentered feminism: Revisiting the "female genital mutilation" discourse*. Compostampa.

Mahmood, S. (2005). *Politics of piety: The Islamic revival and the feminist subject*. Princeton University Press.

Marco, O. (2008). The hijabization process: Some "mindful" bodies uncovered. *Quaderns De La Mediterrània, 9*(9), 201–214

McCall, L. (2005). The complexity of intersectionality. *Signs: Journal of Women in Culture and Society, 30*(3), 1771–1800.

Moghadam, V. M. (2010). *Feminist activism in the Arab region and beyond: Linking research to policy reform and social change*.

Moore, K. M. (2007). Visible through the veil: The regulation of Islam in American law. *Sociology of Religion, 68*(3), 237–251

Moors, A., & Salih, R. (2009). 'Muslim women' in Europe: Secular normativities, bodily performances and multiple publics. *Social Anthropology, 17*(4), 375–378

Muñoz, G. M. (2010). *Esto alimenta a la derecha islamófoba*. https://elpais.com/diario/2010/04/22/sociedad/1271887205_850215.html. 22 April 2010.

Muñoz, M. G., & Grosfoguel, R. (2012). La islamofobia a debate. La genealogía del miedo al Islam y la construcción de los discursos antiislámicos.

Ozouf, M. (1995). *Les mots des femmes: essai sur la singularité française*. Fayard.

Roy, O. (2007). Islam terrorist radicalization in Europe. In S. Amghar, A. Boubekeur, & M. Emerson (Eds.), European Islam: Challenges for public policy and society. CEPS.

Said, E. W. (2002). Orientalismo. 1990 (M. L. Fuentes, Trans.). Debate.

Salih, R. (2009). Muslim women, fragmented secularism and the construction of interconnected 'publics' in Italy. *Social Anthropology, 17*(4), 409–423

Savage, T. M. (2004). Europe and Islam: Crescent waxing, cultures clashing. *Washington Quarterly,* *27*(3), 25–50

Scott, J. W. (2009). *The politics of the veil.* Princeton University Press.

Sibai, S. A. (2010a). *Quítame este velo, porque solita yo no puedo.* Published in www.masdeunavez. blogspot.com.es.

Sibai, S. A. (2018). *La cárcel del feminismo: Hacia un pensamiento islámico decolonial* (Vol. 13). Ediciones AKAL.

Stasi, B. (2004). Laïcité et République. Rapport de la commission de réflexion sur.

Tohidi, N. (2003). "Islamic feminism": Perils and promises. *Middle Eastern Women on the move.*

Volpp, L. (2011). Framing cultural difference: Immigrant women and discourses of tradition. *Differences, 22*(1), 91–110

Zapata-Barrero, R., & Diez-Nicolas, J. (2012). Islamophobia in Spain? Political rhetoric rather than a social fact. In M. Helbling (Ed.), *Islamophobia in the West: Measuring and explaining individual attitudes* (pp. 83–97). London: Routledge.

The Hijab Sign System: Toward a Cognitive Critical Discourse Analysis Theory CCDA

Introduction

The Cognitive Approach, generally, studies how the brain processes information, how it transforms this information into memories, how the brain recalls it as well as uses this information in interaction. The cognitive analysis does not depend on neurological evidence. It relies on the study of behavioral and linguistic (re)actions.

Functionalism, the first generation that merged the Cognitive Approach in language studies, appeared in the 1950s–1960s. J. R. Firth, a British linguist, and his student M.A.K. focused on what language does and how it does it. They gave importance to the language function contrary to Structuralism, which focuses on the elements of language and their combinations. They called their approach Systematic-Functional Linguistics. SFL focused on the social context and observed how language acts in a social context and how language is restrained by it. It considers the language as a strategic, meaning-making resource. Functionalists' novel theory was interpreting the mind independently from the body. They assumed that signs and symbols are meaningless in their abstract form. The human mind attaches meaning to signs and symbols depending on the former rules and attributes they have experienced throughout their lifetime.

The second generation appeared around the 1970s. They focused on individual bodily experiences in interpreting signs. Noam Chomsky's theories, the most sophisticated philosophical linguist of our time, significantly influenced the contemporary cognitive linguistics approach. However, Cognitive Linguistics as a discipline appeared around the 1970s by scholars, such as George Lakoff, Ronald Langacker, and Leonard Talmy. They were more interested in the meaning and cognitive processes than abstract grammar. The CL approach was well established by the publication of Lakoff's *Women, Fire and Dangerous Things*, and Langacker's *Foundations of Cognitive Grammar*.

Cognitive Linguistics aims to explain, or discover, the relation between mind, brain, and body from one hand and the language used to express the meanings of signs on the other side. *Cognitive Linguistics* depends on the "context" as a critical

© Springer Nature Singapore Pte Ltd. 2021
G. Khir-Allah, *Framing Hijab in the European Mind*,
https://doi.org/10.1007/978-981-16-1653-2_4

element to interpret the language choices. Language-context focus paved the way to the *Cognitive Sociolinguistics* approach, which focuses on culture and cultural differences as primary triggers of linguist productions and linguistic variations. Psychologists, philosophers, and anthropologists are increasingly interested in the *Cognitive Sociolinguistic* approach for its capacity to reveal the shared mental structures that are being practiced by society members through language or (group or individual) behavior. Langacker (1999) stresses the need to extend the cognitive approach to sociolinguistics. Since then, there were several attempts to set together with the term *Cognitive Sociolinguistics.*

As this book analyzes the hijab sign system in the European press discourse, I adopted the *Cognitive Sociolinguistic Analysis* as a tool to discover how the hijab is introduced in the Spanish and British national press discourse. I consider that cultural differences, such as secularism versus religion, are primary triggers for the discourse variation on the hijab (between hijab wearers and the hijab-opposer discourse). Writing this chapter was challenging because it focuses on various interrelated cognitive and sociolinguistic approaches. Although I tried, at many points, to correlates these (cognitive and sociolinguistic) arguments to the hijab case studied in this book, I left many other points open to the reader's self-critical reading. I challenge you to reflect on what you have read in the previous two chapters (on hijab visibility and the political discourse) in the shed on these cognitive and sociolinguistic theories.

I have been through another challenge; I wanted to introduce this theoretical chapter attractively and simply to non-linguist readers. As I know that this book is multi-disciplinary, I am quite sure that not all readers are interested in the in-depth theoretical in Cognitive Linguistics review. For this reason, I limit this chapter to simplify the structure of the new Cognitive Critical Discourse Analysis CCDA methodology, which I used in the analysis section.

This chapter will explain the Critical Discourse Analysis approach CDA and Conceptual Metaphor Theory CMT in their simplest form. I used the cognitive sociolinguistic theory to study the social integration of Muslim women in the European context and analyze the social-sign system of the hijab. I will briefly recapitulate the works of Zoltan Kovecses, Antonio Barcelona, George Lakoff, and Mark Johnson on metaphors and mental frames and the literature of Tuen Van Dijk and Christopher Hart on Critical Discourse Analysis and the connection between it and conceptual metaphors, without going through the details such as the semantic and lexical frames[1] or domains mappings in CMT.[2] After going through these theories and approaches, I present my new theory on CCDA.

---

[1] Sullivan (2013).

[2] Clausner and Croft (1999).

Cognitive (Socio)Linguistics

Historical and Contemporary Perspectives

Noam Chomsky combined Cartesian Philosophy with formalist philosophy to create a new philosophical view in his career. From Cartesian linguistics, he adopted some key component in Descartes' view of mind and reason, such as:

- The separation of mind and body: the mind is different and separated from the body.
- Transcendent autonomous reason: the reason is the capacity of the mind, not the body. It works autonomously by its own rules, independently from any bodily control, e.g., emotion and imagination.
- Essence: Everything has an essence that distinguishes it from other things.
- Rationality defines human nature: rationality is a universal essence shared by all human beings. It is what distinguishes us as humans.
- Thought as language: thought is metaphorically understood as language. As reason and rationality are universal, this might lead us to a universal language, and eventually, universal grammar.

From these theories, Chomsky theorized that language is universal and innate. It is an autonomous capacity of mind. The language essence is "universal grammar." The separation between the mind and the body distinguishes humans from other beings and provides them free will. Rationality and freedom occupy the central place, while culture aesthetics and pleasure have no essential role in universal human nature. Accordingly, culture has no vital contribution to language, and the role of the body is totally denied. Chomsky is interested in the purely syntactic essence, innate and universal parameters, shared by all languages, yet this focus underestimates other language features, such as evidential systems, spatial-relation systems, and politeness systems.

The second generation of cognitive science was interested in the notion of embodiment because it determines what and how we think. The term embodiment goes beyond the physical sense of the body to involve every experience, meaning, thought, and language.

Mark Johnson, in his book *The Body in the Mind: the Bodily Basis of Meaning, Imagination, and Reason* (1987), uses the term "body" as a generic form of the embodied origins of the imaginative structures and understandings, such as image schemata and metaphorical structures.[3] In a difference to Objectivism, he focuses on the indispensability of the embodied human understandings for meaning-making and rationality. Objectivism, the abstract philosophical approach, ignores human beings' imagination. The recent version of Objectivism claims that the human embodiment has no significant effect on meaning and rationality.

---

[3] Johnson (2013).

Johnson stresses the experimental structure of meanings and understanding, which repeals the "arbitrariness" theory. He argues that metaphorical projections are not arbitrary. On the contrary, they are based on emotional, historical, social, and linguistic experiences. Besides, Johnson explores the significant role of human imagination in making meaning of, understanding, and reasoning about the world around us. Johnson considers the study of imagination as a critical element to understand human cognition. Again, Johnson's theory goes against Objectivism, which aims to find the meaning of abstract concepts and arbitrary symbols through rules of logic and rationality.

Johnson argues that understanding "imagination" as artistic creativity is a nineteenth-century Romantic view. He argues that meaning and rationality require a comprehensive theory on imagination capable of structuring human experiences and cognition. He asserts that any comprehensive theory on imagination needs to include the following components:

- Categorization: to break up our experiences into simpler patterns.
- Schemata: general knowledge or mental structures.
- Metaphorical projection: the tool by which we project and develop image schemata.
- Metonymy: another tool to project and develop meanings.
- Narrative structure: the unity of the complex communal narrative by which we experience, understand, and order our lives as stories.

Johnson concludes that our imagination structures make our experiences meaningful and control our reasoning about them. Imagination structures are the shared embodied, spatial, temporal, cultural understandings that make our communication mutually understood.

The meaning of anything (e.g., experience, symbol, or a story) is how we understand this thing. We do not understand things individually in a separate manner. We instead understand things as embodied individuals in a linguistic community, such as a culture or a historical context. Meaning-making is a public process that establishes the shared meanings and understandings of the external world for all members of the speech community. As we have read before, cognitive science argues that our body, brain, and imagination are the main unconscious factors in meaning-making.

Meaning-making is done through several processes, from which categorization is the first. All living beings categorize. Animals, even unicell beings, categorize what is food or to move forward or backward. The human neural system inevitably and unconsciously categorizes the world around us. Our minds and bodies decide what we categorize and what categories we already have, and how we structure them. We also create new categories regularly. Mental frames are in the second position in the meaning-making process. Mental frames form the fundamental experiences that are used in metaphorical thought. It is the overall conceptual structure of a "field" or an "experience"; it also defines the semantic relationships among this conceptual structure and the words that express them. For example, the restaurant frame, which characterizes our general knowledge of restaurants, is not only intentional and representative but also propositional. The restaurant frame includes the concepts of a restaurant, waiters, menus, and checks. It contains propositional information: a waiter brings you a list, takes your order, etc.

Conceptual metaphors and metonymy are essential in meaning-making. Lakoff and Johnson (1980) define metaphors through thoughts and reasoning: "the essence of metaphor is understanding and experiencing one kind of thing in terms of another" (1980: 5). They argue that our conceptual system is metaphorical in nature. Metonymy has received less attention in cognitive linguistics than conceptual metaphors even though it is essential to language and cognition, too. Antonio Barcelona (2012) indicates that metonymy is a conceptual projection between two notions, yet, both are in the same common exertion domain. It is a kind of activation of that domain. For example, in *she's just a pretty face*, FACE stands for the person (FACE FOR PERSON).

Polysemy, another process in meaning-making, is to understand multiple related meanings by a single word. The interconnection between mental frames, metaphors, and metonymy might explain the numerous meanings of correlated senses. The several metaphorical projections of the same image schemata generate polysemy. Finally, (social) meanings change over time. Identifying the semantic change is important in meaning-making theory because it reveals the (social, historical, experimental) triggers behind these changes. The first three processes in meaning-making theory, categorization, mental frames, and conceptual metaphors, are the focus of this research.

Cultural forces guide the interaction between human beings. That is, for any communication, individuals initially categorize situations into mental categories. Afterward, they impose, on these categories, forms of talk regulated by the social norms to express interactions and emotions. Zoltan Kovecses, who I follow in this research, describes such categorization as "essential for survival" because these mental categories are the "backbone" of language and thoughts (2006: 17). The interconnection between meaning-making and mental categories is fundamental in any language, and it is traditionally called "feature lists," which indicates what a language's speakers know about abstract concepts. In many of his research, Kovecses (2000, 2003, 2005, 2006) criticizes that "feature lists" may include unrelated confusing structures. He replaces this term with "mental frames." "Frames" are defined as "structured" mental representations of conceptual categories that cannot be given as in "feature lists" (2006: 64). Mental frames are called differently by scholars: scenario, scene, cultural models, cognitive models, or image schemas. However, all of these terms stand for a coherent, categorized structure of human experiences (Johnson, 1987; Kovecses, 2005, 2006; Lakoff, 1987; Lakoff & Johnson, 1980; Ziem, 2014). I use Kovecses' term because I agree with him that "mental frames" provide the "structured" mental representation that other definitions might miss.

George Lakoff notifies that one of the essential cognitive science findings is that people think in terms of mental frames and metaphorical-conceptual structures. Based on Kovecses' and Lakoff's various works, I define mental frames as follows: A mental frame is the cognitive structures that we build to understand the world. Mental frames are imaginary representations and categorizations of the abstract and physical aspects of our life. They are essential for our survival and are unconsciously rooted in our cognitive system. They are not fixed nor stable, yet they hardly change. Mental frames are not separable from the language we receive and produce. The received language contributes to building our mental frames, and we reveal our mental frame through the language we speak.

Cognitive linguists argue that the words we use to talk about any social sign evoke ready-established mental boxes that attribute meaning to that sign. These mental categories cannot go under radical change, neither we can consciously subject them to a process of recategorization. Our experiences can re-shape unconsciously and gradually these categorizations. Simultaneously, the cognitive approach argues that our neural system is unable to go beyond our neural categories and think in an abstract uncategorized manner.

Knowing the fact does not indicate believing in it and working according to it. When the fact does not fit the mental frame that we already constructed through our cultural, or even personal, context, the fact is simply ignored. Lakoff states that the term *"the fact will set you free"* is a lie because even though the fact is clear out there, the human mind denies it if it does not fit the existing mental frame on that issue.

Conceptual Metaphors: Definitions and Properties

Metaphors have been given different definitions because each discipline defines metaphor from its viewpoint. For example, in rhetoric, metaphors are figures of speech. Oxford English Dictionary's 3rd edition revised defines metaphors as "a figure of speech in which a name or a descriptive word or phrase is transferred to an object or action different from, but analogous to, that to which is literally applicable." Unlike rhetoric, cognitive linguistics deals with metaphors from a conceptual perspective. At the beginning of the twentieth century, Ivor Richard (1936) established an entirely new theory of conceptual metaphor that converted it to a significant field of study. He described conceptual metaphor as a fundamental principle of language, which we inevitably use everyday. Lakoff and Johnson's (1980) *Metaphors We Live By* had marked the beginning of this approach. Their book is considered significant and influential because it established the connection between conceptual metaphors and thoughts. They argue that our conceptual system is metaphorical in nature.

Consequently, what we think and what we experience everyday are just matters of metaphors.[4] They set that "the essence of metaphor is understanding and experiencing one kind of thing in term of another" (1980: 5). Antonio Barcelona's definition (2003) coincides with Lakoff and Johnson's. It is based on a mapping process between two conceptual domains: the source domain and the target domain. Barcelona uses

---

[4]Cornell Way (1991) refused Lakoff and Johnson's stress on the conceptual over the literal. She argued that we cannot consider that all our language is conceptual. In every language, there is fixed meaning words that have literal reference and used everyday for granted. Way also argues that the "literal" language is important to set the contrast to the "non-literal" one.

the term "Conceptual Metaphor" to refer to "the cognitive mechanism whereby one experiential domain is partially 'mapped,' i.e., projected, onto a different experiential domain, so that the second domain is partially understood in terms of the first one" (2003: 3). A more straightforward definition is introduced by Kovecses, who states that metaphors are cross-domain mappings, which represent "the relationship between two frames with the notion of A (abstract concept) is B (more physical)" e.g., LOVE IS JOURNEY[5] (2006: 116).

Lakoff and Turner (1989) give importance to "basic conceptual metaphors." They consider them a "common conceptual apparatus," which is shared by the members of a particular culture or subculture. For example, speech patterns used by the (minority or majority) language users on a (minority) practice or sign is one of the "basic conceptual metaphors." Kovecses refers that conceptual metaphors could be tangible processes in our social and cultural practices because of the source domain's capacity in becoming a social, physical reality. For example, in seating arrangement at a formal meeting usually, important people tend to sit more centrally or higher than less important people. Kovecses associates this social phenomenon with the metaphorical structure SIGNIFICANT/IMPORTANT IS HIGHER/CENTRAL and LESS SIGNIFICANT/LESS IMPORTANT IS LOWER/PERIPHERAL (2005: 142). He indicates that metaphors mainly constitute the cultural models or the native understanding of non-physical social, legal, or emotional concepts.

Kovecses lists 12 components of conceptual metaphor (2006, ch:8), yet I will include only those fundamental for this research. Firstly, each metaphor consists of two main domains: the source domain (more physical, represented by the letter B) and the target domain (more abstract, represented by the letter A). The relationship between both is represented as A is B. In other technical words, the target is the source "AFFECTION IS WARMTH" and "LOVE IS JOURNEY." The target domain can be attached to several sources "LOVE IS WAR," "LOVE IS JOURNEY," which is called the range of the target. Secondly, each metaphor acquires an experiential basis, our embodied experience, that remains unconscious most of the time. It helps any language user to understand metaphors easier. For example, we accept substantial metaphors such as "AFFECTION IS WARMTH" without difficulty because the feeling of affection correlates with bodily experience of warmth.

Thoughts are embodied, which means that we understand our ideas about the world and ourselves through our embodied experience of the world and self. Accordingly, we can only understand abstract ideas, e.g., love and life, by projecting them into a physical world, which we are familiar with. It is to say, conceptual metaphors are the outcome of the interaction between cognitive structures and our bodily experience of the world. Thirdly, Mappings between the source and the target domains are taken to be basic and essential. In the metaphor "LOVE IS JOURNEY," mappings are as follows: lovers are travelers, love relationship is a vehicle, progress made in a relationship is distance covered, and so on. Fourthly, there is a connection between the

---

[5]Following the study of Lakoff and Johnson (1980), the capitalized words stand for the conceptual wide understanding of the source and the target domains of metaphors, not the literal meaning of the vocabulary.

linguistic metaphor (rhetoric) and the conceptual metaphor (cognitive). Conceptual metaphors manifest through linguistic expressions.[6] Finally, conceptual metaphors produce cultural models or mental frames which operate in thoughts. They are "culturally specific mental representations of aspects of the world" (2006: 126). The love range of target I have mentioned above is a good example. The different understandings of the target domain, LOVE, depend on the particular meaning in focus. Each of the sources, WAR and JOURNEY, imposes an entirely different understanding of the target LOVE because each depends on the cultural, individual, bodily, and emotional lived experience of being in love. Accordingly, conceptual metaphors can be interpreted only within their cultural context and depending on their social-sign system[7] (Khir-Allah 2019).

Lakoff and Johnson (1980) list three kinds of conceptual metaphors; the first is the orientational metaphors. They are metaphorical structures built on organizing a whole system of concepts with respect to spatial orientations such as up-down and front-back. For example, the expression "I feel *up* today" comes from the fact that HAPPY is oriented UP in the "HAPPINESS IS UP" metaphor. Such metaphorical orientations are not randomly assigned. They are simply grounded on the speaker's physical and cultural experience. As a sequence, these metaphorical structures might vary from one culture to another.

The second is the ontological metaphors. They indicate understanding experiences in terms of objects and substances. These metaphors allow the speaker to treat parts of his/her experience as discrete entities or substances of a uniform kind. The structure of ontological metaphors depends on our experience with the physical objects around us, e.g., MIND IS AN ENTITY is elaborated to be THE MIND IS A MACHINE, e.g., he *broke down*. The range of such metaphors is immense. Besides, they could vary within the cultural context. Some of the most commonly used ontological metaphors are the following: containers metaphors (IN/OUT), entity metaphors (MIND IS A BRITTLE OBJECT, e.g., he *cracked up*), and personification (INFLATION IS A PERSON, e.g., inflation *has attacked* the foundation of our economy, the dollar *has been destroyed* by inflammation, inflammation *has given birth* to a money-minded generation).

Structural metaphors, the third in the list, provide the most abundant source of metaphorical elaboration. They allow the speaker to use one highly designated concept in order to structure another sub-concept. Such kind of metaphors is more flexible than the previous ones. For example, structural metaphors provide us with more understandings of what communication, argument, and war are. Additionally, they are grounded on the systematic correlations with the speaker's experiences, e.g., IDEAS ARE BUILDING, ARGUMENT IS WAR, and LIFE IS JOURNEY.

---

[6]However, Kovecses indicates that identifying what counts as metaphorical expressions and what counts as rhetoric is "an extremely difficult task," but it does not indicate that it is impossible (2006: 122).

[7]Khir-Allah (2019).

Cultural Models, Mental Frames, and Metaphors

Conceptual metaphors attract cognitive linguists' attention for their ability to reveal the mental frames they depend on. There is an integral relationship between our mental frames, conceptual metaphors, our embodied experiences, and our cultural backgrounds. From a cognitive perspective, culture is a shared understanding of the world based on mental frames.[8] Some cultural backgrounds are argued to be universal as in the AFFECTION IS WARMTH metaphor due to the unconscious bodily experience of warmth in human nature. This experience is called primary experience and is believed to be responsible for producing such universal metaphors. However, Kovecses (2005: 4) argues that not all universal experiences necessarily lead to universal metaphors. At the same time, primary metaphors are not inevitably universal. Metaphors are not necessarily based on bodily experience because many are based on cultural variation and cognitive processes of various kinds.

Naomi Quinn disapproves of the need for primary conceptual metaphors in our everyday interactions.[9] She argues that metaphors simply reflect mental frames, and no metaphor is needed to understand abstract concepts such as love and marriage. The understanding of these concepts emerges from basic experiences that structure them. For example, marriage is an expectational structure that is derived from the motivational structure of love. In its turn, love is obtained from "the basic infantile experience between baby and first caretaker."[10] Zoltan Kovecses refers to Quinn's argument as incomplete and lacks evidence.[11] He and Kay Brugge[12] assert that metaphors not only reflect the mental frames but also afford them. Brugge indicates that conceptual metaphors provide us with the mental scaffold on which our thoughts can rest, noting that our thoughts can only go as high as the scaffold permits. We live within the lines that mark the boxes of our mental frames, which become the stage of our lives. These lines, or boxes, can be self-imposed (e.g., inner forces of underestimating or well-estimating of the self) or imposed by others (e.g., the social norms imposed on individuals).

Brugge classifies metaphors into positive and negative metaphors. Positive metaphors provide us with a profoundly liberating frame and all the resources we need to make changes. Negative metaphors can provide a very rich picture of what is going inside and what we want to preserve and keep away from change. To differentiate between the negative and the positive metaphors, especially in media discourse, we

---

[8] Shore (1996).

[9] Quinn (1997).

[10] Quinn also argues that the cultural model content of marriage is reflected by the metaphor of marital compatibility, difficulty, success, risk, and so on. Quinn concludes that these metaphors are derived from "a contradiction that arises inevitably between the expectations of mutual benefit and that of lastingness" (1991: 67).

[11] Kovecses (2005).

[12] Brugge (2011).

need "conscious thought," which works as the stimulating factor in our minds, especially when targeting social minorities and diversity.[13] Our conscious thoughts have
to distinguish between metaphors that reflect the related values of the minority's sign
system and the metaphors that reflect our understanding of their sign system based on
our own values. Conscious thoughts involve the awareness of separate episodes that
occur in different times and places at the moment of dealing with public discourse
or social signs: the past (conscious remembering), the future (conscious planning),
and counterfactual (conscious reasoning) imagined situation (conscious design) and
desired situations (daydreaming).[14] The lack of conscious thoughts by the receptors
(society members) leads to the accumulation of confined (manipulated) metaphors
in our society build by those who control the public and political discourse.[15]

Kovecses argues that any culture and subcultures use more than one set of coherent
mental frames to interpret the world. Accordingly, the contradiction among these
mental patterns on a particular domain of experience or a cultural symbol (hijab
in our case) causes the metaphorical variation across cultures as well as within
the social varieties of the same culture. Kovecses finds out that the main meaning
focus on conceptual metaphors is useful because of its "cultural sensitivity." The
meaning focus of each metaphor constitutes the central and shared knowledge about
the target (abstract) concept; "it also allows us to capture interesting cross-cultural
(or within cultural) shifts in source domains and what they are connected within the
target" (2005: 12). In contemporary societies' complex structures, both conceptual
and linguistic structures are supposed to vary across social diversities within the same
culture. Social divisions, which are essential operators in the group and individual
identity construction, are called "dimensions" such as the class dimension, ethnic
dimension, regional dimension, and subcultural (religious) dimension. The last is the
focus of this book.

Subcultures are a common feature in the current complex societies. A subculture is defined based on the difference between the cultural mainstream dimension,
which is considered the main style, and the subcultural dimension, which involves
behaviors, or a lifestyle, related to a particular social group. Lakoff and Johnson
indicate that subcultures are identified by those who define themselves in contrast
to the mainstream culture. Often, they can be partially recognized by the symbols
and metaphors they use. The self-definition of subculture membership involves the
unique metaphorical structures of essential concepts by which the "separateness" is
marked.

The linguistic performance reveals identities. Eventually, metaphorical structures
vary according to the social diversities within the same culture. It is to say when
children from minor social groups start expressing their identity, they use a different
set of linguistic structures of the mainstream. Even those who join minority sects

---

[13] Baumeister and Masicampo (2010).

[14] Look at Tomasello's (1999) evolutionary perspective of the development of cognition in
humankind, which suggests that 'culture transformed primate cognition into human conscious
thought' (2010: 952).

[15] Steen (2009).

begin using a different set of linguistic structures. As Kovecses maintains, religion is one of the prominent subcultures in current societies. The visibility of the hijab, as we mentioned in the previous chapter, is the most controversial religious sign in Europe. This book studies the variation in the metaphorical understandings of the abstract concepts of the hijab, secularism, and women's sexuality within—and across—Spanish and British cultures.

Kovecses (2005) clarifies that all the components of conceptual metaphors we have read before are involved in the cultural variation. Different social varieties use different but congruent source domains at lower levels of the conceptual organization. Whereas at higher levels, source domains are more likely to be sub-culturally shared. Secondly, the target domain could be conceptualized differently in the same culture or across cultural variations, producing different metaphors. Thirdly, the relationship between the source and the target in variation is set into two types: (a) one social variety can have a specific target domain that is conventionally associated with a set of source domains. This set of source domains is called the range of the target. For example, Kovecses explains that ANGER in the United States is understood as DARKNESS, DOWN, or HEAVY. (b) the scope of metaphor is when a given source domain is associated with different sets of targets in two or more social varieties, e.g., LIFE IS JOURNEY and LOVE IS JOURNEY. Finally, the conceptual metaphor might be shared by both cultural varieties. Yet, mappings may be different. Accordingly, a shared conceptual metaphor among different social varieties commonly displays variation in the metaphorical linguistic expressions based on that metaphor. These variations are notable in the analysis section of this book.

Framing Social Signs: Positionality and Belonging

Our cognitive system inevitably organizes the input information into conceptual patterns. For example, our brain categorizes every person we meet as confinable, amiable, untrusted, or enemy. Cultural "sign systems" are classification or ordering to the world around per rules that depend on oppositions and similarities. It is an essential attitude for human cognition who tends to simplify the world by selectively categorizing our experiences depending on our cultural rules. By this, we safely picture the world as relatively stable, predictable, and orderly. We find unity in its infinite diversity.[16] Categorization is crucial in self-identification and in locating our social positionality (see chapter "Introduction").

Europeans have always built their identity on "we" and "other" positionality (see Floya Anthias' and Thomassen Lasse's theories on identity construction in Chap. 1). This phenomenon is still dominant till today when the Occidental "we" stands in opposition to the Oriental "others." The secular "we" is defined as liberated and civilized in opposition to the Muslim, oppressed, and in need of civilization, "others."

---

[16]Lindesmith et al. (1999).

The visibility of Minorities' identity is profoundly affected by the pre-existing mainstream perceptions on that identity, i.e., the "othering" framing of that identity. It is realizable that when the mainstream framing of the minorities' identity is stereotyped, the majority of that group members assert their identity in public. Evidence of that is the increasing number of European hijab-wearing women in France despite the political restrictions on its visibility (see chapter "Introduction").

Brugge indicates that our thoughts cannot go farther than the scaffold that metaphors afford us. Lakoff and Johnson agree that we cannot make a massive change in our mental system through the conscious act of recategorization even though we are exposed to new mental frames regularly.[17] Those mental frames are part of our experience; it is not an intellectual matter. We cannot go beyond our mental frames and think of a sign or a symbol as a purely uncategorized matter if it acquires a cultural pre-existing established meaning. Our cognitive system simply cannot do this. Accordingly, our notions on social signs and symbols are merely cognitive structures that allow us to, mentally, attribute characteristics to these signs/symbols and reason about them, which creates prototypes.

Prototype reasoning emerges in the framing process. It is "the neural structure that permits us to do some sort of imaginative inferential task relative to a category" (Lakoff & Johnson, 1999: 19). It constitutes a large proportion of the actual reasoning we do; it is expected that we could not function for long without it. Our brain comfortably and rapidly attaches ready-established boxes of meaning and attributes (mental frame) to what it perceives around. Prototypes are where social stereotypes are created and developed. Stereotypes provide us with a snap, unconscious, judgment of people, or symbols around us. Representative features of social groups can be classified as a sign system, and they are subjected to stereotypes. For example, the "food system" is where rules exclude certain foods from being eaten, especially those associated with a dictated ritual of use. Another example is the "garment system" where clothes are written about, photographed, stereotyped, and banned.

So far, we know that humans cannot think of an object without giving it immediately a set of meanings in order to assimilate it as part of our understanding of the world. The point is not how we, individually, understand the sign. Instead, it is about how we, as embedded in a (linguistic) community, in a culture, and a historical context, understand that specific sign (the hijab in this case).[18] The shared public meaning of the hijab sign in Europe is highly contextualized and affected by the mainstream European values such as race, religion, gender, and class; the political context as well. Physical social signs are reflexive, and they are the stimulus of reaction.[19] We use verbal and non-verbal signals as a tool to convey the meaning and the interpretation of these physical symbols.[20]

"Self-categorization" and "positionality" are significant in the analysis of group behavior. De Zalia indicates that individuals develop a shared social categorization

---

[17]Lakoff and Johnson (1999).

[18]Johnson (2013).

[19]DeZalia and Moeschberger (2014).

[20]Allan (2009).

of themselves in contrast to "others" in a given situation, and this becomes the basis of their attitudes and behaviors. We are not independent entities, instead, we are social beings who continually define the friend and the enemy. We divide people into "them" and "us" or into "in-group" and "out-group" depending on specific categories that we find salient. Our ancestors did it that way, too. Lakoff and Johnson noted that we inherit cultural positionality and the meanings attached to it. Along the positionality process, we compare the identity features among our experiences and the pre-existing meanings depending on similarities or differences. If we feel that these features share something familiar with us, we include them in the "in-group" identification, and we feel connected to them. If we perceive them more in common with the "out-group" sign system, we classify them as "others" even though we feel sympathy with them. However, we do not usually hold positive views for those features we perceive as separate from ourselves. Nicolas Winter attributes the systematic discrimination against the out-group to the "in-/out-group positionality" syndrome. He justifies that humans fulfill an intuitive desire by the assertion or the creation of differences even though they don't exist because the meaning of social belonging is constructed through these differences.[21]

"Signs" and "symbols" are used interchangeably in the Lindesmith et al. book titled "Social Psychology,"[22] yet, Carl Hausman,[23] Byron Kaldis,[24] and James Forte[25] distinguish between these terms. Hausman defines a sign as a meaningless abstract icon that stands for something and needs an interpretation. On the contrary, Kalids explains that signs indicate something while symbols stand for something. He adds that a sign can be an index, an icon, or a symbol; the sign is a broader term that can include all of them. Forte extends that a symbol, which can be a word, an object, a gesture, or a style of appearance, is used to represent something other than what it is usually used for. In semiotic, Charles Sanders Peirce (1960) argues that a symbol is meaningless and they have no intrinsic relationship with the idea or the thing it evokes; while a sign as an icon or as an index inherently does. Symbols acquire their meanings from the social conventions that attaches meanings to them. Accordingly, Anjum Alvi explains that to see the hijab as a symbol suggests that the hijab has no meaning, but it acquires its meaning through what it is referred to.[26] She argues for the hijab's inseparability from its reference, the semiotics from the practice, and thoughts from the action. Depending on Forte's theory and Alvi's perspective, and based on the reads in the previous two chapters, I argue that the hijab in the European context is unwelcome as a sign (a religious requirement) because of the secular frame of reference. It is attacked as a symbol when stereotypical colonial meanings are attached to it. I insist that the hijab needs to be treated as a sign first and foremost. As Hausman indicates, it is not a meaningless symbol (an abstract

---

[21] Winter (2008).

[22] Lindesmith et al. (1999).

[23] Hausman (1989).

[24] Kaldis (2013).

[25] Forte (2014).

[26] Alvi (2013).

piece of cloth that needs interpretations).[27] It is a transnational religious sign that refers to the Islamic codes for gender public relations. The hijab is a sign that has a definite criterion (modesty) and utility (reducing the gender identity) in the public sphere. To consider the hijab as a "symbol" is to locate it in the target zone for the populace who will interpret it supportively or disapprovingly. This social process attaches unrelated meanings to the hijab without prior knowledge about the practice or any previous religious or cross-cultural knowledge.

Understanding the "sign system" of the under-analysis culture is essential for objective and accurate findings. Some scholars show acquaintance with the Islamic frame of reference on gender relations and sexuality in the public sphere, such as Hoodfar (1992), Scott (2009), and Hawkins (2003). Yet, the ban-supportive debated on the visibility of hijab at the French public school, e.g., Esposito (1999), Stasi (2004), Alvi (2013), and Beary (2014), interpret the hijab as a symbol understood through the embodied Western, secular, colonial values and frames. The result is packing the hijab in stereotypes and stigmas.

France falls short of recognizing the difference between two diverse sign systems on sexuality in the public sphere. Scott (2009: 170–173) describes these two sign systems as two psychological states: (1) the psychology of denial of the social and political problems that sex and sexuality provoke in the public sphere. The solution is persisting on the sameness as a principle of *laïcité* gender equality. Thus, the hijab is seen as a symbol of the difference between sexes and a symbol of Muslim women's subordination. The psychology of denial forces so many French feminists to abandon their state quo in France and rush to support a law that offered *laïcité* as the ground of gender equality. (2) the psychology of recognition, which is seen in Islamic demands on concealing sexuality and demanding codes on gender relations in the public sphere. Islamic legislations recognize the possible disruptive effects of sexual relationships between men and women. The solution is individual behavioral and dress codes (modesty), which indicates that sexual relations are off-limits in the public space. The hijab is a sign of explicit acceptance of the difference between the two sexes. It is also a statement that sexuality can be celebrated only in private places where women are respected and loved, not based on their physical appearance.

Both of these understandings of the hijab sign system depend on cultural models. The first interprets the Islamic dress code from the French secular frame of reference while the second interprets the hijab within its religious frame of reference. In sociolinguistic cross-cultural studies, it is essential to leave our mental comfort zone, the way we understand the world, and to approach the others' frames of reference. It is difficult to challenge our own mental frames, and it is challenging to accept that there are other ways than mines to understand the world, and they are as correct as yours.

---

[27] Hausman (1989).

Critical Discourse Analysis CDA

Ideology and Language

Ideology is the system of ideas (social, political, or religious) produced by the dominant group, reflecting the group's interests. Dominant ideologies are dominant not only because dominant groups create them but also because they are accepted and practiced by the diverse society members. Ideologies are developed for many reasons; power and social categorization are prominent ones. If power is the control/superiority of one group over other, ideology is the mental dimension of this form of control.

Ideologies are related to social values. They define what is good and what is bad; it draws the social permitted practices and redlines. The specific interpretation of values is the core block of these ideologies' beliefs. They are not arbitrarily organized. They form systems of beliefs, schema-like, that allow us to understand the ideology rapidly. Any group members follow fixed patterns of basic categories of ideological schemata, such as (1) Membership criteria: Who does (not) belong? (2) Typical activities: what do we do? (3) Overall aims: What do we want? Why do we do it? (4) Norms and values: What is good or bad for us? (5) Position: What are the relationships with others? (6) Resources: who has access to our group resources? These categories identify the sense of belonging to a group because ideology can establish a sense of self- (and Other-) representation. It summarizes the collective beliefs and hence the identification criteria of group members.

Communism versus anti-communism, socialism versus liberalism, feminism versus sexism, racism versus antiracism, and pacifism versus militarism are some common ideologies. Following one of these constrains our thoughts (our understanding of the world) within the borders of this specific ideology. Tuen Van Dijk defines ideologies from the cognitive perspective as "the fundamental beliefs of a group and its members" (2013: 7). Van Dijk calls misguided beliefs as "false consciousness." The dominant class, mainly the political discourse, imposes them to legitimate the status quo or conceal real socio-economic problems. Feminists and anti-racists ideologies are "positive ideology," and they are "systems that sustain and legitimize opposition and resistance against domination and social inequality" (2013: 8).

Ideologies are the basis of the social practices of group members. For example, racist ideologies are the basis of discrimination, and ecological ideologies will act against pollution. Conflicts and struggles among social groups assert ideologies and mark "us" against "them." However, Van Dijk argues that ideologies and social practices are two different notions because there is no simple notion of "ideological practices."[28] In the debate on secularism, Jose Casanova distinguishes between secularism as a statecraft principle and secularism as an ideology (2009: 1051).[29]

---

[28] Van Dijk (2009).
[29] Casanova (2009).

As a statecraft principle, secularism is merely some principles of separation between religious and political authorities. It aims to maintain social neutrality and protect individuals' freedom of consciousness and equal democratic participation. Secularism, as a statecraft principle, does not imply any positive nor negative theory on religion. A statecraft principle of secularism becomes an ideology when the State entails a particular theory (or position) on religion, e.g., what it is or what it does.

Discourse(s) on Social Signs

Words are signs that aim to invoke certain understandings about any social, physical, or not, symbol. There is a difference between the language (social institution) and the system of values that gives meaning to words and the speech "discourse." The system of values is an individual and interactional production of selection and actualization. Sociolinguists study the language as a system of representations through which all social phenomena are realized. The language shapes the meaning of social signs as much as the meaning of social signs controls the linguistic choices in the discourse on them. The discourse that gives meaning to social signs is never neutral. It is to say, the meaning of social signs never flows to the linguistic representation. On the contrary, in most cases, the linguistic representation imposes meaning upon the physical or non-physical social signs it represents. Minority signs or symbols obtain different connotations through different discourses within the same culture.

Some discourses are considered more "authoritative" than others. They are propagated more effectively as representative systems over other discourses and are called "dominant discourse." They dominate how social phenomena are thought about and acted toward by society members.

Discourse Hegemony

The semiotic shaping of social experiences is argued to be unconscious by the community members. Still, David Francis and Stephan Hester argue that several meanings on social signs are an outcome of the meaning-imposition of some dominant group upon others for social or any other kind of interest.[30] It is to say, as we see economic hegemony, class hegemony, and political hegemony, there exists semiotic hegemony. Public spheres are controlled and shaped by such hegemony, e.g., what people listen to, speak about, and react against/for. Tuen Van Dijk asserts that those who control the discourse control power because they control people's minds. He indicates that, unless people are inconsistent with their beliefs, enjoy the "conscious thoughts" I mentioned above, recipients tend to accept the beliefs of the discourse

---

[30]Francis and Hester (2004).

they consider "authoritative."[31] Authoritative discourses are hegemonic due to the power assigned to the authors, e.g., minorities' and women's discourse is more often perceived as less credible. In many contexts, participants are obliged to be recipients of hegemonic discourse, to attend it, interpret and learn it as the institutional authors require, e.g., learning material, job instruction, or dictator's discourse.

Most of the time, there is no alternative public discourse that can evoke different mental frames on the same social phenomena. Or maybe, the recipients do not have the knowledge to challenge the dominant discourse they are exposed to. Van Dijk explains that if recipients have no alternative discourse or options but to listen and read a dominant discourse without having additional resources to evaluate it, the recipient lacks the opportunity to think about a social phenomenon from different perspectives.

Critical Discourse Analysis

Van Dijk defines Critical Discourse Analysis as research that primarily studies how social power abuse, group dominance, and political context are enacted, reproduced, and resisted by texts and talks in the social and political discourse. Its main aim is to understand, expose, and combat social inequality. This book's data analysis followed the five requirements Van Dijk sets for any effective CDA. Firstly, CDA should be "better" than any linguistical analysis (the analysis of this book goes beyond the linguistic use of words and go deep to analyze the mental frames the texts stand for). Secondly, it should primarily focus on social problems and polit-ical issues rather than paradigms and fashion (this book's primary focus is a social problem that evokes a political reaction, by which social inequality might be the outcome). Thirdly, CDA needs to be empirically adequate and multi-disciplinary (this research is a multi-disciplinary one that involves social integration, political sovereignty on Muslim women's vestment, feminism, religious diversity). Fourthly, instead of merely describe discourse structures, CDA should try to explain these linguistics structures in terms of properties of social interaction and social structures (the analysis goes deeply into the social dominant mental frames imposed on the hijab and hijab-wearing women through the interactional national press debate on the French ban and national hijab exclusion cases or hijab visibility). Fifthly, and finally, CDA has to focus on the ways discourse structures enact, confirm, legitimate, reproduce, or challenge relations of power and dominance in society (the research analyzes the authoritative voice of the women journalists in the hijab discourse. It also investigates the power relation between the interviewed Muslim women who support the freedom to hijab and other non-Muslim or Muslim women who oppose the practice).

Norman Fairclough notifies that CDA does not aim to analyze the discourse itself but to analyze the dialectical relations between the discourses in general as well as

---

[31] Van Dijk (1979, 2001a, 2001b).

the internal relations in each discourse.[32] Departing from the fact that such analysis depends on several disciplines, he calls CDA a transdisciplinary approach, which indicates that the dialogue between theories and frameworks from different disciplines in the analysis is essential for each development. Fairclough also notes that transdisciplinary CDA should have a transdisciplinary "methodology" rather than "method." He justifies that pre-established methods are not adequate for such analysis. He also identifies the critical approach of CDA manifests to explain areas of social life, which include social wrongs and try to righten them. It analyzes how the "wrongs" might be "rights" and how social and political values categorize social phenomena into these two categories. It also investigates how possible changes might occur.

Discursive Strategies

Critical Discourse Analysis investigates how the story was told and why it was told that way, especially in press discourse that shapes the public mind toward that story. Discursive strategies are essential for the journalists to bring the readers closer or further away from the core idea of the story, empathize with the participant, and highlight his/her discourse as authoritative and trusted. For example, the identification strategies introduce social actors (explicitly or implicitly) according to roles and degrees of salience "mystification." Identification strategies depend on the "scope of reference." For example, the "categorization strategies" are used to represent and identify certain social actors while barring others as the predication subject for the readers. By doing so, readers are pushed to another unconscious discursive strategy: "framing strategies" that inboxes entities, actions, events, processes, or relations into attributions, qualities, or structural properties. Thus, we tend to have all elements clear at reading the press: the negative others, the reliable sources, the amiable, the enemy, etc. Christopher Hart agrees that identifying strategies and framing strategies is a concurrent analysis because identifying participants in particular roles indicates framing them into specific statuses or qualities.[33] Hart also listed another discursive strategy called "positioning strategy." It is about the positioning of social actors/events in relation to one another (deictic) and the positioning of propositions in relation to one's conception of reality (epistemic) or morality (deontic).

In CDA in press discourse, it is essential to analyze the participants' quotations in the storytelling. Ruth Wodak and Michael Meyer explained four types of verbs used in the representation strategies in any discourse (2009: 59–60)[34]: (1) **Neutral structuring verbs** introduce the saying without evaluating it explicitly, e.g., say, tell, ask. (2) **Metaproposicional verbs** mark the author's interpretation of the speaker, e.g., "declare, urge, grumble". These verbs can be assertive to the content such

---

[32]Fairclough (2013).

[33]Hart (2011).

[34]Wodak and Meyer (2009).

as "announce" and "declare." Even the word "complaining" also adds an assertive notion to the speaker. (3) **Descriptive verbs** mark how the participants tell the story, and they categorize the reader's interaction, e.g., whisper and laugh. These verbs mark the manner and attitude of a speaker in relation to what is being said. They signify the attitudes, power relations, and likelihood of truth. (4) **Transcript verbs** indicate the progress of the discourse, e.g., repeat, or relate the quotation to other parts of the discourse, e.g., pause. In the press, the journalist promotes the participant's narration as "s/he added" or "continued" to give the impression that they are offering more information while, in fact, the same point is repeated to be asserted. These representational verbs are used in the press discourse to make certain participants appear more authoritative or subservient, legitimate or non-legitimate. They help define the roles of participants or events even though they might not explicitly state it. They can also mark some participants as having a negative attitude and stigmatize others as friendly or imply moderation and authoritative levels.

Discourse Authority

Cultural authority helps journalists use their interpretation of public events to shape themselves into an authoritative community. This particularity is relevant when so many groups—journalists, politicians, historians—reconstruct a reality to mold external events into preferred forms. Barbie Zelizer indicates the working of discourse authority has made it possible for those who have retold the assassination of John Kennedy's story to shape the American public's memories of that event.[35]

Journalists promote themselves as authoritative and preserve the right to present a reliable version of the world/story (the hijab visibility in this book). They articulate the story through explanatory frames that construct reality but do not reveal the secrets, sources, or methods of such a process. Readers only protest if these frames do not coincide with their codes of collective knowledge.

CDA aims to give authority to those who have been deprived of it. Deborah Cameron states that CDA focuses on the real injustice in the linguistic structures which are used to talk about women.[36] She refers that the intersectional feminist's focus in CDA is to enrich feminist researchers by a new commandment of non-discriminative discourse guidelines, which can restrict the discourse hegemonists in practicing their prejudice in the public sphere. Minorities, as well, maintain a less authoritative voice in press discourse.[37] Van Dijk points out that the European press promotes the elites' discourse, white and autochthones, as the primary source of reliable discourse over the minority discourse, who are perceived as "less credible" and "less authoritative" sources. He continues that white journalists are considered

---

[35]Zelizer (1992).

[36]Cameron (1992, 1995).

[37]See Deborah Cameron's publication and Ehrlich and King (1995).

more expert and more objective in ethnic debates than the experts and leaders who are members of these minority groups. The question is, what level of authority do the hijab-wearing women enjoy in the Spanish and British press?

Authoritative Discourse on the EU Hijab

Mohamed El-Madkouri Maataoui analyzed the dominant and authoritative French discourse on the hijab.[38] He summarized that the discursive representation of hijab visibility in France is assigned to migrants. It is limited to an oppressive sign that goes against the French principle of *laïcité*. This discourse is the dominant one in French press discourse due to the authoritative position of the secular, white, and liberal journalists. It aims to constrain the French community, who share a stereotypical collective memory on the hijab since the colonial era, by one dominant discourse that serves political interests depending on contemporary (well perceived) arguments (ideologies) "secularity and human rights." "Human Rights" argument also serves to assert the Republican unified identity as secular and egalitarian, free from religious signs and discriminatory symbols.[39]

El-Madkouri Maataoui argues that the French journalists' authoritative position toward the hijab and hijab-wearing Muslim women is based on western "prototypes" attached to the European Muslim women because of economic interests, national crisis on identity, and the exclusionary tendency of Euro-Muslims as "Others" (see chapter "Introduction"). Beate Collet refers that the equality principle is a domi-nant discourse in France.[40] However, the hegemonic discourse asserts equality as an abstract concept that takes away the cultural and religious particularity of percipients. Accordingly, French percipients are unable to mentally visualize French, modern, civil, and professional Muslim hijab-wearing women because this image does not coincide with any mental frame on the hijab in the collective memory.[41] I have mentioned before that the dominant secular/liberal feminism rejects Islamic femi-nists' discourse on women's rights and freedom because of its religious frame of reference. Thus, French collective mental framing and neural categorization classify French professional hijab-wearing women as imaginary. As Lakoff indicates, when the fact contradicts the already existing mental frames, the mind simply rejects that fact.

---

[38] El-Madkouri Maataoui (2009).
[39] KhirAllah (2015).
[40] Collet (2004).
[41] Jouili (2009).

Toward a Cognitive Critical Discourse Analysis CCDA

As we have been through, CDA involves action, meaning, cognition, and social structure (Lindesmith et al., 1999; Ponterotto, 2000; Van Dijk, 1977). It is to say, it is necessary to explain the link between the discourse (text) and cognition (mental activities) of processing and categorizing information. Van Dijk notifies that scholars should take these interdisciplinary frameworks seriously because each social group shares specific methods for making sense of the social world.[42] Knowledge and beliefs which are presumed (mainly by the dominant groups), then adopted and practiced by the rest of the community, provoke norm-usage-speech pattern. Accordingly, discourse analytics needs to understand those presumed mental patterns and analyze their manifestation in linguistic production to reach a competent CDA. To sum up, a cognitive approach is required for any comprehensive CDA.

Lakoff and Johnson's (1980) *Metaphors We Live By* had marked the "*before and after*" in the cognitive approach. The significance of their book comes from the establishment of the linkage between conceptual metaphors and thoughts. By doing so, we are capable to profoundly analyze any social-sign system through the conceptual metaphors used in the language (discourse). Conceptual Metaphor Theory (CMT) is generally used to analyze daily unconscious language production in the abstract world such as love, time, anger, etc. The question is: Can we apply CMT in CDA? Christopher Hart (2014: 47) notifies that there might be a problematic relation between CMT and CDA. CMT studies daily apolitical discourse while CDA studies the political and social public discourse. Besides, in CMT, Lakoff and Johnson assert that the experimental linkage between domains in primary metaphors is part of the cognitive unconsciousness. While in CDA, Charteris-Black (2004: 247) states that metaphors are chosen to achieve a specific communication purpose in a particular context; they are not merely "predetermined bodily experience."

If we think of knowledge and discourse as construal, we might overcome these problematic relations between CMT and CDA. Firstly, knowledge and beliefs are presumed (mainly by dominant groups for a particular purpose or need). Then, an appropriate and convincing discourse is imposed on this knowledge and beliefs (the dominant discourse is imposed on the rest of the community). After that, the community builds their experiences, as much as their mental frames, toward these beliefs depending on the information they receive from the dominant discourse. Finally, the built mental frames become part of the community's embodied experience toward this knowledge and beliefs. Accordingly, even if conceptual metaphors in public discourse, as Charteris-Black indicates, are chosen, they are eventually constructing the unconscious thinking of the public minds toward the topic.

I separate between the CMT and what I call Mental Frame Theory (MFT), which analyzes the cognitive boxes that we build and use to understand the world around us. Both are interconnected, and both form an integral part of the Cognitive Approach. Conceptual metaphors of group members on any social sign are efficient in detecting

---

[42] Van Dijk (1993).

their mental frames on it. Yet, I argue that identifying mental structures is not exclusive to CMT. CDA is capable of figuring out the mental frames on the social sign by analyzing the vocabularies that are used to talk about that sign. The analysis of the used vocabularies (the semantic relationships among them and the repetitive use) reveals the mental frames that lie behind them. Such analysis needs to be carried out on a considerable number of data (discourse) to capture the mental frames behind the used vocabularies.

Thus, I created a new theory that joins the Cognitive Approach CA (CMT and MFT), and CDA and I call it: Cognitive Critical Discourse Analysis. CCDA analyzes the linguistic structures on three dimensions: the discursive strategies (mentioned above), the conceptual metaphors, and the vocabulary usages and the mental frames behind them. The results of this triple-dimensional analysis are interpreted within the social, political, and historical context of the discourse. The outcome is a comprehensive analysis that allows us to figure out the cognitive structure that controls discourse production. CCDA will able us to identify the cognitive structures of social inequality and injustice, evaluate them, and detect the cognitive structures behind them. These findings will help academics from several disciplines, and social agents create effective methods to correct these social wrongs.

Analysis methodology in CCDA depends on each researcher's focus and data. As Fairclough indicates, a pre-established methodology cannot be adequate for such transdisciplinary and multi-dimensional analysis. In this book, I carry out CCDA on the press discourse to analyze the national hijab-debate discourse in Spain and the United Kingdom. My focus is the hijab sign, the French ban-law framing, the hijab-wearing women framing, women's sexuality, and social diversity in the national press discourse. I analyze (1) the discursive strategies used in presenting the participants in the debate, (2) the vocabularies used to talk about the hijab, the French ban, the hijab-wearing women, (3) the conceptual metaphors on these three, (4) connect the findings with the social, political, and historical interpretations as much as I can.

Following Lakoff and Tuner's (1989) argument, there is a deep interconnection between social inclusion and exclusion of the hijab and hijab-wearing women (in Spain and the United Kingdom) and the press discourse that activates or deactivates negative mental frames and conceptual metaphors on them. I also argue, depending on Van Dijk's authoritative discourse theory,[43] that Hijab-wearing Muslim women's participation is less authoritative and less reliable than the non-Muslim or non-hijab-wearing journalists. Applying CCDA to the national hijab-debate discourse will allow us to figure out the cognitive structures by which the European mind understands the hijab sign system and values in each context.

---

[43] Van Dijk (2001a).

Conclusion

The Cognitive Approach entails that our neural system cannot think of the world as an abstract uncategorized matter. Conceptual Metaphor Theory (CMT) and Mental Frame Theory (MFT) are useful in social studies because they can reveal the social values and sign systems underlying our way of thinking. Framing values and signs vary from one social group to another; correspondingly, related conceptual metaphors differ as well. Studying the sign system of minorities is essential in social sciences.

Critical Discourse Analysis (CDA) highlights the importance of the political and press discourse in shaping or even controlling the public discourse. Public discourse exercises semiotic hegemony on how people talk about minority groups and understand the minority's public signs. As a studied case, this chapter and the previous one argue that French discourse on the hijab discussed the practice from the *laïcité* frame of reference on gender relations in the public sphere and, then, criticized it. The outcome was to strengthen the prototype-based understanding of the hijab sign and the French hijab-wearing women.

The innovative Cognitive Critical Discourse Analysis (CCDA), which merges the CMT, MFT, and Cognitive Linguistics with CDA, is a triple dimensional and transdisciplinary methodology that aims at finding out the cognitive structures produced by the public discourse. CCDA also aims to identify the cognitive structures behind social inequalities and injustices which manifest in the public discourse. Findings are interpreted within the social, political, and historical context of the discourse. The outcome is a comprehensive analysis of how the dominant discourse impacts framing the collective understanding of social and political phenomena.

References

Allan, K. (2009). *Metaphor and metonymy a diachronic approach*. Wiley-Blackwell.

Alvi, A. (2013). Concealment and revealment. *Current Anthropology, 54*(2), 177–199.

Barcelona, A. (2003). The cognitive theory of metaphor and metonymy. In A. Barcelona (Ed.), *Metaphor and metonymy at the crossroad* (pp. 1–31). Walter de Gruyter.

Barcelona, A. (2012). Introduction The cognitive theory of metaphor and metonymy. In *Metaphor and metonymy at the crossroads* (pp. 1–28). De Gruyter Mouton.

Baumeister, R. F., & Masicampo, E. J. (2010). Conscious thought is for facilitating social and cultural interactions: How mental simulations serve the animal-culture interface. *Psychological Review, 117*(3), 945–971.

Brugge, K. U. (2011). *Planting the impatience*. John Hunt Publishing.

Beary, D. (2014). Pro Wrestling Is Fake, but Its Race Problem Isn't. *Atlantic, 10*.

Cameron, D. (1992). *Feminism and linguistic theory*. Springer.

Cameron, D. (1995). Lost in translation: Non-sexist language. *Trouble and Strife*, 20–28.

Casanova, J. (2009). The secular and secularisms. *Social Research: An International Quarterly, 76*(4), 1049–1066.

Charteris-Black, J. (2004). *Corpus approaches to critical metaphor analysis*. Springer.

Clausner, T. C., & Croft, W. (1999). Domains and image schemas. *Cognitive linguistics, 10*, 1–32.

Collet, B. (2004). Muslim headscarves in four nation-states and schools. In *Civil enculturation. Nation-state, school and ethnic difference in the Netherlands* (pp. 119–146). Berghahn.

DeZalia, R. A. P., & Moeschberger, S. L. (2014). The function of symbols that bind and divide. In *Symbols that bind, symbols that divide* (pp. 1–12). Springer International Publishing.

Ehrlich, S., & King, R. (1995). Gender-based language reform and the social construction of meaning. *Discourse & Society*.

El-Madkouri Maataoui, M. (2009). La imagen del otro en la prensa. Arabia Saudí, Egipto y Marruecos.

Esposito J. L. (1999). Clash of civilization? Contemporary images of Islam in the west. In G. M. Munoz (Ed.), *Islam, modernism and the West: Cultural and political relations at the end of the millennium*. IB Tauris.

Fairclough, N. (2013). *Critical discourse analysis: The critical study of language*. Routledge.

Forte, J. A. (2014). *Skills for using theory in social work: 32 lessons for evidence-informed practice*. Routledge.

Francis, D., & Hester, S. (2004). *An invitation to ethnomethodology: Language, society and interaction*. Sage.

Hart, C. (2011). Force-interactive patterns in immigration discourse: A cognitive linguistic approach to CDA. *Discourse & Society, 22*(3), 269–286.

Hart, C. (2014). *Discourse, grammar and ideology: Functional and cognitive perspectives*. Bloomsbury Publishing.

Hausman, C. R. (1989). *Metaphor and art: Interactionism and reference in the verbal and nonverbal arts*. CUP Archive.

Hawkins, S. (2003) The essence of the veil. In E. M. Caner (Ed.), *The voices behind the veil: The world of Islam through the eyes of women* (pp. 93–106). Kregel Publications Inc.

Hoodfar, H. (1992). The veil in their minds and on our heads: The persistence of colonial images of Muslim women. *Resources for Feminist Research, 22*(3–4), 5.

Johnson, M. (1987). *The body in mind*. Chicago University Press.

Johnson, M. (2013). *The body in the mind: The bodily basis of meaning, imagination, and reason*. University of Chicago Press.

Jouili, J. (2009). Negotiating secular boundaries: Pious micro-practices of Muslim women in French and German public spheres. *Social Anthropology, 17*(4), 455–470.

Kaldis, B. (Ed.). (2013). *Encyclopedia of philosophy and the social sciences* (Vol. 1). Sage.

Khir-Allah, G. (2015). Veiling and revealing identity: The linguistic representation of the Hijab in the British Press. In M. C. La Barbera (Ed.), *Identity and migration in Europe: multi-disciplinary perspectives* (pp. 229–249). Springer International Publishing.

Khir-Allah, G. (2019) Love metaphors in love songs: Cross-cultural comparative study in Arabic and English songs. In M. C. Ainciburu (Ed.), *Actas del IV Congreso Internacional en Lingüística Aplicada a la Enseñanza de Lenguas: en camino hacia el plurilingüismo*. Nebrija Procedia. Available at: https://www.nebrija.com/vida_universitaria/servicios/procedia.php.

Kovecses, Z. (2000). *Metaphor and emotion: Language, culture and body in human feeling*. Cambridge University Press.

Kovecses, Z. (2003). The scope of metaphor. In A. Barcelona (Ed.), *Metaphor and metonymy at the crossroad* (pp. 79–92). Walter de Gruyter.

Kovecses, Z. (2005). *Metaphor in culture: Universality and variation*. Cambridge University Press.

Kovecses, Z. (2006). *Language, mind and culture*. Oxford University Press.

Langacker, R. W. (1999). *Grammar and conceptualization*. De Gruyter Mouton.

Lakoff, G. (1987). *Women, fire and dangerous things: What categories reveal about the mind*. Chicago University Press.

Lakoff, G., & Johnson, M. (1980). *Metaphors we live by*. Chicago University Press.

Lakoff, G., & Johnson, M. (1999). *Philosophy in the flesh: The embodied mind and its challenge to western thought*. Basic books.

Lakoff, G., & Turner, M. (1989). *More than cool reason: A field guide to poetic metaphor*. Chicago University Press.

Lindesmith, A. R., Strauss, A. L., & Denzin, N. K. (1999). *Social psychology.* SAGE Publication, Inc.

Peirce, C. S. (1960). *Collected papers of Charles Sanders Peirce: Edited by Charles Hartshorne and Paul Weiss: Principles of philosophy and elements of logic* (Vol. 1). Harvard University Press.

Ponterotto, D. (2000). The cohesive role of cognitive metaphor in discourse and conversation. *Metaphor and metonymy.*

Quinn, N. (1991). The cultural basis of metaphor. In J. Fernandez (Ed.), *Beyond metaphor: The theory of tropes in anthropology* (pp. 56–93). Stanford University Press.

Quinn, N. (1997). *A cognitive theory of cultural meaning.* Cambridge University Press.

Richard, I. A. (1936). *The philosophy of rhetoric.* Oxford University Press.

Scott, J. W. (2009). *The politics of the veil.* Princeton University Press.

Shore, B. (1996). *Culture in mind: Cognitive, culture and the problem of meaning.* Oxford University Press.

Stasi, B. (2004). Laïcité et République. Rapport de la commission de réflexion sur.

Steen, G. (2009). Deliberate metaphor affords conscious metaphorical cognition. *Cognitive Semiotics, 5*(1–2), 179–197.

Sullivan, K. (2013). *Frames and constructions in metaphoric language.* John Benjamins Publishing Company.

Tomasello, M. (1999). The human adaptation for culture. *Annual Review of Anthropology, 28*(1), 509–529. Available at: http://www.biolinguagem.com/ling_cog_cult/tomasello_1999_human_a daptation_for_culture.pdf.

Tomasello, M. (2010). *Origins of human communication.* MIT Press.

Van Dijk, T. (1977). Context and cognition: Knowledge frames and speech act comprehension. *Journal of Pragmatics, 1*(3), 211–231.

Van Dijk, T. (1979). Cognitive processing of literary discourse. *Poetics Today, 1*(1–2), 143–159.

Van Dijk, T. A. (1993). *Elite discourse and racism* (Vol. 6). Sage.

Van Dijk, T. A. (2001a). 18 critical discourse analyses. In *The handbook of discourse analysis* (pp. 349–371).

Van Dijk, T. A. (2001b). Discurso y racismo. *Persona y sociedad, 16,* 191–205.

Van Dijk, T. A. (2009). *Society and discourse: How social contexts influence text and talk.* Cambridge University Press.

Van Dijk, T. A. (2013). *News as discourse.* Routledge.

Way, E. C. (1991). *Knowledge representation and metaphor* (Vol. 7). Springer Science & Business Media.

Winter, N. J. (2008). *Dangerous frames.* University of Chicago Press.

Wodak, R., & Meyer, M. (2009). Critical discourse analysis: History, agenda, theory and methodology. *Methods of Critical Discourse Analysis, 2,* 1–33.

Zelizer, B. (1992). *Covering the body: The Kennedy assassination, the media, and the shaping of collective memory.* University of Chicago Press.

Ziem, A. (2014). *Frames of understanding in text and discourse: Theoretical foundations and descriptive applications* (Vol. 48). John Benjamins Publishing Company.

Framing the National Hijab in the European Mind (Spanish and British Cases)

Data Review

Introduction

This chapter aims to introduce you to the data analyzed in this book. I consider this chapter essential because it explains the criteria of the data selection, the articles' focus, and the time interval of the Data selection. Although the selection criteria are the same in the Spanish and British contexts, there seems a significant difference in the selected articles, something I would like to share with you in this part of the book before we go into the linguistic analysis of the data.

Selection Criteria and Variables

For the purpose of this analysis, I selected 108 articles, 54 from each press. All of them are written by Spanish and British (Muslims and non-Muslims) women authors. The selected articles cover 13 years, starting in 2003 when the French government started the debate on the ban until 2016.[1] Nevertheless, in 2017, there was a new turn of the debate on hijab at the European level. In March 2017, a decision of the Court of Justice of the European Union made the ban of the hijab at the workplace legal.[2] Such a judicial decision re-inflamed the European debate on hijab, migration, and social integration. The recent publication of Sirin Adlbi Sibai's book (2016), "*La cárcel del feminism*," was discussed in the mainstream Spanish press.[3] In the British context, articles published in 2017 showed an increased number of Islamophobic violence, which manifests in hijab-wearing women's physical attacks in streets. Yet, because of my Ph.D. dissertation's time constraints, these articles published in 2017 have not been included in this research.

---

[1] I stopped at 2016 because I needed to finish the analysis and present my PhD thesis on 2017.

[2] See https://curia.europa.eu/jcms/upload/docs/application/pdf/2017−03/cp170030en.pdf.

[3] Gomez Garcia (2017).

© Springer Nature Singapore Pte Ltd. 2021
G. Khir-Allah, *Framing Hijab in the European Mind*,
https://doi.org/10.1007/978-981-16-1653-2_5

Due to the diversity of the topics involved in the hijab debate, the content is controlled by restricting the subject matters of the selected articles to the followings: (i) the 2004 French ban, (ii) national hijab-exclusion cases at school and workplace, (iii) social and political debate about national hijab and hijab-wearing women, and, finally, (iv) interviews with national hijab-wearing women. Since I hypnotized that the 2004 French ban impacted the hijab debate in the national Spanish and British levels, I included how the mainstream press introduced this ban to the national readers. The hijab exclusion and inclusion cases are all national ones. For example, the Spanish articles on Nadiya Hussain's winning, the hijab-wearing woman in the "Great British Bake Off" TV show, were not selected in the Spanish press. But they are selected in the British press. Another example is the overturn of the hijab ban by FIFA in the 2012 Olympics in London. This topic was selected in the British press but not in the Spanish press.[4]

Jilbab (a traditional long dress) has been included in the analysis of the British press discourse because it has been considered, according to the wearers, as part of hijab modesty requirements, considering that it not a full veil that covers the face. Simultaneously, *jilbab* exclusion cases had a significant impact on the debate of hijab in the British mainstream discourse by both hijab-supporters and hijab-opposers.

The articles that are excluded in the selection process are several, such as the articles written by men journalists, articles published by anonymous journalists (through press agency, e.g., *Efe* in Spain), articles that focus on interviewing hijab-wearing migrants (only Spanish and British hijab-wearing women are included), articles that cover cases of gender violence in migrant Muslim families, and articles on the hijab debate in Iran, Egypt, and Saudi Arabia. Such restriction on the data aims to concrete the analysis focus. The analysis aims at revealing the mental frames and conceptual metaphors of national hijab and national hijab-wearers in the national debate in each social context. It avoids foreign affairs and the migratory dimensions in the hijab debate.

Besides, the sex variable is controlled.[5] All the selected data have been written by women journalists, authors, or interviewee's direct quotations. The rationale of this selection is to examine how women's discourse, in both contexts, shapes the public's mental frames on minority women's visibility. The selection of women's articles also aims to challenge the common perception that hijab-wearing women are dominated by their menfolk and are not capable nor allowed to speak out themselves. Therefore, I selected articles written by women and in which the majority of the contributors and interviewees are women.

Another controlled variable is the nationality of the writers. All women journalists and interviewees have been identified as "British" or "Spanish" women. This identification is made either by checking the journalists' nationalities on the newspaper website or relying on the interviewee's self-identification as British or Spanish

---

[4]Kaleeli (2012).

[5]In case the article is written by both man and woman journalists, the article is chosen because the content of the article is approved by the women writer and it reflects her viewpoint. The citation includes only the women writer in the analysis. In the Innox, the man co–writer is referred to.

citizens in the articles. In some articles, some non-national participants contribute to the hijab debate, especially in the Spanish press. However, these articles are included because the article debates the national hijab.

The data was selected from the mainstream online British and Spanish national newspapers. In the British context, the newspapers are The Guardian, The Independent, BBC, The Time Online, The Telegraph, and The Standard. In the Spanish context, the newspapers are El País, El Mundo, and La Vanguardia. The limited number of Spanish newspapers is due to the sex and content-controlled variables of the articles. Although La Razón and El Diario Publico published many articles on the hijab and hijab-wearing women, they were included because the journalists are men or anonymous. Or because the main topic of the articles is not related to the controlled content. I recognize that the digital press acquires more readers nowadays, such as the Spanish digital newspaper *Libertad*. Yet, the digital press was included because it appeared around 2008. They do not fit in the selection period that starts in 2003.

I collected the first 60 reader's comments on each article, and I analyzed them to see how the activated mental frames in the article are reflected in the readers' comments. Yet, this analysis is not included in my Ph.D. dissertation nor this book. It is to be published in a separate publication because the metaphors in readers' reactions and discussions are of different peculiarities.

I used the following keywords in the search engine on the newspaper's webpage: French ban, hijab, the Islamic veil, and hijab at school. During the articles' selection, I did not use any education center name or any students' names to look for the exclusion cases. I followed this general search method to find out what readers come through in the mainstream press when they search for the French ban law 2004, the hijab, and the hijab-wearing Muslim women.

The analysis is based on Cognitive Critical Discourse Analysis CCDA methodology. In Chapters IV and V, linguistic findings are classified according to the mental frames they activate, re-activate, or de-activate. In Chapter VI, I analyzed the Conceptual Metaphors and discussed them within the frame of reference of the findings of the previous two chapters.

Data Discussion

I categorized the articles into three categories: (1) articles on hijab-wearers' exclusion cases, (2) articles on 2004 french ban social, and political and national hijab visibility debate, (3) Articles are written by and articles interviews national hijab-wearing women. This classification is prominent in the Spanish data because each category contains a considerable number of articles. As the exclusion cases are scarce in the British data, the articles that cover these cases are scarce, too.

Spanish data reveals that hijab-wearing women have no access to the mainstream press discourse, contrary to the British data. It is to say, national Spanish hijab-wearing women, do not publish in the mainstream press. These women publish their articles on Muslim websites such as masdeunavoz.blogsopt.com, and webislam.com. I did not include these articles in the analysis because they are not accessible for the regular national press reader.[6] Another difficulty in collecting the Spanish data is the limited number of women journalists who write on national hijab in the Spanish national newspapers.

In the British context, the difficulties are related to the definition of the mainstream discourse's diverse voices. In the Spanish data, two voices are clearly distinguishable: (1) the mainstream voice, which includes national non-Muslim Spanish (mainstream voice) and outsider non-veiled Muslims or non-Muslims whose mental frames of the hijab reflect a mirror effect of the mainstream's voice, and (2) national Spanish hijab supporters and hijab wearers, both oppose the ban and support the right to practice the hijab. In contrast, a considerable variety of national voices exists in British data: Muslim women oppose the hijab and support the ban, non-Muslim oppose the ban as much as all forms of veilings, but they support religious freedom and multiculturalism within a restricted frame, Muslim women (who wear the hijab or not) defend the hijab practice, Muslim women who oppose the *jilbab*. Due to the abundant number of articles in each category, the "mainstream discourse" is difficult to be restricted to one group. The national hijab-wearing women's article is part of the national press discourse. A second difficulty in analyzing the British data is the imbricated debate on the Islamic dress codes. Although the hijab is the main topic of the selected articles, hijab-opposers blend all the Islamic dress codes in the debate. On the contrary, Spanish data do not frequently mix the full-veil debate with the hijab debate.

Another variation between the British data and the Spanish data is the publishing peak. For example, in 2003/2004, only two articles on the 2004 ban law are found in the Spanish data,[7] whereas eleven articles introduce the 2004 French ban to British readers. The hijab exclusion from public schools in Spain was a significant trigger for the hijab debate in Spain. Thirty-three articles cover the exclusion progress at school or the workplace. These thirty-three articles cover ten exclusion cases, of which eight are at schools: (1) Shaima Saidini: 7-year-old child. Girona, 2007; (2) Nawal and Nahed Amar: 17-year-old. Ceuta, 2007; (3) Lleida Case: 16/17-year-old students. Lleida, 2009; (4) Najwa Al-Malha: 16-year-old student. Madrid, 2010; (5) Arteixo school: 11-year-old child. Galicia, 2011; (6) Usera School: 14-year-old student. Madrid, 2011 (7) Hasna Isslal: 13-year-old. Burgos, 2011; (8) Takwa Rejeb: 24-year-old. Valencia, 2016. Two exclusion cases are at the workplace: (1) Zubaida Barik Edidi: 39-year-old lawyer. Madrid, 2009; and (2) Ana Saidi Rodríguez: an airport employee. Palma de Mallorca, 2010.

---

[6]I collected 17 articles written by Spanish hijab-wearign women and I analyzed them. I did not include them inthis book for the reason I mentioned above. Part of this analysis is published in (KhirAllah 2016).

[7]Moliner (2004) and Etxenike (2004).

The exclusion cases of 2007 have been covered by one article each. The hijab-exclusion had not been a prominent social phenomenon or a vital topic in the Spanish press discourse until 2010 when the case of Najwa Al-Malha had a significant impact on the press discourse. Ten articles covered Al-Malha's case progress. This case initiated the debate on the need to have clear constitutional regulations on the hijab at Spanish schools. I observed that the 2010 French ban of the full veil in the public sphere[8] increased the hijab exclusion cases in the Spanish schools, e.g., four cases in 2010/2011. The 2010 French ban also gave importance to the hijab debate in the Spanish mainstream press. The highest peak of published articles is in 2010 (22 articles) and 2011 (13 articles).

In contrast, the 2004 French ban was a trigger of the national hijab debate in the United Kingdom, but not a trigger for exclusion cases. The 2010 French ban law was not a trigger for the hijab debate in the United Kingdom. Seven articles were found in 2010; five of them are part of the interview series by Arifa Akbar, one article is an interview with a hijab-wearer Rock fan,[9] the last one is written by a hijab-wearing woman who discusses women's rights and equality in the political discourse.[10] In 2011, two articles discussed British national Muslim social issues.[11] It is to say; the 2010 French ban was not a trigger for exclusion discourse in the British national press.

Only six articles are related to exclusion cases in the British press. Three cases are related to hijab-wearers exclusion (a) from a school: Seleena Sabeel, *hijab* Case: 15-year-old student, Peterborough, 2004, (b) from a workplace: an interview with Bushra Noah, *hijab* Case: 19-years-old worker, London, 2007, and (c) A bullying case at a hotel: Ericka Tazi, *hijab* Case: 60-year-old hotel guest, Liverpool, 2009. There are two jilbab cases: (1) Shabina Begum *Jilbab* Case: 16-years-old student. Luton, 2005, and (2) Tamanna Begum *Jilbab* Case: Nursery Worker. Essex, 2015. In the British context, the *jilbab* case of Shabina Begum inflamed the hijab debate in the United Kingdom in 2005.

Interviews in the Spanish press are infrequent: one article is found in 2012 in El Mundo[12] and three interviews in 2015/2016. The interviews revolve around the stereotypes hijab-wearing Muslim women go through in their daily social interactions. There is only one article written by a hijab-wearing Muslim woman in El Mundo.[13] The writer is an ex-journalist in El Mundo, who covered school exclusion cases in previous years. Later, she converted to Islam. In contrast, 14 articles in the British data were written by British hijab-wearing Muslim women (they introduce themselves as such). The high number of hijab-wearing writers is due to the service that The Guardian and The Independent provide to the public. Public figures and academics can send their articles to the newspaper, and these articles are published

[8] See: https://www.legifrance.gouv.fr/affichTexte.do?cidTexte=JORFTEXT000022911670.
[9] Aly (2010).
[10] Mursaleen (2010).
[11] Marrison (2011) and Burchill (2011).
[12] Lidón (2016).
[13] Figueras (2015).

under the online section "comment is free." These writers are public figures and well known in the Muslim community, e.g., Fareena Alam, editor of Q News (the Muslim magazine),[14] and Jana Kossaibati, a YouTuber and blogger.[15] Besides, nine articles are dedicated to interviewing national hijab-wearing Muslim women. The interviews were not limited to the debate on the hijab. The interviews' focus covers different aspects of British Muslims' daily lives, e.g., music[16] and fashion.[17]

Such inclusion of hijab-wearers in Spanish society is scarce. Only one article is found in the inclusion of Fatima Hamad, the first hijab-wearing delegate in Ceuta,[18] whereas more articles addressing hijab-wearing inclusion within the "Britishness" are found, For example, an interview with radio show hijab-wearing presenters in 2005,[19] four articles/interviews on the H&M hijab-wearing model Mariah Idrissi (2015), and one article on The Great British Bake Off winner Nadyiah Hussain (2015).[20]

Conclusion

Even though the same selection criterion is used, and the same controlled variables are applied in both contexts, the data variation is significant. The collected selection criteria reveal the levels of diversity visibility in these two contexts. The British hijab-wearers visibility forms part of national press discourse in the United Kingdom, as writers and interviewees. The Spanish hijab-wearing women do not enjoy significant visibility in the national press, not as writers nor as interviewees. Such inclusion and exclusion are reflected in the numerous exclusion cases in the Spanish context and the few exclusion cases in the British context.

The linguistic analysis of the selected data in the following three chapters will reveal more findings on the visibility of the national hijab and the hijab-wearing women in press discourse. It will also uncover the level of inclusion and exclusion of the hijab-wearing women in the national debate on the hijab, diversity, and women's rights.

---

[14] Alam (2005).
[15] Kossaibati (2009).
[16] Aly (2010).
[17] Khaleeli (2008).
[18] Abad (2007).
[19] Byrne (2005).
[20] Sanghani (2015).

References

KhirAllah, G. (2016). Media discourse Representation on adopting the hijab in Spanish public schools: Islamic veiling and social inclusion and exclusion at Spanish classroom In *Images of women in Hispanic culture* (pp. 173–187). Cambridge Scholar Publishing.

Annex 1

Spanish Articles

Abad, R. (2007). *A la Asamblea con el 'hiyab'*. http://elpais.com/diario/2007/06/17/espana/118203 1209_850215.html. 17 June 2007.

Etxenike, L. (2004). *Tirar de la manta*. http://elpais.com/diario/2004/02/08/paisvasco/107627 2805_850215.html. 8 February 2004.

Figueras, A. (2015). *'¿Por qué se me cuestiona por abrazar esta fe? El islam no es el velo ni el IS ni ningún tipo de terrorismo'*. http://www.elmundo.es/espana/2015/06/24/55797914ca4741a626 8b457d.html. 30 June 2015.

Gomez Garcia, L. (2017). *Emancipación, feminismo e islam*. http://cultura.elpais.com/cultura/2017/ 01/30/babelia/1485772617_744429.html. 30 January 2017.

Lidón, I. (2016). *Vetada en el instituto por su hiyab: "Me dijeron: o te lo quitas o te das baja*. http://www.elmundo.es/comunidad-valenciana/2016/09/16/57dc38c2ca4741b51d8b4676. html. 18 September 2016.

Moliner, E. (2004). *A favor y en contra*. http://elpais.com/diario/2004/09/12/domingo/109495 7850_850215.html. 12 September 2004.

Sibai, S. A. (2016). *La cárcel del feminismo: hacia un pensamiento islámico decolonial*. Akal.

Annex 2

English Articles

Alam, F. (2005). *We must move beyond the hijab*. https://www.theguardian.com/education/2005/ nov/29/highereducation.uk. 29 November 2005.

Aly, R. (2010). *Hijab-wearing women rock!* http://www.theguardian.com/world/2010/feb/14/why-muslim-women-like-hard-rock. 14 February 2010.

Burchill, J. (2011). *Carla Bruni is standing up to the stoners. Lauren Booth just covers up for them*. http://www.independent.co.uk/voices/columnists/julie-burchill/julie-burchill-carla-bruni-is-sta nding-up-to-the-stoners-lauren-booth-just-covers-up-for-them–2067119.html. 4 April 2011.

Byrne, C. (2005). *Heard the one about the Mickey Mouse hijab?* http://www.independent.co.uk/ news/media/heard-the-one-about-the-mickey-mouse-hijab–320202.html. 17 October 2005.

Kaleeli, H. (2012). *Sports hijabs help Muslim women to Olympic success*. https://www.theguardian. com/sport/the-womens-blog-with-jane-martinson/2012/jul/23/sports-hijabs-muslim-women-oly mpics. 23 July 2012.

Khaleeli, H. (2008). *The hijab goes high-fashion*. https://www.theguardian.com/lifeandstyle/2008/ jul/28/fashion.women. 28 July 2008.

Kossaibati, J. 2009. *It is a wrap!* https://www.theguardian.com/lifeandstyle/2009/mar/30/fashion-hijab-muslim-women. 30 March 2009.

Marrison, S. (2011). *The Islamification of Britain: Record numbers embrace Muslim faith*. http:// www.independent.co.uk/news/uk/home-news/the-islamification-of-britain-record-numbers-emb race-muslim-faith–2175178.html. 4 January 2011.

Mursaleen, S. (2010).*The power behind the veil*. https://www.theguardian.com/commentisfree/bel
ief/2010/jan/25/burqa-ban-veil-sarkozy-ukip. 25 January 2010.
Sanghani, R. (2015). *Armistice Day: Great British Bake off winner Nadiya Hussain wears
'poppy hijab'*. http://www.telegraph.co.uk/women/womens-life/11988184/Armistice-Day-2015-
Great-British-Bake-Off-winner-Nadiya-Hussain-wears-poppy-hijab.html. 11 November 2015.

Framing National Hijab in the European Mind: Within and Cross-Cultural Analysis of the British and Spanish Press

Introduction

In this chapter, I carry out a Cognitive Critical Discourse Analysis CCDA on the selected Spanish and British press. I analyze the linguistic expressions that debate the hijab visibility in the Spanish and British public sphere. I go far beyond these linguistic expressions to figure out the mental frames that these expressions (re)activate, de-activate, empower, and/or assert. I depend on the literature of the previous chapters to figure out the historical and contextual factors which operate in the building of these mental frames.

I find six prominent mental frames of the hijab in the data: "Discrimination," "Submission," "Compulsivity," "Concealment," "Religiosity," and "Othering." These mental frames are (re)activated, empowered, and asserted (and sometimes de-activated) in both national press discourse. The analysis will be on two levels sequentially: Micro-Level analysis (each mental frame is discussed within the national press/diversity) then the Macro-Level analysis (I carried a cross-culture comparative analysis).

I use the term "re-activate" to refer to these stereotypical mental frames which the press recycles from the colonial discourse. The term "activate" refers to the new mental frames that are related to the current contextual visibility of the hijab in the Spanish and British public sphere.

Framing Hijab Through "Discrimination"

The "Discrimination" mental frame of the hijab is asserted in both presses through the discourse that casts the piece of cloth as a symbol of (gender) discrimination. It is not a new framing of the hijab. It is a recycled mental framing of the practice since

© Springer Nature Singapore Pte Ltd. 2021
G. Khir-Allah, *Framing Hijab in the European Mind*,
https://doi.org/10.1007/978-981-16-1653-2_6

the colonial and neo-colonial discourse. But are the arguments used to re-active the "Discrimination" mental frame modernized and updated to the twenty-first-century logic?

Spanish "Discrimination" Mental Frame of Hijab

The reference to gender inequality and gender discrimination is extensively used in the social and political debate on the hijab. The linguistic expressions used to assert the "Discrimination" mental frame of the hijab are not innovative or narrative. They are almost parallel and repetitive phrases in the selected data. For example, Ana Del Barrio in El Mundo cited the Minister of Equality's, Bibiana Aído, assertion that "not all cultural practices should be protected."[1] Aído argues, in the Forum of the Alliance of Civilizations, that "those (cultural practices) which promote women inequality should be criticized." She directly refers that hijab is only practiced by women, and Muslim men are free to wear occidental dress "*al modo occidental.*" These declarations are announced by the Minister of Equality in the Forum of the Alliance of Civilization (by whom and in which diversity is supposed to be respected). At the same time, the comparison between the modest dress of hijab-wearing women and the occidental dress draws an inclusive separation between Muslim dress codes (oriental, unmodern, uncivilized, oppressive) and the Spanish one (occidental, modern, civilized, liberating). In the same newspaper, Carmen De Ganuza indicates that the Partido Popular's proposal of a hijab ban at the public school "is to preserve the principle of equality between men and women, recognized by the Constitution."[2] This justification cast the hijab as a discriminative practice. However, De Ganuza ignores the fact that the Spanish Constitution also recognizes the freedom of religion:

> Freedom of ideology, religion and worship is guaranteed, to individuals and communities with no other restriction on their expression than may be necessary to maintain public order as protected by law. (Chapter 2, Section 16:1)[3]

The journalist also ignores the constitutional recognition of the personal image:

> The right to honour, to personal and family privacy and to the own image is guaranteed. (Chapter 2, Section 18: 1)

En El País, the "Discrimination" frame is more direct and more explicitly highlighted. Naiara Galarraga wrote the following subtitle: "Many young Muslims see hijab as a way of self-affirmation while others want to ban it because it is a sign of discrimination."[4] "Many" stands for the few who usually are the partitions, and "others"

---

[1] Del Barrio (2008).

[2] De Ganuza (2008).

[3] The translation of the Spanish Constition is found in the BOE (Boletín Oficial del Estado): http://www.congreso.es/portal/page/portal/Congreso/Congreso/Hist_Normas/Norm/const_espa_texto_ingles_0.pdf.

[4] Galarraga (2010).

stand for the mass rationale. In one of these categories, readers locate themselves. Galarraga cited Sihem Habchi's opinion on the practice, Habchi is the president of Not Whores Not Submissive movement. She re-activates the gender "Discrimination" framing by affirming that "hijab is a discriminative sign because only women have to hide their hair. Having a beard is enough for pious Muslim males." Luisa Extenike indicates in her discussion on the 2004 French ban of the hijab that "identity and cultural traditions [...] are one of the favorite refuges of sexist discriminators."[5] She continues "(hijab-wearing women in France) lived submitted to an imported discriminative code. The same code we rejected in Afghanistan, Saudi Arabia, and Iraq." She concludes that "the origin of many forms of extremisms is discrimination." Extenike's activation of the "Discrimination" mental frame is not innovative. She recycled the neocolonial discourse in her argument.[6]

In El País, Concha Caballero points out that nun's veiling aspires an equal signification of "the *hijad's* (a spelling mistake that conflates *hijab* with *jihad*) sexual segregation."[7] She declares that she is "totally against veils, bonnets, and vestments, which significance is only to convert women to be invisible and humiliated." Caballero states: "there is in all of them clearly discriminatory sexual distinction. Paternalistic arguments about identity do not convince me. Nor I am disposed to call a culture to the merest indication of discrimination." At the beginning of that article, the journalist announces herself as an expert on the topic. Then she cast an entire culture as a "discriminative" one. Readers, who typically have limited access to the topic details, perceive the journalist's viewpoints as a comprehensive summary of the topic.[8] How far would her authority contribute to shaping the readers' minds toward hijab visibility in the public sphere?

Caballero introduces hijab visibility through a wrong analogy between the hijab and the nun's dress code. The temporary nun's head covering is practiced through a particular dress code that distinguishes these women as being part of Divine order and as belonging to a specific social status that renounces earthly pleasures (sexual relations is only one of them). The hijab practice does not stand for such a mystical social attitude. Although the hijab represents piety, modest dress and behavior, commitment to religion, yet none of these implies the renouncement of the earthly pleasures; all pleasures are enjoyed within regulatory (but not restrictive) Islamic criteria. After the wrong spelling of the hijab and the false analogy, the journalist shuts out the door in front of any other argument that might create an alternative mental frame (understanding) of the practice. She stigmatizes the different arguments which support the practice as "*unconvincing.*"

From their authoritative position, El Pais journalists demonstrate notable authoritative discourse on the hijab sign without a deep understanding of its originality and criteria. Refusing to accept alternative framing of the hijab publically and clearly shows not only superiority but also arrogance. Journalists in El Mundo do not use

---

[5]Etxenike (2004).

[6]Haddad (2007).

[7]Caballero (2010).

[8]Pape and Featherstone (2005).

their own authoritative voices to cast the practice as a discriminatory one. They limited their role to transmit the message of the politicians without negating it nor supporting it. To sum up, the Spanish re-activation of the "Discrimination" framing is direct, adopted from the past century, and it is not updated for the twenty-first-century readers.

British "Discrimination" Mental Frame of Hijab

"Discrimination" framing of the hijab in the British press discourse is activated avoiding direct association between the hijab and the term "discrimination." British discourse does not describe the practice as "discriminative." This frame is re-activated through the emphasis on the equality value the 2004 French ban offers. Discussing the 2004 French ban in BBC, Caroline Wyatt indicates that Ghislaine Hudson, "a headteacher who gave evidence to the Stasi commission on secularity, says she understands the concerns surrounding the law, but she believes it is the only way to ensure that all pupils are equal in the classroom."[9] Wyatt does not explain the (religious or gender) discriminative features of the hijab that will be replaced by the equality offered by the ban. The justification of the "Discrimination" framing is left to the personal references and interpretations of each reader. In another article in BBC, Wyatt narrates her conversation with a French friend, Antonio, "a middle-aged, rather conventional French businessman,"[10] about the hijab. The businessman asserts the need for the ban to protect the "liberty, equality, fraternity, and the need to keep France a secular state." The image of Wyatt's friend is conceived as a representative image of French citizens whose viewpoint reflects the French public opinion. The same ambiguous reference to the "Discrimination" frame of the hijab is found in Elizabeth Jones' Article in BBC.[11] The discourse introduces the French ban as "the chance to start on equal footing and receive the same education." In all these three cases, BBC does not refer directly to the hijab as a discriminative practice. The ban's efficiency in providing equality nourishes the "Discrimination" mental frame of the banned item.

In *The Independent*, the "Discrimination" mental frame is re-activated through the "gender inequality" interfered meaning of the hijab. In the article titled "Why is the right of Muslim women to wear the hijab still so controversial in France?"[12] Marie Dhumieres introduces the French ban to the British reader through Thomas Legrand's words, a French political commentator. Legrand explains that the target is not Islam, but "the expression of the sexist practice of religion." He continues that "the vast majority of French people seem to agree, viewing the hijab as a symbol of oppression and inequality between the sexes, and would support laws against it

---

[9] Wyatt (2004).

[10] Wyatt (2003).

[11] Jones (2005).

[12] Dhumieres (2013).

for this reason." Legrand asserts the "Discrimination" framing by considering his viewpoint as representative of the "majority of French people" converting framing the hijab (as sexist) and the ban (as equality supplier) to a national attitude that determines who is French and who is not.

In the British national debate, the discourse also avoids a direct association between the term "discriminative" and the hijab. The "Discrimination" mental frame is activated through the assertion on the national value of gender equality. For example, in The Times Online, gender discrimination is referred to, yet without using the keyword "discrimination." Minette Marin discusses "the challenge the veil presents in the West" in the shed of Seleena Sabeel's case (Peterborough, 2004). Marin praises "the equality of women with men" in the UK and states that the hijab "immediately suggests a belief of system in which women are inferior to men, which is intolerable in here."[13] Marin indirectly stigmatizes the practice as a discriminatory and foreign practice which is not tolerated *here* (activating the "Otherness" mental frame too). However, the jilbab is framed as "discriminative" in Shabina Begum Jilbab Case (Luton, 2005) in *The Independent*. Joan Smith concludes her article by asserting that pupils and their parents at school "want to inhabit a rational world in which men and women enjoy equal rights."[14] Smith's reference to the parents is generic and hypothesizes that they all share her "Discrimination" framing of the jilbab.

In another article published in *The Independent*, Joan Smith includes Muslim women's viewpoints (294 out of 1974 words) about Jack Straw's declarations on the full veil and hijab practices.[15] Straw asked Muslim women to take their veil off because he feels "uncomfortable" when a woman had worn one in his Blackburn constituency office.[16] Smith, in her introduction (1069 words), starts by a story about a full-veiled Saudi Arabian's wife, "or maybe a mistress," who took off her full veil to swim in a bikini in Beirut five stars hotel where she was last summer. Next, she expresses her "loath" to burqa and niqab. Later on, she notifies that Jack Straw's intervention "tells the truth about how many of *us* feel about the veil in all its forms: the hijab, niqab, jilbab, chador and burqa." Here, Joan Smith used the political hijabophobic declaration to publish her hate discourse (*loath*) on the practice. Apart from the fact that Smith joins the distinctive veiling practices into one single frame in the reader's mind, she announces Straw's declarations as representative of the mainstream position toward veiling. The use of (us) excludes the Muslim minority from the British national identity. Stimulating the self-location strategy is also used in El Pais by Naiara Galarraga.[17] Both encourage the reader to process self-locating between the "majority" "us" or the "minority" others." Smith interprets the veil as follows: "the veil protects men from casual arousal. It also establishes women as the sexual property of individual men -fathers, husbands and sons- who are the only

---

[13] Marin (2004).

[14] Smith (2006b).

[15] Smith (2006a).

[16] See https://www.telegraph.co.uk/news/1530717/Take-off-your-veils-says-Straw.html.

[17] Galarraga (2010).

people allowed to see them uncovered [...] (it is) a symbol of inequality." Instead of using the direct vocabulary "discriminative," she explains the discriminative features of the practice. In *The Guardian*, gender discrimination is indirectly referred to by the reference to the trajectory of Western feminism "who has tied up with the freedom to uncover ourselves"[18] (I will go through it in the following frame).

The British re-activation of the "Discrimination" mental frame of the hijab is not limited to the simple association between the practice and the term "discrimination." BBC and *The Independent* used the French "Discrimination" framing of the hijab to justify the French ban to the British reader. They stressed on the "equality" provided by the 2004 French ban. On the British national level, "Discrimination" framing is re-activated by the assertion on the equality principle of the British values, as much as by highlighting the (gender) discriminative features of the practice without using a direct association between the hijab and the term "discrimination." Not all journalists use their authoritative personal voice to address the reader's mind directly. Such authoritative discourse manifested only in Joan Smith's discourse. She took advantage of the political hijabophobic discourse to publish an authoritative hate discourse.

Cross-Cultural Analysis

Both the Spanish and the British discourse re-activate the "Discrimination" mental framing of the hijab. I use the world re-activate instead of activating because it is not a new framing of the hijab. It is a recycled framing form the past century. The "Discrimination" mental framing in each press is not updated with new arguments or contextual facts. It is based on weak argumentation on gender equality without going deeply into the religious gender-relation frame of reference in Islam.

Although the "Discrimination" mental frame is re-activated in both presses, the linguistic strategies of the re-activation differ. The Spanish strategy is indirect in El Mundo, and it is direct in El País. It consists of repetitive usage of the vocabulary "discrimination." Such a strategy is influential in shaping the audience's mind toward hijab visibility; it strengths the stereotypical mental image associated with the indicated symbol, the hijab.[19] When this mental frame gets magnified and rooted, the discourse only needs to "recall in memory" to activate the "Discrimination" mental frame. Based on this fact, the Spanish discourse recalls on the memory of the colonial prejudice on the hijab. It activates the "Discrimination" frame by a simple association between the hijab and the term "discriminative" without any further explanation. In the British discourse, re-activating this frame is based on highlighting the gender discrimination features of the practice in superficial argumentation far away from the religious gender-relation frame of reference in Islam.

---

[18] Walter (2004).
[19] Toolan (2016).

The utilization of the Islamophobic political discourse in the re-activation of this frame slightly differs across these presses. In El Mundo, Ana Del Barrio only narrates the political declaration, and she did not use her personal and authoritative voice to empower or demolish it. However, in the same newspaper, De Ganuza interprets the political attempt to ban the hijab at the public school as a measure to protect gender equality. Both do not use the political declaration to reflect the majority's opinion nor to transmit direct hate speech. In the British discourse, Joan Smith, in *The Independent*, uses the political declarations to publish a hate discourse in the name of the mass majority of the readers.

The negation of the "Discrimination" mental frame by the hijab wearers or hijab supporters is not prominent in both contexts.

Framing Hijab Through "Submission"

The "Submission" mental frame of the hijab is a recycled one too. In this framing, the hijab is not seen as a sign with an inherited meaning itself. It is framed as a submissive tool to subdue Muslim women. The "Submission" mental framing of the hijab is re-activated in both press discourses. In the following, I will analyze the linguistic strategies that re-activate the "Submissive" mental frame of the hijab. I will also reflect on the arguments used to fortify this mental frame.

Spanish "Submission" Mental Frame of Hijab

Understanding the hijab as a submissive practice is recurrently used in Spanish media discourse. It manifests only once in the exclusion cases in El Mundo 2010.[20] Yet, it is more frequent in political and social debate. Maria Peral, who covers the exclusion of the lawyer Zubaida from the court, indicates that the judge "rejected the garment that, according to his reasoning, does not conform with the prestige and dignity of the toga." Peral distanced the judge's opinion from her own. She limited the judge's viewpoint to "his reasoning." She does not use her authoritative position as a journalist to put a final announcement on the incompatibility between the embodied meanings of the two garments: the hijab and the toga.

In social and political debate, the "Submission" mental frame appears in El País and La Vanguardia. No re-activation of this frame is detected in El Mundo. Due to the limited number of the selected articles from the La Vanguardia, El País records a higher score in re-activating the "Submission" mental frame of the hijab. Similar to the Spanish "Discrimination" frame, the linguistic expressions are repetitive and dull. The term "sign of women's oppression" recalls in the memory of the colonial past repetitively without giving a comprehensive definition or shape of that submission.

---

[20]Peral (2010).

For example, In El País, Etxenike indicates that "the veil has too much fabric and too many folds [*mucha tela y muchas vueltas*] but I understand that it is fundamentally a sign of women's oppression."[21] Caballero, in her argument in favor of banning the hijab at school, refers to the need to end all "submissive expressions, of difference or religious symbols."[22] Angeles Espinosa indicates that the interpretations of the practice are "assumed by the European collective subconscious, certainly and unquestionably, to be an external imposition and an indication of women submission."[23] The journalist continues, "-Islamic feminists negate it." Espinosa uses her authority as a journalist to speak, (unmistakenly), on behalf of the "European collective subconscious." The mental positionality toward hijab visibility conditions the membership in this EU collective. Another similar generic discourse on behalf of Europeans appears in Ana Carabajos' article. The journalist indicates that "the public opinion of Europeans, laicists, including feminists, consider that covering women is a submissive act."

Carabajos, to give more validity to the "Submission" mental frame of the hijab, introduces Farah Amara to the reader. Amara is a secretary in the French State and the founder of Not Whores Nor Submissive. She "explains very well the Islamic veil" because she is a Muslim. Carabajos states: "(Amara) considers the hijab an act of submission [*en estado puro*]." Amara's declarations assert Carabajos' argument: "I am a Muslim, and I consider the hijab as a tool of oppression. Its history is attached to, not Islam, but patriarchal societies." In this article, the assertion of the "Submission" frame is not limited to linguistic repetitions. It comes from the credibility given to Amara as a Muslim whose mental frame on the hijab coincides with the "public opinion of Europe" "Submission" mental frame.

Naiara Galarraga's article titled "Hijab of submission or rebellion?"[24] categorizes the hijab into two specific stereotypical frames shutting out any possible third alternative framing. Concha Caballero, who discusses the hijab exclusion cases in Spain, states that if "we were able to separate the Catholic Church from the state, we would have the authority to demand the end of any expression of submission, of difference or religious symbols."[25] Galarraga indirectly refers to the hijab considering it and any other religious symbol as oppressive. This framing is built on the assumption of the hegemonic feminism that frames secularity as modernity and religion as backwardness (see Chapter 1). However, Seba Mahmood answered that feminists who have difficulties in respecting women from other cultures with different traditions rely on an "imaginary freedom," the liberal one (see Chapter 2).

The only negation of the "Submission" frame in El País comes from the "Arabist" Gema Martín Muñoz. She states that "today, it is not the hijab that marks the liberty or the submissive state of Muslim women."[26] Muñoz does not provide the reader

---

[21] Etxenike (2004).

[22] Caballero (2010).

[23] Espinosa (2010).

[24] Galarraga (2010).

[25] Caballero (2010).

[26] Muñoz (2010).

with what marks the liberty or the submission of Muslim women so that the reader can build an alternative frame. She uses the simple negation, which only serves to assert the negated mental frame, as Lakoff explains[27] (see Chapter 3). Besides, her negation of the "Submission" frame loses its credibility as she is introduced as an "Arabista." Such a presenting strategy locates Muñoz in the "others" category; she shares "their" frame of reference (see the "Otherness" mental frame).

In the discourse of 2015/2016, in La Vanguardia, Carian Farreras interviews the philosopher Olga Dominguez. Farreras indicates that Dominguez distinguishes between an original meaning and a new meaning of the hijab. Dominguez explains that the original meaning of the hijab is "submission." She "warns that behind the use of the hijab, there exists an implied interpretation: women are possessed by men."[28] She continues "for those young Muslims, the sign of *hijab* seems to be detached from the submission to men; they try to give it the new significance." Dominguez warns from the new meaning of the hijab, she states that "to change the meaning of an implicit violence symbol, its victims are going to be affected in some way. We run the risk to play in a favor to the Islamic patriarchy." In the first meaning of the hijab, Dominguez re-activates the colonial stereotypes (an oppressive and violence symbol) and announces it as the original frame of reference. Then, she states that hijab-wearers who intend to support a new meaning to the practice are doing a favor for Muslim patriarchy. This particular discourse is manipulating because when readers meet hijab-wearers who negate the "Submission" frame and provide them with alternative mental frames (such as: empowerment, religion, free choice); the reader would keep in mind that those hijab-wearers are potential victims of their own process of creating these alternative frames. Such manipulating discourse also suggests that supporting this free-choice hijab will harm the rest of the hijab victims. It is to say; in Dominguez's discourse, the hijab is understood within the "Submission" frame in both original and new meanings.

Interestingly, Farreras, later on in the same article, interviews hijab-wearing women. These women express the "liberation" aspect of the hijab. However, the reader's mind has been already prepared to cast these women's declarations as manipulated. The Muslim women's arguments evaporate in front of the warnings mentioned above.

To sum up, the "Submission" mental frame is similar to the "Discrimination" mental frame in the Spanish press. It is not recurrent in the exclusion cases discourse nor in El Mundo discourse. The journalists in El Mundo do not use their authoritative voice to arbitrate on the visibility of the hijab as a submissive sign. On the contrary, El País and La Vanguardia re-activate the "Submission" mental frame of the hijab. The journalists in these two presses speak in the name of Europeans and announce their personal framing of the hijab as the unquestionable representative reality.

The linguistic re-activation of the "Submission" mental frame of the hijab is dull and repetitive. It does not explain the shape of the submission nor define it. The discourse depends on the recall in memory strategy. The journalists use the

---

[27] Lakoff (2014).
[28] Farreras (2016).

testimony of "Muslim" or "ex-Muslim" hijab opposer women as eyewitnesses of that (unexplained) submission. Their contribution is a repetition of the exact expressions used by the journalists, e.g., "it is a sign of submission." The journalists controlled their participation by announcing them spokeswomen, authoritative speakers, owner of a trusted discourse. They also stigmatized non-stereotypical frames as deceitful and warned readers of the new meaning of the hijab. The only Spanish contributor who negates the "Submission" frame of the hijab is located within the "others" frame of reference.

British "Submission" Mental Frame of Hijab

The "Submission" frame of the hijab is re-activated in the British press. However, the "Submission" frame is more frequently re-activated at referring to women who practice hijab Unlikely to the "Discrimination" framing of the hijab; all the British newspapers re-activate the "Submission" mental frame by a direct linguistic trigger "oppression." In BBC, the "Submission" frame is directly and clearly outlined in the debate of 2004 French law. Caroline Wyatt narrates her French friend's opinion on hijab visibility at French schools, "'it was degrading to women' he (Antonio) told me." She continues that "'Muslim girls were clearly being oppressed by the headscarf. It was all very dangerous and would lead to no good', said Antoine ominously."

The oppression in the British discourse is not argument-free as in the Spanish one. It is argued and asserted by the activation of another frame of the hijab: the (Sexuality) "Concealment" mental frame (discussed below). For example, in *The Guardian*, Samra Mursaleen, a hijab-wearing woman writer, expressed her worries on Nigel Farage's, UKIP's ex-leader, statements on the hijab. Farage states that the hijab is "something that is used to oppress women."[29] Farage re-activated the "Submission" framing of the hijab due to the sexual concealment it imposes, which is "an affront to women." In Times Online, Minette Marin depends on the (Sexuality) "Concealment" frame of veiling, in general not only the hijab, to re-activate the "Submission" frame of the practice. She said that "the appearance alone of heavily swathed women suggests that there is something about them which must be hidden, secluded, controlled and kept private."[30] In *The Independent*, the "Submission" frame of veiling is re-activated and asserted by the vestment restrictions the veil imposes on its wearers. Joan Smith indicates that "the hijab, niqab, jilbab, chador and burqa" are "symbols of oppression" and "inequality."[31] She adds that the veil, in its all forms, imposes "rules" on women to follow." Smith joins all distinctive kinds of veiling in one abstract sac and stigmatizes them as oppressive. In the same newspaper, Arifa Akbar, who carried out a series of interviews with hijab-wearing and full-veil-wearing Muslims, introduces in the

---

[29] Mursaleen (2010).
[30] Marin (2004).
[31] Smith (2006a).

introduction all different, both for and against, perspectives on veiling practices.[32] Akbar concludes that "for its detractors, the headscarf is simply a form of oppression." The journalist limits the "Submission" frame to the opinion of the veil-opposers; she did not introduce the frame as a representative truth that everybody agrees on. As a consequence, the reader is able to associate the "Submission" mental frame to the hijab opposers instead of being unconsciously identified with this frame as European as the Spanish Press does.

Another argument in the re-activation of the British "Submission" mental frame of hijab is patriarchy. In *The Guardian*, Kate Melville, who comments on Kossaibati's article in which Kossaibati narrates her experience in shopping cloth that matches the hijab criteria,[33] uses the following title: "Muslim Patriarchy Served Well by Hijab."[34] The title directly associates the "Submission" mental frame of the hijab, one of the simplest form of veiling, with the patriarchal submission of the hijab-wearers. In a similar discourse in the same newspaper, Catherine Bennette states "(H)owever modestly sized the hijab, many of us would recognize it -like a nun's wimple- as a clear nuisance and hindrance, and more importantly, as a prominent signifier of women's subservience, enforced at the behest of men."[35] In Bennette's discourse, we see the confusion between the Muslim hijab and nun's veiling criteria, which we found out in the Spanish "Discrimination" frame of the hijab. Bennette introduces her opinion as a representative of the Majority of readers.

In the Telegraph, Sajda Khan asserts the re-activation of the "Submission" mental frame of the hijab through a similar strategy used by Ana Carabajos in El País. Sajda Khan introduces the testimonies hijab opposer "Muslim" or "ex-Muslim" women to give credibility to "Submission" framing of the hijab. Muslim feminists Fatima Mernissi and Nawal El Saadawi view it as "an oppressive symbol of male supremacy."[36] Ex-Muslims, such as Ayaan Hirsi Ali, states that Islam is "a religion which subjugates its women." These contributions are of significant impact on shaping the reader's opinions because they are identified as the critical thinking of the Islamic epistemology by those who escaped the submission.

To sum up, the "Submission" mental frame of the hijab is directly activated in all the British press. Unlikely to the "Discrimination" mental frame, the expression "submission" is directly used. It is re-activated to justify the 2004 French ban to the British reader in BBC. The re-activation of the "Submission" mental frame depends on two arguments: the (Sexuality) "Concealment" mental frame of the hijab (in the *Time* Online and *The Independent*) and on the patriarchy (in *The Guardian* and *The Telegraph*). The testimonies of "Muslim" and "ex-Msulim" hijab opposers were used to assert the re-activation of this recycled mental frame.

---

[32] Akbar (2010a).

[33] Kossaibati (2009).

[34] Melville (2009).

[35] Bennett (2004).

[36] Khan, Sajda, *It is not the hijab which holds women back, but prejudice.* http://www.telegraph. co.uk/culture/tvandradio/great−british−bake−off/11919553/Its−not−the−hijab−which−hol ds−women−back−but−intolerance−and−prejudice.html (8 October 2015).

In the "Submission" framing of the hijab, the British journalists did not use their authoritative position constantly to, directly, impose their opinions on the readers through positional strategies, e.g., we, most of us, etc. The expression "many of us" is used once. At the same time, one narration restricts the "Submission" mental frame of the hijab to the hijab opposers' perspective.

Cross-Cultural Analysis

There are slight differences in the re-activation of the recycled "Submission" mental frame of the hijab across the British and the Spanish press. The activation of the Spanish "Submission" mental frame depends on "recall the memory," i.e., it is merely repetitions of the expression without any clear arguments because the mental frame is rooted in the social cognition. In contrast, the British re-activation of this frame is based on evidence that justifies it; (Sexuality) "Concealment" mental frame and patriarchy.

Despite the absence of the Spanish arguments, journalists announce the "Submission" frame of the hijab as the representative truth about the hijab, and they cast all the different non-stereotypical framings of the hijab as deceptive. In comparison, the British journalists did not take that authoritative stance, although they support their framing with an evidence. The "Submission" mental frame is frequently limited to the opinion of those who oppose the hijab and not as an absolute truth about the practice. The Spanish authoritative discourse restricts the Spanish reader within a pre-monitored and restricted mental space in which they can limitedly think of the hijab visibility. On the other hand, the British less monitored discourse provides readers with mental freedom to think critically and objectively through all the diverse opinions on the hijab.

Journalists who oppose the hijab practice, in both presses, used the testimony of "Muslim" and "ex-Muslim" hijab-opposer women to assert the re-activation of the "Submission" mental frame. These testimonies do not add a significant argument in the re-activation process. Yet they are of a substantial impact on shaping the readers' minds because these testimonies stand for the critical thinking on the Islamic epistemology by those who escaped the submission.

Framing Hijab Through "Compulsivity"

The "Compulsivity" frame indicates that the practice is enforced by Muslim men; it is a related frame to the previous ones "Discrimination" and "Submission." This frame is also re-activated in both presses because it is recycled from the stereotypical colonial discourse. The arguments used to reactive and empower the "Compulsivity" frame depend on the old-fashion patriarchal embodiment of (Arabic) Muslim cultures.

Spanish "Compulsivity" Mental Frame of Hijab

The forced hijab is referred to in both Spanish article categories: the exclusion cases and the political and social debate. Each Spanish newspaper uses specific linguistic strategies to indirectly re-activate the "Compulsivity" frame. For example, in the exclusion cases, El País discourse links the hijab practice to the parental enforcement on the minor. Natalia Iglesias notifies that "the direction of the school asked the parents not to cover the head of their daughter with the hijab"[37] (Shaima Case, Girona, 2007). In this newsàèr, the "Compulsivity" mental frame is re-activated after three years when Rebeca Carranco interviewed the same girl and her mother in the shed of the controversial case of Najwa Al-Malha (2010, Madrid). Carranco indicates that both Shaima and her mother assert the free-choice in the current decision of the practice. However, she continues, "if Shaima wanted to take it off now, it would be ok for her mother. When she has her menstruation, her mother will force her to veil."[38] Carranco demolishes the free-choice framing in her discourse. However, the article's focus was not on the free current choice of Shaima. The constant analogy between Shaima's hijab and Najwa's hijab highlights the enforced parental hijab at the age of puberty, the age of Najwa Al-Malha but not yet of Shaima.

The male presence is another trigger of the "Compulsivity" frame. The discourse in El País declaratively negates the compulsivity through the minor's discourse at the presence of her father. For example, in Fatima's case (2011, Madrid), Fatima announces her free choice of hijab while her father is next to her [se ríe del desparpajo de la chica]. The same exact scenario is pictured in Hasna Isslal's case in the same newspaper.[39] Isslal, sitting in the salon of her house with her father and the rest of the family, assures that "her father, Brahim, asked her many times to take it off." The male presence demolishes the credibility of the "Compulsivity" young girls' negation, and it conveys a stereotypical understanding of the patriarchal nature of the Muslim family.

On the contrary, El Mundo's discourse refers briefly that the hijab is the minor's free choice without any reference to the male presence or any indirect linguistic link to the "Compulsivity" frame. For example, in the case of Najwa, Ana Del Barrio narrates: "Najwa […] ensures that she wears the hijab because of her own decision against her father's will."[40] In 2016, in Takwa Rejeb's case, Inma Lidón quoted Rejeb's views of her veiling choice: "wearing the hijab is a lifestyle I chose freely."[41]

In social and political discourse, the "Compulsivity" frame is more salient and recurrent. The linguistic strategy that re-activates the "Compulsivity" frame varies across the selected newspapers. Rosa Montero, in El País, decisively assumes the males' enforcement of the hijab on women members of the family. She indicates that in the hijab decision, there "intervene the decision of boyfriends, it is to say,

---

[37] Iglesias (2007).

[38] Carranco (2010).

[39] Álvarez (2011c).

[40] Del Barrio (2010a).

[41] Lidón (2016).

machismo."[42] El País asserts the "Compulsivity" mental frame by the Muslim women's testimonies. Their contributions are introduced through the "uncertainty" discursive strategy, as we will see ahead. They are the eyewitnesses of the hijab enforcement. For example, Naiara Galarraga includes in her article a contribution of a young Muslim woman of a Palestinian father, an anonymous non-hijab-wearing eyewitness, who "thinks that all of them (hijab-wearing friends) do it freely."[43] The linguistic expression "think" indicates the uncertainty and potentiality, especially when a member of the vulnerable group utters it. She is, as Van Dijk state, less authoritative and less credible. The reader's mental framing of the free-choice testimony will limit the free-choice hijab to the anonymous Muslim woman's own hypothesis. Maria Sahuquillo, in another article in the same newspaper, quoted the testimony of a 29-year-old Muslim woman, born in Belgium of Turkish parents, who "does not wear the hijab because she is not prepared to it yet"[44] and because she does not want to lose her job. The anonymous witness indicates that "sometimes, she feels lobbied to wear it (the hijab). Mainly, by the family of her father." It is to say, the hijab imposition is not limited to the family head-male pressure, but it extends to male relatives too. Ana Carabajos uses a similar discursive strategy that directly re-activates the "Compulsivity" mental frame. She introduces Nadia Yassine, Moroccan, a leader in the Islamic Justice and Spirituality Movement, who "admits" that "some girls of her family are obliged to cover their head, but many of them decide freely to veil."[45] Another eyewitness in the same article is Chebaa, a member of the Women Emancipation platform in Belgium, who admits that "there are men who obliged their women to veil, but she affirms that they are a minority." Carabajos concludes that Chebaa decided to hijab at 25, "four years after getting married." Although Chebaa referred to the forced hijab cases as a "minority," this faint negation of the "Compulsivity" frame is demolished by Carabajos' comments on Chebaa's hijab decision after marriage. Besides, the discourse introduces Yassine's and Chebaa's contributions through the verb "admit" *[admitir]* by which the contributors are classified as "guilty" for hiding the truth of hijab enforcement in their community. Through this linguistic expression, the journalist is pronounced as the truth seeker.

In addition to the eyewitness strategy, El País re-activates and asserts the "Compulsivity" mental frame of the hijab through the unbalanced ratios between free and enforced hijab. Ana Carbajos indicates that in the "ebb and flow" of the political motivations of veiling, as to defend Muslim identity in front of Islamophobia, "the number of women who plan consciously the decision of wearing or not the veil is a minority." Naiara Galarraga, in the same newspaper, indicates that "the experts in Islam" and the Minister of Justice Francisco Caamaño cannot deny the fact that "today here in Spain, there exist cases of women who are wearing the hijab because

---

[42]Montero (2010).

[43]Galarraga (2010).

[44]Sahuquillo, Maria R. *Integración, si, asimilación, no.* http://www.elpais.com/articulo/sociedad/Integracion/asimilacion/elpepisoc/20080216elpepisoc_1/Tes (16 February 2008).

[45]Carbajos (2008).

they are obliged, yet it is impossible to know how many they are."[46] Comparing these three declarations, we found out that the free choice of hijab is limited to the minority of Muslim hijab-wearers. The unknown number of forced hijab cases is linked to the journalist's authoritative position and the Spanish Minister of Justice. Besides, the number of these cases is left wide open and unknown in their discourse. From a parallel perspective, Concha Caballero argues that "some Moroccan women use the hijab to claim their existence as free women. Yet, along with them, there are millions of women in Muslim countries that are obligated to wear garments that cover them."[47] Caballero blames the "some" free-choice hijab-wearers for all the worldwide enforced hijab cases, which are set to be "millions."

The unbalanced quantity between the free choice and the forced hijab is used as a linguistic strategy to assert the exceptionality of free choice hijab in contrast to the mass compulsory hijab. Every time the first image is created, the second one appears to weigh it down. The proportion of few/some ≠ many/millions re-activate, strengthens, and normalizes the "Compulsivity" frame of the practice. Although the proportion provided by both Yassin and Chebaa is in contrast to what the journalists affirm, the journalists' arguments of the compulsivity frame of the hijab tend to be more reliable and trustworthy because they belong to "Our" circle of trusted sources. As Lakoff (2014) said, people normally tend to feel identified with the linguistic and conceptual representation that coincides with their already existing mental frames. They are easy to understand, comfortably processed, and safely identified with. And as the "Compulsivity" mental frame is a recycled one from the colonial era, Spanish readers tend to believe in the journalists' discourse on the forced hijab by recalling in the memory of the colonial past. To think of the hijab as a free choice needs a change in the mental structures on the hijab sign, and it is a tough mental process for the reader.

Although El Mundo includes the "Compulsivity" frame, it is not as direct as in El País. It is re-activated through the politicians' declarations. The journalists do not involve their authoritative voice in the discourse to assert that frame. For example, Ana Del Barrio quotes the Minister of Equality's, Bibiana Aído, declaration in the forum of The Alianza de Civilizaciones who criticized that "Muslim or Arabic males can wear occidental style while women must wear a long dress that covers their body in addition to a veil on the head that covers their hair."[48] The linguistic expressions "must" indirectly activate the "Compulsivity" frame in Bibiana's declaration, although the imposer is not defined. Del Barrio does not elaborate on this activation. Instead, she included a direct negation by Eduardo Mansur Escudero, the president of the Islamic Council. Escudero "reminded" that "Islam does not impose the use of the veil. It is a right, not an obligation. I do not know any women who wear the veil

---

[46]Galarraga (2010).

[47]Caballero (2010).

[48]Del Barrio, Ana. *De la Vega desautoriza a Aído y dice que el Gobierno respeta la tradición del velo islámico.* El Mundo, 27 June 2008, http://www.elmundo.es/elmundo/2008/06/26/espana/121 4475820.html.

as an imposition." However, the negation would be more credible if a (Muslim) man speaker was not saying it.

In El Mundo, the unbalanced quantity between the free choice and the forced hijab stands in contrast to the El Pais. Rosa Meneses attempts to find the significance and origin of the veil in her article, "What are the significance and the origin of the veil?"[49] She states: "occasionally, it can be that women feel obliged to wear this garment by family pressure of the social environment. But, it is, almost always, their choice." The linguistic expressions "occasionally" for forced hijab and "almost always" for free choice hijab set the free-choice hijab as a norm—however, the forced hijab seems to be unavoidable in the Spanish data.

In 2015–2016, the "Compulsivity" frame was re-activated in La Vanguardia. Carian Farreras activates this frame by questioning the free decision of the practice: "To what extent is covering the head a voluntary act?"[50] In the first part of the article, which involves a social debate on the hijab, the "Compulsivity" frame is re-activated through the contribution of an eyewitness Najat Talha, an ex-hijab-wearer. Talha indicates that it is not easy "to unleash hair in Muslim communities because of social pressure," and she affirms that the pressure is more intense when she is in Morocco. La Vanguardia's reference to the "Compulsivity" frame is generic and does not specify the kind of social pressure or obligation, e.g., religious, identity, patriarchal, or gender role pressure. Besides, the discourse limits the hijab practice to hair concealment, amputating it from its core meaning, criteria, and purposes.

In 2016, El Mundo showed a significant shift in the re-activation of the "Compulsivity" frame. The newspaper includes an explicit negation of this mental frame by Spanish hijab-wearing Muslims. Ana Juarez interviews Naima El-Akil, the president of The Muslim Girls of Madrid Association ACHIME, who "puts on the veil at 25 voluntarily" and Omaima Bouiri, who "voluntarily wears the hijab since she was 13 years old."[51] The discursive narration of the journalist did not manipulate the hijab-wearers' contributions as El País tends to do. Their declarations were neutrally narrated without stereotypical stigmatization or re-activation of the "Compulsivity" frame. Yet, the hijab-wearers' negation of the "Compulsivity" mental frame is mostly short and limited, e.g., "no one obliged me." Such kind of negation is weak; it is called passive negation because it does not support the negation with any argument; consequently, it asserts the negated frame as Lakoff states.

In the same newspaper, Amanda Figueras interviews convert and autochthone Muslim women.[52] None of the interviewees refers to the hijab enforcement nor negates it. In a different article, Figueras, who converted to Islam around 2010, describes her hijab experience as "a personal decision."[53] She converted to Islam while she was still working for El Mundo and adopted the hijab just before she had left the newspaper.

---

[49] Meneses (2010).

[50] Farreras (2016).

[51] Juárez (2015).

[52] Figueras (2012).

[53] Figueras (2015).

To sum up, El País and La Vanguardia re-activate the "Compulsivity" frame of the hijab. It is re-activated indirectly by the male presence in the hijab decision and directly by using the linguistic expression that indicates the hijab enforcement. The discursive strategies that are used to re-activate this mental frame of the hijab are the journalist's assertion of the enforced hijab, Arab and Muslim women testimonies, and the high frequency of enforced hijab around the world. Although these arguments are not related to the Spanish national context, they are used to assert the "Compulsivity" frame in Spain. In Contrast, El Mundo does not re-activate the "Compulsivity" mental frame, and the journalists do not use their authoritative position to manipulate the Muslim women's assertions on the free-choice hijab. Yet, the Spanish Muslim negation is prosaic. It does not elaborate an alternative mental frame for the reader. It is limited to the passive negation of the stereotypical frame.

British "Compulsivity" Mental Frame of Hijab

Framing hijab as an enforced practice on Muslim women is re-activated in all the selected British newspapers. Yet, in the British context, there is significant visibility of educated hijab-wearers in the mainstream press discourse as writers, journalists, and contributors. They assure their free-choice hijab independent from the mainstream non-Muslim journalist's guardianship. The independent discourse of the hijab-wearers in the mainstream makes it difficult to entirely demolish the free-choice hijab framing in the British context. For example, in *The Guardian*, Catherine Bennett re-activates the "Compulsivity" frame four times, giving it primary importance over the "Religiosity" mental frame of the hijab (which I will explain below) and over the free-choice references. Bennett states that the hijab is "enforced by the behest of men [...] (it) has nothing to do with religion."[54] Due to the visibility of the free-choice hijab in the mainstream discourse, Bennett builds her re-activation of the "Compulsivity" frame as follows: first, she states that "Muslim women we see veiled [...] actually want to dress like this, is impossible to refute. Who knows? Maybe, inside all that dark material (hijab and full veil wearers), they are brimming with self-esteem." In this statement, she draws the line between "We" who see the "Other" veiled women, "We" who are skeptical of the "others" claim of free-choice hijab. Next, she continues that "the point that headscarves are, contrary to decadent western propaganda, actively empowering, is generally made by some brainy young professional wearing becoming lace-trimmed hijab. Fine." Here, the journalist continues the binary position between "we" and "other" through the contradiction between the hijab viewpoint and the "western propaganda." Bennets continues, "there must surely be more doubt about freedom of choice when the veil is worn by a child at school. As Adonis wrote, "When one sees girls as young as four years old wearing the veil in the streets of Paris, for example, can anyone seriously claim they are doing this voluntarily?" As Bennett is obliged to recognize the free choice of hijab

---

[54] Bennett (2004).

because of the visibility of the hijab-wearing women in the public sphere, she limits the "Compulsivity" frame to French children's hijab. Bennett blames the national adult free-choice hijab for the children-imposed hijab in France.

The "Compulsivity" frame is re-activated in the British debate on the 2004 French ban in BBC. It serves well to justify the ban law. Wyatt's friend, Antonio, told her that "few women wearing it did so voluntarily. They are forced, he said, by their families and by local imams, who were teaching an increasingly fundamentalist form of Islam to France's Muslim community."[55] In the same article, Samira Bellil, "a 30-year-old Algerian-born French woman is just as passionate as Antoine in her rejection of the hijab." Bellil states: "girls are being pressurized to wear it, as much to protect themselves from the casual violence of the ghetto, as by their families or religious leaders." The linguistic expressions "few" did it voluntarily," they are forced," "enforced," "fundamentalist," and "pressurized" are all triggers of the "Compulsivity" framing of the hijab. This frame, as much as the previous two, is the justification of the French law to British readers.

The "Compulsivity" frame is asserted by undermining and questioning the free-choice assertion expressed by hijab-wearers in the mainstream. For example, in *The Guardian*, Yasmine Alibhai-Brown decreases the credibility of hijab-wearers' free-choice references, she states that "(t)heir choice, even if independently made, may not be fully examined."[56] She questions if a male Muslim child, she saw in the street next to his full veil mother, will be a participant in enforcing hijab on the female members of his family in the future: "She had a baby girl in a pushchair. Her young son was running around. Will the girl be put into a hijab, then a jilbab? Will the son accept that of his sister and wife one day?"

In *The Independent*, Joan Smith mixed the British veiling practice (all different forms) with the Afghan veiling context (Burqa) in her re-activation of the "Compulsivity" mental frame. She starts by the Afghan scene:

(T)he inescapable fact being that the vast majority of women who cover their hair, faces and bodies do so because they have no choice. [...] they wear it because they are afraid of being killed if they don't. Women haven't suddenly gone back to wearing the veil in Iraq because they're pious; they do it because women who are courageous enough to refuse, including a well-known TV presenter, have been murdered by Islamic extremists.[57]

After this mental preparation through violence and enforcement (unproved) references, Smith moves to the British context. She associates between the free-choice and the Muslim male enforcement in making the decision: "Muslim women in this country may be telling the truth when they say they are covering their hair and faces out of choice, but that doesn't mean they haven't been influenced by relatives and male clerics." Smith takes away the agency of Muslim women over their vestment choices. She supports her argument by an announcement of a Muslim man leader, Dr. Mohammed Mukadam, a chairman of the Association of Muslim Schools and principal of the Leicester Islamic Academy, "which is due to receive state funds

[55] Wyatt (2003).
[56] Alibhai–Brown (2015).
[57] Smith (2006a).

next year." Mukadam confirmed that even non-Muslim girls at his school would be expected to cover, he said: "We have a school uniform and that means wearing the hijab and the jilbab." Mukadam's statement is successfully used to assert the "Compulsivity" frame of hijab as much as to draw attention that this hijab enforcement might be funded by the State next year.

The reference to the male presence behind the practice appears in several newspapers. Sarrah Marrison, in The Independence, introduces the interviewee Denise Horsley as follows: "Denise Horsley lives in North London. She converted to Islam last year and is planning to marry her Muslim boyfriend next year."[58] Horsley activates the (Empowering) (Sexuality) "Concealment" frame while telling her hijab-wearing experience; she highlights the respect she acquires from being judged not on her look. She ends up: "It is kind of respect every dad wants for their daughters." Both the journalist's reference to the Muslim boyfriend and the convert's reference to the father activate, indirectly, the "Compulsivity" frame of hijab. The male presence at the hijab decision appears, as well, in BBC. Paula Dear interviews the Pharmacist Saba Naeem, a mother of two, who said she started wearing the hijab later than many women. Naeem indicates that she wanted to practice hijab, but she had never found the support until she got married: "My husband gave me the encouragement I needed, and I came back from honeymoon wearing the hijab. It feels so positive."[59] I do not intend here to say that these declarations by hijab-wearers give evidence to the "Compulsivity" frame. I argue that among all the hijab decision experiences in the United Kingdom, we only find out these, which are supported by a male member in the family.

In Tamanna Begum Jilbab's case, also covered in *The Independent*, Jessica Ware narrates that the school manager asked her to wear a "slightly shorter jilbab that does not cover her feet at work." "She said she would go home and discuss with her family. She afterwards filed a religious discrimination claim with an employment tribunal."[60] The reference to home discussion indirectly calls in memory the (male) family authority over the length of Begum's jilbab. In the other jilbab case of Shabina Begum (Luton, 2005), covered in The Times Online, Minette Marin mentions that Begum was "encouraged by the Islamic organization Hizb ut-Tahrir, with which her elder brother has connections, and which campaigns to segregate the sexes in public institutions such as schools."[61] To sum up, we can see that the Muslim male is always, directly or indirectly, referred to in the process of making a hijab decision or jilbab decision; consequently, the "Compulsivity" mental frame is indirectly re-activated in British readers' minds.

The negation of the "Compulsivity" mental frame appears in both for and against hijab discourses. It is more repetitive, visible, and potent than the Spanish negation. Some potent negations appear in the articles that assert stereotypical mental frames on the hijab and on the women who practice it. For example, in *The Guardian*,

---

[58] Marrison (2011).

[59] Dear (2004).

[60] Ware (2015).

[61] Marin (2004).

Natasha Walter, who praises the French secularism and links women uncovering to enlightenment and professionalism, indicates that she "met many women who had taken to wearing the headscarf out of choice. (I) met young, educated women who had decided to start wearing hijab even though there was no tradition of doing so in their families."[62] Walter's reference to free-choice hijab refers to "the majority" of cases, on the contrary to the Spanish ratio. Walter does not highlight the male presence during the process of making the hijab decision. Walter includes a brief testimony of a hijab-wearing woman who participates in a demonstration in London; Dr. Iman, a pediatrician at Northwick Park hospital, states, "it is my choice."

The negation of "Compulsivity" frame is detected in BBC coverage of the French law.[63] The negation comes from the French hijab-wearing students from Delacroix school in an encounter with the direction to reach a compromise over the French ban. Elizabeth Jones states that all the hijab-wearing students in the meeting "understood very well the feminist arguments condemning many aspects of their faith, but all of them insisted that they were under no pressure at home to wear the veil. In fact, quite the opposite is true. Their parents would prefer to them to de-veil than jeopardize their education." In this report, the negation of the "Compulsivity" frame is not the journalist's viewpoint, as Walter's negation. It is an objective narration of the participants' contributions without using the journalist's authoritative position to assert nor negate the content.

Hijab-wearers' negation of the "Compulsivity" mental frame of the hijab is recurrent in *The Guardian* and *The Independent*. Their negation is not passive negation limited to the denial of the male's enforcement, which is detected in the Spanish press, e.g., "no one obliged me." In contrast, The British hijab-wearers' negation of the "Compulsivity" frame is activated in the narrating of their personal journey with no reference to passive negations. Such discourse provides British readers with alternative experiences that contribute to activating the "Free-Choice" mental frame of the hijab. For example, in *The Guardian*, Rania Cllr Khan activates the "Free-Choice" framing by her "spiritual choice" experience. She indicates that "there are some simple guidelines, but ultimately it is up to individual women to decide what they feel comfortable wearing."[64] Khan empowers her arguments by a British national assertion on women's freedom: "the women's movement in this country has won many important freedoms. One is the freedom to choose what we wear. I exercise that choice every time I put on my headscarf and a set of clothes that are loose-fitting, modest." Khan's discourse is inclusive; she includes the hijab free choice as part of the British female struggle to unconditional liberty. In the same newspaper, Sabbiyah Perves weakens the "Compulsivity" frame by asserting her (religious) free-choice decision. She points out that "just because an individual or a group of people do not think the hijab is mandatory does not mean that this interpretation of the Qur'an

---

[62] Walter (2004).

[63] Jones (2005).

[64] Cllr Khan (2006).

should be enforced upon the rest. That is the beauty of the flexibility of the Qur'an: you take what you choose from it."[65]

In *The Independent*, the hijab-wearing interviewee Soha Sheikh activates the "Free-Choice" framing by denouncing the "Compulsivity" frame: "It must be a choice that is made by the woman, if there are any outside pressures making a woman feel compelled to adopt hijab then that becomes problematic."[66] In the same series of interviews done by Arifa Akbar, the hijab-wearing interviewee Shelina Zahra Janmohamed, the author of *Love in a Headscarf*, denounced the attempts that diminish Muslim women's agency over their vestment choice: "The most offensive suggestion is that women who wear a headscarf have no autonomy, and that it is not a free choice."[67] The interviewee Rajnaara Akhtar, the creator of Protect Hijab Campaign group, negates the "Compulsivity" frame through repetitive linguistic expressions that activate the "Free-Choice" frame. She avoids using the passive negation, e.g., "free choice," "chooses," and "voluntarily" are repeated eight times out of 747 words.[68] The de-activation of the "Compulsivity" frame in the British context is creative, assertive, and more effective than the Spanish passive negation. It depends on activating a new alternative, the "Free-Choice" mental frame.

The mainstream press discourse shows that the "Compulsivity" frame is not limited to the cognitive framing of the practice. It turns to be a social behavior to react with the visibility of the hijab. The hijab-wearers declare that they need to be in a constant awareness to detect this cognitive framing in their interlocutor's perception and negate it. For example, in the case of H&M model Mariah Idrissi, the Telegraph indicates that Idrissi had "asked her parents before she could take part in the H&M shoot."[69] In a contrastive discourse in *The Independent*, Idrissi "denies reports that she had asked permission from her parents before taking part in the shoot, saying she had just asked for advice. Her parents were 'relaxed Muslims,' she said, and there was no pressure for her to wear the hijab." In *The Guardian*, Syima Aslam, Bradford sales and marketing executive, narrates her experience when she decided to practice hijab:

> I spent a week visiting clients and explaining that the next time they saw me I would be wearing a scarf and, as we were post 9/11, there would be no bomb under it! What I found most surprising was that the majority of people assumed I was about to get married. In actual fact, I had been married for four years and the decision to don a scarf was completely personal. It did not seem to occur to people that I may be taking this step of my own volition.[70]

This experience might prove how deep the "Compulsivity" frame of hijab is in the British mainstream mind. Even though costumers are in contact with a free-choice decision, it turns difficult for them to assimilate it because it contradicts the already rooted stereotypical mental frame.

---

[65] Perves (2013).

[66] Akbar (2010a).

[67] Akbar (2010c).

[68] Akbar (2010b).

[69] Sanghani (2015a).

[70] Aslam (2014).

To sum up, the "Compulsivity" frame in the British press is re-activated in all the British newspapers. It re-activated to justify the French ban for British readers. The discursive strategies depend on the projection of the forced political hijab in Afghanistan into the British context. Against-hijab journalists blame the British free-choice hijab of all the forced-hijab cases across the world. Male members of the family are used as triggers of this frame in the storytelling of the hijab-wearers' experiences. This discourse strategy depends on the call in memory to the patriarchal stereotypes imposed on Muslim cultures. *The Independent*, *Times* Online, and BBC link the free-choice decision to a family male member. Both *The Independent* and *The Guardian* underestimate the hijab-wearers autonomy and agency over their vestment choices.

The social categorization, "we vs. others," is complex in British discourse. Hijab opposers identify their voice as the representative voice of the British mainstream. They use the pronoun "we" to determine their position on the contrary to the "others" imposed hijab practice. As much, the Muslim hijab-wearers use the multicultural British "we" to celebrate women's freedom to wear what she chooses.

The de-activation of the "Compulsivity" frame of the hijab appears in both for and against hijab articles. Hijab-opposers' discourse refers to the existence of a free-choice hijab without discursive manipulation. The visibility of educated, trained, and independent hijab-wearing women in the British national press created an alternative frame on the hijab: "Free-Choice" mental frame. The hijab-wearers' articles are independent from the secular journalists' revision or manipulation. They are the owner of their discourse and of their experience. The "Free-Choice" frame is not a passive negation of the stereotypical "Compulsivity" frame. The "Free-Choice" mental frame of the hijab is activated in *The Guardian* and *The Independent*.

Cross-Cultural Analysis

In both presses, the "Compulsivity" mental frame is a re-activation depending on colonial arguments. In the British press, the "Compulsivity" mental frame of the hijab is re-activated in all the selected newspapers while in the Spanish press, El Mundo does not. Both presses discourse projects the worldwide forced hijab cases into the national debate and blames the national free-choice hijab of the forced-hijab cases across the world.

The discursive strategies that re-activate and empower the "Compulsivity" frame slightly differ. Although both presses use the male family members' visibility to refer to the enforcement, El País and La Vanguardia use direct linguistic expressions to re-activate the "Compulsivity" frame. The British discourse, more frequently, refers to the male religious family member as an indirect trigger of the "Compulsivity" frame depending on recall on the memory strategy, readers will recall on the colonial memory on Muslim culture as patriarchal. Journalists in El País and La Vanguardia empower the "Compulsivity" framing of the hijab by testimonies of ex-Muslims and ex-hijab-wearing women as much as by the testimonies of anonymous migrant

Muslim women; even though the debate is on the national hijab. There is no testimony by a hijab-wearing Spanish woman before the 2015/2016 articles. In the British press, hijab-wearing women have access to writing in the national press.

Unlike the British press, the Spanish press demonstrates a controlled de-activation of the "Compulsivity" mental frame. It is to say, the contribution of the hijab-wearing women in the national press in 2015/2016 is controlled by the (secular) journalists. The hijab-wearers de-activation is limited to passive negation without any elaboration to an alternative frame. Their contribution is limited negations, and it is manipulated by the journalist's introductory discourse, which prepares the reader's mind not to fully believe in what the hijab-wearing women think of their decision. On the contrary, the British hijab-wearing women's contribution was not manipulated because they write their own articles in the national press. Their de-activation of the stereotypical "Compulsivity" frame is not a passive negation. It is done through the activation of an alternative mental frame, the "Free-Choice" frame. This activation is based on the British national arguments of liberty and women's rights.

Framing Hijab Through "Concealment"

The experiential basis of the "Concealment" mental frame is derived from the hijab concealment of the body parts. This frame is another recycled frame from the colonial discourse. The "Concealment" is not strictly limited to the physical body. It extends to conceal other aspects of Muslim women, as we will see below. The "Concealment" framing in the colonial period aimed to construct an imaginary "curtain," as Meyda Yegenoglu (1998: 48–49) indicates. This curtain was used by the colonizer to hide the truth about the Orient in the past. It aims to turn the hijab-wearers into "an object of curiosity or marvel, and an exterior target or threat." But why would the twenty-first-century discourse cling to this curtain? What is the cognitive understanding of the "Concealment" mental frame in the British and Spanish press discourse?

Spanish "Concealment" Mental Frame

The equivalent Spanish verb to the English verb "to wear" is *llevar* and the equivalent Spanish verb to the English verb "to practice" is *practicar*. However, the Spanish discourse used none of these verbs to express the act of practicing the hijab. The used verbs, in a high frequency, are *"ocultar su cabello"* (to hide the hair), *"cubrir,"* and *"tapar"* (to cover). These vocabularies are the trigger for the re-activation of the "Concealment" frame. In the articles of El Mundo and El Pais published in 2015/2016, the use of these verbs is reduced, and the verb *llevar* appears, yet, La Vanguardia maintains the high frequency of the "Concealment" framing verbs.

In the exclusion school cases of hijab-wearing students, the trigger of the conflict is the limited understanding of hijab as a simple head covering that conceals the hair.

Understanding the hijab as simply a headcover strips away the first and foremost criteria or the practice: a religious demand. The internal regulations of several Spanish schools prohibit covering the head for disciplinary reasonings. When the school direction goes behind the confined "Concealment" frame and interpret hijab through the "Religiosity" frame, the conflict is resolved, and an extension "except for a religious motive" is added to the internal school regulation. The conflict is solved in Shaima Saidini's case (Girona, 2007) and Usera school's case (Madrid, 2011). However, when the school direction and/or school council's understanding of the hijab was strictly confined to the (hair) "Concealment" frame, without giving a chance to other embodied understandings, the hijab might stand for, the conflict turned on fire. The hijab-wearing minors needed to change their schools, e.g., Najwa Al-Malha case (Madrid, 2010), Arteixo school case (Galicia, 2011), and Takwa Rejeb case (Valencia, 2016).

The (hair) "Concealment" framing of the schoolgirls' hijab extends to conceal the personality of the hijab-wearers along with their human aspect. The "Concealment" frame takes away the significant contributions of the hijab-wearers. Their narrative on the exclusion experience does not seem necessary. In most cases, they are not interviewed to hear their story or to understand their practice. The (hair) "Conceal-ment" mental frame in the school cases justifies the absence of significant repre-sentations and/or valuable interventions of hijab-wearers in the public discourse. In school cases, Najwa Al-Malha was not interviewed nor her motivations of the practice were investigated (Sotero and Bécares, 2010a), (Del Barrio 2010a), (Belvar 2010), (Figueras, 2011c), and (Álvarez and Cembrero, 2010a; Álvarez and Garriga, 2010c). The same concealment of the "covered" student is detected in Arteixo case (Galicia, 2011) (Obelleiro, 2011e). In workplace exclusion (Peral, 2010) and (Belaza 2010), the excluded lawyer was completely absent as well.

In the political and social debate, the "Concealment" frame is equally re-activated recurrently across the three newspapers. The debate of the hijab revolves around the right of Muslim women "to cover" or "not to cover" (Carbajos, 2008) and (Moliner, 2004), the first Muslim delegate in Ceuta has her hair "covered" (Abad 2007a), the right of "covered" Muslim women to "uncover" (Del Barrio, 2008), (Espinosa, 2010), (Caballero, 2010) and (Gallego-Díaz, 2010); and the restriction on human rights imposed by the practice of "covering" (Carbajos, 2008). In the political and social debate, hijab-wearers are concealed from the scene, too. They are dehumanized and described as "Islamic women" in El Mundo,[71] in El País,[72] and in La Vanguardia.[73] The adjective "Islamic" is normally associated with objects, not humans, such as an Islamic Center, an Islamic organization, an Islamic Law, and an Islamic veil. The link between "Islamic" and "Muslim women" could be one of two options, none of them is positive: it is either objectifying the "concealed" Muslim women, i.e., to

[71] De Ganuza (2008).

[72] Espinosa (2010).

[73] Quelart, Raquel, *He conocido a mujeres muy felices detrás del velo.* http://www.lavanguar dia.com/salud/20111212/54239960536/beatriz−goyoaga−entrevista−meditacion−velo.html (12 December 2011).

dehumanize them and frame them as objects who have no personality, no active mind, insignificant as Yegenoglu mentioned above; or to link, indirectly, female Muslim students to the Islamization and Islamic (political or extremists) movements; the enemy.[74]

In El País, the re-activation of the "Concealment" frame of the hijab overlaps with the re-activation of the "Concealment" frame of the hijab-wearers, which I will discuss in the next section. In this chapter, I will spot the light on the (Identity) "Concealment" framing of the hijab in the Spanish press. The hijab-wearing women before 2015/2016 are mainly anonymous due to their concealed hair. And I refer only to the hair, not to the face-covering in the case of full veil practices. For example, in El País, the debate on the enforced hijab, the "Compulsivity" frame, included Najat El-Hashmi, Leonor Morino, Randa Achmawi, Siham Habchi, and Nawal El Saadawi; all are Academic and/or head of social organizations and movements. Most importantly, they all support the stereotypical frames on the hijab practice, which the newspaper intends to assert.[75] The hijab wearers and hijab supporters were the following: The first is an anonymous "Spanish Muslim." The second voice is another anonymous voice of a 20-year-old girl of a Palestinian father and Spanish mother. The third voice is by another anonymous migrant woman; she works in domestic cleaning per hour. These three voices were added in the article to create an, apparently, an objective debate about hijab with diverse pros and contra contributions on the topic.

To sum up, the Spanish embodied framing of the hijab is frequently limited to the act of covering the head and hair. This does not indicate that it is not framed, at all, as a religious practice. As we will see below, it is sometimes framed through "Religiosity." The "Concealment" framing of the hijab is clear in the used linguistic expressions to refer to the practice. El Mundo and El País show a tendency to replace the conceal-ment verbs by dressing up or practicing verbs in the 2015/2016 discourse. However, La Vanguardia shows consistency in re-activating this frame. The re-activation of the (hair) "Concealment" framing of the hijab is the trigger of the exclusion cases at the public schools. Religious liberty is guaranteed in Spanish public school, yet the internal regulation prohibits the head covering to identify the students. The "Con-cealment" mental framing of the hijab overlaps with the "Concealment" frame of the hijab-wearing women in the national press. The hijab-wearing women in the discourse before 2015/2016 are anonymous, and their contributions are insignifi-cant. The "Concealment" mental frame of the hijab extends to conceal the women behind it. Hijab-wearers are dehumanized and objectified in the national press before the 2015/2016 discourse.

---

[74] KhirAllah (2015).
[75] Galarraga (2010).

British "Concealment" Mental Frame of the Hijab

The linguistic expressions used to re-activate the "Concealment" frame of the hijab are not limited to the verb "covered up" as in the Spanish discourse. Diverse linguistic expressions assert the "Concealment" frame of the hijab and all types of veiling such as: "swathed" and "masked" (Marin, 2004), "large swathes of cloth" (Chowdhury, 2005), "shrouded" (Malik, 2006), "Islamic headgear" and "Islamic dress drag" (Burchill, 2011), "abbreviated drapery" (Bennett, 2004), "enveloping folds" (Orr, 2005) and "the life of layering" (Kossaibati, 2009) because, as we have mentioned before, the debate of hijab in the British press conflates all Muslim dress together. Kate Melville opines, in *The Guardian*, that the hijab-covering causes movement restrictions. Kate indicates that she is "always amazed by hijab-wearing women's limited capacity for hearing what's going on around them, stepping out into traffic, apparently oblivious of other people."

The "Concealment" mental frame of the hijab is shared with both for and against hijab discourse. In a difference to the Spanish (Identity) "Concealment" framing, both British social verities agree on the covered entity; it's the Muslim women's sexuality. Yet, each discourse re-activates and nourishes the (Sexuality) "Concealment" mental frame differently.

However, the Spanish(Hair) "Concealment" framing of the hijab appears once in the selected data in the exclusion case of Bushra Noah (London, 2007). Due to the professional requirements (hairdresser), employees are demanded to display their physical image, especially the hair. Sarah Desrosiers, the salon owner, understood the hijab as a simple headcover "if someone came in wearing a baseball hat or a cowboy hat, I'd tell them to take it off while they are working." Desrosiers states, "I sell image – it's very important - and I would expect a hairstylist to display her hair because I need people to be drawn in off the street." In this case, the hijab is framed as a (Hair) "Concealment" practice in the British press.

(Sexuality) "Concealment" in the hijab-contra discourse is understood as "offensive," "discriminatory," "affronting," and "degrading" for women who practice it. For example, in The Time Online, Minette Marin indicates that "the sight in this country of women, particularly of young girls, heavily swathed and covered up as if they were not capable of going about as freely as a man. That there is something about them needs to be hidden. It is genuinely offensive both to the informed and to the uninformed. The big headscarf is not quite so startling as the enormous burqa or the birdlike Arab masks, but its message is the same."[76] Marine stigmatizes all the veiling forms under the same stereotypical framing: (Offensive) (Sexual) "Concealment" frame. In *The Guardian*. Samra Mursaleen describes the hijab as "an affront to women,"[77] and Natasha Walter asks, "why should we show respect to people

---

[76] Marin (2004).

[77] Mursaleen (2010).

who would love to restore female invisibility in this country?"[78] All these narrations activate, directly or not, the (Offensive) (Sexual) "Concealment" framing of the practice.

In *The Independent*, Joan Smith associates the "Religiosity" frame of the veil to the (Sexuality) "Concealment" frame. She states that there is "abundant evidence" that "the stricter forms of Islam have major problems with sexuality.[79]" In the jilbab case, Smith states that both Begum, who chooses jilbab for school, and Cherie Booth, Tony Blair's wife who supported Begum's right to wear a jilbab, "should acquaint themselves with the sexuality disgust expressed by Islamic authorities who argue in favor of covering girls and women. They condemn women who 'flaunt' themselves in push-up bras.[80]" Smith's discourse stigmatizes the Islamic perspective on sexuality visibility in the public sphere as misogynic and problematic. While Scott opines that the Islamic perspective is another ontological understanding of the pros and cons of the sexuality visibility; in which Islam provides potential solutions (see Chapter 3).

In the re-activation of the British "Concealment" mental frame, the hijab wearers are dehumanization, and their potentials are underestimated. For example, in *The Independent*, Marie Dhumieres criticized the French attention to the fabric and the carelessness toward the women who practice it. Yet, Dhumieres does not picture the hijab-wearers as practitioners. She introduces them as hidden objects under the hijab. She states, "French should maybe take some time to think about why they really care so much, and maybe forget for a second what they believe 'the hijab' represents and think about the women under them." Hijab-wearers acknowledge being dehumanized after practicing the hijab. They explained that they are ignored by their friends or by the business owners after they started the practice. For example, Soha Sheikh indicates that "a lot of friends started to ignore" her after she dons the veil.[81] The H&M model Mariah Idrissi, a model for H&M, indicates that because of the (Sexuality) "Concealment" mental frame of the hijab, she was not taken seriously in the fashion world before. She states, "It always feels like women who wear hijab are ignored when it comes to fashion. Our style, in a way, hasn't really mattered, so it's amazing that a brand that is big has recognized the way we wear hijab."[82]

British Muslim hijab-wearing women de-activate the (Offensive) (Sexuality) "Concealment" framing through the activation of an alternative frame. They agree on the (Sexuality) "Concealment" framing of the hijab, but they consider it (Empowering) and not (Offensive). In *The Guardian*, *The Independent* and BBC, Hijab-wearing women activate the (Empowering) (Sexuality) "Concealment" frame of the hijab independently from its religious references. Very few hijab-wearers associate the "Religiosity" frame of the hijab with the (Empowering) (Sexuality) "Concealment" frame. For example, in *The Guardian*, Samra Mursaleen discusses the question of sexual equality from an authoritative position as Muslim, and as hijab-wearer, she

---

[78] Walter (2004) and Bennett (2004).

[79] Smith (2006a).

[80] Smith (2006b).

[81] Akbar (2010d).

[82] Sanghani (2015a).

states, "from my point as a Muslim woman" and "in my experience."[83] Mursaleen argues that "it is the veil which affords that (sexuality) equality." She continues that the hijab is "an empowering force rather than an oppressive one." The writer maintains that "(hijab-wearers) are in full command of their bodies. With their outer beauty hidden from view, what is exposed instead is their mind and inner qualities and so in any interaction with men they are valued not just for how they look. This attire also sends out a message that a woman is chaste and modest and that she does not want her sexuality to enter into the interaction in the slightest degree." For Mursaleen, the (Sexuality) "Concealment" is not only (Empowering) but also (Liberating).

Similar activation of the (Empowering) (Sexuality) "Concealment" mental frame is found in Natasha Walter's article in the same newspaper. Walter re-activates the "Discrimination" frame of "covering up" through contrasting the practice and the liberation trajectory of western feminists.[84] After that, Walter interviews a hijab-wearing woman in London demonstrations against the French ban. Her interviewee Salma Yaqoob, the chair of Birmingham Stop the War Coalition, asserts the (Liberating) (Sexuality) "Concealment" frame. She states that hijab-wearers "are valued for their intellectual rather than their looks which is actually very liberating." In *The Guardian*, Rania Cllr Khan indicates that she "feel(s) liberated from worry about hair, clothing and makeup."[85] In *The Independent*, the interviewee Denise Horsley, 26-year-old convert and a dance teacher, explains her experience in assimilating modesty as follow: "I started dressing more modestly - foregoing low cut tops and short skirts - but before I donned a headscarf I had to make sure I was comfortable on the inside before turning my attention to the outside. Now I feel completely protected in my headscarf. People treat you with a new level of respect, they judge you by your words and your deeds, not how you look."[86] In BBC, the hijab-wearing student, Rumana Habeeba, refers that the "hijab allows interactions between men and women to be free and safe. Relationships can then be based on intellect and nothing else."[87] In the same article, Pharmacist Saba Naeem states that the hijab aims "to preserve a woman's modesty. It means you are not just a sex symbol - you have something to offer other than just your looks."

(Empowering) (Sexuality) "Concealment" mental frame of the hijab is activated as a counter-mental frame of "Submission" and "Discrimination" framing of the practice. Hijab-wearing writers and interviewees did not passively negate these stereotypical frames. Instead, they provide wholly new and contrastive arguments for readers to think critically about.

Similar argumentation appears in Nadiya Takolia's article in *The Guardian* titled "*The hijab has liberated me from society's expectations of women*."[88] Takolia explains her motivation of the hijab practice, "reading feminist literature and

---

[83] Mursaleen (2010).

[84] Walter (2004).

[85] Cllr Khan (2006).

[86] Carter (2009).

[87] Dear (2004).

[88] Takolia (2010).

researching stories of women's lives in the sex industry. From perfume and clothes ads to children's dolls and X-Factor finals, you don't need to go far to see that the woman/sex combination is everywhere." Takolia decided to veil to "reject" the social expectation of her as a woman; she states "It makes many of us feel like a pawn in society's beauty game – ensuring that gloss in my hair, the glow in my face and trying to attain that (non-existent) perfect figure. Subconsciously, I tried to avoid these demands – wearing a hat to fix a bad-hair day, sunglasses and specs to disguise a lack of makeup, baggy clothes to disguise my figure. It was an endless and tiresome effort to please everyone else." She extends that the modest criteria and the rejection of sexuality submission of women can be adopted as an ideology by non-Muslims, and it is not necessarily linked to religion; she detached the practice from the "Religiosity" mental frame.

In *The Guardian*, the comic writer and aid worker Shaista Aziz wrote an article about "the best comments 'whiteys' make over the years to hijab."[89] She listed six situations, only one of them (the final one) is not made by a "whitey." Out of the five cases, two occurred with women and the other three with men. The focus of the white men's comments was related to Aziz's sexuality concealment. The first one is an unknown "40s who (she) has never met before." Aziz narrates: "(he) grabs hold of my shoulders. Before he moves into plant kisses in my checks". He justified his act "I have never kissed a hijabi women before." The second one is "a male boss leaning in very close to (me) and lowering his voice to sound seductive 'so Aziz. I am ever going to see your hair?" The third one is when a male workmate told her, "I can see a bit of your hair. Are you trying to flirt with me? Do you need to go home and pray now that I have seen your hair?" These comments show that those men find it difficult to assume that they are denied their granted prerogative to see the physical shape of Aziz. Western men are used to having the open visual access to women's sexuality in the public sphere. They are accustomed to look unrestrictedly to the women's hair, curves, or hips. Yet, the hijab concealment of the body parts reduces the men's visual access to Muslim women's bodies to those parts that the woman decides to make visible to men. This practice decreases the men's authorities and increases the women's authorities over their bodies (see Chapter 3).

The contradiction between the re-activation of the (Offensive) (Sexuality) "Concealment" and the activation of the (Empowering) (Sexuality) "Concealment" framing of the hijab emerges from the contradiction on sexuality interpretation in the public sphere. Although many western feminist movements criticized the sexual objectification of women, they fall short of accepting the hijab (Empowering) (Sexuality) "Concealment" framing. As Scott (2009: 156) indicates, when the debate is on the hijab, equality is used as synonymous with "sexuality emancipation" and displaying the women's bodies. Lakoff (2014) explains that when human beings have contrastive mental frames about the same concept (or social phenomena), they, eventually, opt to stick to what their brains are used to because the change the mental frame of any social concept is exhausting. In this case, they stick to the colonial stereotypical framing of the hijab; "Discrimination," "Submission," and (Offensive)

---

[89] Aziz (2014).

(Sexuality) "Concealment" framings. The hijab-wearers activation of the (Empowering) (Sexuality) "Concealment" framing is based on the western feminists' arguments on liberation and women's freedom. Yet, the against-hijab discourse ignores the potential reasoning in the hijab-wearers' arguments and casts the "Concealment" frame as an (Offensive) to women. In the selected data, hijab opposers decrease the credibility of (Empowering) (Sexuality) "Concealment" mental frame. For example, Kate Melville, in *The Guardian*, asks Jana Kosaibati, who wrote about shopping tips for modest cloth, "isn't wearing 'style' or 'beautiful' clothes a challenge to the rules?[90]" A similar question appears in the same newspaper by Yasmin Alibhai-Brown. She disputes that "some young Muslim women argue that veils liberate them from a modern culture that objectifies and sexualizes women. That argument is appealing; but if credible, why would so many hijabis dress in tight jeans and clinging tops, and why would so many Muslim women flock to have liposuction or breast enhancements?"[91] Although these arguments are appealing and in need to be answered and discussed, the attention here is the constant balming of hijab-wearers of other cases, such as forced hijab cases, or diversities that exist in the practice.

To sum up, the British "Concealment" mental frame of the hijab is not limited to the hair covering. Although this understanding appears once, it was due to the contextual workplace exclusion in a hairdresser salon. The British "Concealment" framing in both pro and contra-hijab discourse (re)activates the (Sexuality) "Concealment." Yet, the embodied understanding of the (Sexuality) "Concealment" varies within these two discourses. The against-hijab discourse re-activates the colonial (Offensive) (Sexuality) "Concealment" mental frame of the hijab while the pro-hijab discourse, the discourse of British hijab-wearers, activates the (Empowering) (Sexuality) "Concealment" framing. The hijab opposer journalists deform the Islamic perspective on women's sexuality in the public sphere and stigmatize the Islamic religion as misogynic. The hijab-wearers depend on the Islamic approach in concealing the sexuality identity in the public sphere. However, they do not necessarily activate the "Religiosity" framing. They consider the practice empowering for women because it provides them with total authority over their bodies.

The hijab-wearers were dehumanized in the re-activation of the (Offensive) (Sexuality) "Concealment" mental frame. They were referred to as objects under the hijab. The contra-hijab discourse recycled this mental frame to empower the "Submission" framing of the hijab. Hijab-wearers activate the (Empowering) (Sexuality) "Concealment" mental frame as an alternative framing of the following stereotypical frames: "Discrimination," "Submission," and (Offensive) (Sexuality) "Concealment" mental frames. They used the western arguments on freedom and women's liberty to empower this frame; it is to say, the negation of the stereotypical frames was not limited to passive negation.

---

[90] Melville (2009).

[91] Alibhai–Brown (2015).

Cross-Cultural Analysis

There are significant differences between the re-activation of the "Concealment" mental frame across the Spanish press and the British press. The "Concealment" framing of the hijab is confined to the hair covering in the Spanish press discourse; such framing is the trigger of exclusion cases at Spanish public schools. The linguistic expressions that re-activate this frame are limited and repetitive. In contrast, the British re-activation of this frame evolves around (Sexuality) "Concealment" and not limited to the hair covering. Yet, the embodied understanding of the (Sexuality) "Concealment" varies within the British discourse. The against-hijab discourse re-activates the colonial (Offensive) (Sexuality) "Concealment" mental frame of the hijab. In contrast, the pro-hijab discourse, the discourse of British hijab-wearers, activates the (Empowering) (Sexuality) "Concealment" mental frame.

In both press discourses, Muslim women are dehumanized and underestimated in the re-activation of the "Concealment" frame. They are referred to as an object behind or under the hijab. Yet, the Spanish "Concealment" mental frame conceals the identity and the voices of the hijab-wearing women. They are excluded from the public debate on the hijab. Even in 2015/2016, where hijab-wearers gain some visibility in the press discourse, their contributions were short and controlled by the journalist's narrative. The British dehumanization of the hijab-wearers in the re-activation of the "Concealment" framing of the hijab is not a concealment of the hijab-wearers visibility because they are engaged in the civil, professional, and public life. They publish articles in the mainstream press to express their own mental frames on the practice and other diverse aspects of life. The British dehumanization of hijab-wearers is limited to attaching objective attributes to the hijab-wearers.

In the Spanish press, there is no significant de-activation of this stereotypical mental frame. The invisibility of the hijab-wearers is an outcome of the "Concealment" framing of the hijab. On the contrary, the British hijab-wearing women are involved in the public debate on hijab, and they de-activate the stereotypical frame by activating (Empowering) (Sexuality) "Concealment" framing. The importance of this activation is an outcome of the cultural diversity in the British public sphere. It enriches the population's perspectives on the diverse patterns of dealing with sexuality, and it implants in them the respect of the diverse form to negotiate women's sexuality in the public sphere.

Framing Hijab Through "Religiosity"

The hijab, as a practice, is a religious one (Ch: II). As a sign, the hijab is not a meaningless symbol that needs an interpretation. It is a religious, transnational, sign first and foremost (Ch: III). The "Religiosity" frame of the hijab is not recycled because in the colonial discourse, the practice was not linked mainly to Islamic religion. It was better introduced as a part of cultural traditions to the European audience. At the same time, the (neo) colonial era, Islam, under the term of Islamism or Islamist movements, was not shaped yet as the shared international enemy as it is in this century.

Spanish "Religiosity" Mental Frame of Hijab

The "Religiosity" mental frame of the hijab is activated in the exclusion cases defended by the lawyer Ivan Jimenez Aybar, a doctor professor of ecclesiastical rights in Barcelona. He defended Najwa Al-Malha's right to practice the hijab at school in 2010. After this case, he became the lawyer of many excluded hijab-wearing students, such as in Arteixo's case (Galicia, 2011, Usera's Case (Madrid, 2011), and Hasna Isslal's case (Burgos, 2011).

Jimenez Aybar is the first who activates the "Religiosity" frame of the hijab in the selected Spanish press discourse. He activates it, repetitively, in all the cases, in all the articles, and across both newspapers, El País and El Mundo. Jiménez Aybar argues that the hijab is not a simple headcover that conceals the student's identity. He asserts that the hijab forms part of the religious and social identity of its wearers. He argues that the religious-social identity is acknowledged by the Interior Ministry that accepts hijab in the national identification documents. Aybar constantly points out that an internal school regulation cannot be above the Constitutional Law of religious liberty. Accordingly, the ban of the hijab at school goes against the Constitution and it is illegal (Figueras, 2011a, b, c, d), (Álvarez, 2011a, c), (Obelleiro, 2011a, c). The "Religiosity" frame, activated by Jimenez Aybar, repeals the "Concealment" framing of the hijab, which was the rationale behind the hijab ban at some public schools.

Before 2015/2016, there was no coherent activation of the "Religiosity" mental frame by hijab-wearing students due to their limited participation in the articles that covers their exclusion. In the case of Hasna Isslal (Burgos, 2011), El Mundo did not interview the student.[92] The debate was limited to the arguments of the school direction and the lawyer, whether it was legitimate to ban the practice or not. On the contrary, El País interviewed the student in her house; however, in the next chapter, we will see how this interview asserted stereotypical framing on Hijab-wearing women. The student activated the "Religiosity" frame, briefly explaining her veiling motivations: "first is my religion."[93] This is the only detected quotation or a reference to the "Religiosity" frame by hijab-wearers in exclusion cases before 2015/2016 in both newspapers. The hijab-wearers who were interviewed in some articles (Álvarez, 2011b), (Figueras, 2011a), (Abad 2007b), (Barik Edidi 2009), and (Carranco 2010); were asked about the incident of the exclusion, mostly introduced to assert stereotypical frames on them, such as the presence of the father next to the student in the activation of "Compulsivity" frame.

---

[92]Figueras (2011d).

[93]Álvarez (2011c).

In the inclusion case of Fatima Hamed, the first hijab-wearing delegate in Ceuta, there were no references on her hijab motivations even though her hijab was the prominent issue of the article.[94] The hijab motivation was not covered in the case of the two sisters Nawal and Nahed Amar.[95] As Ceuta is framed from a distant position in the Spanish public discourse (see Chapter 1), the founded discourse considers the hijab as a peculiar aspect in Ceuta's social frame.

The activation of the "Religiosity" frame by the discriminated hijab-wearing students appears in the 2015/2106 exclusion cases: Takwa Rejeb, who was excluded from her institute (Valencia, 2016) and Ana Saidi Rodriguez who was excluded from her workplace (Palma de Mallorca, 2016). The significant shift in the discursive strategies in these cases is mainly the visibility of the hijab-wearer protagonists in the discourse. They argue and defend their own mental frames of the hijab. In Valencia case, covered in EL Mundo by Inma Lindón, Rejeb indicates that the internal regulation of the institute should include "respect to the other, to religious liberty and to learn how to coexist (with difference)."[96] At the end of the article Monica Oltra, the vice-president of the Consell in Valencia, declares that "hijab is a religious, culture and a gender sign, similar to the pendant we put to girls and not to boy." These two activations of the "Religiosity" frame indirectly re-activates the "Othering" mental frames at once, e.g., "the other" and "we." However, this re-activation of the "Othering" frame is not exclusive; it is inclusive of the difference.

Ana Saidi Rodriguez activates the "Religiosity" frame to assert her right to hijab in the Spanish Constitution. Yet, both El Mundo and El País employ Saidi Rodriguez's "Religiosity" frame to justify the decision of the Company, Acciona, which asserted the "acconfessional politics of the company."[97] En El Mundo, Irene Velasco asserts the "Religiosity" frame of Saida practice in order to make it easy for the reader to understand Acciona's exclusion of the employee. Velasco reasons that "hijab, the veil that is practiced by Muslim women who follow the religious precepts that Islam dictates, causes them severe problems at work." Accordingly, the journalist stigmatizes the practice as problematic, shifting the reader's attention away from Acciona's conflictive attitude in refusing the hijab visibility between their employees. In El País, Lucia Bohorquez quotes Acciona's assertion on the company "neutral professional image," which legitimates their exclusion of hijab practice. However, Saidi Rodriguez asserts earlier that "along the last couple of years, the company allowed crosses, tattoos and pendulous. They have never said anything."[98] Acciona's lawyer, Tania Hierro, argues that "to ban the veil of Saidi is legitimate and it does not violate any right." In these two cases, we can notably realize that the activation of the "Religiosity" framing by Spanish Muslim hijab-wearing women is used, by the journalist or by the entity, to justify the exclusion in the 2015/2016 discourse.

---

[94] Abad (2007a.

[95] Abad (2007b).

[96] Lidón (2016).

[97] Bohorquez (2016 and Velasco (2016).

[98] Bohorquez (2016).

In the social and political discourse, the "Religiosity" frame is well activated, attacked, and, then, de-activated. In El Mundo, this frame appears only once in Rosa Meneses' article titled *"What is the origin and the meaning of the veil?"*[99] Meneses intends to figure out the truth about the practice as it turns to be "a European issue where prejudice and stereotypes affect the debate." She starts the article from the famous *hijab* semantic meaning, then, includes quotations from the Quran (surah: 24 and 33). Her interpretations of the Quranic text are the following: "Therefore, the Quran refers that women (have to) cover with a cloak '*jilbab*' to be recognized. Then, it is a matter of a social status of free women, in that era, to be different from slave women who were not allowed to wear jilbab". Meneses continues that the hijab in the "XX century and the first years of the XXI has become a key question of the emancipation of Muslim identity." So far, the activation of the "Religiosity" mental frame is shaky and faltering. No profound arguments are made. The religious embodied criteria of the hijab are located in the Quranic text and reduced to the *jilbab* and to the social status of "that period of time." The contemporary hijab is given an instrumental function: the "emancipation of Muslim identity." She does not refer to the identity that is being emancipated? The religious one or a social one? Meneses continues that "wearing the veil is a symbol of identity for women who live in occidental countries. They use it as a way to be faithful to their origin, far away from their land." Successfully, Meneses de-activates the shaky "Religiosity" frame (which is transnational) and re-activates the "Othering" mental frame of the hijab linking the practice to the migrant home-sick women; stigmatizing all the hijab decisions of converts and second or third generations, as foreigners.

El País activates more frequently the "Religiosity" frame of the hijab. The purpose behind this activation varies, yet it always works for empowering recycled stereotypical frames of the practice. Besides, the "Religiosity" mental frame of the practice is not limited to the hijab. It overlaps all veiling styles together in the social and political discourse, and it serves well as a trigger to activate the (Extremist) "Religiosity" mental frame. For example, Solidad Gallego-Diaz supports the school's right to exclude the hijab-wearing students because of the internal ban law of head covering. The structure of this article is confusing. Although the focus of the article, which consists of 671 words, apparently is directed to the hijab exclusion, the discourse dedicates the first four paragraphs to the full veil outside Spain. The journalist links this religious practice to extremism three times in these three paragraphs (349 words). After that, the journalist dedicates one paragraph for the urgent need to ban the full veil in Spain (81 words). The last two paragraphs (229 words) discuss the right of Spanish schools to preserve their internal rules untouched. In a similar activation to (Extremist) "Religiosity" frame, Gallego-Diaz starts her article introducing Houda Shaarawi, who always fought against Burka and niqab because they are considered "an imposition destined to extremist ideology."[100] She backs up Shaarawi's interpretation: "(the full veil) is a political tendency of right extremism […] for many of them (female form *muchas*) it is simply a sort of uniform to proclaim a very concrete

---

[99]Meneses (2010.

[100]Gallego−Díaz (2010).

militant ideology." The mix between the full veil and hijab is not in vain. It is meant to classify the hijab in the "bottom list"; the journalist continues: "the veil that covers only the hair does not provoke any real conflict."

A direct activation of the (Extremist) "Religiosity" frame in hijab debate is found in Rosa Montero's article published in 2010.[101] Montero reflects on the Bishops Conference that supported POSE position which defended the "use of the Islamic veil" as part of the religious liberty in Spain. The journalist asks: "do not they think that there is something frankly negative in defense of the extremity of hijab?" The use of "extremity" as an adjective to the practice stigmatizes it as a sign of religious extremism. Ana Carabajos activates, too, the (Extremist) "Religiosity" frame in the subtitle: "The Islamic veil that the minister Aído criticizes wins visibility among youth- for tradition, but also as a militant gesture." The association between the attribute "Islamic" and expressions of militancy activates the (Extremist) "Religiosity" frame in the readers' perception of the hijab visibility in the public sphere.

Another employment of the "Religiosity" mental frame in the social and political debate in El País is promoting the need to pass a ban law on religious signs at schools, imitating the 2004 French ban (Etxenike, 2004), (Carbajos 2008), (Sahuquillo, 2008), (Caballero 2010) and (Galarraga, 2010). Naiara Galarraga discusses the pros and contra of the 2004 French ban through the activation of the "Religiosity" frame. Galarraga indicates that Sami Nair, a French essayist; Mohamed Bensalah, a professor at Oran University (Argelia); and Nawal El Saadawi, an Egyptian writer; three of them "reject the Islamic veil and, of course, any other religious symbol." Such discourse discusses the hijab as the central problematic religious sign to be banned; then, it refers to other religious signs as an extension that aims to hide the racist aspect of the discussion. Concha Caballero takes advantage of the "Religiosity" frame to criticize the State's relationship with the Christian church and to highlight the government inability to separate religion from the State as France did: "If we were able to derogate the [Concordato con la Santa Sede], place order for the confessionalism principle at schools, eliminate the religious symbols in Administration and limit back religion to faith and consciousness sphere -where it was not supposed to be allowed to leave- we would have the authority to demand the end of any submissive expression, of difference or of religious symbolism." Caballero's recognition of the "Religiosity" frame of the hijab is activated only to assert the need to conceal religion (the hijab) from the public sphere as France does.

Ana Carabajos activates the "Religiosity" frame is politicized. It is to say, Carabajos activates this frame on political references: "political-religious ebb and flow," "in Europe, far from the political and religious issues, the veil is a fashion that sweeps [arrasa]" and "similar arguments are heard from the mouth of women from particular political trace or religious passion." In this article, the hijab-wearer's activation of the "Religiosity" frame is done by the wife of a Hezbollah clergyman,

---

[101] Montero (2010).

Samah: "the religion is a determinant factor." Carabjo's article activates the (Polit-ical) "Religiosity" frame of the hijab, which is a critical cognitive basis in framing the (political) enemy of the State we have mentioned in the first chapter.

In La Vanguardia in 2015/2016, the "Religiosity" mental frame is activated by Carina Farreras' "The New Meaning of the Veil: Increased the number of Muslims (female) with academic title who want to express their religion."[102] The link between "academic" formation and "religious" practices in the title suggests certain incom-patibility between both. I will go into the details of the activation of the "Igno-rance" mental frame of the hijab-wearing women in the following chapter. Yet, I will focus here on the de-activation of the "Religiosity" mental frame of the hijab. Farreras quotes Spanish university professors Silvia Carrasco, a doctor in Social anthropology at UAB, Dolores Bramón, a doctor in Semitic Philosophy in UB, and a "major expert in the topic in Catalunya." Carrasco and Bramón agree that Muslim women mistakenly think of the hijab as "a religious" practice; the truth is the hijab is "an identity or cultural affirmation." The declaration of these non-Muslim women (secular-authoritative) on the origin of the hijab is more reliable than the testimony of the hijab-wearing women (religious-less authoritative). Their declarations de-activate the "Religiosity" frame of the hijab and activate the "Othering" frame: it is the traditions of "others." Farreras continues that "(in Spain) the lack of clear criteria on the manifestation of religious signs […] causes harm to the girls who want to wear the veil." Ferreras de-activates the "Religiosity" frame of the hijab by experts in a direct reference to the hijab and activates the same frame to refer to the lack of Spanish political legislation on religious symbols in the public sphere. In the second part of the article, Ferreras interviews two Spanish academic hijab-wearing youth: Najat Driouech and Ramia Chaoui. Both explain the hijab motivations as personal decisions related to religious and spiritual factors. Both activate the "Religiosity" frame: "spiritual decision," "modesty for God," and having "a [*revelador*] dream indicates veiling." However, this activation has been weakened by the introduction of the article, which I explained before. The introduction casts the hijab-wearers as deluded by the original meaning of the practice.

In El Mundo 2015/2016 discourse, the "Religiosity" frame is activated by the hijab-wearing journalist Amanda Figueras. She is an ex-journalist in El Mundo, and she narrates her experience in converting to Islam without converting the hijab to the main plot of the article; she doesn't write a lot about it, almost only 229 out of 2259 words. She states: "It is my personal choice […] the veil is only a detail. Quran speaks a little about it. But once again, we hold fast to this issue. We forget that Islam is held in the heart, not in the outfit."[103] Figueras' activates the "Religiosity" frame at a minimal level, and she asserts the free-choice references. The "less religious" and "more personal" assertion is a counter-argument against the ban supporters' who constrain the hijab framing to "Religiosity."

To sum up, the "religiosity" mental frame of the hijab in the Spanish press is activated by secular journalists more than being activated by hijab-wearing women.

---

[102]Farreras (2016).

[103]Figueras (2015).

Before 2015/2016, hijab-wearers in the exclusion cases were not asked about the hijab's motivations or what the hijab means for them. All the interviews in El Mundo and El País evolve around the exclusion storytelling. In the cases after that date, hijab-wearers gain more space in the national press; they start to activate the "Religiosity" frame on their hijab decision.

The secular activation of the "Religiosity" mental frame is shaky and cloudy. It is mainly activated in the articles which hypothetically aim is to question the original meaning of the practice away from stereotypes and prejudice. However, it is not based on religious texts or religious criteria. It is based on what the journalist thinks of the religious meaning of the hijab. The Spanish hijab-wearing women were not given an authoritative voice to speak out about their "Religiosity" framing without discursive manipulation by the journalists. The only article in which a hijab-wearing woman has an authoritative voice on her hijab decision is in El Mundo in 2015. It is written by a Muslim ex-journalist who slightly activates the "Religiosity" frame and asserts the free choice of the practice.

The activation of the "Religiosity" frame in the social and political discourse is used to defend a contra-hijab argument. El Mundo (before 2015/2016) and La Vanguardia (in 2015/2016) activate the "Religiosity" frame to empower the "Other-ing" framing of the hijab. While El País activates the (Extremist) "Religiosity" frame and the (Political) "Religiosity" frame of the practice. Both framings blame the government of her incapability to ban the practice as the French government did. They are essential cognitive structures in the process of framing the enemy of the State. The (Political) and (Extremist) "Religiosity" frames are activated in the process of using the hijab as an instrument-of-fear. As Ramadan indicates, such framing is part of hasty announces that lack social awareness and in-depth analysis. Such discourse casts the hijab-wearing women as fundamentalists, extremists with a polit-ical (foreign) agenda, and it announces them a threat to be protecting the nation from.

British "Religiosity" Mental Frame of Hijab

The "Religiosity" frame is activated and de-activated by direct linguistic expressions in the British press. It is not pure religious framing. As in the Spanish press, the "Religiosity" framing of the British hijab is politicized. BBC, *The Guardian*, and *The Independent* activate the (Political) "Religiosity" frame and the (Extremist) "Religiosity" frame of the hijab in the justification of the French ban law. British readers are open to diversity and would not easily assimilate the french governmental hegemony on the French Muslim women's vestment (Wyatt, 2003), (Walter, 2004), and (Riddell, 2003). The British discourse links extremism and fundamentalism to the French hijab to give legitimacy to the French ban. Thus, the law is announced as a political response to the Islamist movements. Caroline Wyatt, on BBC, cites UMP deputy Jerome Riviere who declares that "the law is not about suppressing religious freedom [...] we do not have a problem with religion in France, we have problem with the political use by a minority of religion. France's secular nature was being challenged by small minority of hardline Islamist. We have to give a political answer to what is a political problem."[104] In this citation, the framing of the French ban is clearly framed as a needed procedure to protect national security. In The Times Online, Marin Minette refers to the tension between the hijab and the French values. It is "a challenge to laïcité" because "religion should be kept out of public life." She projects the French values on the British context, and she states that the debate on these values cannot be "complacent about." It is not because the United Kingdom accepts religious diversity. Instead, Marin criticized the "struggle to defend secularism," which she describes as useless as long as the government supports the church. She asserts the need to "defend" secularism in the United Kingdom because the "alternative is so dire." The alternatives are the "Islamists proposals" and "fundamental Christians" who abandon the universal principles of human rights. The result is a "struggle between militant forms of different religions over the final say on sexual relationships, crime and punishment, education and forging policy." Maine activation of the (Political) and (Extremist) "Religiosity" frame of the hijab visibility is not limited to Islam. It includes the Christian religion too. Mary Riddell, in *The Guardian*, activates, as well, the (Extremist) "Religiosity" frame in the French ban debate. She points out that Bernard Stasi's report "alludes grimly to 'extremist groups'."

In the debate on the British context, the (Extremist) "Religiosity" frame is activated through direct linguistic expressions as "radical Islamic," "fundamentalist," and "extreme Islam," along with reference to Hizb-ut-Tahrir and Al-Muhajiroun group in the discourse, which are introduced as radical Islamic groups. For example, in the case of Selena Sabeel (2004), covered in *The Times* Online, Minette Marin mentioned the "radical Islamic group Al-Muhajiroun" as a supportive group to hijab practice at the British school. The article revolves around religious freedom at British school and the need to draw "the line of tolerance."

The (Extremist) "Religiosity" frame is activated, too, in the British *jilbab* debate. In both jilbab cases, Some journalists assert the religious motivation of these young women; others stigmatize it as an extremist and radical practice. For example, in *The Independent*, Hester Lacey indicates that Shabina Begum "claimed" that she was denied her "right to education and to manifest her religious beliefs." In the same newspaper, Sara Cassidy cites Begum's description of her *jilbab* as an "adherence to"[105] her religion. In the other case of *jilbab* (2015), which is covered in *The Independent*, Jessica Ware introduced Ms. Tamanna Begum as "a devout Sunni Muslim." Ware explains that *jilbab* is a requirement of the Muslim girl's "morals and beliefs." The conflict occurs because it is "against her morals and beliefs" to wear a shorter garment and that she had suffered discrimination because of her "ethnic or cultural background." Joan Smith links Shabina Begum's "Religiosity" frame and extremism; Smith indicates that "Muslim extremists want a society in which women are denied the status of full citizens." She describes the House of Lord's

---

[104]Wyatt (2004).

[105]Cassidy (2005).

previous decision against Begum as needed: "the decision marked the moment in The United Kingdom when the state, faced by religious extremism, drew a line." The journalist concludes the article by empowering the (Extremist) "Religiosity" frame at schools: "Under a government that is recklessly expanding the number of faith schools, religious extremists have spotted an opportunity. As so often since Tony Blair became Prime Minister, it has been left to the House of Lords to act, halting a dangerous process under which fundamentalists seek to extend their influence on state education." The debate on the hijab automatically leads to the debate of extremism, unconsciously, turns to be a debate on (Muslim) religious visibility in the public sphere. In the same case, Marin Minette, in The Times Online, points out the support of the Al-Muhajiroun group to the jilbab case. She asserts the malicious orientations of the group: "It is striking that the demonstrators with leaflets outside the Luton school were from Al-Muhajiroun, the group which notoriously celebrated the slaughter of September 11 and which wants to establish a worldwide Islamic state."[106]

The (Extremist) "Religiosity" frame includes converts' hijab as well. In *The Independent*, Julie Burchill discusses the veil of Lauren Booth, "who now she can no longer make a shilling from being related by marriage to Tony Blair." Burchill tells that Booth works on an Iranian channel.[107] She quotes an Iranian website in the exile: "Has this woman gone mad? [...] In donning the hijab, she is kowtowing to the very fundamentalism." In the case of Erick Tazi (Liverpool, 2009) covered in *The Guardian*, the convert sued the hotel owners for calling her a "terrorist" because of her hijab.[108] The case of Tazi is an outcome of the activation of the (Extremist) "Religiosity" frame in the press. The Hotel owners interpreted Tazi's hijab sign as a religious extremist practice according to what they read in the press and they called her names accordingly.

However, In *The Independent*, Katey Guest and Merry Wyn Davies criticize the political use of the (Extremist) "Religiosity" frame of hijab.[109] They discuss the Home Office Minister Hazel Blears' declarations, which state that people of "Islamic appearance must accept being stopped and searched disproportionately- in the interest of public safety." Blears' declarations come after "Tony Blair talked of 'several hundred' people in Britain intent on terrorism." Both political declarations reflect the direct activation of the (Extremist) "Religiosity" frame of the hijab in the political discourse, which I will not go deep in it because the political discourse is not the focus of this book. But I would like to remind the reader that such discourse uses the hijab visibility in the Euro-public sphere as an instrument-of-fear in the political agenda (see Chapter 1). The interviewee, Inayat Bunglawala, a spokesman for the Muslim Council of the United Kingdom, responded that "it is hard to believe there are no other motives behind Hazel Blears' comments. Are they using Muslims as an

---

[106]Marin (2004).

[107]Burchill (2011).

[108]Carter (2009).

[109]Guest, Katey and Merry Wyn Davies, *The Muslims next door,* http://www.independent.co.uk/news/uk/this−britain/focus−the−muslims−next−door−527359.html (6 March 2005).

easy target to scare the public?" In BBC, Wyatt points out that excluding Muslims is what "drives some Muslims into the arms of Islamic fundamentalists."

From a different perspective, some hijab-wearing women activate the "Religiosity" mental frame of the hijab as an assertion on its trans-nationality as a religion. By which, They de-activate the "Othering" framing of the hijab as a regional-cultural specific (an outsider). In the activation of the "Religiosity" frame of the hijab, the hijab-wearers assert a religious territory-independent dimension in the hijab sign. For example, in BBC, Paula Dear interviews the pharmacist Saba Naeem who indicates that hijab "is a religious duty" and the microbiology student, Monowara Gani, who states that "the covering of the head is something that is commanded by God, not man […] I can't explain why, it's something between me and God. I think it was the best decision I ever made."[110] In Arifa Akbar's series of interviews in *The Independent*,[111] the interviewee Suha Shikh, a library assistant, frames the veil as "something in our religion," "my own choice," and "criteria I have to meet" (repeated twice). In The Standard,[112] the article covers the exclusion case of the stylist Bushra Noah in a job interview at a hairdressing salon in London. Noah narrates her veiling experience from the "Religiosity" frame: "wearing a headscarf is essential for my beliefs." Helen Carter, in *The Guardian*, cites Ericka Tazi's framing of her hijab: "it is part of my faith."[113] Carter refers to it as a "traditional Islamic dress" in the article rather than a regional-cultural dress.

At the same time, some hijab-wearers de-activate the "Religiosity" frame in *The Guardian* and *The Independent*. It is a counter-discourse aim to de-activate the (Extremist) "Religiosity" framing in the mainstream discourse. De-activating the "Religiosity" frame of the hijab is normally associated with a justification that provides readers with alternative reasoning on the hijab. For example, in *The Guardian*, Nadiya Takolia does not limit the de-activation of the "Religiosity" frame to passive negation. She associates her veiling motivation to the British values of women empowerment; she states, "wearing the hijab doesn't have to be about religious dedication. For me, it is political, feminist and empowering."[114] She elaborates, "not religion, is the motivator here. I am not one of these women". Takolia spot the light on the common (Extremists) "Religiosity" framing oh her hijab which manifests through daily humor or jokes; she said, "one friend joked that I was officially a 'fundamentalist'" (when she practiced the hijab). In the same newspaper, Sabbiya Perves discusses an interview in Daily mail with Today program's first Muslim presenter. The interview, as Perves states, "contained some basic understandings and a disturbing subtext."[115] Perves, as a response to the stereotypical framing of the hijab in that interview, displays her own mental frames from an authoritative position as a hijab-wearing Muslim woman. She states, "my reason for wearing the hijab

---

[110]Dear (2004).

[111]Akbar (2010d).

[112]Bentham and Davis (2007).

[113]Carter (2009).

[114]Takolia (2010).

[115]Perves (2013).

is not because I think God ordered it [...] I love wearing the hijab because I like
the idea that anyone who sees me will identify me as a Muslim. I wear it because I
know it forces people to listen to my words and to look beyond my aesthetics. I know
this from experience." Both Takolia and Pervez give more importance to (Sexuality)
"Concealment" framing of the hijab than the "Religiosity" framing. They do not
aim only to decrease the intense relationship between the practice and the "extremist" discourse; they also try to debate about the hijab thorough the British values
of women empowerment and liberty. These values are easier to be understood by
British readers who the majority might have no religious affiliation.

In a coincide de-activation to the "Religiosity" mental frame, Fareena Alam's, an
editor of Muslim magazine Q News, published an article in *The Independent* about
the Imperial College's ban on the full veil for security reasons. The decision of the
college has conflated the terms of full veil and headscarf, causing "significant distress
among British Muslims."[116] Alam states: "agony could have been avoided had the
report been more accurate." Hijab is seen as a "spiritual commitment," but Muslim
women "do not fixate about it. They just make their decision and get in with it [...] it is
neither the sum total of their identity nor does it indicate a uniform understanding of
Islam." In the case of *jilbab*, in *The Independent*, Shamim Chowdhury de-activates
the "Religiosity" frame of *jilbab* as a required garment. She states, "modesty is
paramount, but beyond that Islam does not dictate dress code."

To sum up, the "Religiosity" frame in the British press discourse is activated
and de-activated, in direct linguistic expressions, by both social varieties in all the
selected newspapers. It is not a recycled framing from the colonial discourse. The
Contra-hijab discourse activates the "Religiosity" frame for political agenda. In the
justification of the French ban, BBC activates the (Political) "Religiosity" frame
that links the French Muslim hijab to foreign political agenda. Such framing helps
the British reader, who is used to diversity, to classify the discriminatory law that
controls the Muslim women's choice of vestment as needed for national security. On
the British hijab, the contra-hijab discourse activates the (Extremist) "Religiosity"
frame. The linguistic strategies that activate the (Extremist) "Religiosity" frame are
direct linguistic expressions or indirect through the link between the hijab/jilbab-
wearing women and Muslim associations, which are introduced as "radical" in *The
Guardian*, *The Independent*, and *The Times* Online. The (Extremist) "Religiosity"
framing of the hijab is a cognitive base on which the political agenda depends to
use the hijab visibility as an instrument-of-fear to control the people. It is framed
as an extremist outsider that intimidates the unity of the British values, even the
multicultural value.

The for-hijab discourse, by the hijab-wearing women, activates the "Religiosity"
frame as much as it de-activates it. Those who activate the "Religiosity" frame of
the hijab aim at de-activating the "Othering" mental frame of the hijab through the
assertion on the religious territory-independent dimension of the practice. The hijab-
wearers who de-activate the "Religiosity" frame aim to de-activate the (Extremist)
"Religiosity" framing of the practice. Both the activation and de-activation of the

---

[116] Alam (2005).

"Religiosity" frame by the British hijab-wearing women are based on solid on religious freedom and women's empowerment in the context of the British values. They are not passive negations of stereotypical frames of the practice. The "Religiosity" frame is de-activated through the activation of the (Empowering) (Sexuality) "Concealment" frame. The activation and the de-activation of the "Religiosity" frame by hijab-wearers are found in *The Independent, The Guardian,* and the Standard.

The varieties of activation and de-activation of the "Religiosity" frame of the hijab by hijab opposers and by hijab wearers in the British national press reflect the authoritative voice and the engagement of British hijab-wearers in the national press and reflect the richness of the national debate on the hijab.

Cross-Cultural Analysis

There are few similarities in the "Religiosity" framing of the hijab across the two contexts analyzed above. For example, the contra-hijab discourse in both contexts activates the (Extremist) "Religiosity" frame in the national hijab debate. Both paved the way to use the hijab as an instrument-of-fear in the political agenda. Yet, the Spanish discourse activates the (Extremist) and (Political) "Religiosity" frame on the Spanish context considering the hijab as a foreign agenda in both framings. They use the visibility of the hijab in the public sphere as an instrument-of-fear to call for a ban law similar to the French one. In comparison, the British discourse activates the foreign (Political) "Religiosity" frame to justify the French ban law in 2004 and the (Extremist) "Religiosity" frame to debate the national hijab.

Contra-hijab journalists in both contexts blame the government's relationship with the Christian Church. In the Spanish context, the contra-hijab discourse considers this relation the only obstacle to banning the hijab visibility at Spanish public school. In the British context, the (Extremist) "Religiosity" frame includes Christianity, too. It is not limited to Islamic hijab visibility.

The discursive strategies in activating the (Extremist) "Religiosity" frame are direct linguistic expressions in both contexts. Yet, in the Spanish contra-hijab discourse, the hijab is first recognized as a religious practice in a superficial argument; then, it is stigmatized as radical and extremist. Whereas, in the British discourse, the hijab is directly stigmatized as thus. It is because the hijab practice is already recognized in the British context as a religious practice. But in the Spanish context, the dominant perception of the practice is "an Arabic cultural-patriarchal-traditional dress." As it is not comprehensive to stigmatize a wide range of Arabic countries' traditions as "extremist" or "radical," the journalists are in need to clarify, in a general way, this detail to the reader "it is a religious practice" then they stigmatize it as "extremist" and "radical."

A salient difference across those two contexts is the visibility of the authoritative hijab-wearing women in the British context and the invisibility of this voice in the Spanish context. The activation of the "Religiosity" frame in the Spanish context is done by secular journalists, and Muslim hijab-wearers are concealed from the debate. They are not given the authority to tell their perspectives and experience about the practice. Whereas, in the British context, hijab-wearing women participate actively in activating and de-activating the "Religiosity" frame through well-argumented discussion. The de-activation of the "Religiosity" frame aims, first, to de-activate the "Othering" frame of the hijab due to the transnational dimension of religion. It also aims to de-activate the (Extremist) "Religiosity" framing of the hijab. The British Mulism de-activation of the "Religiosity" frame is not limited to passive negation. It depends on the activation of the (Empowering) (Sexuality) "Concealment" of the hijab.

Thus, the hijab-wearers in the Spanish national debate have prevented the access to tell their own story. Spanish secular journalists announce themselves as spokeswomen on behalf of a Spanish Muslim woman whose voice is concealed. These journalists explain the Muslim women's religious demand, interpret her vestment choice, and provided Spanish readers with "comprehensive" answers on the practice. On the contrary, the British hijab-wearers are engaged in the national hijab debate as much as the secular journalists are.

Framing Hijab Through "Othering"

The "Othering" frame of the hijab is not a new framing of the practice. It is a continuum from the colonial discourse that de-estimated the "other" Muslim women. It is a recycled and re-activated mental frame. "Othering" the hijab is inseparable of "Othering" women who practice it. In the hijab-abstract interpretations, the hijab is framed through "Religiosity" frame in order to assert the notion of secular Europe "us" in contrast to the hijab "other." Accordingly, the visibility of the hijab arouses the debate of the "others" cultural visibility, and it intensifies the need to protect "ours."

Spanish "Othering" Mental Frame of Hijab

The Spanish coverage of the hijab-exclusion cases relates the hijab motivation to the students' affiliation with their parents' country of origin. It also introduces these cases as separated migratory-related incidents rather than a social reality in Spanish diversity. For example, in Shaima's case, covered in El País, Otero, the supervisor of the scholastic absentee investigation, calls for "tolerance" and asks the school direction to respect "the use" of the veil.[117] The call of "tolerance" frames the practice as an undesirable (intruder) social phenomenon that needs to be tolerated. As Thomassen indicates, "tolerance," as a term motivates the "undesirable" embodied

_____

[117]Iglesias (2007).

experience because people usually tolerate what they do not like. In the same news-paper, Rebeca Carranco draws a direct link between the student's hijab motivation and the Arabic context, especially the Moroccan. Carranco quotes Shaima: "I had seen on Arabic TV some girls with the veil."[118] Shaima's mother said: "she covered for the first time in Morocco. She went with her grandmother to the mosque." In both quotations, the hijab is associated with the "other" country traditions that is brought into Spain. Interestingly, this is the only time when a Muslim student's motivation to hijab is being cited. This citation re-activates the "othering" framing of the hijab by The hijab practitioners.

In the case of Najwa, Ana Del Barrio, in El Mundo, limits the case to the Moroccan Muslim minority in the title of her article: "Moroccans demand the Community intervention in the case of Najwa."[119] The debate of the case is almost restricted to ATIME (Association of Moroccan Workers). In the same newspaper, Christina Galafate refers to the hijab of Najwa as an outsider that "landed on Facebook."[120] The article refers to a supportive campaign that collected signs to ask Esperanza Aguirre, the president of the Madrid Community at then, to support Najwa Al-Malha's right to education and religious liberty. Both journalists discuss and present the cases away from the Spanish mainstream involvement. Both isolate the case of Najwa from Spanish social reality and re-activate the "Othering" frame of the hijab.

The analysis detects that both El Mundo and El País re-activate the "Othering" frame of the practice at schools. Even in the 2015/2016 discourse, the "Othering" frame is re-activated. The case of Saidi Rodriguez, covered in El Mundo by Irene Velasco, is discussed with Spanish Muslims: Yonaida Salem, a president of the intercultural association of Mellie, and Amanda Figueras, a Muslim journalist.[121] Although both are Spanish Muslims, yet, they were introduced as the Muslim "others" (I will discuss "Othering" frame of hijab-wearers in the next chapter). In the Institute case of Takwa Rejeb, covered in El Mundo by Inma Lidón, Monica Oltra, the vice-president of the Consell in Valencia, declares that "hijab is a religious, cultural and gender sign, similar to the pendant we put to girls and not to boy." Although Oltra's narration seems to be supportive to Rejeb, she frames the hijab through binary frames: "Religiosity" and "Othering" frame. Oltra's comparison between the religious/culture practice and the pendant "we put" indicates the separateness of the two compared elements. In other words, it is their hijab and our pendant. Although the discourse indirectly re-activates the "othering" frame, the debate in Rejeb's case is not limited to any social minority group as it tends to be before 2015. Instead, the supportive voices were Olter and Francisco Solans (the lawyer of SOS Racism). The discourse indicates that "her case has reached Sindic de Greuges y del Defensor del Pueblo. It is to say, Rejeb's case is the only case in the selected data where members of the mainstream (non-Muslim) Spanish in power support Spanish women's right to hijab, consider the practice as an aspect of Spanish diversity.

---

[118]Carranco (2010).

[119]Del Barrio (2010a).

[120]Galafate (2010).

[121]Velasco (2016).

The "Othering" frame of the hijab in the social and political discourse is re-activated mainly through the "politics of migration" involvements and the "debate importation" techniques. For example, in El Mundo, Carmen de Ganuza starts the article by drawing a link between the hijab practice and migrant politics, "Popular Party strongly gambles in its politics of immigration. As much as to dare to restrict the use of the Islamic veil of Muslim children in Spanish schools."[122] She closes the article asserting the re-activation of the "Othering" frame. She indicates that the motivation of the new political proposal is "deciding to specify to the maximum these 'principles' and 'Spanish costumes.'" Such discourse explicitly sets "our" costumes in contrast to the hijab practice of "others."

In El Mundo, Ana Del Barrio covers the case of ONG Campaign that intends to break stereotypes that obstacle the hiring of hijab-wearing Muslims.[123] The article introduces hijab-wearing women's employment problems as a migrational issue. The campaign is organized by a Moroccan Association (ATIME). The article is relatively short (338 words) with a one-sided contributor, the president of ATIME. This article builds its argument on the separation between Spanish society "us" and the hijab-"Moroccan"-women "others." The discourse draws that line using reciprocal discourse: "To animate Spanish company to contract Muslim women who wear the veil," "they suffer from labor discrimination that restrains their integration in Spanish society." Every time "Spanishness" is mentioned, hijab-wearing women were mentioned as the opposition, as a separate entity from the entire us, that struggle to enter in, not as a part of "Spanishness" who try to make their own life as all Spanish women do.

The Minister of Equality, Bibiana Aído, declarations on the forum of "Alliance of Civilizations" re-activates the "Othering" of the hijab in direct linguistic expressions that separates between "us" and "them." Aído states that "Arab or Muslim males can wear occidental clothes while women must wear long dresses that cover their bodies. They also need to wear the veil on the head to cover the hair" "not all cultural practices should be protected and respected," and those practices "that promote inequality of women must be criticized." In addition, "they should arbitrate the necessary elements that contribute to eliminate it." This political discourse promotes the otherness of the practice. It rejected the fact that the hijab is a Spanish Muslim practice. It is instead categorized as an Arabic practice. The minister of Equality conflates together "Arab" and "Muslim" cultures; she uses the conjunction "or" instead of "and" by which she refers that even non-Arabic Muslims will share these "patriarchal" thoughts. In the same article, De la Vega, the first vice-president of the government, links the hijab practice to "cultural traditions," which does not violate individual liberty, and it needs to be respected. It is to say; both contributors re-activate the "Otherness" frame, Aído calls for its elimination while De La Vega calls for respect.

In the same newspaper, Rosa Meneses explains the practice through "imported debate" and "imported experiences" techniques. These techniques indicate that the hijab practice is discussed within "other" (Arabic) countries by "other" (Arabic)

---

[122]De Ganuza, (2008).

[123]Del Barrio (2010b).

participants. These techniques frame the hijab visibility as an outsider imported to Spain by others. For example, Meneses explains the hijab as follows: "in Kuwait, Emirates, and Qatar, it is a social status symbol to be distinguished from the rest." Here, the hijab is attached to Arabic traditional vestments. Meneses specifies its meaning in European countries, but not Spain in specific. She says, "women who live in Occidental countries, they use it (the hijab) as a way to stay faithful to their country of origin, away from their land" or as "a way of being cool without it contravenes progenitors' traditions." Both of these hijab motivations re-activates the "Othering" frame. They exclude the practice from the European social reality and stigmatizes its practitioners as "Others."

In El País, "imported experience" and "imported debate" techniques are used. Solidad Gallego-Diaz includes two Egyptian speakers, Hoda Shaarawi and Mona Eltahawy, to debate whether the hijab needs to be regulated by law or not; the article is titled "The Veil does not Deserve a Law." Although the debate emerges because of the exclusion cases in Spanish public schools, the entire debate has not included any Spanish speakers or experts to discuss if the hijab needs a law or not. This methodological exclusion of Spanish voices in the hijab debate is an attempt to frame the hijab debate away from "La Hispanidad."

The social and political debate in El País re-activates the "Othering" frame recurrently. The discourse picture the hijab as an outsider practice introduced to Spain by migrants, for political purposes. Angeles Espinosa indicates that veiling is "an external imposition." The discourse stresses on "our" Spanish frame in opposition to the outsider imposed hijab four times along the article: "our society is sufficiently independent of all religions," "(...) or a husband imposes veiling on any Spanish or foreigner who resides in our country," "(the ban) is against the foundation of our liberty" and "our democratic values are strong enough to prevent a bonnet or a veil from threatening it." Several articles in El Pais, starting from the title till the conclusion, spins around the same axis of re-activating the "Othering" frame of the hijab, e.g., (Montero, 2010), (Moliner, 2004), (Galarraga, 2010), (Caballero 2010), (Carbajos 2008), and (Sahuquillo, 2008). It is quite important to draw your attention that the selected articles for this study focus on the Spanish national hijab and not on migrants issue. It is to say, the title of these articles the overall focus is the hijab in Spain. Yet, the discursive techniques are re-activating the "Othering" frame constantly. For example, in Maria Sahuquillo's articles, all the participants are introduced as migrants or daughters/sons of migrants in Spain and outside Spanish national borders: Said Kirlani, the president of the Association of Moroccan University Students, has been in Spain for six years; Salah Sharif, a counselor at Dar Il Salam Foundation, reached the United Kingdom in 1991 and he has the British nationality (a distant inclusion in Europe "us"), and Batul was born to Turkish parents and lives in Belgic. The only Muslim voice who has not been stigmatized as a foreigner is Riay Tatary, the (male) president of UCIDE.[124]

---

[124]Sahuquillo, Maria R. *Integración, si, asimilación, no,* http://www.elpais.com/articulo/sociedad/Integracion/asimilacion/elpepisoc/20080216elpepisoc_1/Tes (16 February 2008).

In the debate on Bibiana Aido's declarations about the Islamic dress code (which we have mentioned earlier), Carbajos justifies Aidos's perspective through for and contra-arguments on the hijab.[125] The participants are as follows: (I followed the order of appearance, and I used Carabjos' introductory words): The Islamic authorities of Spain (anonymous); Bibian Aido, the Minister of Equality, "is disposed to challenge the political correctness in order to make her message heard"; Nadia Yassine from Rabat, a leader of the Justice and Spirituality Movement, persecuted by Moroccan government; Angelica Oballe, a German 21-years-old girl who "has converted to Islam since hardly few months and she migrated to the Proximate Orient"; Mina Chebaa, 38 years old, a member in a platform of Muslim women emancipation in Belgic; Fadela Amara, a Secretary of the French Government and a founder of Not Whores Nor Submissive organization that fights against the use of the veil; Samah, a 20 s girl from Beirut, married to a clergyman of Hezbollah; Liz Ercevik, a Turkish feminist from Istanbul; Maria Teresa Fernández De La Vega, the vice-president of the government.

The Spanish participants are the women politicians who get minimal discourse (82 words for both out of 1853 total words) and whose political declarations are the trigger of the article. All other participants are not Spanish nor related to the Spanish social actuality. The article restricts the Spanish mainstream or Muslim minority involvement and re-activates the "Othering" frame of the hijab. Carabajos indicates that the veil is a sign of (outsider) identity; she said, "if the occident does not want them (Muslim women), they turn their back, and they cling to traditions." Accordingly, hijab practice is a way to announce the detachment of European society.

In 2015/2016, the discourse continues in re-activating the "Othering" framing. However, Spanish experts are included in the national hijab debate. In La Vanguardia, Carian Farreres interviewed Spanish Academic speakers: Silvia Carrasco, a doctor in Social anthropology at UAB, Dolores Bramón's, a doctor in Semitic Philosophy in UB, and Olga Dominguez, a philosopher.[126] Yet, their discourse maintained the activation and re-activation of stereotypical mental frames of the hijab. We have been through these mental frames above.

To sum up, The "Othering" mental frame is re-activated in picturing the exclusion cases as an isolated migrational crisis rather than an indicator of the crisis in Spanish social diversity. The "Othering" frame is re-activated by representing the Spanish students as children of migrants and relate the hijab motivation to "other" (Arab or Muslim) cultural traditions. Both El Mundo and El Pais consider that hijab visibility in public schools is an issue related to migration policies. Both El Mundo and El Pais sustain the "Othering" frame of the practice in the 2015/2016 discourse.

In the Social and political debate, the separation between "we" and "others" was drawn and sustained. The political and social debate re-activates the "Othering" frame of the hijab through the "imported debate" and "imported experiences" techniques. These techniques indicate that the hijab practice is discussed within "other" (Arabic) countries by "other" (Arabic) participants. These techniques frame the hijab visibility

---

[125]Carbajos (2008).
[126]Farreras (2016).

as an outsider imported to Spain by others. To conclude with, The "Othering" frame of the hijab is constructed in the readers' embodied experience through the direct image schemata of the hijab "entrance" to the Spanish society or by debating the hijab with migrants or other-nationality speakers in order to exclude the hijab from the Spanish social reality. The de-activation of the "Othering" frame by hijab-wearers is controlled by journalists, limited to simple statements in minimal words.

British "Othering" Mental Frame of Hijab

The "Othering" frame of the hijab in the British selected data is re-activated differently from the Spanish one. In the British context, the "Othering" mental frame is not re-activated only by "imported debate" techniques. It is re-activated by the stress on the "Britishness" prejudice of "Our multicultural British," "British tolerance," and "British values," e.g., (Elkin, 2013), (Khan, 2015), (Walter, 2004), and (Riddell, 2003). These terms are used repeatedly in the discourse to stigmatize the hijab practice, as much as to criticize the intolerant French ban. The "Othering" mental frame is re-activated and de-activated in the British press, as we will see below.

The activation of the "Othering" frame manifest, similar to the Spanish activation, through othering the debate by the hijab opposers. Several journalists include outsider images of hijab or burqa and project them on the British context, yet they are not as intensive as in the Spanish press. For example, in *The Guardian*, Yasmin AliBhai-Brown presents herself as "practicing 'though flawed Shia Muslim."[127] She mixes the Arabic and Iranian social practices in the British hijab. AliBhai-Brown introduces the following scholars: Qasim Amin and Riffat Hassan, and feminists who "claimed to be visible" and "fight for equality," Huda Shaarawi, Fatima Mernissi, and Nawal El Saadawi; they are all Egyptian, Moroccan, and Iranian. AliBhai-Brown indicates that "they rightly saw the veil as a tool and symbol of oppression and subservience." She indicates that "purity," as a belief, is "backed up by Saudi Arabia and other Gulf states. Deobandi revivalists, funded by Arab money, now run more mosques in the United Kingdom than any other Muslim subgroup."

Catherine Bennett, in *The Guardian*, re-activates the "Othering" frame, too.[128] Bennett starts her article by the fall of the Taliban and praises Cherie Blair's support to the oppressed Afghan women who lost their human rights. Then, she mentions the French ban that "has traveled to Britain." The hijab and the ban are pictured as outsiders; they do not belong to the British social reality. Bennett wonders: "is the abbreviated drapery pinned to the heads of some Muslim schoolgirls entirely unrelated to the restrictive burqa? And if not, should we be smiling on this particular expression of cultural difference?" In this discourse, Bennett indirectly links between the British schoolgirls' hijab and the Taliban's burqa. She answers her own questions after 581 words (out of 1007 words). Bennett cites Adonis, "the Arabic world-leading

---

[127] Alibhai−Brown (2015).
[128] Bennett (2004).

poet," an expert by belonging, and who asserts the non-religious meaning of the hijab. She notes: "despite what the fundamentalists would have us believe, nowhere in the Quran or hadith is there a single, unequivocal passage that imposes the veil on Muslim women. Their view is based on a different reading of the text." The journalist states that "The wearing of a hijab, that ostensibly mild statement of cultural difference, is, Adonis argues, harmfully socially divisive: It is, in fact, the symbol for a desire for separation: it means we refuse integration. Moreover, as he reminds us, such overt demonstrations of difference may have nothing to do with religion." The repetitive de-activation of the "Religiosity" frame is an attempt to detach the practice from the universal religious practice and to emphasize on the cultural-dependence "Othering" frame of the hijab.

In the same newspaper, Natasha Walter introduces the hijab debate through the comparison between the occidental feminism, which "has been tied up with the freedom to uncover ourselves" and the veil enforced in Iran and Afghanistan, two countries the journalist visited before, where veiled women, according to her, are oppressed. This article is discussed more in the following chapter of the hijab-wearing women framing.[129]

In *The Independent*, Joan Smith opens up the article by a clear division between the West and Islam. She starts by Samuel Huntington's thesis which divides the world "into two camps, western and Islamic, and he assumes that their values are different, if not mutually hostile.[130]" After that, she re-activates the "Compulsivity" frame of veiling within the Saudi Arabia social context; she states, "It is imposed on reluctant women in Saudi Arabia by clerics like Grand Mufti Sheikh Abdul Aziz al-Sheikh." Smith points out that in Saudi Arabia, authorities "are not noticeably sympathetic to foreign visitors who reject the veil as a manifestation of shame culture: so much for respecting other people's values." The journalist indirectly refers that the enforced hijab on foreigners in Saudi Arabia justifies the enforced unveiling of "foreigners" in occidental countries. Right after that, Smith argues that the French ban is no more than an attempt to protect the national values as Saudi Arabia does with its values. She states, "Chirac's tough stance has come about because his Government sees demands that Muslim girls be allowed to wear hijab in state schools as a calculated challenge to *laïcité*." Accordingly, Smith first excluded the practice from the European context, then justifies its ban in France. The third argument is on the British context; Smith continues, "It is a debate Britain cannot afford to be complacent about. We will struggle to defend secularism for as long as the Government refuses to dismantle the established church, blasphemy laws and state-funded Christian, and now Muslim, schools." The journalist blames the State for its relationship with the Christian church, which obstacles the use of "secularism" to stop Islam spread in Britain.

In the Times Online, Marin Minette re-activates the "Othering" mental frame, too. Minette states that the hijab is "strongly associated with cultures and countries which deny women the vote, equality under the law [...]."[131] Minette continues that

---

[129] Walter (2004).
[130] Smith (2004).
[131] Marin (2004).

"the insistence on the headscarf here, or in France, is quite clearly an insistence on identifying with those cultures. As a result, it looks like a rejection of British culture." She re-activates the "Othering" frame by interpreting the practice as a sign of rejection to the British values and relating it to the patriarchal agenda. She continues, "Young British Muslims show some signs of resisting assimilation more than their parents."

The linguistic expressions "to resist" and "to reject" are recurrent triggers for the "Othering" frame. These two expressions frame the hijab into, not simply the "other" yet, the opposing and conflicting "other." This mental frame contains an antagonistic dimension. In the French law debate, BBC, Wyatt's friend, Antonio, re-activates the (conflicting) "Othering" frame. Wyatt states the "he said they (Muslim women) were rejecting French values and French culture and identifying themselves with their co-religionists in other countries instead, even insisting on wearing the headscarf to school."[132] The hijab visibility at French public school is the ultimate social rejection which needs to be regulated and controlled by law. Mary Riddell, in *The Guardian*, cites Bernard Stasi, who states that "extremist groups" are "testing the Republic and pushing certain people to reject France and its values."[133] Riddell projects the French (conflicting) "Othering" frame on the British context. She said that "we are not as different as we should be. Le Pen-style nationalism has its echo in Britain, where more girls from the 1.6 million Muslim population are abandoning the diaphanous scarves of their grandmothers and becoming hijab-wearers at puberty, partly through solidarity with the global diaspora, but also, maybe, as a sign of separateness." Both hijab motivations "diaspora" and "separateness" re-activate the "Othering" frame of the British hijab. AliBhai-Brown, In *The Guardian*, repetitively asserts the (conflicting) "Othering" frame of hijab, the title is "As a Muslim woman, I see the veil as a rejection of progressive values."[134] AliBahai-Brown insists that "veiled women have provoked confrontations over their right to wear veils, in courts, at schools and in colleges and workplaces. But I regard their victories as a rejection of social compromise [...] a good number have thrown themselves into political Islam to resist and combat western hegemonies – or so the story goes." It is to say; the (Conflicting) "Othering" frame is re-activated by (1) stigmatizing the hijab as a sign of rejection to the (total of) French or British values, (2) by announcing the hijab as a sign of belonging to foreign political agendas.

British hijab-wearing writers and interviewees restrict the "rejection" the hijab might imply to the sexual visibility in the public sphere. They do so by activating and empowering the (Sexuality) "Concealment" mental frame of the hijab. According to them, the practice does not reject British culture; the practice rejects the liberal culture that objectifies women and turns them into sex objects. The rejected "elements" manifest only in *The Guardian* due to the high visibility of hijab-wearers writers. Takolia specified that her hijab rejected the liberal social expectation of her as a female. She states, "sure the hijab was not the only way to express my feelings and frustrations, but knowing that our interpretation of liberal culture embraces, if not encourages,

---

[132]Wyatt (2003).

[133]Riddell (2003).

[134]Alibhai−Brown (2015).

uncovering, I decided to reject what society expected me to do, and cover up."[135]
Alam indicates that hijab becomes a "powerful political symbol"; it is "an emblem
of resistance to a dominant culture that objectifies women's bodies."[136] Akhtar states
that Muslims can "fully integrate without assimilating the British community."[137]
She narrates her own experience: "I am different, I'm Muslim. A lot of my values are
British, but where they contradict Islam, then they will be Islamic values." Accordingly, the resistance of the hijab is not British values as a whole because these women
assert that they hold these values. The resistance and the rejection the hijab implies
for them is limited to the liberal values that objectify women's body.

The "Othering" frame is re-activated in the jilbab debate by Deborah Orr, in *The
Independent*. She re-activates the "Othering" frame of the *jilbab* in the first paragraph
of her article. She describes it as an Arabic pre-Islamic dress, she says, "somebody
ought to tell Shabina Begum, who took her school to court in order to win the right
to wear the jilbab, that the draping of women's bodies in enveloping folds is an
Arab custom that predates Islam."[138] Orr highlights the political use of the case, the
activation of the (Extremist) "Religiosity" frame: "Now it emerges that Begum had
contacts with an extremist Islamic group set up by the militant cleric Omar Bakri
Mohammed." She reveals the uneasy feeling of the Muslim community about the
case, which "is going to make life in Britain harder for them rather than easier. The
awful thing is, I fear that this is exactly what it was designed to do. It's already, after
all, working like a charm". Guest and Merry quote a hijab-wearing Muslim British
public figure, statements which re-activate the "Othering" frame of the jilbab.[139]
The first Speaker is Fareena Alam, "the editor of Muslim magazine Q News," who
states, "I'm very happy for Shabina, but I'm upset about the whole case. The jilbab
is an Arab dress. It is completely wrong to suggest that the shalwar kameez is not
[an Islamic] proper dress. And it is wrong that we have to compete with Arabs to
be [considered] proper Muslims." The second voice is Fauzia Ahmed, "a research
fellow in sociology at Bristol University," she "thinks the issue is not Islamic, but
cultural." Ahmed adds that "a lot of Muslim women are very tired of the idea that
what they wear is the single most important and defining issue for them."

Hijab-wearing women declaratively re-activate the "Othering" frame of the *jilbab*
in their articles. They refuse to consider the jilbab as an "Islamic" dress. For them, it
is one of the vestments that matches the Islamic criteria and which can be replaced by
the shalwar kameez. Hijab-wearers de-activate the (Extremist) "Religiosity" frame of
jilbab (Luton, 2005). They re-activate the "Othering" frame considering it an Arabic
traditional cloth. In the Independent. Shamim Chowdhury uses an outsider Saudi
Arabian scene to introduce the jilbab debate "At the Masjid-al-Haram, the holiest of
mosques in the sacred city of Mecca, thousands of Muslims flock daily to perform

---

[135] Takolia (2010).

[136] Alam (2005).

[137] Akhtar (2004).

[138] Orr (2005).

[139] Guest, Katey and Merry Wyn Davies, *The Muslims next doo*, http://www.independent.co.uk/
news/uk/this−britain/focus−the−muslims−next−door−527359.html (6 March 2005).

pilgrimage and offer prayers. The women among them are modestly dressed in accordance with the laws of the faith. Large swathes of cloth cover even the finest strand of hair, and unassuming garments disguise any hint of body shape."[140] Chowdhury asserts the association of *jilbab* to that specific social context; she continues, "but here the uniformity ends." She lists the different dress codes in the diverse Muslim community; "colorful salwar kameezes" of Pakistanis and "flower-printed capes" of Somalis; "modesty is paramount," but it is not limited to specific dress. Chowdhury argues that the alternative school uniform, Shalwar kameez is an Islamic alternative that fits modesty criteria.

British "tolerance" is questioned in the re-activation of the "Othering" frame. For example, in *The Independent*, Smith considers the court decision to the favor of Luton school as "the decision marked the moment in Britain when the State, faced by religious extremism, drew a line."[141] She re-activates the (Extremist) "Religiosity" frame as a tool-of-fear and asserts the importance of setting limits to "tolerance." In Time Online, Minette Marin also mentions the "line" of tolerance twice. She indicates that "the truth about the hijab is far from simple. It presents a serious challenge to the West. It challenges our ideas of what's most important in our own culture and the points at which we draw the line of tolerance."[142] More ahead in the article, she indicates that "we are beginning to be inclined to draw the line of tolerance. We are beginning to feel, after years of misguided multiculturalist propaganda about diversity, that what we must emphasize is similarity. There is a growing feeling that the host culture should stand up for itself as the common culture and be less tolerant of the intolerant." Such discourse asserts the incompatibility of Muslims and the British values; besides, it stigmatizes those who practice the hijab/jilbab as intolerant to the mainstreamers.

In a contrastive discourse, Marry Riddell, in *The Guardian*, asserts the multiculturalist identity to the United Kingdom. She states that "British multiculturalism seems strong. Rabinder Singh, a High Court judge, sits in a turban. The hijab is part of the Metropolitan police officer's uniform."[143] Natasha Walter, in the same newspaper, activates the "Othering" frame of the hijab as much as the need to tolerate it.[144] Walter concludes her article as follows: "but if we really believe in tolerance, then of course that must include even tolerating behavior we find alien. And if we believe in women's self-determination, then we must also respect those choices that are not our own." The linguistic expression "alien" and "not our own" are direct triggers of the "Othering" frame of the hijab within the "multicultural" British. The practice is included as the practice of "others" and not as part of the British social reality.

The "Othering" frame of hijab is de-activated by the hijab-wearing women who associate the British hijab to fashion and elegancy. The assertion on the smart appearance is recurrent in the British data, which aims to break down the stereotypical image

---

[140]Chowdhury (2005).

[141]Smith (2006b).

[142]Marin (2004).

[143]Riddell (2003).

[144]Walter (2004).

of the "archaic veil"[145] as much as to break down the association between the hijab criteria and other worldwide cultural forms of it. For example, Akbar's interviewee in *The Independent*, Rajnaara Akhtar, points out that the hijab is not what people think as "drab and dreary" because "modesty does not exclude a smart appearance. The two are equally compatible."[146] In the same series of interviews, Shelina Zahra asserts the smart appearance "I do not want to look like I am living in the 19th century. I have never liked wearing black scarves and black coats."[147] Soha Sheikh indicates that she tries "not to stick to black but wear various colors and make them fashionable."[148]

In *The Guardian*, Khaleeli's article is entirely dedicated to the hijab fashion in autumn 2008.[149] The interviewee is Jana Kossaibati, a blogger, "the UK's first style guide for Muslims." She expresses that there are two types of hijabs: "head-scarves that reflect (their) cultural heritage" and "the mixing techniques from all over the Muslim world with newly created styles to complement Western clothes." Kossaibati states, "what kind of message are you sending out if you look drab or missy?" Kossaibati writes an article in the same newspaper introducing herself as follows: "bleary-eyed and weary as I am after long nights spent with my nose buried in a book. Welcome to the sartorial challenges of a 19-year-old hijab-wearing Muslim medical student."[150] In her article, she discusses the summer challenge "is to keep covered, keep cool, and look good." Kossaibati provides shopping tips and fashionable modesty recommendations.

The hijab-wearers assert the fashionable aspect of their hijab to de-activate the "Othering" frame of the hijab. However, hijab opposers attack the fashionable-hijab discourse. Hijab opposers argue that since the hijab indicates the concealment of sexuality, and since the hijab-wearing women call to treat them on what their personality is and not on how their physical appearance looks like; why would Muslim women pay attention to or care about the smart look?

To sum up, the "Othering" frame in the British press is re-activated by various discursive techniques depending on the focus of the hijab debate. In the French ban debate, BBC and *The Guardian* activate the (Conflicting) "Othering" frame. Both newspapers picture the practice as a sign of resistance to French secular values and a sign of belonging to forging political agenda. This picture is imported into the British national hijab in *The Guardian* and *The Independent*. The hijab is framed as the vestment of "others" (Arabs and Afghans). The Times Online re-activates the "Othering" frame of the hijab without attaching it to any specific forging country. British hijab-wearing women activate the (sexuality) "Concealment" mental frame of the hijab to assert that they only reject the liberal values that objectify women's bodies. In *The Guardian* and *The Independent*, they de-activate the "Othering" frame of the

---

[145] Akbar (2010b).

[146] Akbar (2010b).

[147] Akbar (2010c).

[148] Akbar (2010d).

[149] Khaleeli (2008).

[150] Kossaibati (2009).

hijab by asserting the fashionable aspect of the hijab outfits that copies contemporary colors and styles.

The re-activation of the "Othering" frame of the hijab spots the light on the British "multiculturalism" and "tolerance." It uses the colonial discourse in othering Muslims (hijab-wearers in particular) and questions the limits by which Muslim visibility is going to be tolerated in the multicultural United Kingdom. *The Independent* and *Time* Online criticize "tolerance" and ask for setting a limit to it. The Independent blames the state of its relationship with the Christian church because it obstacles the adoption of secularism in front of Muslim visibility. *The Guardian* asks to respect multiculturalism and tolerance while stigmatizing the hijab-wearers as (alien) others.

Hijab opposers re-activate the (Extremist) "Religiosity" frame of jilbab, as we have seen above. However, hijab-wearers de-activate this framing by the re-activation of the "Othering" mental frame of jilbab. They de-associate the "Religiosity" frame from the garment and limit it to Arabic traditional cloth in the Independent.

Cross-Cultural Analysis

The "Othering" frame of the hijab is re-activated in both contexts. There seem to be a few similarities in the activation of this mental frame. Both contexts used the "imported" image of "oppressed" women in Afghanistan and Saudi Arabia to the national debate of the hijab. Both contexts asserted the "we" in opposition to "they." The Spanish "we" was not clearly defined. Although some Spanish journalists define it as "secular," Spain is not a secular country. The Spanish "we" stands for the occidental feminist movement and women's liberation process in opposition to foreigner and outsider "others." While the British "we" is more defined as "multicultural."

Both re-activate the (Conflicting) "Othering" frame of the hijab. It is to say; both press discourse considers the hijab a sign of rejecting the national values and the accomplishments of women's rights on the national level. However, the Spanish "we" stands, consistently, against the foreigner, oppressed, suspicious "other," who comes to Spain, rejects its values and causes the social disorder. Whereas, the British "we" stand in opposition to insider "others." the discourse does not generate an image schema that pictures them coming from out of borders. They are from inside; they reject the British values and cling to foreign agenda by practicing the hijab.

In the Spanish context, the hijab exclusion cases are numerous, whereas, in the United Kingdom, they are limited. Othering the hijab in the exclusion cases in the Spanish context is systematic and extensive. The discourse aims to "other" the national debate and picture the exclusion cases as isolated phenomena related to immigration issues. Several articles debate the hijab with several participants, none of them Spanish. This discursive strategy is not seen intensively in the British context—the hijab exclusion cases in Spain framed as fragmented cases to conceal the Spanish diversity crisis. In the British press, Othering the hijab is not a significant frame in the hijab exclusion cases. Yet, it is re-activated in the jilbab exclusion cases (by for hijab and against hijab participants.) British multiculturalism and tolerance are debated and questioned in the British context.

In both presses, the re-activation of the "Othering" frame manifests through othering the debate by the hijab opposers. Their discourse includes outsider images of hijab or burqa to project these interfered meaning. Foreigners from other countries were interviewed and introduced as legitimate analysts on the hijab visibility in Spanish public schools. Although this discursive technique appears in the British press, it is less intensive and not repetitive as in the Spanish one. As I mentioned before, the Spanish discourse attempt by this strategy to exclude the national factor of the debate. It was until 2015 when Spanish national analysts appear to debate the hijab visibility in Spain.

The de-activation of the "Othering" frame in the Spanish press by hijab-wearers appears after the 2015–2016 discourse as limited and controlled interventions by the journalist. The de-activation is limited to simple statements and reduced to a few words. In contrast, the de-activation of the "Othering" frame in the British press is rich and argumentative. Hijab-wearers write their proper articles to talk about fashionable hijab and to empower the "Religiosity" mental frame of the hijab to assert the practice universal aspect. They activate the "Othering" frame on the jilbab visibility in British public schools to detach the practice from the (Extremist) "Religiosity" frame, which is activated by the against-jilbab in the mainstream discourse.

Conclusions

The colonial discourse on hijab is still dominant in the Spanish and British press discourse. Only one frame (the "Religiosity" frame) out of six frames in this analysis is not a recycled frame on the hijab practice. The British discourse against hijab seems more politically correct and less stigmatizing hijab-wearing women than the Spanish press. It uses indirect discourse techniques to activate the "Discrimination" and "Submission" frames. However, it depends on the recall-on-the-memory strategy. Readers will recall the colonial memory of Muslim culture as patriarchal.

The hijab is being used in both national presses to support the political discourse that uses the hijab visibility in the public sphere as a way to activate fear. The frame "Religiosity" is activated in connection with extremist religious movements. Secular journalists from both countries blame their government for establishing a relationship with Muslims because this relationship prevents the State from legislating against the hijab as the French government did.

The 2004 French law had a significant effect on British and Spanish national debate on the hijab. Yet, in the Spanish case, the hijab is not given much space until the first exclusion case occurred in the national arena. The French ban is praised and seen as a good example to follow to protect Spanish national values and maintain public order. The British context differs due to the multicultural social structure. British women journalists highly justified the French ban to British readers (who are used to diversity) to conceal the discriminatory aspect of the ban. Some against-hijab journalists consider the French ban an excellent example to follow, while others acknowledge that it goes against British values. However, both call for tolerance.

The invisibility of the hijab-wearing women in the Spanish national debate is significant. The mainstream journalists engage on gender equality, women's right, women's vestment in Islam based on incohesive arguments. Despite their lack of information about Islam, they set themselves as authoritative spokeswomen on behalf of the hijab-wearing women, whose voices are absent. The more recent participation of hijab-wearing women in the debate is limited and manipulated. As a consequence, Spanish readers are not used to diverse mental framings of the hijab. It is difficult for Spanish readers to think of the hijab as part of the Spanish social diversity because they are not exposed to different ways of framing it. The instruments to think critically are missing because of the monocular frames provided in the press. Hijab-wearing women resort to writing in personal blogs and Muslim magazine, yet their voice is still limited to the community which logs in these platforms.

On the contrary, British readers have access to both for and against hijab discourse in the national press. Hijab-wearing women have access to write on their own experiences, their success, and their political opinions on the State policies. They activate, de-activate, and re-activate frames on their hijab, and public debate on them is open. British readers have the opportunity to read the arguments of both sides and critically think of the hijab visibility in the British national public sphere.

References

Haddad, Y. (2007). The post-9/11 hijab as icon. *Sociology of Religion, 68*(3), 253–267.
KhirAllah, G. (2015). Veiling and revealing identity: The linguistic representation of the hijab in the British Press. In *Identity and migration in Europe: Multidisciplinary perspectives* (pp. 229–249). Springer.
Lakoff, G. (2014). *The all new don't think of an Elephant! Know your values and frame the debate.* Chelsea Green Publishing.
Pape, S., & Featherstone, S. (2005). *Newspaper journalism: A practical introduction.* Sage.
Scott, J. W. (2009). *The politics of the veil.* Princeton University Press.
Thomassen, L. (2011). (Not) Just a piece of cloth: Begum, recognition and the politics of representation. *Political Theory, 39*(3), 325–351.
Yegenoglu, M. (1998). *Colonial fantasies: Towards a feminist reading of Orientalism.* Cambridge University Press.

Annex 1

Spanish Articles
Abad, R. (2007a). *A la Asamblea con el 'hiyab'.* http://elpais.com/diario/2007/06/17/espana/118 2031209_850215.html. 17 June 2007.

Abad, R. (2007b). *Este velo es para siempre" Vuelven a clase las alumnas del colegio ceutí obligado por Educación a aceptar el 'hiyab'.*http://elpais.com/diario/2007/10/11/sociedad/1192053613_8 50215.html. 11 October 2007.

Álvarez, P. (2011a). *A clase con el velo.* http://sociedad.elpais.com/sociedad/2011/10/18/actualidad/ 1318888806_850215.html. 18 October 2011.

Álvarez, P. (2011b). *Mi velo sí entra en clase.* http://elpais.com/diario/2011/10/19/madrid/131902 3459_850215.html. 19 October 2011.

Álvarez, P. (2011c). *Renunciar al velo islámico sería como quitarme la piel.* http://elpais.com/dia rio/2011/10/23/sociedad/1319320802_850215.html. 23 October 2011.

Álvarez, P., & Cembrero, I. (2010a). *Estalla el debate sobre legislar el uso del pañuelo islámico en clase.* http://elpais.com/diario/2010/04/22/sociedad/1271887203_850215.html. 22 April 2010.

Álvarez, P., & Garriga, J. (2010c). *Aguirre ficha de asesor al director del centro que vetó el velo de Najwa.* http://elpais.com/diario/2010/05/25/sociedad/1274738410_850215.html. 25 May 2010.

Barik Edidi, Z. (2009). *Encuentro* http://www.elmundo.es/encuentros/invitados/2009/11/3898/ index.html. 11 November 2009.

Belaza, M. C. (2010). *El Supremo decidirá sobre el uso del "hiyab"* en los juicios. http://elpais. com/diario/2010/01/15/sociedad/1263510007_850215.html. 15 January 2010.

Belvar, M., & Blasco, P. (2010). *El instituto de Pozuelo no modifica sus normas e impide a Najwa ir con veil.* http://www.elmundo.es/elmundo/2010/04/20/madrid/1271786689.html. 21 April 2010.

Bohorquez, L. (2016). *Que me obliguen a quitarme el velo es como arrancarme mi propia piel.* http://politica.elpais.com/politica/2016/12/20/actualidad/1482237712_030858.html. 20 December 2016.

Caballero, C. (2010). *Un velo y una toca.* http://www.elpais.com/articulo/andalucia/velo/toca/elp epiespand/20100424elpand_10/Tes. 24 April 2010.

Carbajos, A. (2008). *Más musulmanas con velo. ¿Porque quieren?* http://www.elpais.com/articulo/ sociedad/musulmanas/velo/quieren/elpepisoc/20080628elpepisoc_1/Tes. 28 June 2008.

Carranco, R. (2010). *No me quito el 'hiyab' porque no quiero.* http://elpais.com/diario/2010/04/22/ sociedad/1271887206_850215.html. 22 April 2010.

De Ganuza, C. R. (2008). *El Partido Popular propondrá prohibir el uso del velo en todas las escuelas.* http://www.elmundo.es/elmundo/2008/02/08/espana/1202448607.html. 8 February 2008.

Del Barrio, A. (2008). *De la Vega desautoriza a Aído y dice que el Gobierno respeta la tradición del velo islámico.* http://www.elmundo.es/elmundo/2008/06/26/espana/1214475820.html. 27 June 2008.

Del Barrio, A. (2010a). *Los marroquíes exigen la intervención de la Comunidad en el caso de Najwa.* http://www.elmundo.es/elmundo/2010/04/16/madrid/1271421715.html. 16 April 2010.

Del Barrio, A. (2010b). *El velo no me limita para trabajar, que no te limita a ti para contratarme.* http://www.elmundo.es/elmundo/2010/12/21/espana/1292933868.html. 22 December 2010.

Del Barrio, A. (2010c). *Los musulmanes anuncian acciones legales contra el colegio de Pozuelo.* http://www.elmundo.es/elmundo/2010/04/21/madrid/1271852171.html. 21 April 2010.

Espinosa, A. (2010). *En mi clase había una monja.* http://elpais.com/diario/2010/04/23/sociedad/ 1271973602_850215.html. 23 April 2010.

Etxenike, L. (2004). *Tirar de la manta.* http://elpais.com/diario/2004/02/08/paisvasco/107627 2805_850215.html. 8 February 2004.

Farreras, C. (2016). *Los Nuevos Significados del velo.* http://www.lavanguardia.com/vida/201 60717/403268947566/universitarias-musulmanas-velo-hiyab-expresion-religion.html. 18 July 2016.

Figueras, A., & Piantadosi, G. (2011a). *Me echaron de un examen y del instituto por llevar el 'hiyab'.* http://www.elmundo.es/elmundo/2011/09/30/madrid/1317407926.html. 3 October 2011.

Figueras, A. (2011b). *La menor expulsada de un examen por el 'hiyab': 'Dicen que me lo invento y me hago la víctima.* http://www.elmundo.es/elmundo/2011/10/04/madrid/1317750847.html. 6 October 2011.

Figueras, A. (2011c). *El instituto que echó a una niña por llevar 'hiyab' acepta que pueda seguir utilizándolo*. http://www.elmundo.es/elmundo/2011/10/17/madrid/1318888325.html. 19 October 2011.

Figueras, A. (2011d). *El director que prohibió ir con el velo a clase podría ser acusado de prevaricación*. http://www.elmundo.es/elmundo/2011/10/27/castillayleon/1319714393.html. 27 October 2011.

Figueras, A. (2012). *La angustia de decir que eres Musulmán*. http://www.elmundo.es/elmundo/2012/04/27/espana/1335521507.html. 29 April 2012.

Figueras, A. (2015). *'¿Por qué se me cuestiona por abrazar esta fe? El islam no es el velo ni el IS ni ningún tipo de terrorismo'*. http://www.elmundo.es/espana/2015/06/24/55797914ca4741a626 8b457d.html. 30 June 2015.

Galafate, C. (2010). *Crean un grupo en Facebook para apoyar a Najwa*. http://www.elmundo.es/elmundo/2010/04/23/madrid/1272044565.html. 23 April 2010.

Galarraga, N. (2010). *¿Velo de sumisión o de rebeldía?* http://elpais.com/diario/2010/04/23/sociedad/1271973601_850215.html. 23 April 2010.

Gallego-Díaz, S. (2010). *El velo no merece una ley*. http://elpais.com/diario/2010/04/25/domingo/1272166236_850215.html. 25 April 2010.

Iglesias, N. (2007). *La Generalitat obliga a admitir en clase a una menor con 'hiyab'*. http://elpais.com/diario/2007/10/02/sociedad/1191276010_850215.html. 10 Feburary 2007.

Juárez, A. S. (2015). *Musulmanas y tan españolas como vosotras*. http://www.elmundo.es/yodona/2015/02/28/54ef5340ca4741216d8b4578.html. 28 Feburary 2015.

Lidón, I. (2016). *Vetada en el instituto por su hiyab: "Me dijeron: o te lo quitas o te das baja*. http://www.elmundo.es/comunidad-valenciana/2016/09/16/57dc38c2ca4741b51d8b4676.html. 18 September 2016.

Meneses, R. (2010). *Cual es el significado y el origen del Hiyab*. http://www.elmundo.es/elmundo/2010/04/21/madrid/1271853528.html. 22 April 2010.

Moliner, E. (2004). *A favor y en contra*. http://elpais.com/diario/2004/09/12/domingo/109495 7850_850215.html. 12 September 2004.

Montero, R. (2010). *Ahí le duele*. http://elpais.com/diario/2010/04/27/ultima/1272319201_850215.html. 27 April 2010.

Muñoz, G. M. (2010). *Esto alimenta a la derecha islamófoba*. http://elpais.com/diario/2010/04/22/sociedad/1271887205_850215.html. 22 April 2010.

Obelleiro, P. (2011a). *La familia de la niña de Arteixo invoca una norma estatal que permite el velo*. http://elpais.com/diario/2011/02/26/galicia/1298719096_850215.html. 26 Feburary 2011.

Obelleiro, P. (2011b). *Educación avala la prohibición del velo en clase a una niña*. http://elpais.com/diario/2011/02/25/galicia/1298632692_850215.html. 25 Feburary 2011.

Obelleiro, P. (2011c). *La Xunta anula la sanción a la niña del velo por un defecto formal*. http://elpais.com/diario/2011/03/11/sociedad/1299798012_850215.html. 11 March 2011.

Obelleiro, P. (2011d). *La 'niña del velo', excluida de la fiesta de fin de curso*. http://elpais.com/diario/2011/06/23/sociedad/1308780009_850215.html. 23 June 2011.

Obelleiro, P. (2011e). *El director del colegio de Arteixo impide a la niña del 'hiyab' entrar a recoger las notas*. http://elpais.com/diario/2011/06/23/galicia/1308824289_850215.html. 23 June 2011.

Peral, M. (2010). *Permitir el 'hiyab', facultad de cada juez*. http://www.elmundo.es/elmundo/2010/02/09/espana/1265687043.html. 9 Feburary 2010.

Sahuquillo, M. R. (2008). *Integración, si, asimilación, no*. http://www.elpais.com/articulo/sociedad/Integracion/asimilacion/elpepisoc/20080216elpepisoc_1/Tes. 16 Feburary 2008.

Sotero, P. D., & Bécares, R. (2010a). *El Ministerio de Educación apela a respetar las creencias de los alumnos*. http://www.elmundo.es/elmundo/2010/04/16/madrid/1271434711.html. 16 April 2010.

Velasco, I. (2016). *Tengo el derecho a trabajar con velo*. http://www.elmundo.es/sociedad/2016/06/10/5756a1bd468aeb14228b45b8.html. 10 June 2016.

Annex 2

English Articles

Akbar, A. (2010a). *The many faces behind the veil* (Introduction). http://www.independent.co.uk/news/uk/this-britain/the-many-faces-behind-the-veil-1865772.html. 13 January 2010.

Akbar, A. (2010b). *The many faces behind the veil* with Rajnaara Akhtar. http://www.independent.co.uk/news/uk/this-britain/the-many-faces-behind-the-veil-1865772.html. 13 January 2010.

Akbar, A. (2010c). *The many faces behind the veil* with Shelina Zahra JanMohamaed. http://www.independent.co.uk/news/uk/this-britain/the-many-faces-behind-the-veil-1865772.html. 13 January 2010.

Akbar, A. (2010d). *The many faces behind the veil* with Soha Sheikh. http://www.independent.co.uk/news/uk/this-britain/the-many-faces-behind-the-veil-1865772.html. 13 January 2010.

Akhtar, R. (2004). *Britain for me is a safe place.* https://www.theguardian.com/uk/2004/nov/30/islamandbritain1. 30 November 2004.

Alam, F. (2005). *We must move beyond the hijab.* https://www.theguardian.com/education/2005/nov/29/highereducation.uk. 29 Novenber 2005.

Alibhai-Brown, Y. (2015). *As a Muslim woman, I see the veil as a rejection of progressive values.* https://www.theguardian.com/commentisfree/2015/mar/20/muslim-woman-veil-hijab. 20 March 2015.

Aslam, S. (2014). *To hijab or not to hijab- A Muslim businesswoman's view.* http://www.theguardian.com/uk/the-northerner/2012/dec/10/hijab-muslims-women-islam-business-bradford-niqab-burka. 21 May 2014.

Aziz, S. (2014). *Laugh, not at my hijab please.* http://www.theguardian.com/theobserver/she-said/2014/apr/01/laugh-not-at-my-hijab-please. 1 April 2014.

Bennett, C. (2004).*Why should we defend the veil?"* http://www.theguardian.com/world/2004/jan/22/gender.schoolsworldwide. 22 January 2004.

Bentham, M., & Davis, A. (2007). *Hairdresser sued in row about headscarf* http://www.standard.co.uk/news/hairdresser-sued-in-row-about-headscarf-6657648.html. 8 November 2007.

Burchill, J. (2011). *Carla Bruni is standing up to the stoners: Lauren Booth just covers up for them* http://www.independent.co.uk/voices/columnists/julie-burchill/julie-burchill-carla-bruni-is-standing-up-to-the-stoners-lauren-booth-just-covers-up-for-them-2067119.html. 4 April 2011.

Carter, H. (2009). *Guest asked whether her hijab meant she was a terrorist, court told.* https://www.theguardian.com/uk/2009/dec/08/hijab-hotel-alleged-abuse-trial. 8 December 2009.

Cassidy, S. (2005). *Schoolgirl banned from wearing Muslim dress wins appeal.* http://www.independent.co.uk/news/education/education-news/schoolgirl-banned-from-wearing-muslim-dress-wins-appeal-527023.html. 3 March 2005.

Chowdhury, S. (2005). *We have more urgent issues to fight for than dress codes.* http://www.independent.co.uk/voices/commentators/shamim-chowdhury-we-have-more-urgent-issues-to-fight-for-than-dress-codes-4576.html. 4 March 2005.

Cllr Khan, R. (2006). *The hijab does not restrict it-it liberates.* https://www.theguardian.com/lifeandstyle/2009/apr/07/letters-hijab-islam-women. 7 April 2009.

Dear, P. (2004). *Women vow to protect Muslim hijab.* http://news.bbc.co.uk/2/hi/uk_news/3805733.stm. 14 June 2004.

Dhumieres, M. (2013). *Why is the right of Muslim women to wear the veil still so controversial in France?* http://www.independent.co.uk/voices/comment/why-is-the-right-of-muslim-women-to-wear-the-veil-still-so-controversial-in-france-8575052.html. 16 April 2013.

Elkin, S. (2013). *Common sense and respect for children in hijabs, please.* http://www.independent.co.uk/voices/comment/common-sense-and-respect-for-children-in-hijabs-please-8437433.html. 3 January 2013.

Guest, K., & Davies, M. Y. *The Muslims next door.* http://www.independent.co.uk/news/uk/this-britain/focus-the-muslims-next-door-527359.html. 6 March 2005.

Jones, E. C. (2005). *Muslim girls unveil their fears.* http://news.bbc.co.uk/2/hi/programmes/this_world/4352171.stm. 28 March 2005.

Khaleeli, H. (2008). *The hijab goes high-fashion.* https://www.theguardian.com/lifeandstyle/2008/jul/28/fashion.women. 28 July 2008.

Khan, S. (2015). *It is not the hijab which holds women back, but prejudice.* http://www.telegraph.co.uk/culture/tvandradio/great-british-bake-off/11919553/Its-not-the-hijab-which-holds-women-back-but-intolerance-and-prejudice.html. 8 October 2015.

Kossaibati, J. (2009). *It is a wrap!* https://www.theguardian.com/lifeandstyle/2009/mar/30/fashion-hijab-muslim-women. 30 March 2009.

Malik, M. (2006). *This veil fixation is doing Muslim women no favors.* https://www.theguardian.com/commentisfree/2006/oct/19/religion.immigration. 19 October 2006.

Marin, M. (2004). *Cry freedom and accept the Muslim headscarf.* https://www.thetimes.co.uk/article/comment-minette-marrin-cry-freedom-and-accept-the-muslim-headscarf-tcxvm85lhqd. 1 Feburary 2004.

Marrison, S. (2011). *The Islamification of Britain: Record numbers embrace Muslim faith.* http://www.independent.co.uk/news/uk/home-news/the-islamification-of-britain-record-numbers-embrace-muslim-faith-2175178.html. 4 January 2011.

Melville, K. (2009). *Muslim patriarchy served well by hijab.* https://www.theguardian.com/world/2009/apr/04/hijab-niqab-islam-muslims. 4 April 2009.

Mursaleen, S. (2010). *The power behind the veil.* https://www.theguardian.com/commentisfree/belief/2010/jan/25/burqa-ban-veil-sarkozy-ukip. 25 January 2010.

Orr, D. (2005). *Blairism is simply Thatcherism administered by do-gooders.* http://www.independent.co.uk/voices/commentators/deborah-orr/blairism-is-simply-thatcherism-administered-by-do-gooders-527246.html. 5 March 2005.

Perves, S. (2013). *Mishal Husain and the Veil: What the Daily Mail was really trying to say.* https://www.theguardian.com/uk-news/the-northerner/2013/oct/08/mishal-husain-veil-daily-mail. 8 October 2013.

Riddell, M. (2003). *Veiled threats.* https://www.theguardian.com/world/2003/dec/14/religion.britishidentity. 4 December 2003.

Sanghani, R. (2015a). *H&M advert features first Muslim Model in a hijab (finally).* http://www.telegraph.co.uk/women/womens-life/11898632/HandM-advert-features-first-Muslim-model-in-a-hijab-finally.html. 29 September 2015.

Smith, J. (2004). *What lies beneath the veil.* http://www.independent.co.uk/voices/commentators/joan-smith/what-lies-beneath-the-veil-8833948.html. 25 January 2004.

Smith, J. (2006a). *The veil is a feminist issue.* http://www.independent.co.uk/voices/commentators/joan-smith/joan-smith-the-veil-is-a-feminist-issue-419119.html. 8 October 2006.

Smith, J. (2006b). *Our schools are no place for Jilbab: Or for Creationists.* http://www.independent.co.uk/voices/commentators/joan-smith/joan-smith-our-schools-are-no-place-for-the-jilbab-or-for-the-creationists-6105619.html. 26 March 2006.

Takolia, N. (2010). *The hijab has liberated me from society expectations of women.* https://www.theguardian.com/commentisfree/2012/may/28/hijab-society-women-religious-political. 28 May 2012.

Walter, N. (2004). *When the veil means freedom.* https://www.theguardian.com/world/2004/jan/20/france.schoolsworldwide1. 20 January 2004.

Ware, J. (2015). *Muslim nursery worker loses appeal to wear jilbab gown at work because it is a 'tripping hazard'.* http://www.independent.co.uk/news/uk/home-news/muslim-nursery-worker-loses-appeal-to-wear-jilbab-at-work-because-it-is-a-tripping-hazard-10317739.html. 13 June 2015.

Wyatt, C. (2003). *Liberty, equality and the headscarf.* http://news.bbc.co.uk/2/hi/programmes/from_our_own_correspondent/3334881.stm. 20 December 2003.

Wyatt, C. (2004). *French headscarf ban opens rifts.* http://news.bbc.co.uk/2/hi/europe/3478895.stm. 11 Feburary 2004.

Framing National Hijab-Wearing Women in the European Mind: Within and Cross-Cultural Analysis of the British and Spanish Press

Introduction

European Muslim women cannot be understood as one homogenous group. Although they have Islam as a shared religion, their ethnic origins, local contexts, and cultural backgrounds play an essential role in their self-identification and self-categorization. However, the European discourse on Muslim women put them all on one sack as if the religious dimension in their identity can erase all the ethnic and social differences. As if it is rational to classify women in Europe as Atheist women and Christian women.

Angeles Ramirez indicates that Muslim women's image schemata in Spain today is based on the colonialized Moroccan Muslim women's image due to the colonial relationship between Spain and Morocco.[1] The hijab-wearers' visibility in the Spanish public sphere is recent and is somehow restricted to Moroccan nationality. Although there are Palestinian, Syrian, and Pakistani communities, Muslim women are framed by first sight as Moroccans or of Moroccan origins. Muslim women's visibility in the United Kingdom is older, started since WWI, and WWII,[2] and it is more diverse. The ethnicity of Muslim women in the United Kingdom is varied and significant: "Indian, Pakistani, Bangladeshi, Turkish, Lebanese, Palestinian, and Iranian." The question is, How is the visibility of these women framed in the national Spanish and British press at the beginning of the twenty-first century?

This chapter does not differ from the previous one on the methodological level. I carried out a Cognitive Critical Discourse Analysis CCDA on the selected article to analyze the hijab-wearing women's visibility in the national (Spanish and British) public sphere. I study the mental frames that are (re)activated, de-activated, empowered, and/or asserted. I depended on the previous chapters' literature to figure out the historical and contextual factors that operate in the building of these mental frames.

I find four mental frames of the hijab-wearing women: "Ignorance," "Oppression," "Othering," and "Indiscipline." These mental frames are (re)activated, empowered,

---

[1] Ramirez (2010).

[2] Gilliat-Ray (2010).

© Springer Nature Singapore Pte Ltd. 2021
G. Khir-Allah, *Framing Hijab in the European Mind*,
https://doi.org/10.1007/978-981-16-1653-2_7

and asserted (and sometimes de-activated) in both national press discourse. As I did in the previous chapter, the analysis will be on two levels sequentially: Micro-Level analysis (each mental frame is discussed within the national press/diversity) then the Macro-Level analysis (I carried a cross-culture comparative analysis).

I also use the term "re-activate" to refer to these stereotypical mental frames which the press recycles from the colonial discourse. The term "activate" refers to the new mental frames related to the current contextual visibility of the hijab in the Spanish and British public sphere.

Framing the Hijab-Wearing Women Through "Ignorance"

Framing hijab-wearing women through "Ignorance" indicates that they lack the knowledge to enjoy the civilized national life pattern. This mental frame is a recycled one from the colonial discourse. It is re-activated by the hijab opposers in both Spanish and British press. However, it is re-activated differently across both press discourses, as we will see below. It is quite important to point out that framing the hijab-wearing coincides with framing the signifier, the hijab.

Spanish "Ignorance" Mental Frame of Hijab-Wearing Women

The Spanish "Ignorance" mental frame of hijab-wearers is re-activated indirectly by several discursive techniques. The re-activation of this frame is extensive in El Pais in both articles categories: the exclusion cases and the social and political discourse. One of these discursive techniques, in exclusion cases, is highlighting the Spanish language skills of the excluded students' mothers. Rebeca Carranco mentions the mother's language difficulties: "the mother does not speak Spanish, her daughter is translating the communication."[3] Carranco continues that "the mother of Shaima had not even heard [*ni se habia enterado*]" of the case of Najwa Al-Malha in Madrid; and "Shaima does not know what to opine." Both the mother and her daughter are pictured as disoriented and ignorant of the social context they live in. The journalist makes sure to tell the reader about the TV choice of the mother and her daughter, Arabic channels. Shaima's motivation for practicing the hijab does not provide any significant argument "I do not want to take it off because I do not want to." She seems that she has no clue why she wants to practice the hijab. All of these details about the mother and her daughter frame both through "Ignorance." Another similar re-activation appears in the case of Hassna Isslal. Pilar Alvarez referred to the mother's language deficiency, "her mother, Khadija (37), who has not learned Spanish after five

---

[3]Carranco (2010).

years in Spain".[4] Referring to these mothers' Spanish language deficiency, reframe them like others (activating the "Othering" frame of hijab-wearing women). Simultaneously, this discursive strategy might activate a sense of language superiority on these women, as if those who do not speak fluent Spanish are less educated than those who do.

However, let's compare Alvarez's introduction of Isslal's mother to the mother of the excluded student in Usera school, who does not practice the hijab. We find out that the Spanish language skills of the latter are not necessary anymore.[5] Yet, Álvarez indicates that the Usera student's mother is a housewife even though Figueras in El Mundo indicates that "the mother works out home and does not use the veil."[6] Interestingly enough, both newspapers are keen on classifying Muslim women in hijab-wearers or non-hijab-wearers categories: the mothers, the cousins, or even the Muslim classmate. In the case of Usera, the student's cousins are referred to as unveiled. This classification provides mental orientation for the reader to frame the mentioned women in according to the characteristics of each category: Non-hijab-wearing (modern) women and hijab-wearing (traditional) (ignorant) women.[7]

In the political and social debate, the "Ignorance" frame of the hijab-wearing women is re-activated through a different discursive strategy. The social and political discourse uses the "insignificant and superficial presentation" technique extensively in El País. Such a presentation was also used for the hijab supporters. They are framed in opposition to the professional/academic experts who oppose the hijab practice and argue in favor of the French ban. For example, Muslim women who support Najwa's right to religious liberty and education are Yoniada Selam and Amparo Sanchez.[8] Both are well known in the Spanish Muslim community and maintain a significant social role. Yonaida Selam is a president of the Intercultural Association of Melilla, a writer, and a public figure. Amparo Sánchez is the (first Spanish woman) president of the Islamic Center of Valencia. However, Álvarez does not narrate much about them. Selam, who states that the hijab is "a sign of identity," is presented merely as a member of "an intercultural association." Sánchez Rosell is introduced as follows: "another woman [Otra mujer], Amparo Sánchez Rosell, has been moving. From the Islamic Cultural center of Valencia, she is planning a caravan trip of women to Madrid." Such a presentation underestimated the Muslim women who support the hijab right is not a coincidence. It is part of discursive strategies to assert the insignificance of Muslim women who practice hijab or support the women's free choice of vestment.

---

[4]Álvarez, Pilar (c). *Renunciar al velo islámico sería como quitarme la piel.* El País: 23 October 2011. http://elpais.com/diario/2011/10/23/sociedad/1319320802_850215.html.

[5]Álvarez, Pilar (b). *Mi velo sí entra en clase.* El País, 19 October 2011. http://elpais.com/diario/2011/10/19/madrid/1319023459_850215.html.

[6]Figueras and Piantadosi (2011).

[7]Ramirez (2010).

[8]Álvarez and Cembrero (2010a).

The presentation strategy has an essential role in re-activating the "Ignorance" mental frame of hijab-wearing women in the Spanish press. Against-hijab participants are presented as active women with academic titles and successful careers; in contrast, hijab wearers and hijab supporters are not. For example, I compare the presentation of the hijab wearers and the hijab supporters to the presentation of the hijab opposers in El Pais. Luisa Etxenike, in "*Tirar la Manta.*"[9] introduces the Not Whores Nor Submissive movement as a trusted voice in the hijab debate "(their voice is) loud and clear" and "their evidence is probative." Their argument opposes the hijab practice, which coincides with the stereotypical colonial discourse of the newspaper. In another appearance of this movement, in Ana Carabajos' article, Amara, the founder of the movement, is introduced as a qualified voice to "explain very well" the origin of veiling practice.[10] Amara's mental frame on the hijab is a copy-paste of the newspaper's stereotypical agenda: "[She] consider the veil an act of submission in its purest form." Carabajos quotes Amara: "I am a Muslim, and I consider the veil an instrument of oppression."

In this article, Carabajos interviewed different women from opposite perspectives; for and against the hijab. The voices who supported the hijab are presented as follows: (1) the Muslim leaders' reaction to Aído's declaration is "short and decisive," and they "transfixed her (Aido)" with statements. (2) a general reference to Muslim women as "progressive and conservative," who are "moan(ing)" their right to veil, they "consider and assure- no one can take away their right of veiling," and they "presume" that their culture "cares about inner beauty." (3) Samah "thinks" and "her words are eloquent" when she states that "males are different, they always have a desire to sex. They should not be provoked". The linguistic expressions "moan" and "presume," which are used to introduce Muslim women's arguments, indicate uncertainty and assumptions more than decisiveness and clarity. The only decisive argument is found in Samah's voice, cross seas, who asserted men's sexual desire, a needed stereotypical notion to assert women subjection and sexual discrimination of the practice. This Discursive "quotation" strategy consists of picking the quotations that support the article's aim. None of these three voices includes an academic-expert argument.

On the contrary to this insignificant presentation, the hijab opposer participants are: (1) Aído "the Minister of equality is disposed to challenge the political correctness to make her message heard," (2) Amara "considers" and "explains very well"; Ercevik, a Turkish feminist from Istanbul, "sustains" (twice) and "adds" and De La Vega "points out." The vocabularies, which introduce the participants' contributions from both groups, are critical in re-activating the "Ignorance" mental frame. The vocabularies stigmatize the hijab supporter and hijab-wearers' argument as unsure and suspicious, whereas asserting the legitimacy and validity of the hijab opposer's contributions.

---

[9]Etxenike (2004).

[10]Carbajos (2008).

In another article written by Naiara Galarraga, we find a similar uneven presentation of women's voices.[11] The women participants in the for and against discourse are well selected in order to create a manipulated scene that re-activates and empowers the "Ignorance" mental frame of the hijab wearers and the hijab supporters. The hijab opposers are of academic profiles: (1) Najat El Hashmi, 30 years old, a "Catalan writer" woman born in Morocco. She was Muslim, and now she is an atheist. Galarraga introduces Najat in a similar presentation of Carabajos' to Amara: "she is one of those Spanish who can speak knowingly about the hijab [*con conocimiento de causa*]." (2) Randa Achmawi, a diplomatic correspondent of Ahram Hebdo diary. Both Al-Hashim and Achmawi argue that the hijab practice is part of the adolescent identity crisis and disorientation at young Muslims. Such discourse also activates the "Indiscipline" frame, which we will cover at the end of this chapter. (3) Sihem Habchi, the president of the Not Whores Nor Submissive movement. She says that "the veil is a sign of discrimination because only women have to wear it." (4) Nawal El Saadawi, an Egyptian writer "famous for her opposition to the hijab and her support to the hijab ban." She wrote to Galarraga by email that "in all countries, occidental and oriental countries, separating education from religion [....] is essential for true democracy." These four (ex) Muslim women are Academic and/or head of social organizations or movements who support stereotypical frames of the hijab: it is a symbol of disorientation, a spiritual caprice, a symbol of discrimination against real liberty and true democracy.

The second category of women in this article includes hijab supporters. Najwa, the protagonist, is not included. They are as follows: (1) an anonymous Muslim woman "Spanish Muslim." Her contribution is introduced through well designed discursive quotation strategy: the journalist first points out that no one can calculate how many women are forced to practice the hijab. She continues: "However, a Spanish Muslim adds 'there is too much syndrome about the Muslim husband.'" The anonymous Spanish Muslim's argument is minimal, brief, and almost insignificant. It does not provide any negation on the enforced hijab, nor she clarifies her argument with an extra explanation. (2) a 20-years-old girl of a Palestinian father and Spanish mother. The anonymous voice warns of the dangerous alternative for Najwa, which is ignorance: "For this young [girl], the worst thing that might happen to Najwa is to have to stay at home. Then, she says, 'they condemn her to ignorance, to get married soon, etc.'" (3) anonymous woman works in domestic cleaning per hour (which highlights that she might not have a contract). She is not linked to any nationality or country. Galarraga quotes Bernabé López, a History professor in Islam at the Autónoma University of Madrid, "he says that a Muslim woman in his neighborhood, who works in house cleaning per hours talked to him about the issue 'she sees what is happening to the girl as aggression because she also wears the veil.'" The woman's opinion lacks objectivity or credibility because of her anonymity and the subjective link established between Najwa's hijab and this women's hijab. These three voices are added in the article to create a sense of multipartiality in the hijab debate. However, this unequal presentation serves to re-activate and assert the "Ignorance" frame of

---

[11] Galarraga (2010).

hijab wearers and hijab supporters. The three voices are Muslims and anonymous with no academic description. Those three voices are intentionally introduced to fill the gap in the readers' minds that might ask for the "other's" viewpoint. Such manipulated discourse neatly, unconsciously, classify hijab-wearing women into the "Ignorance" frame in the readers' mind.

You might have recognized the connection between the "Ignorance" frame of hijab-wearing women and the "Concealment" frame of the hijab in the Spanish press. In the previous chapter, we discussed that the hijab conceals the women's visibility from the Spanish public life. In a reciprocal relationship, the "Concealment" frame of the hijab is justified by the "Ignorance" frame of the hijab-wearers, and the "Ignorance" frame explains their limited insignificant contributions in social and political debate.

As a result, the journalists, who are all women in the selected data, set themselves as spokeswomen on behalf of Muslim feminine using the "I" pronoun to opine on the topic. For example, Etxenike writes her article, titled *"Tirar la manta,"*[12] because of her sense of responsibility to reflect on the hijab ban in the neighbor France. She states: "from this neighborhood, today, I appoint some reflection (supportive in the majority) on the law that is designed to ban the veil and other ostensible religious signs at public schools." At the end of the article, she indicates: "I will not end the article before I talk about the other depth of the topic: The sphere in which this law is applied, the school." Empar Moliner starts the article pronouncing herself the professional whose opinion matter to explain and understand the French ban law.[13] She states: "the life of a professional [opinador] is not a rosy road," "I do not have a solution so there will be no touching [...]" in reference to gender separation in Saudi Arabia, "it does not sound to me logical the phrase [...]" and "I find it good that girls and boys see each other hair mutually." The same self-assignment as a professional appears in Montero's article.[14] The journalist introduces her ideas as follows: "it looks for me," "I believe," and "I think that." Journalists also set the speakers whose ideas assert the stereotypical frames as spokeswomen, as we have seen above in the analysis. Gallego-Díaz presents Hoda El Shaaraw as follows: "(she) decided to rip off the veil which covered her face when she moved in public spaces. [....] (she) is educated women implicated in the political battles; she fought for that Muslim women do not wear the burka or niqab."[15] All of these discursive strategies provide the journalists and the hijab opposers with legitimacy and authority. Simultaneously, it rips away the hijab-wearing women's right to participate in the debate equally.

In La Vanguardia, Raquel Quelart interviews Beatriz Goyaoaga, a general coordinator of the Art of Living ONG in Spain and Latin America.[16] The ONG fights against stress and seeks to get a peaceful world. The title *"I have met very happy women behind the veil"* indicates that the interview revolves around the hijab and

---

[12]Etxenike (2004).

[13]Moliner (2004).

[14]Montero (2010).

[15]Gallego-Díaz (2010).

[16]Quelart (2011).

Muslim women. Surprisingly, the analysis detected that out of 1697 words, only 232 words related to the hijab at the end of the interview; and 44 words are related to Burka. In total: 274 words (2 questions for each veiling practice out of 26 questions). The rest of the meeting tackles many different questions about stress, meditation, lifestyle, travels, and essential moments in Beatriz Goyoaga's life. However, these 274 words have sufficient weight to occupy the title, which does not represent the article's content. Quelart refers to Goyoaga as an "expert in Islamic women" right before she asks her about the veil: "You are considered an expert in Islamic women. Do you see it ok that many of them wear a veil?". Announcing the participant's expertise in the hijab debate is another discursive strategy that legitimate her contribution as much as it provides her with an authoritative voice. Goyoaga re-activates the "Ignorance" frame of the hijab-wearers in her answer: "before, I thought that living behind the veil is a huge trauma. but it is not like this. They do not know any other thing. They feel very happy." Accordingly, Goyoaya, the expert, indicates that hijab-wearers she met do not know about alternative lifestyles, and they are happy with what they have gotten. She concludes that "if these women do not agree. [...] They, by themselves, should go out to reclaim permission not to wear the veil." In other words, it is "their" lifestyle, "their" problem, and they need to deal with it.

In 2015/2016, the discourse in El País and El Mundo steps forward to include scattered voices of academic hijab-wearers who has been excluded from the workplace and the institute and who defend their right to hijab, work, and study (Bohorquez, 2016; Figueras, 2012, 2015; Juárez, 2015; Velasco, 2016). Hijab-wearers' contributions indicate their awareness of the "Ignorance" frame imposed on them in the public sphere. For example, Omaima indicates that the school's headmaster "was astonished last year" when she was given an honorary degree.[17] She continues: "The results of the Moroccan of the neighborhood did not make sense for him." Omaima's good grades are conflictive because it does not fit with the "Ignorance" frame he builds on the hijab-wearers. Such mental conflict makes it difficult for Spanish mainstreamers to accept an educated Muslim as a norm. Both Omaima and Naima (interviewed in this article) indicate that people tell them they are "exceptions" because they are successful and motivated women. The Spanish mainstream mind cannot shift to the idea that Muslim women can be as successful as the norm. Figueras highlights the rigidity of the "Ignorance" mental frame in the Spanish mainstream minds. She states that when people know about her reversion to Islam, they do not make an effort to know her motivation: "prejudice wins. It is easier to think that some *[moros le habrian comido la cabeza]* than to make questions".[18] She continues that society had given her credit for independence when choosing her career, work, house, and boyfriend. But when she chose Islam, society stripped away its trust and stigmatized her as a manipulated woman. Besides, the journalist is aware of the authoritative unilateral discourse of some feminist journalists; she specifies the "feminist tendencies who consider that Muslim women are incapable of speaking out for ourselves and feel the necessity to liberate us."

---

[17] Juárez (2015).
[18] Figueras (2015).

However, in 2015/2016, La Vanguardia maintains the discursive strategies that re-activate the "Ignorance" frame. For example, Carina Farreras, in her article: "The New Meaning of the Veil: Increased the number of Muslims (female) with an academic title who want to express their religion,"[19] links between "academic" and "religion." The focus matter of the title suggests the incompatibility between them. It is an indirect indication that, typically, practicing the hijab is not assigned to educated women. The article quotes Spanish university professors to debate the hijab visibility in the Spanish public sphere: Silvia Carrasco, a doctor in Social anthropology at UAB, and Dolores Bramón, a doctor in Semitic Philosophy in UB and a "major expert in the topic in Catalunya." Given the academic and professional authority to talk about the topic, Carrasco and Bramón agree that Muslim women mistakenly think of the hijab as "a religious" practice; the truth is it is "an identity or cultural affirmation." These declarations de-activate the "Religiosity" frame of the hijab and re-activate the "Othering" frame: it is the traditions of "others." The journalist concludes the first part of the article by quoting the philosopher Olga Dominguez who sets out the "original meaning" of the hijab practice: "the submission to the man." Dominguez explains that "for these young women, the symbol of the veil seems to be detached from the submission to men, creating with it a new meaning." She "warns": "giving a new meaning to a symbol is not an automatic process that can be done at your convenience." Dominguez asserts the stereotypical meaning of the hijab through what she calls the "original meaning," yet, she keeps the new meaning of the hijab practice obscured. The journalist introduces Dominguez's opinion on the untold new meaning by the verb "warn," indicating the danger that evolves around it. Farreras asserts Dominguez's quotation and explains the worries of the new meanings of the hijab: "For Dominguez, a symbol that expresses implicit violence cannot change its meaning without affecting its victims in some way. "We run the risk of playing in favor of Islamic patriarchy."

In this article, what the journalist and the philosopher create in the reader's mind is the following: (1) The hijab means first and foremost oppression. (2) When the hijab wearers youth claim that they are not oppressed, they are fooled by patriarchy, and they are doing a favor to it by practicing the hijab. The second part of the article follows this mental preparation; the interviews with Spanish academic hijab-wearing youth: Najat Driouech, licensed in Arabic Philology, a master in cultural Identity Construction, Diploma in Social Work, post-master in Immigration, Identity, and Religion. She participates in Catalan University international congresses and in European and American congresses. Ramia Chaoui, licensed in Business Administration and Direction in UB. She is born and educated in Catalunya. Najat Talha, will start the first grade of Social Work at Girona University. She followed formative sessions about Social Integration and Work with the Mayor of Figueres. She was born in Figueres, and Jihan Dahou, who has not had any presentation. The academic career of these women was mentioned in opposition to the pre-2015/2016 discourse. Both Driouech and Chaoui are hijab-wearers, and both explain the hijab motivations

---

[19]Farreras (2016).

as personal decisions related to religious and spiritual factors, activating the "Religiosity" frame of the hijab. They say that the hijab is a "spiritual decision," "modesty for God," and having "a [*revelador*] dream indicates veiling."

However, all these motivations have been already cast to be false by the experts above. They have already stigmatized the religious motivations as mistaken, limiting it to cultural identity manifestation. Dominguez's warnings (the danger of attaching new meanings to the hijab) cast away all the young girls' arguments as a dangerous attempt that serves patriarchy. Such cognitive manipulation in introducing the visible academic hijab-wearers promotes unobjective debate that maintains the "Ignorance" frame of the hijab-wearers active along with the article. It sticks in the mind that these women do not know what they are talking about. In the same article, Chaoui refers to the "Ignorance" frame, among others, imposed on her in the public sphere: "you see it in their eyes (mainstreamers) when they look at you: poverty, analphabetism, war, oppressed woman, without studies." Driouech narrates that in a conference of migrants in Europe where she has a 30 min' contribution, a Euro MP asked her why she wears the veil. The academic women's limitation in an international conference to merely woman with a piece of cloth on the head underestimates her academic and professional career.

To sum up, the "Ignorance" frame of hijab-wearing women, in social and political debate, is re-activated in El País through various discursive strategies: (1) highlighting the students' mothers' inability to speak the Spanish language in the school exclusion cases, (2) The manipulated presentation of the hijab wearers and hijab supporters in comparison to the professional presentation to the hijab opposers in the social and political debate. This manipulation aims to create a multipartial discussion on the hijab. It looks inclusive to hijab-wearers, yet, the inclusion is systematically controlled to re-activate the "Ignorance" mental frames on these women. (3) the concealment (anonymity) of women's social role and presenting them as insignificant individuals whose declarations are superficial and inconsequential. This mental frame's re-activation in readers' minds justifies these women's anonymous contributions in the articles (empowering the "Concealment" framing of the hijab). Besides, it justifies the authoritative discourse of Western spokeswomen who lecture Muslim women, analyze their religion for them, and talk on their behalf.[20] (4) The cognitive manipulation of the readers' minds before they are exposed to the controlled hijab-wearers' participation in the mainstream press discourse. Both El Pais and La Vanguardiause this strategy even in the post-2015/2016 discourse. (Reliable) (academic) (white) against-hijab participants' arguments were introduced to repeal the less authentic, less reliable, hijab-wearing women's arguments.

Muslim visibility in the post-2015/2016 discourse, even though manipulated, might shake the rigid "Ignorance" frame imposed on them. The hijab-wearing participants show awareness of this framing through real stories they have been through. However, their contributions were limited and controlled by the journalists, except the article written by Amanda Figueras en El Mundo.

---

[20] Ahmed (1982) and Jouili (2009).

British "Ignorance" Mental Frame of Hijab-Wearing Women

The British "Ignorance" mental frame of hijab-wearing women is re-activated by indirect discursive strategies. It is less intensive in the Spanish re-activation because of the national visibility of high-profile hijab-wearing women in the United Kingdom public sphere; who works in hospitals (Walter, 2004), magazines (Alam, 2005), Radio stations (Byrne, 2005), libraries (Akbar, 2010c), etc. The British "Ignorance" frame of hijab-wearing women is not imposed on them as an essential feature of their character. Instead, it is limited to the wrong decision of practicing the hijab or *jilbab*. In a similar discursive strategy to the Spanish press, the re-activation of the "Ignorance" frame of hijab-wearers depends on raising suspicions on the "real" motivation of the practice. It is seen as doing a favor to Islamist and extremist groups. For example, in The Independent, Joan Smith refers that the *jilbab*-wearing student (Shabina Begum. Luton, 2005) and her supporters, including Cherie Booth, as "misguided" by the Islamic authorities who express "sexual disgust" and "argue in favor of covering girls and women."[21] Smith, in another article, refers to the backwardness decision of hijab, which is imposed on women through history: "Islam isn't alone in this: for centuries, Christianity laid down similar conditions but the Enlightenment, of which feminism is an integral part, successfully challenged such rigid divisions between the sexes."[22]

In a similar discursive strategy to Ferraras, Smith highlights the incompatibility between enlightenment and (Sexuality) "Concealment" framing of the hijab. She depends on the re-activation of the "Discrimination" and "Oppression" frame of the practice. Smith says that the high-profile hijab-wearers who "cover themselves" "are demonstrating their acceptance of an ideology that gives them fewer rights than men and an inferior place in society." In the third article, Smith includes an "impassioned denunciations" of "women in Muslim countries, some of whom go as far as describing women who wear hijab as brain-washed."[23]

The cognitive strategy that casts the hijab decision as a wrong and misleading one is the principal axes in the re-activation of the "Ignorance" frame of hijab-wearers in the British national sphere. Such framing underestimates the (sexuality concealment) decision. It announces the European standards of gender relations as exemplary and cast the "other" Muslim standards on gender relations as the opposite (un-enlightened or ignorant of liberty and equality values). Thus, hijab-wearers are accused of being unable to see the practice's discriminative aspect due to their cultural inclinations, patriarchal domination, or mind-shortness. The British re-activation of the "Ignorance" frame of hijab-wearing women does not stigmatize them as ignorant individuals, as we see in the Spanish context. This frame is confined to the practice decision that accepts the "discriminated" aspect of the practice. Sexuality exposure in the public sphere is tied to women's liberty and enlightenment.

---

[21] Smith (2006b).
[22] Smith (2006a).
[23] Smith (2004).

A similar reference to the misleaded decision appears in The Times Online. Minette Marin indicates that "it is essential to allow Muslim schoolgirls to dress in whatever way they think their religion demands, wrongly or rightly, and however much liberals may illiberally object."[24] The practice motivation is limited to what these girls "think" of their religious demands and not to Islamic religious demands. The linguistic expressions "wrongly or rightly" create skepticism around the correctness of the hijab decision. Marin concludes the article with Qassim Amin's warnings in 1899. Amin asserts the incompatibility between the hijab practice and modernity: "unless Muslims embraced modernity and equality, the future be bleak. We are in bleakness now, and few dare to speak up for its values." This statement stigmatizes hijab-wearing women as un-moderns and as a coward to call for it. In the Guardian, the "Ignorance" mental frame is re-activated in Kate Melville's article. Melville indicates that the hijab is imposed by "the Muslim patriarchy to make sure that women waste their time, remain ignorant, and never quite focus for long enough on things that really matter."[25] In this statement, there is a visible direct framing of the hijab-wearing women as amalgamated in ignorance.

In the British data, there has been an association between uncovering and professionalism/independence. For example, such an association is seen in Smith's discourse above. In The Guardian, Natasha Walter also indicates that feminism in the West is "tied up with the freedom to uncover ourselves."[26] The discourse links women's hat a century ago to the women's traditional role in society at that time (indoors). She indicates that taking off the hats, gloves, and long skirts were "tied up to a larger struggle to come out of their houses, to speak in public, to travel alone, to go into education, into works, and into politics, and so on to be independent." According to this mental frame, the levels of body exposure in the public sphere reflect the level of women's independence. She states that any "journey of self-determination for women" goes through the same trajectory: "moving bareheaded into public sight," which reflects the "independence of mind and body."

Even though the "Ignorance" frame is not extensive in the British, Hijab-wearing writers and interviewees narrate their experience of the "Ignorance" frame imposed on them by the British mainstream. For example, in The Guardian, Syima Aslam, "Bradford sales and marketing executive who is a 43," narrates her experience as follow:

> I couldn't quite forget a few post-hijab meetings, small in number but significant in my head, where people I had met with a colleague would talk only to my colleague. I would have to muscle in, and they would realize halfway through the meeting that I was the one with the required expertise. One particular gentleman spent the entire meeting talking to a point slightly to one side of my head, which I found most disconcerting.[27]

Her experience reveals two mental categorizations imposed on her by the mainstreamer: first, the "Concealment" frame due to her sexuality concealment; second,

---

[24] Marin (2004).

[25] Melville (2009).

[26] Walter (2004).

[27] Aslam (2014).

the "Ignorance" frame. Both end up marginalizing the hijab-wearers in the British public sphere.

In The Independent, Ciar Byrne interviews two sisters Faiza and her sister, who present a radio show, *The Islamic Hour*, broadcast by the Manchester community radio station ALL FM. In their show, Faiza told the listeners her post-hijab experience: "People start treating you a little bit differently. I got pulled over by a policeman, and he spoke to me like I was dumb. He was talking to me like I was three years old. I felt like saying, just because I'm wearing the hijab doesn't make me stupid."[28]

In the British context, high-profile educated British hijab-wearing women participate in social and political debates (writers and interviewees) in the Independent and the Guardian, including those articles which show stereotypical discourse on the hijab. For example, Dr. Iman, a pediatrician at Northwick Park hospital, and Salma Yaqoob, the chair of Birmingham Stop the War Coalition, are interviewed by Walter in the Guardian. He links between the bareheaded women and the independence of mind and body.[29] Fareen Alam and Fauzia Ahmed, a research fellow in sociology at Bristol University, are interviewed in Guest and Davies' article in The Independent.[30] As well, we read a series of interviews with academic, social activists hijab-wearers in the Independence (Akbar, 2010a, b, c). The hijab-wearing writers have the opportunity to engage in the national mainstream press, especially in The Guardian. They published their own articles, such as Maleiha Malik, "a lecturer in law at King's College London and author of feminism and Muslim Women,"[31] Fareena Alam, an editor of Q News, The Muslim magazine,"[32] and Jana Kossaibati, a medical student and YouTuber.[33] In addition to the hijab-wearing interviewees and writers, the British context includes hijab-wearing famous public figures, such as H&M model Mariah Idrissi and the winner of Great British Bake off 2015 Nadiya Hussain (Khan, 2015; Sanghani, 2015a, b) in The Telegraph and (Aly, 2015) in The Guardian. It is to say, re-activating the "Ignorance" frame of hijab-wearing women did not conceal the hijab-wearers' free, un-manipulated, participation in the mainstream discourse and the British public sphere as we have seen in the Spanish press.

To sum up, the British "Ignorance" frame of hijab-wearing women is almost restricted to the ignorant choice of accepting the gender discrimination of the practice. It is not re-activated as the main feature of the hijab-wearers. It is re-activated in the Independent, Times Online, and The Guardian. The discursive (cognitive) strategies depend on raising doubts around the "real" hijab decision, accusing the hijab-wearers of being deceived by the Islamist and radical groups.

The re-activation of the "Ignorance" frame depends on the re-activation of "Discrimination" and "Oppression" frames of the hijab. It also depends on the (Offensive) (Sexuality) "Concealment" frame. The discourse links between professionalism and

[28] Byrne (2005).

[29] Walter (2004).

[30] Guest and Davies (2005).

[31] Malik (2006).

[32] Alam (2005).

[33] Kossaibati (2009).

unveiling. It sets the European values on gender relations as exemplary and cast "other's" values on gender relations as destitute of feminist liberation movements and enlightenment. In The Independent and The Guardian, the hijab-wearers' experiences confirm being ignored at work as if they were concealed or less professional than their workmates.

Cross-Cultural Analysis

The "Ignorance" mental frame of the hijab-wearers is re-activated in both Spanish and British press. We find several similar discursive strategies to re-activated, yet; there seem to be slight differences. For example, both presses raise doubts in the readers' minds about the accurate or original meaning and motivation of the hijab. Both presses link it to Islamist and radical movements. They also stigmatized the decision of the hijab-wearers as "deceived." Both presses depend on stigmatizing framings of the hijab to empower the "Ignorance" framing of its wearers, such as the "Discrimination" and "oppression" frame.

Both discourses establish the link between the "Concealment" frame of the hijab and the ignorance of the hijab-wearers. However, in the previous chapter, the Spanish "Concealment" features are not defined. Yet, it concealed the visibility of the hijab-wearers in the national debate on the hijab. The Spanish discursive strategies are severe; the discourse concealed her name, professional career, and humanity. Such concealment boosted the reliability of the "Ignorance" framing of the hijab-wearers, and it legitimates the authoritative position of the white non-muslim journalist to speak on her behalf. On the contrary, the "Concealment" framing in the British context is reduced to the (sexuality) "Concealment." Accordingly, the "ignorance" frame's re-activation depends on the following equation: More sexuality concealed, the less professional the Muslim women are.

In the British discourse, the "Ignorance" frame is limited to the hijab decision but not as a prominent feature of the hijab-wearing women, as we see in the Spanish press. British journalists argue against the practice as much as the hijab-wearers argue for the liberty to practice hijab in the national press. In the Spanish context, Hijab-wearers are concealed and accused as ignorant of the language or the social context. Even the Muslim visibility in the 2015/2016 discourse was manipulated by the journalist who interviews them.

Both press discourses (as Ferraras en El Pais and Smith in the Independent) point out the incompatibility between enlightenment and the hijab practice. The British discourse supports its argument with a general reference to the euro- and the national feminist labor to liberate women from religious and traditional oppression. Whereas the Spanish argument considers the French movement Not whores not submissive as an exemplary example of such liberation. Several members of this movement have been interviewed and introduced as legitimate and expert participants in the debate.

In the Spanish discourse, I find some discursive strategies that are not seen in British discourse, such as othering the hijab-wearers by the reference to the mother's language difficulties, the anonymous presentation of the hijab-wearing participants, and the manipulated contributions of the hijab-wearers. These strategies play an essential role in presenting a "hypothetical" balanced debate on the hijab, where participants from all sides have an opportunity to participate. It also legitimates the authoritative voice of the hijab opposers' discourse.

Hijab-wearing women in both contexts narrate their experience of the "Ignorance" frame imposed on them by the mainstream. In the Spanish context, the hijab-wearing women appear in post-2015/2016 discourse in limited quotations. On the contrary, The British hijab-wearers participate in publishing their proper articles in the national press describing their experience and debates such as discriminative behavior. Their visibility in the public sphere as public figures, social activists, and employees is reflected in the national press.

Framing the Hijab-Wearing Women Through "Oppression"

The "Oppression" framing of the hijab-wearing women is an inevitable extension of the "Oppression" framing of the hijab. It is a colonial framing of both the hijab and who practice it. The "Oppression" mental frame is re-activated in both press discourses.

Spanish "Oppression" Mental Frame of Hijab-Wearing Women

The Spanish re-activation of the "Oppression" framing of the hijab-wearers is recurrent. Yet, the oppressor is not limited to the hijab. The oppressor varies according to the focus of the article.

In the Exclusion cases, the "Oppression" frame is re-activated on the excluded girls: "Oppressed-by-Exclusion" frame. This mental frame is found in El Mundo, which covers the bullying that hijab-wearers went through, in contrast to El País, which keeps this aspect in most cases uncovered. For example, in a meeting with Zoubaida Barik Edidi in El Mundo, the court's excluded lawyer refers that she "was discriminated" by the judge's act who has not given her a chance to explain that she is used to attending the court with her hijab on before.[34] The judge told her, "this is my hall, and here I command." The article is an open interview in which the public sends their questions by email or message, and she answers. Eight participants of 26 demonstrate their support to and sympathy with Zubaida. They classified the judge's act as "discriminatory," "ignorant," "arbitrary," "despotic," and "intolerable." These linguistic expressions indicate sympathy with the affected hijab-wearers, who is mentally framed as "Oppressed-by-Exclusion."

---

[34] Barik Edidi (2009).

In the Usera case, covered in El Mundo, Amanda Figueras covers the minor's abuse when she decided to practice hijab. The hijab-wearer says:

> they shouted at me for anything. A professor (female) closed the door at my face, literally. Another one (female) said she is not going to answer any of my questions because I play the "victim." They do and say all of this in front of my class," and "they humiliated me.[35]

These behaviors show the un-professionality of the school staff and frame the minor in the "Oppression-by-School" frame. Interestingly, Pilar Álvarez covers the same case in El País, yet she skips the bullying and the abuse the young girl went through.[36] In contrast, she writes that the family is happy, celebrating the school council's decision that voted to modify the internal rule. She sustained the perfect image of *convivencia* protected by the school direction. Álvarez indicates that the father is "very thankful" for them and for the director (female) who gives them "all of her support."

In Hassna Isslal case, covered in El Mundo, Amanda Figueras activates the "Oppression-by-School" frame. The family denounced the school because the minor was "harassed by many teachers."[37] The father says: "the damage they are causing to my daughter is unrecoverable." Álvarez en El País introduces the case from a completely different mental frame. It activates the "Othering" frame of hijab-wearers, which will be discussed below. Álvarez replaces the "Oppression-by-School" frame with the "Oppression-by-Patriarchy" frame. She quotes the school director (male): "This man is like Agamemnon. He sacrifices his daughter, so ships have wind."[38] Accordingly, the minor is framed as a victim of cultural rituals or patriarchal practices.

The "Oppression-by-Exclusion" frame is found once in El País in the Arteixo case covered by Paola Obelleiro. The first three articles on the case narrate the progress of the exclusion and assert the total support of the Galician Government to the autonomous decision of the school (Obelleiro, 2011a, b, c). The school director prevented the hijab-wearing minor (12 years old) to attend the end-course party. He claimed that he sent her school file to the other school that morning, so she is no more a student of this center. However, the director of the other school said that he did not receive those documents. The Arteixo director told the minor: "you are no longer a student of this school." In the fourth article on the same case, there is an indirect reference to the head master's abusive treatment. The "Oppressed-by-school" frame is re-activated by the lawyer's quotation and not by the journalist's own words.[39] Jimenez Aybar describes the abusive school treatment as "barbaric" and "a personal revenge." This is the only context in which El País re-activates the "Oppression-by-School" mental frame on the hijab-wearing girls.

The "Compulsivity," the "Oppression," and the "Discrimination" frames of the hijab implicate, necessarily, that the practice oppresses the hijab-wearing

---

[35] Figueras (2011a) and Figueras and Piantadosi (2011).

[36] Álvarez (2011a, b).

[37] Figueras (2011c).

[38] Álvarez, Pilar (c). *Renunciar al velo islámico sería como quitarme la piel.* El País: 23 October 2011. http://elpais.com/diario/2011/10/23/sociedad/1319320802_850215.html.

[39] Obelleiro (2011d).

women. The "Oppression-by-Hijab" mental frame is re-activated in El País and La Vanguardia. For example, Solidad Gallego-Díaz indicates that the burqa and niqab are used to "subjugate women."[40] Caballero indicates that "Million" of Muslim women are persecuted if they "set free their hair and ideas."[41] Etxenike narrates the oppressing lifestyle of hijab-wearing students at home. They enjoy the French ban; "they go to school, to liberty of gymnastic, playing in the mixed break yard, they follow certain classes of natural science."[42] She extends the "Oppressed-by-Hijab" frame to include all hijab-wearers in France, not only the students; she states: "(They) live submitted to imported discriminative codes." The same mental frame is re-activated in Espinosa's discourse "(the veil) a sample of submitting women."[43] These discursive strategies re-activate an inescapable relation between the hijab stereotypical frames and the hijab-wearers. Etxenike re-activates the "Othering" frame of the hijab, "imported," to assert the European guiltlessness in that oppression. It also indirectly enforces the superiority of European Standards on freedom.

The "Oppression" frame of hijab-wearers is also re-activated by the references to patriarchy in the debate; "Oppression-by-patriarchy." En El Pais, Maria Sahuquillo re-activates this frame through a real story told by a teacher in Algeciras, Juan Martinez. He states that his workmate "wears the veil," Shahuquillo quotes him: "and I know that she eats in the kitchen while her husband and kids eat in the dining room. I do not want to have such a thing in Spain."[44] Again, we notice that the woman referred to is anonymous, silent, hijab-wearer, and oppressed. In the same newspaper, Ana Carbajos uses the colonial discursive strategy to frame hijab-wearing women. she points out that "from one side, the occident invaded Kuwait and Afghanistan to liberate women. On the other side, Muslim leaders [*instrumentalizar*] used their bodies to strengthen (their) national identity."[45] She continues that in America, "they do not have better luck." According to Carabajos, being a Muslim woman implies being oppressed and misused by national and international forces, inside or outside doors. Carabajos re-activates another dimension of the "Oppression" frame in her defense of Aído's criticism of women Islamic dress code: the "Oppression-by-Culture" frame. She asks: "why the Islamic males and Mayas do not have to hold the burden of the cultural identity and, in contrast, they (females) have to demonstrate [*como la prueba mas rotunda*] that these cultures exist?". Habichi sustains the "Oppression-by-Culture" frame in Galarraga's article.[46] Such re-activation empowers the de-activation of the "Religiosity" frame of the hijab. It detaches the hijab from its values in the gender-public-relations framework and limits

---

[40]Gallego-Díaz (2010).

[41]Caballero (2010).

[42]Etxenike (2004).

[43]Espinosa (2010).

[44]Sahuquillo (2008).

[45]Carbajos (2008).

[46]Galarraga (2010).

the hijab to an abstract cultural practice used to oppress women. The "Oppressed-by-Culture" framing of the hijab-wearers, as well, er-activates the "Othering" frame of the hijab and the hijab-wearers.

In the 2015/2016 discourse, La Vanguardia sustained the "Oppression" mental frame's re-activation in Ferreras' article.[47] Olga Dominguez, the philosopher, explains the two meanings of the hijab, which we covered before. She states that in both senses, hijab-wearers are victims and ignorant of this patriarchal oppression; she says: "to change the meaning of an implicit violence symbol, its victims are going to be affected in some way. We run the risk to play favor to the Islamic patriarchy." Dominguez joins together the "Oppression-by-Hijab" (by considering the hijab the tool of oppression) and the "Oppression-by-Patriarchy" in one discursive narration.

The "Oppression" frame's de-activation is detected only in one article written by Ana Juárez in El Mundo[48] in 2015/2016. Juárez interviews hijab-wearing women who show their awareness of the "Oppression" frame they are limited to by the mainstream. The interviewees de-activate this mental frame by the direct negation of the frame, using the negation adverb (not), and by narrating segments of their own life to prove the "Oppression" frame incompatibility. Naima El-Akil states: "Do not look at me as a poor girl who doesn't think and she is under the veil; I am not a terrorist, you might think that I am a submissive woman." Chadia Lemrani points out: "I am not blinded; I do not live under the authority of my husband. I am the one who chose him." Chadia indicates that she had to quit her job because of her baby girl, "to contract a babysitter will somehow equal the salary. A lot of Spanish mothers do the same, and they are not questioned, but, yes, I am." The "Oppression" frame's de-activation is not as powerful as its re-activation, not only due to the low frequency. The "oppressed" and "victimized" image schemata of Muslim women denies the agency of hijab-wearers, their autonomy to have a critical perspective on their own situation. By re-activating the "Ignorance" mental frame, hijab-wearers' perceptions are taken to be false consciousness.[49]

To sum up, the "Oppression" frame of hijab-wearing women in the Spanish press has different features across the newspapers, depending on the article's focus. In the Exclusion cases, El Mundo re-activates the "Oppression-by-Exclusion." In contrast, El Pais tends to hide this exclusion aspect and re-activates the "Oppression-by-Patriarchy" frame by highlighting an enforced hijab image.

The re-activation of the colonial frames on the hijab inevitably re-activates the "Oppression" frame of the hijab practitioners. El Pais re-actives, in the political and social debate, the "Oppression-by-Hijab," "Oppression-by-patriarchy," and "Oppression-by-Culture." These frames empower the "Othering" framing of the hijab and the hijab-wearers, and they assert the Spanish guiltlessness in the "Oppression." La Vanguardia sustains the re-activation of these frames in the 2015/2016 discourse. The de-activation of the "Oppression" mental frame is found only in El

---

[47]Farreras (2016).

[48]Juárez (2015).

[49]Bullock (2003).

Mundo in the 205/2016 discourse. It is a simple negation in low frequency. The "Ignorance" frame of the hijab-wearers awaken such de-activation.

British "Oppression" Mental Frame of Hijab-Wearing Women

The British "Oppression" mental frame of hijab-wearers is re-activated in the debate of the legitimacy of the 2004 French ban on BBC. The colonial frame is re-activated by asserting that the ban law protects Muslim schoolgirls from their parents' cultural impositions. For example, Elizabeth Jones covers an encounter between hijab-wearing students and the direction of their French school Delacroix in Drancy, a suburb northeast of Paris.[50] The encounter aims at reaching a compromise between the French ban and the practice. Eric Finot, a teacher, says, "we are thinking of those girls who we could maybe protect a little bit at school […] This law is here to protect those girls who are obliged to do things they don't want to do - not to be forced into marriage, not to wear the veil." In the same newspaper, Wyatt points out that Ghislaine Hudson, "a headteacher who gave evidence to the Stasi commission on secularity," understands the Muslim families' worries about the law. He says: "We have to work with our teachers, we have to work with the students, the families, we have to explain to them that this is a law for their own protection."[51] Hudson re-activates the "Ignorance" frame of hijab-wearers and their families. He needs to "explain" to them the target of the ban because they do not get it. Again, such discourse promotes the superiority of the European values over the "others'" values of vestment and gender relations. Waytt supports Hudson's framing of the law as a protector; she continues "and that's a view supported by some French Muslims, some of whom came to France partly because it is a secular state in which religious belief is kept a private matter." She supports this argument by (anonymous) Muslims to give it validity and assertion. In the British discourse, the determiner "some" is used to refer to the (oppressed) students at French school on the contrary to the Spanish determiners "the majority" and "millions" which are used for the same purpose.

Afghan women are used to re-activating the "Oppression" mental frame of hijab-wearing women in the British context even though they wear a different Islamic dress, the burqa, and they are also not related to the British nor French social contexts (on which the debate evolve). For example, in The Independent, Joan Smith re-activates the "Oppression" frame of British Muslim women on Afghan women's gloomy image. She states that Afghan women and Iraqi women are wearing the enforced dress code because "they are afraid of being killed if they do not" or "being murdered."[52] Smith projects this oppression scene onto the British context setting the hijab as the oppressive tool in a similar Spanish re-activation of "Oppression-by-Hijab." Smith continues: "I loathe the niqab and the burqa when I see them there.

---

[50] Jones (2005).

[51] Wyatt (2004).

[52] Smith (2006a).

And I can't pretend I don't find them equally offensive on my local high street." Smith re-activates the "Oppression-by-Hijab" of the hijab-wearers depending on the colonial discursive strategy that considers the hijab-wearers as in need of salvation. At the same time, she joins all different Islamic dresses in one sac.

In The Guardian, Natasha Walter re-activates the "Oppression" frame of the hijab-wearers following the same methodology. In her visit to Afghanistan, she narrates that she met "desperate women to take off the burqa, including one who had been beaten almost to death by the Taliban for showing her hair. These women wanted to take the same path that women in the west took, and in the face of even greater hurdles." Walter empowers the European cultural superiority by considering the Western feminist's path as an exemplary that Afghan women are eager to follow. She continues: "they wanted to be free of such hampering laws, despite the anger of the men around them and taunts of immodesty and irreligiousness. We must support them. Their struggle is real.[53]" Walter projects the social disorder and women's suffering in Afghanistan (which are some of the colonial outcomes) to attach meaning to British hijab-wearing women.

Walter and Smith re-activate the "Oppression-by-hijab" and "Oppression-by-Patriarchy" frames in their discourse. Such re-activation is related to the "Other-ing" frame of the hijab (the practice of others) and to the "Compulsivity" mental frame of the hijab. These frames on the hijab and on its practitioners justify the Western foreign political performance in Afghanistan in the past as much as justify the French political sovereignty over women agency over their bodies/sexuality in the public sphere. Walter and Smith are not the only journalists who recycle the colo-nial discourse to re-activate the "Oppression" frame of the hijab-wearing women in Europe. Catherine Bennett, in The Guardian, also follows the same methodology in re-activating the "Oppression" frame.[54] Bennett highlights Mrs. Blairs' preoccupa-tion with the oppressed and discriminated Afghan women "shortly after the fall of Taliban" and her affection to grant them "human rights." Blairs states that "they need opportunities, self-esteem, and esteem in the eyes of their societies." Such discur-sive strategies frame Muslim women through the "Oppression-by-Patriarchy" and announce the Western authorities as liberating, caring, and supportive to Muslim women. Bennett cites Walter's superiority of Western women's vales of uncovering; she states: "as Walter said, 'The whole trajectory of feminism in the west has been tied up with the freedom to uncover ourselves.'" She continues that Muslim women are to be blamed for their oppression in the United Kingdom: "It is the choice of some women in Britain to force marriage on their unwilling daughters. Or genital mutila-tion. Both practices have, occasionally, been defended by western feminists putting multiculturalism before human rights." Accordingly, the "Oppression" mental frame of hijab-wearers in the British press is not limited to the "Oppression-by-Patriarchy." It is an "Oppression-by-Volition" of Muslim women.

---

[53] Walter (2004).
[54] Bennett (2004).

Blaming Muslim women of her "Oppression" appears in other British articles such as in Yasmin Alibhai-Brown's in the same newspaper, the Guardian.[55] She faults the hijab-wearers in the United Kingdom of women's worldwide submission cases. She blames the free-choice hijab-wearers in the United Kingdom of the "women in Iran, Saudi Arabia, Afghanistan, Pakistan, Iraq, and even the west, who are prosecuted, flogged, tortured or killed for not complying. This is not a freestanding choice—it can't be." Alibhai-Brown projects the "Oppression" frame from out-borders into the British context: "although we hear from vocal British hijabis and niqabis, those who are forced cannot speak out. A fully burqaed woman once turned up at my house, a graduate, covered in cuts, burns, bruises, and bites. Do we know how many wounded, veiled women, walk around hidden among us? Sexual violence in Saudi Arabia and Iran is appallingly high, as is body dysmorphia."

Jumping between the British contexts and other foreign contexts (Saudi Arabia and Iran) confuses the fact that the hijab in the United Kingdom is a British social reality and not related to the other social contexts. It is a national phenomenon with different particularities. This discursive strategy depends on the "Othering" frame of the hijab and the hijab-wearers. At the same time, Alibhai-Brown associates the burqa concealment of the body with physical abuse concealment. The discourse re-activates the "Oppression" mental frame on British hijab-wearing women and blames the free-choice hijab of worldwide Muslim women oppression.

Blaming the free-choice hijab appears in The Independent, too. Julie Burchill blames Lauren Booth for her hijab decision. She states that Booth's hijab decision "ignores the savage states persecution of free-thinking women while having enjoyed fully all the freedom the West has to offer."[56] Again, the superior image of Western liberty is highlighted. The journalist continues stating that "some girls strip off for the camera, some veil up for murderous, gynophobic, theocratic dictatorship!" Burchill refers to the Shah of Iran. Thus, she underestimates Booth's free choice to don the hijab and links it to another cause: pleasing a foreign male dictator. Questioning Booth's hijab motivation re-activates the "Ignorance" mental frame on her. The journalist takes away Booth's agency on her decision and reduces them to a manipulated practice by men in power.

In The Independent, Joan Smith introduces the movement Not Whores Nor Submissive as an outcome of France's patriarchal Muslim community. She re-activates the "Oppression-by-Patriarchy" frame of Muslim women; such oppression was the reason why this movement appeared. She says: "Intimidation and family pressure play a role in the French banlieue where the Not Whores Nor Submissive movement was set up by Muslim women to oppose racism by the French and the strict Islamic identity imposed on them by fathers, uncles, and brothers."[57] The British discourse does not include the movement recurrently nor present its members as the authoritative spokeswomen as the Spanish discourse does. Smith introduced them by their "courageous march through Paris."

---

[55] Alibhai-Brown (2015).

[56] Burchill (2011).

[57] Smith (2006a).

The "Oppression" frame is de-activated by hijab-wearers by several discursive techniques. The de-activation is not limited to simple negation as the Muslim women do in Spanish discourse. Of course, the difference is related to the accessibility of the British hijab-wearers to the press mainstream discourse. For example, on the BBC, Paula Dear writes about a European campaign to protect Muslims' right to wear hijab.[58] The pharmacist Saba Naeem narrates her independent life as a counter-discourse of the "Oppression" frame: "I am a professional woman who works. I am involved in many activities in my own right."

The de-activation of the "Oppression" frame depends on the (Empowering) (Sexuality) "Concealment" mental frame of the hijab. For example, Nadiya Takolia, in The Guardian, points out that "many of us feel a pawn in society's beauty game [...] trying to attain that 'non-existent' perfect figure".[59] She continues

This is not about protection from men's lusts. It is me telling the world that my femininity is not available for public consumption. I am taking control of it, and I don't want to be part of a system that reduces and demeans women. Behind this exterior, I am a person – and it is this person for which I want to be known.

Takolia de-activates the "Oppression" framing of the hijab-wearers by activating the "Oppression" framing of women subjected to sexuality consumption in liberal values.

In The independent, the de-activation of the "Oppression" frame of Muslim women manifests in the series of interviews made by Arifa Akbar (2010a, c). Rajnaara Akhtar points out the stereotypical frame, de-activates it by the national visibility of professional hijab-wearers, and activates the "Religiosity" framing of the hijab. She states:

Even though there has been work done to counter these stereotypes, I think the view that women in hijab are somehow oppressed, or have been forced into some form of archaic dress, is still the most prevalent one. The reality is that you have a lot of well educated young women choosing to adopt hijab because when they go down the path of trying to find out more about their religion and their identity, they actually chose a form of modesty, which may include hijab.[60]

Soha Sheikh does not limit her de-activation of the "Oppression" frame by simple negations. She says: "When we talk about headscarves, the first thing that comes into a lot of people's heads is 'oppressed woman.' It's hard for some people to accept that it's a sign of liberation. You don't always have to conform to a certain stereotype or fashion statement."[61] As Akhtar does, Sheikh also points out the "Oppression" frame imposed on hijab-wearers directly, and she argues about it.

British hijab-wearing women are aware of the "Oppression" frames imposed on them. Their everyday experiences show how the public mind perceives their visibility. Nadiya Hussain states: "When I began to wear a headscarf, one friend split no hairs,

---

[58]Dear (2004).

[59]Takolia (2010).

[60]Akbar (2010a).

[61]Akbar (2010c).

telling me I was bending to 'male enslavement.'"[62] This behavior indicates that this friend understands the hijab through the "Oppression-by-Patriarchy" frame. In the same newspaper, another experience is told by Shaista Aziz, a comic writer and aid worker.[63] In her article, she narrates the best comments "whiteys" made over her hijab. "Whitey" male's comments indicate that they understand the hijab through the (Sexuality) "Concealment" frame, which we covered before. "Whitey" women's comments reveal their inability to grasp the amount of suffering imposed on Aziz by the practice, the "Oppression-by-Practice" frame. The first woman in Aziz's article is an aid worker who constantly asks Aziz: "so do you feel hot in there? I mean, you must feel hot?" The second is a female boss in London who told Aziza, "I dreamt you removed your hijab and stopped fasting during Ramadan because it all got too much for you." Both narrations reflect the "Oppression-by-Hijab" mental frame. Both women face difficulties in mentally framing the practice as an enjoyed free choice. While the first one reduced Aziz's suffering to the hot weather, the second considered the hijab practice and fasting Ramadan as heavy loads on Aziz.

In The Independent, Hijab-wearers argue that the religious hierarchy based on women's vestment choice is used as a trigger in the hijab opposer discourse to re-activate the "Oppression" frame of hijab-wearers. For example, in The Independent, Shamim Chroudy disapproved of begum's decision of jilbab at school while the shalwar kameez is available as an alternative school uniform. She states:

> by bickering among ourselves in public over who is most appropriately dressed, all we achieve is to give the bigots even more ammunition with which to attack us. We also play into the hands of sanctimonious Western feminists who continue to churn out tired, arrogant arguments about how the hijab is oppressive and enslaving.[64]

In another case, Maria Idrissi, the hijab-wearing model in H&M, points out that "women making the comments about modesty were the reason British society still sees Islam as oppressive to women."[65] It is to say; they consider the debate on which is the "perfect" modest dress among British Muslims works in favor of the re-activation of the "Oppression" framing of the hijab-wearers.

To sum up, the "Oppression" mental frame is re-activated in the British press discourse. In BBC, the "Oppression" framing of the hijab-wearers legitimate the French ban. BBC, the Independence, and the Guardian picture the hijab-wearing Muslim women as oppressed due to the practice and patriarchy culture; they re-activate the "Oppression-by-Hijab," and "Oppression-by-Patriarchy" frames, respectively. The discourse depends on Afgan women's colonial image to empower the "Oppression" frame of British national Hijab-wearers. The "Othering" and the "Compulsivity" frames of the hijab serve well in re-activating the "Oppression" frame of the practitioners. Altogether, these stereotypical frames justify French sovereignty over French women's sexuality in the public sphere. The "ignorance" frame is part

---

[62] Aly (2015).

[63] Aziz (2014).

[64] Chowdhury (2005).

[65] Mortimer (2015).

of the "Oppression" frame of the hijab-wearers. They are ignorant of the liberty they miss.

The Guardian and the Independent re-activate the "Oppression-by-Volution" frame in which they blame the hijab-wearing women for all the forced hijab cases. They also question the motives behind the hijab decision. The movement Not Whores Nor Submissive is considered as an outcome of the Muslim patriarchal oppression.

The de-activation of the "Oppression" mental frame is not limited to simple nega-tion. Hijab-wearing women are aware of the "Oppression" frame imposed on them. They de-activate it by sharing segments of their life in BBC; they draw reference to the visibility of British professional hijab-wearers in the Independent, and they reverse the "Oppression" frame by the activation of the "Oppression-by-Sexuality-Objectification" mental frame in liberal values. They also write about the comments they receive in their daily life.

Cross-Cultural Analysis

The re-activation of the "Oppression" mental frame in the Spanish and British presses is almost similar. Both contexts (El Pais, La Vanguardia, BBC, the Guardian, and the Independent) re-activate the "Oppression-by-Hijab" and "Oppression-by-patriarchy." The discourse drives out the Spanish and British involvement in the oppression of the hijab-wearing women. In the exclusion cases in Spanish contexts, only El Mundo re-activates the "Oppression-by-Exclusion" frame.

The re-activation of this stereotypical frame depends on the previously mentioned stereotypical frames on the hijab. The Spanish discourse depends on the "Other-ing" frames of the hijab and the hijab-wearing women. In comparison, the British discourse depends on the "Compulsivity," "Othering," and (Sexuality) "Conceal-ment" frames of the practice and its practitioners. In the British discourse, there is an acknowledgment of the free-choice hijab; accordingly, they re-activate the "Oppression-by-Volition" frame.

Both the Spanish and British presses established a connection between the "Igno-rance" frame and the "Oppression" frame of the hijab-wearers. In the Spanish press, the "Ignorance" frame is more elaborated than the British one. Consequently, the de-activation of the "Oppression" frame in the Spanish press is more superficial. The invisibility of the hijab-wearers in the Spanish mainstream press sets the hijab opposers as authoritative speakers; members of Not Whores Nor Submissive are one of these. Whereas the British discourse considers this movement as an outcome of the oppression practiced on Muslim women. The British de-activation of the "Oppres-sion" mental frame is narrative, not limited to simple negation as in the Spanish press. British hijab-wearers share segments of their life; they argue about the perspectives of women's oppression.

Framing the Hijab-Wearing Women Through "Othering"

The "Othering" frame of the hijab-wearers is not separated from the "Othering" frame of the hijab. It is a recycled frame. The colonial relationship with Muslim countries in the past century is still conquering the current Spanish and British Muslim generations' framing.

Spanish "Othering" Mental Frame of Hijab-Wearing Women

The "Othering" mental frame of the hijab-wearers is re-activated through various discursive strategies. One of the linguistic "Othering" in the exclusion cases can be the repetitive use of exclusionary attributes to refer to the hijab-wearers, such as "excluded," "expelled," and "separated." Such expressions create that mental and spatial division between "us" (inside the public sphere/included participants) and "them" (outside the public sphere/excluded others). In the exclusion cases, the hijab-wearers are referred to as follow: "the expelled minor,"[66] "she is no more expelled,"[67] "expelled" and "separated,"[68] "separated from her classmates,"[69] "the expelled student,"[70] "the expelled hijab-wearing kid,"[71] and "[*vetada*] (banned) from the institute."[72] These examples are representative of endless attributes used to refer the hijab-wearers in the exclusion cases. Although the journalist is only narrating the progress of the case, she establishes the cognitive categorization of who is in and who is out; who is welcomed inside the public sphere and who is unwelcomed/excluded.

A second discursive strategy that re-activates the "Othering" frame of the hijab-wearers is the constant reference to the hijab-wearers or her parents as "Moroccan," in both papers and all cases. The only exception is found in El Pais in Najwa Al-Malha's case (Madrid, 2010). Álvarez refers to the Al-Malha as "Spanish Muslim"[73] and "of Spanish nationality."[74] On the contrary, El Mundo refers to Najwa Al-Malha as follows: "a 16-year-old girl from Moroccan origin,"[75] "(She) was born in Spain to a family of Moroccan origin,"[76] "The student of Moroccan origin," and "the Moroccan girl."[77]

---

[66]Figueras (2011a) and Figueras and Piantadosi (2011).

[67]Álvarez (2011b).

[68]Sotero and Bécares (2010a).

[69]Álvarez and Cembrero (2010b).

[70]De Ganuza (2008).

[71]Obelleiro (2011d).

[72]Lidón (2016).

[73]Álvarez and Garriga (2010).

[74]Álvarez and Cembrero (2010c).

[75]Sotero and Bécares (2010a).

[76]Del Barrio (2010a).

[77]Belvar and Blasco (2010).

Such stigmatization of Spanish-born students empowers the social categorization of these girls/women as "migrants" "others" instead of recognizing them as part of the new Spanish social reality. They were born in Spain, educated in Spanish public schools, and they speak the *Castellano* as their mother tongue. For example, in the case of Shaima, which is covered only in El País, the first published article on the case by Natalia Iglesias (2007) did not include any national stigmatization.[78] However, in the second article in 2010, in which the girl and her mother were interviewed on the shed of Najwa's case, Rebeca Carranco re-activates the "Othering" frame repetitively.[79] Both women are attached to Arabic TV at home and to the summer vacation in Morocco. Besides, Carranco repeats their following statement three times along the article: at the beginning, in the middle, and at the end: "(if the school will not accept the veil), we will go back to Morocco." Carranco's article maps both Muslims (the girl and her mother) as outsiders who have no interest in living or integrating in Spain, yet, they want to enforce their "cultural" (and not religious practices) on the Spanish public sphere. Associating the practice to cultural tradition is another re-activation of the "Othering" frame of the hijab-wearing women. In Arteixo case (Galicia, 2011), which is also covered only in El País, the student and her family are anonymous Morrocan, "the student of Moroccan origin."[80] In the article, Obelleiro states that the family spent May vacation in "their country of origin, Morocco,"[81] by which the journalist links the girl and her family to an outsider culture.

Establishing the connection between the hijab-wearing students and the "outsider national contexts" aims to frame the exclusion cases as migrants' affairs instead of directing the difficulties and challenges in Spanish social diversity. It wards off the readers' attention on the national discrimination that the Spanish Muslim women go through and convert it to the migrants' refusal to integrate in Spain. For example, Pilar Álvarez, En El Pais, re-activates the "Othering" frame of the entire family. She narrates the migratory trajectory of the family.[82] The family is from "Tangier, a city surrounded by mountains" (an abridged countryside image-schemata is generated especially for those who have never been there). The student is a friend of another migrant "Colombian" girl. They talk about "their things and laugh." At home, where the meeting takes place, the journalists picture the house image of a dependent migrant "others": the cuscus, the numerous children, the unemployed father with "a lot of free time to dedicate to the case," and the "ignorant" or "uneducated" mother who does not speak the language. These details are not arbitrary included in the article to an exclusion case from the public school. They aim to re-activate the "Othering" framing of the hijab practitioner and her family.

In the exclusion case of the lawyer Zubaida, Monica Belaza, in El País, highlights the lawyer's Moroccan origin.[83] Peral Maria en El Mundo does not present the lawyer

---

[78] Iglesias (2007).

[79] Carranco (2010).

[80] Obelleiro (2011c).

[81] Obelleiro (2011e).

[82] Álvarez (2011c).

[83] Belaza (2010).

Zubaida at any moment in the article that covers the exclusion.[84] In the meeting with the public in EL Mundo, the participants point out her Moroccan origin.[85] Six participants out of 26 referred that the lawyer needs to consider Spanish norms, the host country, of secularity, and aconfessionality. They indicate that the religious practice of veiling needs to be limited to the private sphere. The lawyer answers that "Spain protects the right to religious freedom," and she clarifies that Spain is not "a secular country." She states that no law prohibits the hijab in the court. One participant praised her courage to stand in front of the judge and answer him. He wonders why she does not "use this courage to liberate women in Morocco." The lawyer answers that she lives in Spain, her daughters are born in Spain. She is licensed in Spain law at a Spanish university. She cannot practice her faculty in Morocco. One (female) participant states that she would not choose a hijab-wearing lawyer to represent her because of the negative stereotypes about the hijab. Even though few in number, the participants' interventions reflect the mental framing of the audience to the lawyer's hijab. Their comments and questions are a simple reflection of what they have been exposed to in the public discourse. The lawyer's faculty and professionality are questioned and untrusted due to her decision to conceal her sexuality. She is also asked to "go back" to Morocco, where the participants think she and her hijab practice belong.

In Ceuta cases, the "Othering" frame's re-activation is not direct because Ceuta is, theoretically, a Spanish territory. In the exclusion cases, El Pais discourse creates a distance between the Spanishness "Us" and the Ceutan-ness. In Nahed and Nawal's case, Rocio Abad does not refer to the student's Spanishness.[86] The entire context is discussed within the Ceuta enclosed borders. The same distance is created in presenting Fatima Hamed, "the winning of the first hijab-wearing delegate in Ceuta."[87] Abad limits this case to the Ceutan community using linguistic expressions such as "in Ceuta" and "Ceutan society." Abad ends up the article commenting that the Ceutan assembly is "representative" to the Ceutan community. There was no reference to the Spanish community throughout the discourse, nor the Spanish "us" emerged. Even the success of Fatima Hamed is framed as a success of the Ceutan woman and not a national Spanish woman's success; "It reflects the advancement of Ceutan women." Hamed is compared to a Muslim hijab-wearing delegate in Melilla, Salima Abdeselam. At any moment, Abad includes a Spanish national dimension in Hamed's and Abdeselam's hijab visibility.

In El Mundo, Amanda Figueras refers to the minor in the Usera case as "a 14-year-old, Spanish" regarding the father's origin, a "Ceutan."[88] In another article, Figueras introduces the same student as follows: "as Spanish as any Maria and

[84]Peral (2010).

[85]Barik Edidi (2009).

[86]Abad (2007b).

[87]Abad (2007a).

[88]Figueras and Piantadosi (2011).

Isabel."[89] The father, as Figueras indicates, "of Spanish nationality."[90] The reference to the document-nationality re-activates the "Othering" frame of the father; he is not Spanish (Spanish father), he joined it. In this case, in El País, Pilar Alvarez indicates that the student's father "was born in Ceuta."[91] Both Figueras and Álvarez's discourse creates a distance between the sense of Spanishness and the Ceutan father.

In the cases that happened in 2015/2016, The discourse slightly differs. It is more inclusive in El Mundo. For example, in Takwa Rejeb's case, Inma Lidon quotes the SOS lawyer, who says: "she is not a kid. She is a 24-year-old young girl of Spanish nationality."[92] The inclusion of Rejeb is similar to Ceutan inclusion, based on documental inclusion in the Spanish "us." In the case of Ana Saidi Rodriguez, Irene Velasco writes in El Mundo: "(She is) Spanish, a daughter of a Moroccan father and her mother from Albacete."[93] She includes the young woman in the Spanish "us," maintaining the reference to the father's origin. In the same case in El Pais, Lucia Bohorquez mentions the father's last name and does not refer to the Spanish mother's last name to frame her as a daughter of a migrant and strip away her legitimate Spanish half.[94]

In social and political discourse, the "Othering" frame of the hijab-wearers is re-activated in similar linguistic strategies that re-activate the "Othering" frame of the hijab. It is to say, the outsider practice of the outsider practitioners. The debate of the hijab does not include the hijab-wearing women within the Spanish social diversity. The debate, more specifically in El País (Carbajos, 2008; Galarraga, 2010; Moliner, 2004) depends on outsider arguments; then, it projects these foreign arguments on the Spanish context and draws conclusions. For example, in Galarraga's article, the Muslim hijab-wearing contributor, who works per hour and sympathizes with Najwa Al-Malha, is introduced first as "Moroccan" and second as a hijab practitioner, "she is also veiled."[95] Najwa's support is mentally framed within her national and cultural belonging to the same minority (migratory) group of Najwa.

In Sahuquillo's article, the hijab debate was linked to immigrants and immigration issues.[96] The Muslim speakers are all migrants or set to be daughters/sons of migrants re-activating the "Othering" frame along with the article. In this article, we will need to quote the whole debate (1618 Words) if we need to spotlight the linguistic expressions that re-activate the "Othering" frame of hijab-wearing women. I will quote the following: "the host countries," (twice) "Muslim who live there," "the host country accepts the presence of foreigners," "[...] the problem is that a lot of immigrants have to get a job," "According to Integration Politics of Immigrant of European Commission [....] the Muslim community feels adaptive enough to the Spanish life

---

[89] Figueras (2011a).
[90] Figueras (2011b).
[91] Álvarez (2011a, b).
[92] Lidón (2016).
[93] Velasco (2016).
[94] Bohorquez (2016).
[95] Galarraga (2010).
[96] Sahuquillo (2008).

and costumes," "We always ask the migrant to act, and we forget that the society closes its doors," "We have to stop thinking of the migrant as temporal manpower and take them in consideration of citizenship terms," "This is integration, the host society accepts the presence of the foreigners," etc. Such discourse re-activates the "Othering" frame of hijab-wearing women and all the Muslim communities in Spain. The hijab practice is framed as a cultural practice that migrants brought with them, e.g. "(…) incorporate the common baggage foreigners bring with them."

In El Pais discourse, it is a significant argument to debate the visibility of the cultural hijab instead of the Islamic religious hijab. It detaches the practice from the universality of religion and from the religious-right argument in Spain. However, even when the hijab is seen as a religious sign of its wearers, the discourse asserts the separation between the practitioners and the Spanish "us." For example, Concha Caballero warns from religious discrimination if the hijab is banned and the other religious symbols are accepted. She argues: "Those who denounce the veil on foreign heads (*cabezas ajenas*) but defend the bonnet and the crucifix on their own are not defending regulations or laws of our country, but they are practicing the grossest (*la mas burda*) Islamophobia and sowing discord in the classrooms."[97] Although Caballero is aware of the Islamophobic stigmatization of the hijab exclusion, she re-activates the "Othering" frame of the hijab-wearers because of their religious visibility. She uses the "us" and "them" categorization.

The "Othering" frame is re-activated in reference to the non-Muslim hijab supporter participants in the hijab debate. Those participants were described as "Arabists" in both newspapers. For example, El Mundo introduces Luz Gomez Garcia, the writer of "Dictionary of Islam," as the "Arabist."[98] Gomez Garcia re-activates the "Concealment" frame of the hijab from a linguistic perspective that does not coincide with The Spanish stereotypical "Concealment" frame discussed in the previous chapter. She explains that the hijab was used to separate the Khalifa from the public. She does not stigmatize the practice nor supported it. El País introduces Gemma Martin Muñoz, the director of "casa Árabe," as "the Arabist Muñoz."[99] Othering Muñoz is due to her support for the rights to education and religious freedom of schoolgirls. She "has it clear." She also de-activates the "Oppression" frame of the veil. Jeronimo Paez also was described as the "Arabist" in El Pais. He established a relation between the hijab and identity formation that can be part of the Spanish society: "(the veil is) a sign of identity," and it is "acceptable in our society."[100]

The "Arabist" stigmatization of those speakers decreases their credibility as objective commentators due to their involvement in, or belonging to, the "other's" social contexts. Accordingly, their unbias declarations on the practice or their negation of the stereotypical frames are not as reliable and trusted as those who are introduced as experts, ex-Muslim, or professional. A similar "Othering" frame to the contrastereotypes voices is re-activated in introducing the European convert, Oballe. The

---

[97]Caballero (2010).

[98]Meneses (2010).

[99]Muñoz (2010).

[100]Montero (2010).

"Jerusalem" background and the "Kohl" in her eyes re-activates the "Othering" frame instantly. Before introducing Oballe's quotations, Carabajos states, "she immigrated to the Orient [Proximo]."[101]

In contrast to the "Othering" framing of hijab supporter, hijab opposers' inclusion is salient in El País. Naiara Galarraga includes Najat EL-Hashmi, not only the Catalan community, in the Spanish "us" because her mental frames of the hijab coincide with those stereotypical frames (re) activated in the newspapers. Galarraga refers to the Morrocan origin of El-Hashmi: "a Catalan writer born in Morocco," but then, she describes her as follows: "Spanish from Moroccan" parents. Galarraga emphasizes that El-Hashmi is an authoritative and reliable commentator on the hijab: "She is one of those Spanish women who can speak about the hijab because of her full knowledge (of the topic) [conocimiento de causa]."[102] In the same article, Najwa, born and raised in Spain, was described as "Spanish from Moroccan parents." Although we have the "Moroccan" reference in both presentations, El-Hashmi was linked to the Morrocan land. She left behind by migrating to and assimilating the Spanish frame of reference; she was described as a "Catalan writer." In presenting Najwa, the reference to the parents' origin activates the Moroccan family role in raising their daughter according to "their" own culture. While Carabajos included El-Hashmi in the Catalan community even though she was born in Morroco and migrated to Spain, Rebeca Carranco never included Shaima (a hijab-wearing student) in the Catalan community even though she was born in Catalunya. Carranco referred to the Catalan accent in the student's Castellano, yet, she did not refer to her as a Catalan student.[103]

Ceuta has its portion of the "Othering" frame in the political and social debate. In El Mundo, Carmen De Ganuza draws a distance between the Spanish "us" and Ceuta and Melilla. She uses the Popular Party's proposal to modify Equality Law. The Law excludes Ceuta and Mellia; she states: "the new regulation aims to specify and protect Spanish principles and costumes […] The exception will benefit the regions mostly populated by Muslims, such as Ceuta and Melilla."[104] There is an indirect separation between the Spanish "us," which needs to be protected, and Ceuta and Melilla. In El País, the "Othering" frame of Ceuta and Melilla is less indirect. Solidad Gallego-Díaz, who highlights the importance of banning the full veil in Spanish territory, refers to Ceuta and Melilla as "of Spanish sovereignty." Gallego-Díaz announces the superiority of Spain "us" over the "other" controlled and marginalized regions due to the visible religious identity.[105]

Before 2015/2016, Spanish journalists in the selected articles do not include any significant Spanish hijab-wearing contributors. In the 2015/2016 hijab debate, hijab-wearers gained more visibility in the national press. However, the three presses of this study maintain the re-activation of the "Othering" frame. For example, in La Vanguardia, Carian Farreras opens the article by the assertion on the migratory origin

---

[101] Carbajos (2008).

[102] Galarraga (2010).

[103] Carranco (2010).

[104] De Ganuza (2008).

[105] Gallego-Díaz (2010).

of the Spanish Muslim generation: "The daughters of those Muslim emigrants who came into our country in the 90s are stepping the university; and very soon, they will look for a job where they will practice their apprenticeship."[106] Muslims and Moroccans are synonymously used in Ferreras' discourse, which implies that all Muslims in Spain are Moroccan, and all Moroccans are Muslims: "we do not see veiled-women employees in companies, at schools, at hospitals, etc., even though there are 214.000 Moroccans in Catalonia". The journalist classifies the Muslim students in opposition to children of Catalan parents: "(these young girls) have received the same education as their classmates of Catalan parents;" and in opposition to non-Muslim migrants: "and other young males of their social community, form sons/daughters of non-Muslim foreigners and of course from other sons/daughters of Christian parents who are born here." Such categorization frames the hijab-wearing young women as (more) different from foreigner Christian "others."

The Muslim interviewees in the article are Najat Driouech, Ramia Chaoui, Najat Talha, and Jihan Dahou. None of them is introduced as Spanish, although the discourse indicates that Chaoui was born in Barcelona (and she has a DNI), and Talha is born in Figueres. Both Driouech and Chaoui, hijab-wearers, point out the mainstreamers' "Othering" mental frame imposed on them in daily life. Driouech states: "automatically, I stop being Najat the student, licensed, mother, a workmate […] and I am turned to be the recent arrival that I need to be integrated." Although the article exposes the difficulties that Spanish hijab-wearers go through because of the "Othering" frame imposed on them, it practices the same mental frame by not mentioning their Spanish or Catalan identity.

In El País, Bárbara Ayuso indirectly re-activates the "Othering" frame on Spanish converts in the title: "From Maria to Maryam: this is how a 29-year-old Spaniard converted to Islam."[107] The title creates an image schema of spatial transition from one state to another, from the Spanish "us" "Maria" to Muslim "others" "Maryam." Ayuso closes the article with the assertion on the contrasting elements in the convert's new identity: "Now she tries to combine her heritage and her choice, the hijab, and the bare head. It is Maryam, but also Maria." There is an insistence on the separation between the Spanish-heritage and bare-head Maria from one side and hijab-wearing Maryam from the other side. The discourse reduces the entire religious heritage (Islam) to the hijab practice announcing it as the main and almost the only changing factor in the transition from Maria (us) to Maryam (others).

In El Mundo, Amanda Figueras re-activates the "Othering" frame of the hijab-wearers in the same indirect discursive strategy.[108] Figueras introduces Mariam El Moden, a nursery assistant, as follows: "the Moroccan Mariam El Moden, 22 years old," "Even Though she lives in Alemannia with her husband, she was born and lived her youthfulness in Spain." Figueras does not acknowledge the Spanish aspect of Al-Modem's identity. The heritage that El Moden obtained being born, lived,

---

[106]Farreras (2016).
[107]Ayuso (2016).
[108]Figueras (2012).

and studied in Spain is demolished, and her parents' origin and her husband's (new family) location were the main focus of her identity/belonging.

In another article in El Mundo, Ana Juarez interviews three Muslim girls: Naima El-Akil, "A woman of Moroccan parents, migrated in the 60s. She is licensed in Law and Journalism at Carlos III University. She is one of four founders of the Association of Muslim Girls in Spain (ACHIME);" Omayma Bouiri, "a 16-year-old student of baccalaureate. She is born in Spain to Moroccan parents;" and Chadia Lemrani: "a Moroccan origin with Spanish nationality. She has been in Spain for ten years. She is married to a Spanish convert and has three children."[109] In the first two presentations, the Moroccan parents are prominent, which refers to their parenting role in raising their daughter according to their heritage. The third interviewee's belonging to the Spanishness (la hispanidad) is limited to the official document.

In the 2015/2016 discourse, Spanish hijab-wearing women are given more visibility in the national press discourse. They explain their awareness of the "Othering" frame imposed on them by the mainstream. They state that difference is the main trigger of the "Othering" frame. For example, Mariam El Moden narrates the challenge of finding a residency for her nursing internship and of finding a job after graduation; she says: "it is not for religion nor the veil. They (Spanish people) simply do not like who is different from them."[110] In the same article, Habiba, a convert, indicates that "many of us think that Spain is tolerant. I used to think like that. But when you are different, you understand, you feel that there is still a lot of rejection." El-Akil affirms that she has no problem in being part of Spain; she states: "yet, the problem is not me. It is how others see me. They do not accept that we are equal."[111]

Amanda Figueras, who converts to Islam later on in her career, asserts the "difference" sensitivity in Spain.[112] Throughout her article (2259 words), she repeats four times that "In Spain, they do not like the different [En España no gusta lo diferente]." Figueras sets a distinction between two kinds of Islam in Spain. She states that "Islam is the worst of the worst when it is related to the Islam of immigrants with difficulties, of women whose vestment different to the established rules, of the terrorists who said they are Muslims. Nevertheless, there is Islam that does not annoy; of the successful football players or elite Arabic women." She continues: "the society does not accept the different, and me, I do not have money, and I am not a fashion-star." Figueras points out that "it is not easy to be different in Europe." She refers that she has "a friend who works in a political party- not the Popular Party- and she hides her belonging to Opus Dei, a friend who works in Metro Madrid who hide that he is Muslim, a journalist friend who is Jehovah Witness, and she keeps it hidden […] Is this Europe that we are proud of? We have to assure that liberty is for all, also for the different, we have to be an example." Figueras explains that the rejection of difference is due to the fear of it. She perceives such fear from her parents: "I recognize that they still have fears."

---

[109] Juárez (2015).

[110] Figueras (2012).

[111] Juárez (2015).

[112] Figueras (2015).

Despite the "Othering" frame imposed on hijab-wearing Spanish women in the mainstream discourse, they identify themselves as Spanish. They also refer to the Spanish community as "our" and "us." El-Akil and Bouiri speak about their lives, experiences, and their future in Spain as follows: "women who are Spanish [...] in our neighborhood and our systems" and "I am proud to be Spanish and (proud) of Spain."[113]

To sum up, the "Othering" frame of the Spanish hijab-wearing women is re-activated extensively in all Spanish newspapers, in both article categories (exclusion cases and social and political debate), and before and in the 2015/2016 discourse. The first and foremost discursive strategy that re-activates this frame is the constant reference to the parents' origin. In the exclusion cases, El País uses additional discursive strategies to empower the "Othering" frame of the hijab-wearers. El País draws a reference to where the family spends the summer vacation (en Morroco) and narrates the family's migratory journey.

The social and political debate counts on non-Spanish contributors to speak out for the hijab-wearing women's motivation of the practice. El País imported forgeries' arguments into the Spanish social instead of meeting and giving voice to Spanish hijab-wearers. The discourse de-activated the "Religiosity" frame (a universal religious practice) to re-activate the cultural "Othering" frame of the practitioners. Once, El País activates only once the "Religiosity" frame of the practice to cast it as the religion of the "other."

The "Othering" frame in the Spanish press is not limited to the hijab-wearers from migratory origins. The "us" and "others" social categorization and the documental national belonging to Spain are repetitive discursive strategies in El Pais and La Vanguardia. The "Othering" frame is also re-activated in reference to non-Muslim hijab supporter (who are described as Arabists) and Spanish converts in El Mundo and El País. It is also re-activated to refer to Ceuta and Mellia, which are excluded from Spanishness *(la hispanidad)* because of these regions' high Muslim population. On the contrary, hijab opposers are included in the Spanish community even though they were born and raised out of borders.

The hijab-wearers, who appears in the 2015/2016, explain their awareness of the social exclusion practiced on them. They use "us" and "our" to refer to the Spanish community. They state that difference is the trigger of the "Othering" frame because Spain rejects and fears the difference.

British "Othering" Mental Frame of Hijab-Wearing Women

The "Othering" frame in the British discourse is mainly re-activated by the positionality discursive strategy, the repetitive use of the constructive "we" and "our" pronouns. In the British context, the "we" and "others" categorization is not a unilateral ethnocentric "Othering." The pronoun "we" delineates the interfered meaning of

_____
[113]Juárez (2015).

the "other," depending on the speaker's orientation. For example, the French ban-law debate outlines "our" multicultural United Kingdom in opposition to the "others" intolerant French Republic. Othering the ban law used by Muslims and non-Muslims; by hijab supporters and hijab opposers, as we will see below. The "our" multicultural British is used by hijab opposers to delineate Islam tolerance in the United Kingdom, as we have seen in the previous chapter. Hijab-wearers use "we" and "our" to refer to both the British Muslim community and the British community as a whole.

For example, in The Independent, Marie Dhumieres indicates that the British debate over the Islamic dress at school is limited to the full-face veil.[114] She continues that Shadow Chancellor Ed Balls argues in January 2010 that "it is not British to tell people what to wear in the streets." Dhumieres re-activates the "Othering" frame of the French ban law. However, she re-activates the "Othering" framing of hijab-wearers by limiting the debate on migration. Dhumieres states: "The French and the British have dealt with immigration and cultural diversity in two very different ways. While both push equality, the French live for "neutrality"—let's all hide our differences—and the British prefer to go with assumed multiculturalism—live and let live. In the Times Online, Minette Marin asks, "Why not let Muslim schoolgirls wear their head coverings to school? It is not as though they are demanding the right to flaunt themselves, like many other British girls, in microskirts."[115] In Marin's argument, "Muslim schoolgirls" are compared to "British girls" as if they do not belong to the same *Britishness*. She continues: "Britain has a tradition of tolerance of which we are rightly proud, and our presumption must be in favor of freedom and of the free expression of religious belief." In this article, Marin uses the "we" pronoun seven times: "Britain has a tradition of tolerance of which we are rightly proud," "we have never insisted on keeping schools strictly secular; on the contrary, we have overtly religious schools," "where we are beginning to be inclined to draw the line of tolerance. We are beginning to feel, after years of misguided multiculturalist propaganda about diversity, that what we must emphasize is similarity." The question is, what social diversities are included in Marin's "we"? The "our" possessive pronoun is used to exclude the hijab practice form the "us" interfered meaning. She states: "It (the hijab practice) challenges our ideas of what's most important in our own culture and the points at which we draw the line of tolerance." Accordingly, this exclusion includes hijab practitioners, too.

Not all the contributors in the French ban debate re-activate the "Othering" frame of the French ban. For example, Natasha Walter in The Guardian expresses her admiration, as a representative of the British "we," of the French separation between religion and the State, she declares: "I wish that we in Britain shared such idealism about the value of secularism."[116] Walter used "we" ten times in the national hijab debate. Yet, the pronoun "we" excludes the "other's" and the "outsider's right to practice hijab. Walter states: "we find it (hijab) so hateful," "we should support them (women in Afghanistan)," "we should not be easily seduced (by the ban law)," "if we

---

[114]Dhumieres (2013).

[115]Marin (2004).

[116]Walter (2004).

believe in tolerance," "we find alien," "we believe in women's self-determination,"
"we also need to respect those choices," "we hold that idea (the feminist propaganda
of free-choice)" and "we should take a stand against those who would force women."
Such discursive strategy asserts class hierarchy as much as re-activates the "Othering"
frame on British hijab-wearers.

In the British context, the "Othering" frame of hijab-wearing women is re-
activated by importing the image of veiled Muslims (hijab, burqa, or niqab) from
different parts of the world into the national debate on hijab-wearers in the United
Kingdom. I have explained this discursive strategy in the re-activation of the "Oppression" frame, in which the Afghan women's social context was used as a trigger.
This strategy indicates that what applies to the Afghan women applies to British
Muslim women. Another indirect discursive strategy to re-activate the "Othering"
frame of hijab-wearers is picturing the visibility of hijab-wearers "in" the United
Kingdom. Such representation activates the "outsider" dimension in their presence.
For example, in The Guardian, Catherine Bennett praises the "trajectory of feminism in the west [...] to uncover."[117] Then, she states that "in other parts of the
world women risk prison or beatings for the same freedom." Directly after that, she
questions, "Why should we show respect to people who would love to restore female
invisibility in this country?". Bennett connects the practice to outsider discriminatory
and oppressive factors as much as she marks it as an introducer "in this country."
Husna Abbasi, in the Guardian too, outlines the difference between hijab-wearers'
choice and British "us," she states that "even if hijab-wearing is a genuine choice,
does it make it obligatory for us to respect it?"[118] In The Independent, Joan Smith
does not refer to hijab-wearers as British. Instead, she says: "Muslim women in this
country may be telling the truth when they say they are covering their hair and face
out of choice, but that doesn't mean they haven't been influenced by relatives and
male clerics."[119] Yet, in the same paragraph, she refers to the influential Muslim male
as British "Just how prescriptive some British Muslim men are on this subject was
revealed in a startling exchange on last week's Moral Maze on Radio 4". The interviewee, a Muslim male, is Dr. Muhammad Mukadam, chairman of the Association of
Muslim Schools and principal of the Leicester Islamic Academy, who declared that
the hijab would be compulsory as a part of the school uniform. It seems more comfortable to include Muslim men into the Britishness, even if he announces imposing the
hijab in school uniform, than including the free-choice hijab-wearing women. In
The Independent, Katy Guest and Merry Wyn Davis indicate that "While Muslim
presence is changing [...] Britain is also changing the Muslims who live here."[120] In
all of these narrations, British Muslims in general and British hijab-wearing women
in specific are referred to as outsiders who live "in" the United Kingdom and not as
British; outsiders who are imposing their hijab on the British identity.

---

[117]Bennett (2004).
[118]Abbasi (2004).
[119]Smith (2006a).
[120]Guest and Davies (2005).

The "Othering" frame is re-activated in the discourse that refers to coverts. For example, in The Independent, Julie Burchill introduces Lauren Booth Form the "Othering" Iranian frame. Booth's hijab decision is linked to the "murderous, gyno-phobic, theocratic dictators."[121] Booth is described as "a good example of a hypocrit-ical woman" who is "no longer" related to Tony Blair by marriage, who "works for the Iranian-funded television channel Press TV – headscarf and all!". Her religious visibility and the broken in-law relationship with Tony Blairs stands for a broken relationship with "Britishness" as a whole.

Re-activating the "Othering" mental frame by the reference to the migratory origins of the hijab-wearers is used to justify the French ban in the BBC. The journalists introduce the French Muslim by reference to their parents/grandparents' migrational origin. For example, Caroline Wyatt refers to the young French Muslim students as follows: "young Muslims of immigrants, they say, they have a dual iden-tity - both French and Muslim - and they blame France for failing to accept its newer citizens."[122] Wyatt introduces the French ban as a tool that hides the Muslim migrant's visible identity in the French secular public sphere. The ban law sizes their public identity to be only "French." In another article also published in BBC, she introduces her friend, Antonio, a middle-age, "rather a conventional business-man" who indicates that "it was the second and third generation of French-born Muslims, many of whom live in the big city suburbs—effectively ghettos—who seem to him increasingly 'un-French.'"[123] The businessman's declaration about the Muslim generation in France sounds authoritative and out of the experience. Wyatt asserts Antonio's "Othering" frame of the marginalized Muslim migrant and their descendants in France; she states:

> France's failure over the past 40 years or so has been to dump those immigrant families into high-rise ghettos, where desperation over unemployment and poverty is boiling over into alienation. A whole new generation of young people is choosing to reject French values, just as they feel France has rejected them. Only now are politicians beginning to wake up and ask what has gone wrong. How can France offer real equality to all, making it more than just a word inscribed on all the national public buildings?

Although Wyatt refers to the French government's involvement in marginalizing the French Muslim community, the discourse highlights French Muslims' rejection of the French values. She also considers the French ban of the hijab at school is the first step to improve Muslim's social situation. This discursive strategy categorizes the Muslim rejection of the French ban as a rejection of the French values. While in fact, the rejection of the hijab ban is a rejection to abandon their religious identity, which is a legitimate right in the UDHR[124]. Such discourse recycles the colonial policies that focused on Muslim women's vestment in social reforms in the colonies. Women's

---

[121] Burchill (2011).

[122] Wyatt (2004).

[123] Wyatt (2003).

[124] See article N:18 in the Universal Declaration of Human Right.

unveiling was the only social advancement in the colonies, while the economic and social problems were not on the colonizer's political agenda.[125]

"Othering" the French hijab-wearers, "unFrench," is based on the French gender-relation sovereignty, which is considered the best system to organize public relations between sexes. Therefore, "those who did not conform to it were by definition inferior and therefore could never be fully French."[126] French Muslims who resist the ban law are stigmatized as "unFrench," while those migrants who support the ban are included in the "French" belonging sense. Wyatt states: "And that's a view supported by some French Muslims, some of whom came to France partly because it is a secular state in which religious belief is kept a private matter."[127]

In the British contexts, we recognize two categories in the British "we": the hijab-opposers' "we" and the hijab-wearers' "we(s)" Each includes particular social components and excludes others. The British Muslim "we" contains two subcategories: the British Muslim "we" and the out/group mainstream "we." For example, in the Guardian, Maleiha Malik asserts the Muslim women (in-group belonging) "we." She state: "we Muslim women who welcome the debate about women's status in Islam, to have feminist alliance with other women to challenge the misuse of power by Muslim men" and to offer 'our own' perspective on both women's advances and setbacks in the west".[128] In The Independent, Shamim Chowdhury uses the British Muslim "we" in the discussion of the case of Shabina Begum (Luton, 2005): "we Muslims have exposed ourselves to even more anti-Islamic sentiment".[129] She indicates that the case "distorted set of priorities" of Muslim and represented them as "fragmented," "bogged down with dogma," and "grieving on one lone school-girl." The case gives "the bigots even more ammunition with which to attack us". In addition, Chowdhury points out the discrimination that Muslim go through in daily interaction: "we are being stopped and searched, arrested randomly and held in custody without a charge" and "many of us are apt at, verbally abused, vilified, criminalized and demonized." She states that "we need to be standing strong, display a united front against the mounting hostilities we face every single day." The "we" categorization in Malik and Chowdhury's dsicourse is built on the abuse that the in-group is exposed to in the public sphere. The discrimination against the Muslim minority empowers the in-group belonging. The discriminated "we" is constructed in opposition to the out-group discriminator "others."

The second British Muslim "we" assert the out-group belonging: the British belonging. For example, in Ciar Byrne's article published in The Independent, Faiza, the radio presenter, criticizes the media "Othering" of hijab-wearing women. She states that "whenever you see women in hijab on the news, it's because of some

---

[125]Muñoz (2010) and Haddad (2007).

[126]Scott (2009).

[127]Wyatt (2004).

[128]Malik (2006).

[129]Chowdhury (2005).

tragedy in a Muslim country. We don't see Muslim women in headscarves on East-Enders or The Bill."[130] In The Guardian, Remona Ali, whose article discusses the British hijab-wearing successful public figures in 2015, indicates: "featuring women in this way is something I find empowering, and confidence-boosting, and it nurtures that old British Muslim sentiment of 'belonging.' I hope it will render Muslim women less 'them' and more 'us' and will promote a shift from a minority complex to a majority mindset."[131] Rania Cllr Khan, in The Guardian, uses the out-group "we" categorization in her argument on women's freedom to vestment: "The women's movement in this country has won many important freedoms. One is the freedom to choose what we wear!"[132] This discourse activates British "we" in which Muslims enjoy an equal sense of belonging as non-muslims.

To sum up, the re-activation of the "Othering" mental frame of hijab-wearers in the British press is indirect. It was re-activated mainly by "we" and "other" positionality. In the justification of the French ban in BBC, the "Othering" frame is re-activated on the French hijab-wearers, and the ban law is framed as a political attempt built on goodwill to improve Muslims' integration in France. In the Independent, the "Othering" frame is activated on the intolerant French, which contradicts British multicultural values. The Guardia asserts the need to put a line for tolerance. On a national level, the "Othering" frame is re-activated through "we"/"other" positionality. The discourse strategies are the migration-reference in the hijab debate, the use of the preposition "in" (the United Kingdom) to refer to British Muslims, the creation of a contradictory relationship between the hijab and the British values. In the British context, "Othering" the hijab is more recurrent than "Othering" the hijab-wearers.

There are multiple positionalities in the British press due to the participants' diversity in the national press discourse. There is the British tolerant "we" in opposition to the Intolerant French "others," the British (librated) "we" in opposition to the (British) Muslim "others," the British Muslim "we" in opposition to the British discriminator "other," and the British Muslim inclusive "we" that includes all the diversity in the United Kingdom social structure.

Cross-Cultural Analysis

The re-activation of the "Othering" frame of the hijab-wearing women is more direct and more repetitive in the Spanish press than in the British one. However, both presses use similar linguistic strategies to re-activate it. For example, both contexts use the image of the Afghan and Arabic oppressed veiled women in the national debate of the hijab practice. By such, the foreigner dimension is imposed on the visibility of the national hijab-wearer in both social contexts.

---

[130] Byrne (2005).

[131] Aly (2015).

[132] Cllr Khan (2006).

Both press discourses establish the link between the hijab debate and migration policies. There was a constant reference to the hijab wearers' parents' migrational origins in Spanish discourse because Spain is witnessing the first Spanish Muslim generation. When the Spanish belonging is mentioned, it is limited to documental belonging "of Spanish nationality." In the British context, as the Muslim generation is enough to be stigmatized as such, the reference to the hijab-wearers was limited to being Muslims who live "in" the United Kingdom.

Both social contexts re-activate the "Othering" frame of convert women. However, the Spanish discourse dedicates phrases and articles to this re-activation. It reduces their religious and spiritual transition to the hijab practice and establishes a positionality between the convert's Spanish heritage and the new religious affiliation. The British context was limited to one case, whose "Othering" is related to political affiliation to Iran.

Both press discourse indicates the hijab-wearing women's refusal to integrate into the national identity by practicing the hijab. The Spanish press re-activates this aspect of the "Othering" frame continuously and directly in the social and political debate. On the contrary, the British press uses the indirect discursive technique by referencing the French Muslim resistance to integrate into the French community.

Both press discourses use the "we" and "other" positionality in re-activating the "Othering" Frame. In the Spanish context, There is only the mainstream (librated) (dominant) "we" in opposition to migrant oppressed Muslim "others." It was until 2015/2016 that we find the Spanish Muslim inclusive "we" by the hijab-wearing interviewee. The British positionality is more complex and more diverse due to its diversity in the national press discourse. There is the British tolerant "we" in opposition to the intolerant French "others," the British (librated) "we" in opposition to the (British) Muslim "others," the British Muslim "we" in opposition to the British discriminator "other," and the British Muslim inclusive "we" that includes all the diversity in the United Kingdom social structure.

Framing the Hijab-Wearing Women Through "Indiscipline"

The "Indiscipline" mental frame is a new framing of the hijab-wearing women re-activated in both presses; however, it is more intensive in the Spanish press. The "Indiscipline" framing picture the practice as a social-order breaker and categorizes it as a practice against the established rules. This frame is not recycled from the colonized discourse. It is a new mental frame that emerges from the hijab-wearers' visibility in the national public sphere.

Spanish "Indiscipline" Mental Frame of Hijab-Wearing Women

The "Indiscipline" framing of hijab-wearers is extensively activated in the Spanish press. It depends on the internal school law that bans the head covering, which prevented Muslim students from practicing the hijab. The previously mentioned "Concealment" frame of the hijab, limiting the practice to simple headcover, triggers the "Indiscipline" frame of hijab-wearers. By activating the "Indiscipline" mental frame, school direction, feminists, socialists, and politicians could justify the abrupt exclusion, expelling, and separation of the minors from the classroom. One of the discursive strategies to assert the validity of the "Indiscipline" mental frame in the Spanish press highlights the minors' critical age (as teenagers). The discourse establishes a link between teenagers' dress codes, teenagers' identity disorientation, and the practice. By activating the "Indiscipline" and the "Concealment" framing of the hijab, the minor's expulsion is being justified by the public opinion.

The first time the "Indiscipline" mental frame of the hijab-wearers is activated in the selected articles was in the case of Najwa Al-Malha (Madrid, 2010). In El Mundo, the reference to the school's internal law of baning head-covering is repeated in (Sotero and Bécares, 2010a), (Del Barrio, 2010a, b). The linguistic expressions that activate this frame are repetitive and symmetric: "she was separated from the class because of wearing the veil" and "in the building's internal parts, it is not allowed to use hats or any other garment that covers the head." In El País, the same linguistic expressions are used by Álvarez who covers Najwa's case (Álvarez and Cembrero, 2010a, b, d; Álvarez and Garriga, 2010).

In Arteixo case, El País asserts the "Indiscipline" frame by using linguistic expressions that cast the hijab-wearing student as guilty for breaking the school's internal law. For example, Obelleiro opens the article as follows: "It looks unstoppable that the new primary school of Arteixo decides, on Monday, to sanction with the expulsion of three days, as a minimum, an 11 years old student because she wears the veil."[133] The discourse introduces the school decision as "unstoppable" "because of breaking the vestment norms." Expressions as "sanctioned" and "expelled" are the trigger of the "Indiscipline" frame. The journalist continues explaining the internal legislation of the head-covering ban with an assertion on the educative center's autonomous nature. The same image schema of "sanctioned student" is repeated with the same order in the many articles written by the same journalist: (Obelleiro, 2011a, c, e, 2012).

In the Usera case, the discourse in El Mundo asserts the "discomfort" which the hijab practice causes to the school direction.[134] In Amanda Figueras' two articles, the discourse is almost repetitive.[135] Figueras states that the girl is a "good student" but "(E)verything had changed when she practiced veiling"; she got "innumerous light

---

[133]Obelleiro (2011b).

[134]Figueras and Piantadosi (2011).

[135]Figueras (2011a, b).

errors," and she is "shy" and has a "low voice." Her veiling motivation is "the pride of her father." In El País, Pilar Álvarez presents the same student as "not delinquent," and her veiling is "not a whim."[136] Both attributes are exaggerated attributes for a 14-year-old student whose crime is practicing the hijab. Álvarez quotes the minor's motivation for the hijab: "I am an adolescent; I wear what they tell me not to wear." We can see that the profile of the student widely varies across these two newspapers. The indiscipline revolutionary student portrayed in El País does not match with the shy and intelligent student described in El Mundo.

In Hasna Isslal case, Álvarez in El País indicates that the school director acknowledges the "Religiosity" frame of the hijab, yet, he rejects the religious practice because it conceals the identity of the student, by which he gives priority to the identity "Concealment" frame of the practice. He states: "It is an indiscipline issue; it is not to value (the) faith."[137] Figueras in El Mundo asserts the internal law of the school that justifies the separation: "students can not cover their head in the interior building."[138] In the case of Takwa Rejeb, in El Mundo, the same rigid interpretation of the institute's internal norms is provided to the reader: "Covering the head is not allowed unless for illness requirements."[139] Inma Lindón indicates that the school director refused "to make a smoother" interpretation of the norm and to include a religious exception. She states that "having the headcover violates the center's internal regulation, which strictly prohibits it."

In the workplace exclusion case of Ana Saidi Rodriguez, the aconfessional laws of the company are broken by Saidi Rodriguez's practice. In El Mundo, Irene Velasco states that Saidi Rodriguez is "sanctioned five times for going to work with the veil."[140] The Human Resources manager in Acciona Airport Services, Victorio Nuñez, justifies the sanctions in two arguments "exclusive uniform" and "banning the use of religious and political symbols." Velasco indicates that he avoids the use of the word "hijab" or the "veil." It is an attempt by the manager to assert the general company rules and to avoid targeting the hijab directly. In El País, Lucia Bohorquez indicates that the company "sanctioned her (Saidi Rodriguez) for veiling seven times" and "they have suspended her salary for various weeks."[141] All these sanctioning procedures are justified through the internal law of the schools and companies. Yet, none of the journalists argues or elaborates on Religious freedom, which is guaranteed by the Spanish Constitution, nor questions if the school's internal law can be above the constitution. These arguments were only mentioned by the lawyer of the school girl Jemenez Aybar. The journalists did not elaborate on them.

---

[136]Álvarez, Pilar (a). *A clase con el velo.* El País, 18 October 2011. http://sociedad.elpais.com/sociedad/2011/10/18/actualidad/1318888806_850215.html.

[137]Álvarez, Pilar (c). *Renunciar al velo islámico sería como quitarme la piel.* El País: 23 October 2011. http://elpais.com/diario/2011/10/23/sociedad/1319320802_850215.html.

[138]Figueras (2011c).

[139]Lidón (2016).

[140]Velasco (2016).

[141]Bohorquez (2016).

In social and political debate, the "Indiscipline" frame is activated by the journalists or the hijab debate contributors. In El Mundo, the Interdisciplinary frame of the hijab-wearers is activated by the politicians' declarations. Carmen de Ganuza quotes Mariano Rajoy, who was not satisfied with the school's decision to accept the hijab-wearing student (Shaima: Girona, 2007). She states: "Rajoy criticized the acceptance of the 'blackmail' of the student."[142] De Ganuza previously, in the same article, has re-activated the "Othering" frame by establishing a connection between the hijab visibility and migration.

In El País, the "Indiscipline" frame of hijab-wearers is activated through two different linguistic strategies. The first linguistic strategy is similar to the one used in the exclusion cases. It is based on the assertion of the broken school's internal laws. For example, Solidad Gallego-Díaz asserts that "schools have the right to include among its regulations the requirement that their students do not cover their heads in class that they do not wear short pants."[143] She continues, "it does not seem that it makes sense to make an exception for the fact that this headdress is related to religious belief. What is clear is that no one denies that teenager the right to receive an education. It will be enough if she finds another school in which head covering is not prohibited." Gallego-Diaz concludes her article by defining the responsibilities of this conflict. She states: "The problem is with their parents who have not bothered to find out the internal rules of that particular school or to find one that meets their demands, and not of society as a whole (*y no de la sociedad en su conjunto*)."

Rosa Montero asserts the priority of school internal norms; she argues, "if the girl goes to a school which bans wearing anything on the head, then, obviously, she cannot use the hijab in class Do not you want to normalize it? This is normal."[144] She also adds: "do not tell me that education should be given the priority and, for so, to accept hijab. Sorry, this form, justly, part of education: put limits to the guys, teach them that there are rules." Both journalists, Gallego-Diaz and Montero, assert the school's internal law's priority over the students' right to religious freedom. At the same time, they frame the Hijab-wearing students and their parents as the problem to cast off the school's responsibility.

The second linguistic strategy that activates the "Indiscipline" frame of hijab-wearers in El Pais is the assertion of students' "critical" age. Repetitively, the discourse in the exclusion cases referred to them as "adolescent": "la adolescente," "la menor," and "la joven." In the social debate, this frame of reference is used to assert the "disorientation" which teenagers go through at this age. Galarraga titles her article as follows: *Veil of submission or rebellion?* By the title, the journalist limits the framing of the hijab, and its practitioners, to only two frames, "Submission" or "Indiscipline." El-Hachmi, interviewed in the article, indicates that "the case of Najwa can be a phase if we do not convert it to a circus. Time will tell."[145] El-Hachmi summarizes her ex-hijab experience as follows: "it was a time when I

---

[142] De Ganuza (2008).

[143] Gallego-Díaz (2010).

[144] Montero (2010).

[145] Galarraga (2010).

was very disoriented, with many identity problems." Naiara Galarraga comments on El-Hachmi's experience: "she took it off. For a long time, she knew that vestment does not tell who you are". Another contributor in the same article supports the "disorientation" argument. Galarraga seems to be determined about the "disorientation" argument. She supports her argument by Leonor Morino's opinion, a UAM professor. Galarraga states: "it has not been so far when teenagers filtered with the idea of being nuns. (the professor says) 'It was a moment of Mysticism, looking for purity.' Perhaps, this is the case of Najwa". Later in the article, El-Achmawi narrates her daughter's case and adverts from the "disorientation" which girls go through at the moment of wearing a hijab. El-Achmawi states that "her friends began to take the step of putting on the hijab" at the age of 15. She recommended her daughter to think over it because "turning back is very difficult. The teenager thought about it. And in the end, she decided that no. She remained as she was, until today." El Achmawi's argument limits the hijab practice to a social-cultural tradition in Eygpt, a fashion to be followed between teenagers. This (outsider) fashion, which goes against the Spanish school internal regulations, pushes the hijab-wearers to break the rules. The same argument appears in Maria Sahuquillo's discourse. Nadia Yassine indicates that "the veil is a fashion that [arrasa]. Teenagers watch models on TV, and they like it."[146]

To sum up, the "Indiscipline" mental frame of hijab-wearers is activated in both El Mundo and El País. In the exclusion cases, the activation of the "Indiscipline" frame depends on the activation of the identity "Concealment" frame. Even when the "Religiosity" frame of the hijab is activated, the "Concealment" framing wins over, and the "Indiscipline" frame conquered the argument. In the exclusion cases, El Pais shows more extensive efforts to activate the "Indiscipline" Frame of the hijab-wearing students and employees than El Mundo. However, both presses assert on the school's internal law autonomy. None of the presses argues on the religious rights of Muslim students.

In the social and political debates, El Mundo uses politicians' declarations to activate the "Indiscipline" frame of the hijab-wearing students. In El Pais, the journalists participated directly in the activation of this frame. They use experts' declarations to empower and assert such framing of the hijab visibility in the Spanish school. The hijab is framed as a fashionable outsider garment used by "disorientated" Muslim teenagers who pass through identity problems. This outsider fashion is brought into the Spanish public school, breaking the internal law of these schools. The real responsible are the parents who are demanding the acceptance of the hijab visibility instead of paying attention to the school's internal norms.

---

[146]The same argument used by Rebeca Carranco who related Shaima's hijab to the Arabic TV programs; Carranco (2010).

British "Indiscipline" Mental Frame of Hijab-Wearing Women

The "Indiscipline" mental frame of hijab-wearers is not a dominant nor asserted mental frame in the British discourse. This frame is not frequent. In the British data, because there are few exclusion cases, most of those are related to *jilbab*. The hijab is included in the school uniforms, and there are no problems in practicing it at British public schools.

In the Independent, there has been one article on the exclusion of a hijab-wearing Seleena Sabeel (Peterborough, 2004). The student is represented through the "Indiscipline" mental frame by Sarah Cassidy.[147] Cassidy narrates that the headteacher of science who has an "unblemished record" faces an "accusation" by a student with a "poor behavior" record that includes "violence and abuse." The student "alleged" that she suffered "a cut neck" when "Ms. Dick 'forcibly' took her hijab from her head." The teacher's behavior is introduced within quotations to limit its reference to what the student says. It is to say; it creates a distance between the journalist's discourse and the student's allegation. Cassidy justifies "the incident that leads to the allegations" happens when Sabeel "was told to change her hijab" because it was not of the school uniform. The discursive strategy gives the teacher privilege over the students, casting the student's behavior and her version of the story as suspicious.

Yasmin AliBahi-Brown activates the "Indiscipline" mental frame of hijab-wearers who, according to her, provoke problems whenever they are visible: "I have been at graduation ceremonies where shrouded female students have refused to shake the hand of the chancellor. Veiled women have provoked confrontations over their right to wear veils, in courts, at schools and in colleges and workplaces."[148] She negates Muslim women the freedom to decide over their vestment and the freedom to build their own gender-relation system.

In the *jilbab* exclusion cases, the activation of the "Indiscipline" mental frame of the *jilbab* wearer is activated by (hijab-wearing) Muslims and non-Muslim. For example, in the case of Shabina's *jilbab* (Luton, 2005), Shamim Chowdhury in The Independent, refers that "this case was not about government policy. It was one girl's dispute with her school over a uniform code".[149] She uses linguistic expressions that activate the "Indiscipline" mental frame: "She broke the school's uniform code."

There has been one link between the hijab practice and identity assertion mentioned by a former hijab-wearer. Nusrat Hussain, in Arifa Akbar series of interviews, associates the hijab practice of "large number" of Muslims to the lack of self-esteem as a person: "For a large number of women, covering their hair gives them something, women who otherwise might not have a strong sense of identity. It is a personality thing. If you are not strong as a person, you use it".[150] Hussain, as former hijab-wearer, projects her experience on a "large number" of the hijab

---

[147]Cassidy (2004).

[148]Alibhai-Brown (2015).

[149]Chowdhury (2005).

[150]Akbar (2010a).

practice as if her "law esteem" at the moment of practicing the hijab is the norm of the Muslim youth.

To sum up, the "Indiscipline" mental frame of the hijab-wearers in Brith press is in both The Independent and The Guardian, in one in each. The jilbab visibility is framed as "Indiscipline" because British public schools offer hijab and shalwar kameez among the school uniform possibilities.

Cross-Cultural Analysis

In the "Indiscipline" Mental frame of the hijab-wearing women, there are prominent differences between the Spanish press and the British press. The "Indiscipline" frame is recurrent in the Spanish press because several schools' internal laws prohibit the head's covering for identification reasons. In contrast, the hijab's inclusion in the school uniform in British schools decreases this frame's activation in the British press.

The Spanish press activates the "Indiscipline" frame to justify the exclusion of the hijab-wearing students from their schools and the hijab-wearing employees from their workplaces. Both hijab-wearers and their parents are framed as the causes of the problem to cast off the responsibility of Spanish education centers or companies, which in theory, have to respect the Spanish constitutional law that protects the religious liberty of students and employees. This constitutional law was not mentioned nor argued about in the Spanish national press. We do not see similar discursive strategies in the British national press. It is due to the British inclusion of hijab visibility in the public school uniform and in the workplace. On the contrary, the activation of the "Indiscipline" frame of the jilbab-wearing student is not seen in the Spanish press because there is no similar case in Spain.

Conclusion

The colonial discourse on hijab-wearing women is prominent in the British and press discourse. Only one frame, "Indiscipline," out of four is a new frame, whereas the three others are recycled. However, the British discourse is more politically correct and indirect in the re-activation of stereotypical frames.

The French ban was a significant trigger in the British hijab debate. It is highly justified in BBC, although it is not seen as an example to be followed. In contrast, the French ban does not appear in the Spanish press until 2007 when it is retrieved as an example to be followed when the first exclusion cases emerged at Spanish public schools.

The Spanish press shows a highly controlled discourse, in which stereotypical frames of hijab-wearers are activated. The stereotypical frames on hijab add to those on hijab-wearers to provide Spanish readers with a biased image schema in which hijab-wearers are located and limited to. The "Ignorance" and the "Oppression" frame of the hijab-wearers justify her concealment and empower the "Concealment" framing of the hijab. It looks like an equation with no other logic than "if a woman wears the hijab, she is oppressed and ignorant." Hijab-wearing women are depicted as unable to speak out for themselves. Hijab-wearing women are represented as oppressed within the family, at school, and in the workplace. We never find an empowered hijab-wearing woman in the Spanish press.

All of these stereotypical frames of hijab and hijab-wearers justify the authoritative voice the hijab opposer journalists enjoy. On the contrary, British discourse doesn't conceal the hijab-wearers' voice because of the practice. The "Ignorance" and "Oppression" frames are limited to the choice of concealing the body, which is understood as an offensive practice by hijab opposers.

The image of Afghan women in the national hijab debate is prominent in both discourses. It re-activates many stereotypical framings on the national Muslim women, even on converts. The Spanish discourse employs several discursive techniques to re-activate the "Othering" frame of the hijab-wearers. The discourse casts off the Spanish community's responsibility to accept religious diversity and blame the patriarchy of Afghan social life (as a representative of the Muslim world). The outcome is a systematic control and manipulated discourse designed to maintain the colonial discourse on hijab-wearers, denying Spanish social responsibility and diversity. The "Indiscipline" frame in Spanish discourse serves to picture the practice as a temporary whim and stigmatizes hijab-wearers as law-breakers instead of arguing on these women's right to religious freedom protected by the Spanish constitutional system.

The inclusion of Muslim diversity in the British multicultural context is reflected in the national hijab debate. "Othering" the hijab-wearers is not direct nor extensive as in the Spanish discourse. The diversity in the British national press reveals several social positionalities, in which inclusion and exclusion depend on the speaker's attitudes toward the hijab. Instead, in the Spanish press, we find the well-trained Spanish hijab opposer's "we" in opposition to the anonymous Muslim "others." Spanish hijab-wearing women in the Spanish press have no space to express themselves freely in the national press. Their agency over their body, image, faith, and thoughts is taken away by the hijab opposer journalists' sovereignty.

References

Ahmed, L. (1982). Western ethnocentrism and perceptions of the harem. *Feminist Studies, 8*(3), 521–534.

Bullock, K. (2003). *Rethinking Muslim women and the veil: Challenging historical and modern stereotypes*. The International Institute of Islamic Thought.

Gilliat-Ray, S. (2010). *Muslims in Britain*. Cambridge University Press.

Haddad, Y. (2007). The Post-9/11 Hijab as icon. *Sociology of Religion, 68*(3), 253–267.

Jouili, J. (2009). Negotiating secular boundaries: Pious micro-practices of Muslim women in French and German public spheres. *Social anthropology, 17*(4), 455–470.

Ramirez, A. (2010). Muslim women in Spanish press: Subaltern image. In F. Shirazi (Ed.), *Muslim women in war and crisis: Representation and reality.* University of Texas Press.
Scott, J. W. (2009). *The politics of the veil.* Princeton University Press.

Annex 1

Spanish Articles
Abad, R. (2007a). *A la Asamblea con el 'hiyab'.* http://elpais.com/diario/2007/06/17/espana/118 2031209_850215.html. 17 June 2007.
Abad, R. (2007b). *"Este velo es para siempre" Vuelven a clase las alumnas del colegio ceutí obligado por Educación a aceptar el 'hiyab'.* http://elpais.com/diario/2007/10/11/sociedad/119 2053613_850215.html. 11 October 2007.
Álvarez, P. (2011a). *A clase con el velo.* http://sociedad.elpais.com/sociedad/2011/10/18/actualidad/ 1318888806_850215.html. 18 October 2011.
Álvarez, P. (2011b). *Mi velo sí entra en clase.* http://elpais.com/diario/2011/10/19/madrid/131902 3459_850215.html. 19 October 2011.
Álvarez, P. (2011c). *Renunciar al velo islámico sería como quitarme la piel.* http://elpais.com/dia rio/2011/10/23/sociedad/1319320802_850215.html. 23 October 2011.
Álvarez, P., & Cembrero, I. (2010a). *Estalla el debate sobre legislar el uso del pañuelo islámico en clase.* http://elpais.com/diario/2010/04/22/sociedad/1271887203_850215.html. 22 April 2010.
Álvarez, P., & Cembrero, I. (2010b). *Mi hija seguira en el mismo instituto y con hijab.* http://www.elpais.com/articulo/sociedad/hija/seguira/mismo/instituto/hiyab/elpepu soc/20100423elpepisoc_3/Tes. 23 April 2010.
Álvarez, P., & Cembrero, I. (2010c). *La justicia examinará la expulsión de Najwa de un colegio por llevar 'hiyab'.* http://elpais.com/diario/2010/09/03/sociedad/1283464807_850215.html. 3 September 2010.
Álvarez, P., & Cembrero, I. (2010d). *La justicia examinará la expulsión de Najwa de un colegio por llevar 'hiyab'.* http://elpais.com/diario/2010/09/03/sociedad/1283464807_850215.html. 3 September 2010.
Álvarez, P., & Garriga, J. (2010). *Aguirre ficha de asesor al director del centro que vetó el velo de Najwa.* http://elpais.com/diario/2010/05/25/sociedad/1274738410_850215.html. 25 May 2010.
Ayuso, B. (2016). *De María a Maryam: así se convirtió al islam una española de 29 años.* El País. 16 July 2016. http://politica.elpais.com/politica/2016/06/23/actualidad/1466664764_761081.html.
Barik Edidi, Z. (2009). *Encuentro.* http://www.elmundo.es/encuentros/invitados/2009/11/3898/ index.html. 11 November 2009.
Belaza, M. C. (2010). *El Supremo decidirá sobre el uso del "hiyab" en los juicios.* http://elpais. com/diario/2010/01/15/sociedad/1263510007_850215.html. 15 January 2010.
Belvar, M., & Blasco, P. (2010). *El instituto de Pozuelo no modifica sus normas e impide a Najwa ir con veil.* http://www.elmundo.es/elmundo/2010/04/20/madrid/1271786689.html 21 April 2010.
Bohorquez, L. (2016). *Que me obliguen a quitarme el velo es como arrancarme mi propia piel.* http://politica.elpais.com/politica/2016/12/20/actualidad/1482237712_030858.html. 20 December 2016.
Caballero, C. (2010). *Un velo y una toca.* http://www.elpais.com/articulo/andalucia/velo/toca/elp epiespand/20100424elpand_10/Tes. 24 April 2010.
Carbajos, A. (2008). *Más musulmanas con velo. ¿Porque quieren?* http://www.elpais.com/articulo/ sociedad/musulmanas/velo/quieren/elpepisoc/20080628elpepisoc_1/Tes. 28 June 2008.
Carranco, R. (2010). *No me quito el 'hiyab' porque no quiero.* http://elpais.com/diario/2010/04/22/ sociedad/1271887206_850215.html. 22 April 2010.
De Ganuza, C. R. (2008). *El Partido Popular propondrá prohibir el uso del velo en todas las escuelas.* http://www.elmundo.es/elmundo/2008/02/08/espana/1202448607.html. 8 February 2008.

Del Barrio, A. (2010a). *Los marroquíes exigen la intervención de la Comunidad en el caso de Najwa.* http://www.elmundo.es/elmundo/2010/04/16/madrid/1271421715.html. 16 April 2010.

Del Barrio, A. (2010b). *Los musulmanes anuncian acciones legales contra el colegio de Pozuelo.* http://www.elmundo.es/elmundo/2010/04/21/madrid/1271852171.html. 21 April 2010.

Espinosa, A. (2010). *En mi clase había una monja.* http://elpais.com/diario/2010/04/23/sociedad/1271973602_850215.html. 23 April 2010.

Etxenike, L. (2004). *Tirar de la manta.* http://elpais.com/diario/2004/02/08/paisvasco/107627 2805_850215.html. 8 February 2004.

Farreras, C. (2016). *Los Nuevos Significados del velo.* http://www.lavanguardia.com/vida/201 60717/403268947566/universitarias-musulmanas-velo-hiyab-expresion-religion.html. 18 July 2016.

Figueras, A. (2011a). *La menor expulsada de un examen por el 'hiyab': 'Dicen que me lo invento y me hago la víctima.* http://www.elmundo.es/elmundo/2011/10/04/madrid/1317750847.html. 6 October 2011.

Figueras, A. (2011b). *El instituto que echó a una niña por llevar 'hiyab' acepta que pueda seguir utilizándolo.* http://www.elmundo.es/elmundo/2011/10/17/madrid/1318888325.html. 19 October 2011.

Figueras, A. (2011c). *El director que prohibió ir con el velo a clase podría ser acusado de prevaricación.* http://www.elmundo.es/elmundo/2011/10/27/castillayleon/1319714393.html. 27 October 2011.

Figueras, A. (2012). *La angustia de decir que eres Musulmán.* http://www.elmundo.es/elmundo/2012/04/27/espana/1335521507.html. 29 April 2012.

Figueras, A. (2015). *'¿Por qué se me cuestiona por abrazar esta fe? El islam no es el velo ni el IS ni ningún tipo de terrorismo'.* http://www.elmundo.es/espana/2015/06/24/55797914ca4741a626 8b457d.html. 30 June 2015.

Figueras, A., & Piantadosi, G. (2011). *Me echaron de un examen y del instituto por llevar 'hiyab'."* http://www.elmundo.es/elmundo/2011/09/30/madrid/1317407926.html. 3 October 2011.

Galarraga, N. (2010). *¿Velo de sumisión o de rebeldía?* http://elpais.com/diario/2010/04/23/soc iedad/1271973601_850215.html. 23 April 2010.

Gallego-Díaz, S. (2010). *El velo no merece una ley.* http://elpais.com/diario/2010/04/25/domingo/1272166236_850215.html. 25 April 2010.

Iglesias, N. (2007). *La Generalitat obliga a admitir en clase a una menor con 'hiyab'.* http://elpais.com/diario/2007/10/02/sociedad/1191276010_850215.html. 10 February 2007.

Juárez, A. S. (2015). *Musulmanas y tan españolas como vosotras.* http://www.elmundo.es/yodona/2015/02/28/54ef5340ca4741216d8b4578.html. 28 February 2015.

Lidón, I. (2016). *Vetada en el instituto por su hiyab: Me dijeron: o te lo quitas o te das baja.* http://www.elmundo.es/comunidad-valenciana/2016/09/16/57dc38c2ca4741b51d8b4676. html 18 September 2016.

Meneses, R. (2010). *Cual es el significado y el origen del Hiyab.* http://www.elmundo.es/elmundo/2010/04/21/madrid/1271853528.html. 22 April 2010.

Moliner, E. (2004). *A favor y en contra.* http://elpais.com/diario/2004/09/12/domingo/109495 7850_850215.html. 12 September 2004.

Montero, R. (2010). *Ahí le duele.* http://elpais.com/diario/2010/04/27/ultima/1272319201_850215. html. 27 April 2010.

Mortimer, C. (2015). *Mariah Idrissi: H&M's first hijab-wearing model says her work 'isn't immodest'.* http://www.independent.co.uk/news/uk/home-news/mariah-idrissi-hms-first-hijab-wearing-model-says her-work-isnt-immodest-a6673901.html. 30 September 2015.

Muñoz, G. M. (2010). *Esto alimenta a la derecha islamófoba.* http://elpais.com/diario/2010/04/22/sociedad/1271887205_850215.html. 22 April 2010.

Obelleiro, P. (2011a). *La familia de la niña de Arteixo invoca una norma estatal que permite el velo.* http://elpais.com/diario/2011/02/26/galicia/1298719096_850215.html. 26 February 2011.

Obelleiro, P. (2011b). *Educación avala la prohibición del velo en clase a una niña.* http://elpais.com/diario/2011/02/25/galicia/1298632692_850215.html. 25 February 2011.

Obelleiro, P. (2011c). *La Xunta anula la sanción a la niña del velo por un defecto formal.* http://elp
ais.com/diario/2011/03/11/sociedad/1299798012_850215.html. 11 March 2011.
Obelleiro, P. (2011d). *La 'niña del velo', excluida de la fiesta de fin de curso.* http://elpais.com/dia
rio/2011/06/23/sociedad/1308780009_850215.html 23 June 2011.
Obelleiro, P. (2011e). *El director del colegio de Arteixo impide a la niña del 'hiyab' entrar a recoger
las notas.* http://elpais.com/diario/2011/06/23/galicia/1308824289_850215.html. 23 June 2011.
Obelleiro, P. (2012). *Declara ante el juez el director que prohibió el velo islámico.* http://elpais.
com/diario/2011/06/23/galicia/1308824289_850215.html. 13 January 2012.
Peral, M. (2010). *Permitir el 'hiyab', facultad de cada juez.* http://www.elmundo.es/elmundo/2010/
02/09/espana/1265687043.html. 9 February 2010.
Quelart, R. (2011). *He conocido a mujeres muy felices detrás del velo.* http://www.lavang
uardia.com/salud/20111212/54239960536/beatriz-goyoaga-entrevista-meditacion-velo.html. 12
December 2011.
Sahuquillo, M. R. (2008). *Integración, si, asimilación, no.* http://www.elpais.com/articulo/sociedad/
Integracion/asimilacion/elpepisoc/20080216elpepisoc_1/Tes. 16 February 2008.
Sotero, P. D., & Bécares, R. (2010a). *El Ministerio de Educación apela a respetar las creencias
de los alumnos.* http://www.elmundo.es/elmundo/2010/04/16/madrid/1271434711.html. 16 April
2010.
Takolia, N. (2010). *The hijab has liberated me from society expectations of women.* https://www.
theguardian.com/commentisfree/2012/may/28/hijab-society-women-religious-political. 28 May
2012.
Velasco, I. (2016). *Tengo el derecho a trabajar con velo.* http://www.elmundo.es/sociedad/2016/
06/10/5756a1bd468aeb14228b45b8.html. 10 June 2016.

Annex 2

English Articles
Abbasi, H. (2004). *Trapped or liberated by the hijab?* https://www.theguardian.com/world/2004/
jan/21/gender.religion. 21 January 2004.
Akbar, A. (2010a). *The many faces behind the veil.* with Rajnaara Akhtar. http://www.independent.
co.uk/news/uk/this-britain/the-many-faces-behind-the-veil-1865772.html.
Akbar, A. (2010b). *The many faces behind the veil* with Shelina Zahra JanMohamaed.* http://
www.independent.co.uk/news/uk/this-britain/the-many-faces-behind-the-veil-1865772.html 13
January 2010.
Akbar, A. (2010c). *The many faces behind the veil.* with Soha Sheikh. http://www.independent.co.
uk/news/uk/this-britain/the-many-faces-behind-the-veil-1865772.html. 13 January 2010.
Alam, F. (2005). *We must move beyond the hijab.* https://www.theguardian.com/education/2005/
nov/29/highereducation.uk. 29 November 2005.
Alibhai-Brown, Y. (2015). *As a Muslim woman, I see the veil as a rejection of
progressive values.* https://www.theguardian.com/commentisfree/2015/mar/20/muslim-woman-
veil-hijab. 20 March 2015.
Aly, R. (2015). *How the hijab-and H&M- are reshaping mainstream British culture.* http://www.
theguardian.com/commentisfree/2015/sep/28/hijab-h-and-m-mainstream-culture-great-british-
bake-off-diversity. 30 September 2015.
Aslam, S. (2014). *To hijab or not to hijab- A Muslim businesswoman's view.* http://www.the
guardian.com/uk/the-northerner/2012/dec/10/hijab-muslims-women-islam-business-bradford-
niqab-burka. 21 May 2014.
Aziz, S. (2014). *Laugh, not at my hijab please.* http://www.theguardian.com/theobserver/she-said/
2014/apr/01/laugh-not-at-my-hijab-please. 1 April 2014.

Bennett, C. (2004). *Why should we defend the veil?* http://www.theguardian.com/world/2004/jan/22/gender.schoolsworldwide. 22 January 2004.

Burchill, J. (2011). *Carla Bruni is standing up to the stoners. Lauren Booth just covers up for them.* http://www.independent.co.uk/voices/columnists/julie-burchill/julie-burchill-carla-bruni-is-standing-up-to-the-stoners-lauren-booth-just-covers-up-for-them-2067119.html. 4 April 2011.

Byrne, C. (2005). *Heard the one about the Mickey Mouse hijab?* http://www.independent.co.uk/news/media/heard-the-one-about-the-mickey-mouse-hijab-320202.html. 17 October 2005.

Cassidy, S. (2004). *Teacher in headscarf case cleared of racial assault on Muslim Girl.* http://www.independent.co.uk/news/education/education-news/teacher-in-headscarf-case-cleared-of-racial-assault-on-muslim-girl-63962.html. 12 March 2004.

Chowdhury, S. (2005). *We have more urgent issues to fight for than dress codes.* http://www.independent.co.uk/voices/commentators/shamim-chowdhury-we-have-more-urgent-issues-to-fight-for-than-dress-codes-4576.html. 4 March 2005.

Cllr Khan, R. (2006). *The hijab does not restrict it-it liberates.* https://www.theguardian.com/lifeandstyle/2009/apr/07/letters-hijab-islam-women. 7 April 2009.

Dear, P. (2004). *Women vow to protect Muslim hijab.* http://news.bbc.co.uk/2/hi/uk_news/3805733.stm. 14 June 2004.

Dhumieres, M. (2013). *Why is the right of Muslim women to wear the veil still so controversial in France?* http://www.independent.co.uk/voices/comment/why-is-the-right-of-muslim-women-to-wear-the-veil-still-so-controversial-in-france-8575052.html. 16 April 2013.

Guest, K., & Davies, M. W. (2005). *The Muslims next door.* http://www.independent.co.uk/news/uk/this-britain/focus-the-muslims-next-door-527359.html. 6 March 2005.

Jones, E. C. (2005). *Muslim girls unveil their fears.* http://news.bbc.co.uk/2/hi/programmes/this_world/4352171.stm. 28 March 2005.

Khan, S. (2015). *It is not the hijab which holds women back, but prejudice.* http://www.telegraph.co.uk/culture/tvandradio/great-british-bake-off/11919553/Its-not-the-hijab-which-holds-women-back-but-intolerance-and-prejudice.html. 8 October 2015.

Kossaibati, J. (2009). *It is a wrap!* https://www.theguardian.com/lifeandstyle/2009/mar/30/fashion-hijab-muslim-women. 30 March 2009.

Malik, M. (2006). *This veil fixation is doing Muslim women no favors.* https://www.theguardian.com/commentisfree/2006/oct/19/religion.immigration. 19 October 2006.

Marin, M. (2004). *Cry freedom and accept the Muslim headscarf.* https://www.thetimes.co.uk/article/comment-minette-marrin-cry-freedom-and-accept-the-muslim-headscarf-tcxvm85lhqd. 1 February 2004.

Melville, K. (2009). *Muslim patriarchy served well by hijab.* https://www.theguardian.com/world/2009/apr/04/hijab-niqab-islam-muslims. 4 April 2009.

Sanghani, R. (2015a). *H&M advert features first Muslim Model in a hijab (finally).* http://www.telegraph.co.uk/women/womens-life/11898632/HandM-advert-features-first-Muslim-model-in-a-hijab-finally.html. 29 September 2015.

Sanghani, R. (2015b). *Armistice Day: Great British Bake off winner Nadiya Hussain wears 'poppy hijab'.* http://www.telegraph.co.uk/women/womens-life/11988184/Armistice-Day-2015-Great-British-Bake-Off-winner-Nadiya-Hussain-wears-poppy-hijab.html. 11 November 2015.

Smith, J. (2004). *What lies beneath the veil.* http://www.independent.co.uk/voices/commentators/joan-smith/what-lies-beneath-the-veil-8833948.html. 25 January 2004.

Smith, J. (2006a). *The veil is a feminist issue.* http://www.independent.co.uk/voices/commentators/joan-smith/joan-smith-the-veil-is-a-feminist-issue-419119.html. 8 October 2006.

Smith, J. (2006b). *Our schools are no place for jilbab. Or for Creationists.* http://www.independent.co.uk/voices/commentators/joan-smith/joan-smith-our-schools-are-no-place-for-the-jilbab-or-for-the-creationists-6105619.html. 26 March 2006.

Walter, N. (2004). *When the veil means freedom.* https://www.theguardian.com/world/2004/jan/20/france.schoolsworldwide1. 20 January 2004.

Wyatt, C. (2003). *Liberty, equality and the headscarf.* http://news.bbc.co.uk/2/hi/programmes/from_our_own_correspondent/3334881.stm. 20 December 2003.

Wyatt, C. (2004). *French headscarf ban opens rifts.* http://news.bbc.co.uk/2/hi/europe/3478895.stm.

Conceptual Metaphors in the Hijab Debate: Multi-Dimensional Analysis in the Spanish and British Press Discourse

Introduction

One of the aims of this book is to follow the Cognitive Critical Discourse Analysis CCDA methodology (see Chapter 3). In the previous chapter, I used Critical Discourse Analysis CDA to find out the cognitive structures that control the perception of the hijab and the hijab-wearing women in the Spanish and British press. In this chapter, we will go through Conceptual Metaphors Theories CMT in order to reach a deep and overall understanding of the entire cognitive scene. This chapter will analyze the conceptual metaphors used to talk about several components in the hijab debate, such as social diversity and the ban law.

This chapter does not go into an in-depth linguistic analysis because the study is not purely linguistics. The focus will be on the mappings between the source domain and the target domain of seven leading metaphors. I call the analysis in this chapter "multi-dimensional" because it goes on several dimensions; within culture dimension (dominant and minority discourse) and across cultures dimension (Spanish and British discourse). The analysis also finds out the relationship between these metaphorical structures and the mental frames discussed above. It is a vertical dimension that goes beneath the linguistic structures to reveal the cognitive structures that control the press discourse in-depth.

I classified the Spanish and the British press findings according to the source domains of the used metaphors. The analysis revealed seven shared domains in the debate of hijab in both European contexts, which are: (1) CONTAINER, (2) PERSONIFICATION, (3) SYMBOLISM, (4) TOOL, (5) ENTITY, (6) JOURNEY, and (7) WAR. These source domains stand for primary metaphorical structures that control the abstract components' framing in the Spanish and British national hijab debate. I call the metaphors in these seven sources *leading metaphors* because each contains several sub-metaphors that construct it. These sub-metaphors are called entailments.

In the following, I will go through each source domain, analyzing the Spanish and British (dominant and minority) mappings of this domain. I followed Lakoff and

© Springer Nature Singapore Pte Ltd. 2021
G. Khir-Allah, *Framing Hijab in the European Mind*,
https://doi.org/10.1007/978-981-16-1653-2_8

Johnson's study (1980) in the capitalization of the metaphor domains. It stands for the entire cognitive structure that lies underneath that concept. In this chapter, I use the term *minority discourse* to refer to the hijab-wearers' and the hijab supporters' discourse. And I use the term *dominant discourse* to refer to the hijab opposers' discourse that enforces the colonial stereotypical frames of hijab and hijab-wearing women.[1] I depend on the findings of the previous chapters in this classification.

CONTAINER

The CONTAINER source domain indicates a "spatial orientation" in terms of "in" or "out." It is a particular space that you have access into, a CONTAINER filled with homogenous but not necessarily identical elements. There is a possibility to have "ghettos" and "foreign" components in the CONTAINER. According to Lakoff and Johnson (1999), this classification is not arbitrary. It comes from the physical and cultural experience that shapes our cognitive system. In both European varieties, the source domain CONTAINER is used to understand the public sphere's abstract concept. PUBLIC SPHERE IS A CONTAINER metaphor is shared by the Spanish and British dominant and the Spanish and British Muslim minority discourses. The linguistic trigger of this metaphor is the proposition "in."

In the Spanish context, both social varieties (the dominant and the Muslim minority's discourse) use the following entailments (mappings) in the PUBLIC LIFE IS A CONTAINER metaphor: SOCIAL DIVERSITIES ARE COMPONENTS, CONNIVANCE, or COEXISTENCE *(CONVIVENCIA)* ARE BUILDING, GHETTOS ARE DANGEROUS NEIGHBORHOOD. All the hijab debate participants call for the steadiness and homogeneity of this CONTAINER and warn from the dangerous ghettos. For example, a Muslim contributor states: *"Todo lo que hemos construido a favor de la convivencia lo están destruyendo"*[2] (Everything we have built in favor of coexistence is being destroyed). Coexistence is understood as the outcome of the building construction in the CONTAINER. These buildings are being destroyed by the successive political and media stereotypical stigmatizations of the hijab practice. Homogenous and ghettos are understood as entities in the CONTAINER. They need to be preserved and equilibrated. For example, The HOMOGENOUS IS ENTITY entailment: *"'las autoridades públicas' tienen que ayudar a conseguir esa ponderación y equilibrio"*[3] ('public authorities' have to help achieve this steadiness and balance). The GHETTOS ARE DANGEROUS NEIGHBORHOOD entailment: *"Ocurre lo mismo en España? ¿Cómo evitar que se formen los temidos guetos?"*[4] (Is the same happening in Spain? How to prevent the dreaded ghettos from being formed?).

---

[1] In this classification, I depend on the findings of the previous two chapters.
[2] Del Barrio (2010a).
[3] Sotero (2010).
[4] Sahuquillo (2008).

Although some entailments of the PUBLIC SPHERE IS A CONTAINER metaphor are shared by the dominant and the minority discourse in both European contexts, the frame of reference of these entailments varies. In the following, we will go through these differences and variations.

Possession and Accessibility to OUR CONTAINER

In the Spanish context, the dominant (mainstream) discourse indicates the possession of the CONTAINER. The abstract concept of the *public sphere* is attributed to another abstract concept, *the culture*. Spanish culture is understood as POSSESSED ENTITY in the CONTAINER. SPANISH CULTURE IS A POSSESSED ENTITY entailment is used by Spanish journalists who produce the Spanish national press dominant discourse. This entailment's linguistic triggers are the repetitive use of "our culture" and "our values." As we see in the "Othering" frame of the hijab-wearing women, Spanish Muslims are excluded from that sense of possession. Accordingly, the dominant discourse maps the CONTAINER metaphor as follows: PUBLIC LIFE IS OUR CONTAINER. This sense of possession of the public sphere by the dominant discourse justifies their control over who has the right to be in and how "others" must be visible.

A similar exclusion appears in the British hijab debate. The *public sphere* is also attributed to the abstract concept *culture*: BRITISH VALUES ARE A POSSESSED ENTITY. British Muslim minority is denied possessing this ENTITY. British journalists who used the stereotypical frames on the hijab and the hijab-wearing women announce themselves as the CONTAINER owners. For example, "it (hijab) challenges our ideas,"[5] and "Our schools are no place for the jilbab."[6]

There is a difference between the dominant British understanding of the PUBLIC SPHERE IS A CONTAINER metaphor and the Spanish one. The British CONTAINER is diverse and multicultural, e.g., "Our multicultural British."[7] Therefore, "integration" is needed. But still, the hijab visibility is not accepted by the dominant discourse as part of this multicultural CONTAINER, e.g., "Why should we show respect to people who would love to restore frame invisibility in this country?"[8] and "In this country, unlike France, the debate about Islamic dress has been muted—largely, I think, out of politeness and a reluctance to criticize ethnic minorities."[9]

In comparison, Spanish dominant discourse does not join between *diversity* and *Spanish culture* terms. *Diversity* is perceived as "difference," and it is not lionized in the Spanish CONTAINER. In the Spanish dominant discourse, the access to the

---

[5] Marin (2004).
[6] Smith (2006b).
[7] Elkin (2013).
[8] Bennett (2004).
[9] Smith (2006b).

CONTAINER is conditioned to those who share the dominant discourse's stereotypical frames on the hijab and hijab-wearers. Although there are no direct metaphorical entailments, the results on the "Othering" frame of the hijab-wearing women in the previous chapter prove it.[10] "Othering" hijab-wearers and hijab-supporters indicate their exclusion from the CONTAINER possession.

Spanish hijab-wearers use the CONTAINER metaphor, too. They assert that *difference* is an undesirable ENTITY in the Spanish public sphere: DIFFERENCE IS A REJECTED ENTITY IN THE CONTAINER. The linguistic triggers of this entailment are "rejection" and "do not want to accept." For example, *"pero cuando tú eres la diferente comprendes, sientes, que sigue habiendo mucho rechazo"*[11] (But when you are the different one, you understand, you feel, that there is still a lot of rejection); *"Si me preguntan si estoy integrada digo que sí. Pero el problema no es mío o tuyo, es cómo me ven los otros, no quieren aceptar que somos iguales"*[12] (If they ask me if I am integrated, I say yes. But the problem is not mine or yours, it is how others see me, they do not want to accept that we are the same); and *"mi Islam no me hace daño, sino porque la sociedad no acepta al diferente"*[13] (My Islam does not harm me, but it is because the society does not accept the difference).

Convert women use the entailment DIFFERENCE IS A SCARY ENTITY IN THE CONTAINER. The linguistic trigger of this entailment is "fear." For example, *"Quiere protegerles (sus padres), porque reconoce que aún tiene miedo"*[14] (I want to protect them (the convert's parents). Because I recognize that they are still afraid) and *"No hay mala intención, sólo miedo"*[15] (There is no bad intentions, only fears).

It is to say, Hijab-wearing women, despite their limited contribution to the articles, indicate that the Spanish CONTAINER does not include diverse components as the British multicultural CONTAINER. The Spanish CONTAINER contains identical elements of "OUR" Spanish particular culture. It is a CONTAINER that reflects the mirror image in thoughts and the visibility among its members. Amanda Figueras extends that it is not only Muslims who are categorized as different; her Opus Dei and Jehovah's Witness friends hide their differences, too.[16]

Hijab-wearers' self-inclusion in the Spanish CONTAINER is detected in the articles published in 2016,[17] e.g., "our schools," "our system," and "our society."[18] In contrast to the dominant's CONTAINER, the Spanish hijab-wearers understand the Spanish public sphere as a diverse CONTAINER that includes all Spanish social

---

[10]We have discussed the domiant "Othering" of hijab-wearing muslims in general and of coverts, Ceutan Muslims in particular. We also discussed the "Othering" of hijab supporters.

[11]Figueras (2012).

[12]Juárez (2015).

[13]Figueras (2015).

[14]Ayuso (2016).

[15]Figueras (2015).

[16]Ibid.

[17]Spanish hijab-wearing women were included in the national debate in 2015/2016.

[18]Juárez (2015).

diversities. According to Jihan Dahou, a Muslim interviewee, diversity is a beautiful ENTITIES in the CONTAINER. She states: *"las dos culturas que habitan en mí (Tanger y Atl Emporda). Siento que soy una pieza de Zelij, los mosaicos árabes hechos a partir de azulejos, y me encanta."*[19] (The two cultures inhabit in me (Tanger y Atl Emporda). I feel like I am a piece of *"Zelij,"* the Arabic mosaic made by printed tile, and I love it). According to Dahou, DIVERSITY IS MOSAIC BUILDINGS decorates the CONTAINER with joy and originality as much as a Mosaic piece does. However, this metaphor is not repetitive. It is mentioned only once in an article published in 2016.

On the contrary, the British Muslim hijab-wearers repetitively express their possession to the multicultural CONTAINER and the British values, including the free-choice hijab's respect. They use the entailment BRITISH VALUES IS A POSSESSED ENTITY in the CONTAINER. For example, "our liberal values are surely flexible enough to take this in stride. You don't have to love it to acknowledge someone else's freedom to wear it".[20] Sajda Khan states that "we need to keep upholding our core value of respecting diversity, which means showing respect for and being tolerant of different faiths and cultures."[21]

Barriers to the CONTAINER

The access to the public sphere is limited to what the owners of the CONTAINER presume proper for the CONTAINER's members. In the dominant discourse, the CONTAINER owners limit the elements that can be visible in the CONTAINER and those that cannot. For example, in the Spanish CONTAINER, *difference* is seen as a barrier to be an equal member in the CONTAINER, DIFFERENCE IS A BARRIER. It is to say, the abstract concept of *difference* is understood as a tangible entity, a physical separation between hijab-wearing women (or even any minority as Figueras declares) and the Spanish public sphere and Spanish values. In comparison, *difference* is not a barrier to the British CONTAINER because it is multicultural. It is the hijab practice that is reduced to be a tangible barrier by the dominant discourse.

The BARRIER entailments of the CONTAINER metaphor vary across the dominant discourse and the minority discourse in each European context, as we will see below.

THE HIJAB IS A BARRIER

The dominant hijab debate in the Spanish press discourse does not mix between the hijab and other traditional veiling forms such as burqa or niqab. The debate of the

---

[19]Farreras (2016).

[20]Alam (2005).

[21]Khan (2015).

hijab is limited to the practice of the hair covering. That is why the BARRIER is limited to the hijab; HIJAB IS A BARRIER. The British hijab debate conflates the hijab practice with the other traditional veiling forms. That is why the barrier is not limited to the hijab practice. It includes all veiling practices such as burqa or niqab; THE VEIL IS A BARRIER. For example, "The sight in this country of women, and particularly of young girls, heavily swathed and covered up [...] their clothing is a barrier between them and the world and between them and us"[22] and "The veil in its various forms signals that women have conditional access to public space."[23] The linguistic expressions that indicate this entailment are various, e.g., "barrier" and "conditional access" in the already mentioned examples. Besides, the hijab is pictured as think entities that separate the women's body from the public sphere, e.g., "Islamic headgear" and "Islamic dress drag,"[24] "abbreviated drapery,"[25] "enveloping folds."[26]

In the Spanish dominant discourse, the linguistic expression "behind" is the trigger of THE HIJAB IS A BARRIER metaphor. The hijab is a BARRIER that hides women behind it, e.g., *"antes pensaba que vivir detrás del velo era un gran trauma"*[27] (before, I thought that living behind the veil is very traumatic) and *"tras el pañuelo se puede esconder mujeres capacitadas con muchos conocimientos"*[28] (behind the veil, there can be hidden qualified women with a lot of knowledge). Accordingly, the hijab is not a BARRIER between women and their education or training. It is a BARRIER between the women and the public sphere where they need to display their professionalism. In the exclusion cases, the hijab is the only barrier to enter the Spanish classroom, the Spanish court, or the Spanish workplace. The hijab is understood as a rigid cover: HIJAB IS A SOILD COVER, e.g., *"tapar, cubrir"* (cover) refers to the hijab practice and hijab-wearing women. For example, *"[...] después de que la dirección de la escuela solicitara a sus padres que no le cubrieran la cabeza con el hiyab."*[29] ([...] after the school adminstration asked her parents not to cover (their daughter´s) head with the hijab) and *"[...] en abril pasado por incumplir las normas del colegio que prohíbe acudir a las aulas con la cabeza tapada con cualquier gorro o paño"*[30] ([...] last April for breaking the school rules that prohibit going to classrooms with your head covered with any hat or cloth).

The hijab-wearing women use the BARRIER entailment in the hijab debate. The BARRIER is not between them and the public sphere; it is between their sexuality and the social interaction in the public sphere, e.g., "This attire also sends out a message that a woman is chaste and modest and that she does not want her sexuality to enter

---

[22]Marin (2004).

[23]Smith (2006a).

[24]Burchill (2011).

[25]Bennett (2004).

[26]Orr (2005).

[27]Quelart (2011).

[28]Del Barrio (2010a).

[29]Iglesias (2007).

[30]Obelleiro (2011).

into the interaction in the slightest degree."[31] Due to the limited contribution of the
hijab-wearing women in the Spanish press, I could not find such similar mappings in
the selected articles. As Scott indicates, the western standards of public interaction
take for granted the accessibility of women's sexuality; the hijab practice denies them
this accessibility. Although sexuality does not appear in the metaphors' structures in
the Spanish hijab debate, the mental frame analysis proves that to conceal women's
sexuality by the hijab practice is to conceal these women's visibility behind A SOLID
COVER.

STEREOTYPES ARE BARRIERS

The minority discourse, in both European contexts, uses the STEREOTYPES ARE
OBSTACLES entailment. In this entailment, stereotypes are seen as tangible obstacles ad barriers to be avoided, e.g., *"evitar prejuicios"*[32] (avoid stereotypes) and *"fue
depositando pequeños guijarros en el camino."*[33] ("they" were depositing small
pebbles on the road). For Spanish hijab-wearers, this BARRIER does not prevent
them the access to the CONTAINER; it makes access more difficult.

British hijab-wearers use the STEREOTYPES ARE BARRIER entailment as
well. They understand stereotypes as a solid entity to be crashed and destroy. For
example, "What also frustrated me about the piece was how it suggested that if you
are a hijab-wearer, you have many glass ceilings to shatter,"[34] "It's not the hijab which
holds women back, but prejudice,"[35] and "the perception of the hijab as a symbol of
backwardness holds back women far more than the scarf itself ever could."[36] In the
British hijab debate, Islamophobia is also part of the BARRIER entailment; ISLAM-
OPHOBIA IS A BARRIER, e.g., "In western countries, the main thing blocking
Muslim women from participating in society is not Islam but Islamophobia."[37]

THE BAN LAW IS A BARRIER

This entailment appears in the exclusion cases discourse in the Spanish context. It
is not used in the British discourse because such ban law does not exist. The hijab
ban law at Spanish public schools and workplaces is understood as a BARRIER that
prevents young girls and women from entering the public sphere, the CONTAINER.
THE BAN LAW IS A BARRIER entailment is repetitive in the school exclusion
articles. The linguistic triggers of this entailment are *"apartar"* (apart), *"separar"*

[31] Mursaleen (2010).
[32] Barik Edidi (2009).
[33] Ayuso (2016).
[34] Perves (2013).
[35] Khan (2015).
[36] Ibid.
[37] Ibid.

(separate), "aislar" (isolate), *"impide a la joven asistir la clase"* (impede the adoles-
cence to attend the class). Since the hijab-wearing students and women have limited
access to the press discourse, there is no elaboration nor significant mappings of this
entailment. BAN LAW IS A BARRIER metaphorical entailment is not found in the
British hijab debate because the hijab is not banned at the national level.

Personification

Personification allows us to make sense of symbols, or abstract concepts, in human
terms. We can understand them on the basis of the speaker's motivations, goals, and
actions (Lakoff and Johnson 1980). The concept, or symbol, can be given human
aspects or attributes to deal with or look at it as a PERSON. Both the Spanish and the
British dominant and minority discourse used the PERSONIFICATION metaphor to
understand the hijab sign in the public sphere, the CONTAINER. Yet the entailments
of the PERSONIFICATION metaphor are not necessarily shared, as we will see
below.

THE HIJAB IS AN UNDESIRABLE PERSON

Both the Spanish and the British dominant discourses use the HIJAB IS AN UNDE-
SIRABLE PERSON entailment. In the Spanish dominant discourse, the hijab is
understood as a person that (asks to step into classrooms) *"pide paso en las aulas."*[38]
It is to say, hijab-wearing women's personality, humanity, is dissolved and reduced
to the hijab-PERSON who wants to enter the CONTAINER.

This PERSON is not welcomed in the Spanish classroom: "no hay sitio en el
aula para Najwa y su hiyab"[39] (there is no room in the classroom for Najwa and her
hijab." The hijab PERSON is not welcomed in the British dominant discourse, too,
e.g., "if I loathe the niqab and the burqa when I see women wearing them in Iraq and
Afghanistan, it would be hypocritical to pretend I don't find them equally offensive
on my local high street"[40]; and "Many women in the west find the headscarf deeply
problematic […] we find it so hateful".[41] Again, we see that the mix between the
Islamic dresses in the British hijab debate permits us to replace the target THE HIJAB
with the broader term THE VEIL.

THE VEIL IS UNDESIRABLE PERSON metaphor reflects the impact of the
hijab visibility in the CONTAINER. The Spanish dominant discourse uses this email
in the exclusion cases but not in the social and political debate. For example, Ana

---

[38]Galarraga (2010).

[39]Álvarez and Cembrero (2010).

[40]Smith (2006a).

[41]Walter (2004).

Saidi, the employee in Acciona, narrates that she becomes an undesirable employee after deciding to practice the hijab. The British discourse points out the UNDE-SIRABLE PERSON entailment more frequently than the Spanish discourse. The frequency varies because, in the British context, hijab-wearing women use this metaphor, whereas, in the Spanish context, hijab-wearers do not enjoy equal access to the national press. They express the mainstream reaction on their hijab visibility, e.g., "When I spoke to her on the phone, she offered me a trial day. But when I turned up, she looked at me in shock. She asked if I wore the headscarf all the time. She kept repeating, 'I wish you told me over the phone'"[42] and "I was recently told by an elderly white jeweler that he would never employ a Muslim girl wearing a hijab as his customers would stop buying from him [...] There is always that nagging fear at the back of our minds: will they refuse us the job once they see the hijab?".[43] A similar experience of the UNDESIRABLE PERSON entailment is told by Mariah Idrissi Model; the journalist narrates that "She did not think they would hire a woman in a hijab."[44] The common linguistic trigger of this entailment is the negation of hijab visibility in the workplace.

THE HIJAB IS AN ADOPTED CHILD

THE HIJAB IS AN ADOPTED CHILD entailment can be illustrated through the following mappings: hijab decision is as important/serious as an adoption decision, it is an individual and women's decision, it is a decision that involves a commitment to that new factor in the woman's life, and it involves a responsibility to take care of it; when the hijab is "adopted," it is as precious and as loved as the adopted child. Muslim women are proud of their veils as mothers are proud of their adopted children. Both Spanish and British contexts use the same mappings of this shared entailment.

In the Spanish context, THE HIJAB IS AN ADOPTED CHILD entailment is used by the dominant discourse in order to highlight the un-readiness of the young students to go through the hijab experience. For example, Achmawi states, *"Es una decisión seria que una debe adoptar cuando es madura"*[45] (It is a serious decision that one must make when mature). In the context of that article, which points out the adolescent's revolutionary attitude when deciding to hijab (the "Indiscipline" frame), Achmawi enforces the immaturity of the adoptive mother.

In the British context, this metaphor is mainly used and mapped by the hijab-wearers. They refer to the hijab practice as "adoption,".e.g., Akbar (2010a, 2010b), Malik (2006) and Byrne (2015). They are aware of the fact that it might impose some difficulty in professional life due to the hijab rejection in the public sphere, UNDESIRABLE PERSON. But, for them, it is similar to the difficulties that appear

---

[42] Bentham and Davis (2007).

[43] Perves (2013).

[44] Mortimer (2015).

[45] Galarraga (2010).

at having a child, e.g., "It must be a choice that is made by the woman […] The reality is that you have a lot of well educated, young women choosing to adopt hijab"[46] and "Although personally, I had decided that I wanted to adopt the hijab, I was worried that professionally it would become a stumbling block on my career path."[47]

The HIJAB IS AN ADOPTED CHILD entailment includes the love relationship between the mother and the child, e.g., "In essence, my hijab and I are in a long-term relationship, which is about love rather than convenience."[48] This relationship also includes the mothers' pride, e.g., "as Muslims, we are proud of the hijab."[49] In the Spanish context, the ADOPTED CHILD entailment is not used. The analysis could not figure out if Spanish hijab-wearers do not use this metaphor because they do not share this metaphorical understanding of the hijab as the British hijab-wearers. Or because they might have the ADOPTED CHILD metaphorical understanding, but their limited contribution does not reflect it. There is one reference to the hijab compromise by Ramia Chaoui. She tells her work interview experience, she says: "*Les dije: 'me encanta este trabajo, no se van arrepentir si me cogen, pero tengo un compromiso con el velo'*"[50] (I told them: I love this job, you won't regret it if you hire me, but I have a commitment to the veil). However, this only reference is not an indication of the existence of the ADOPTED CHILD entailment in the discourse of the Spanish hijab-wearers.

THE HIJAB IS AN IDENTITY SWIPER

This metaphor appears only in the Spanish dominant discourse. It is used by school authorities who supported the ban law in exclusion cases. THE HIJAB IS AN IDENTITY SWIPER metaphor indicates that the hijab takes away the identity of those who adopt it. The internal law of Spanish public school use this metaphor, e.g., "*El reglamento del centro incluye un artículo que impide "la utilización en el interior de los espacios de gorras pañuelos u otras indumentarias que dificulten la identificación de los alumnos*"[51] (The regulations of the center include an article that prevents the use of caps, scarves, or other clothes that make it difficult to identify the students in the interior buildings.) This internal law is repeated through almost the exact linguistic expressions in Álvarez (2011a), Figueras (2011a, c) and Álvarez (2011b). The linguistic trigger is almost the same, "make it difficult to identify." However, THE HIJAB IS AN IDENTITY SWIPER entailment coincides with THE HIJAB IS AN UNDESIRABLE PERSON entailment. The hijab person swipes away women's identity and converts them to covered entities.

---

[46] Akbar (2010b).
[47] Aslam (2014).
[48] Ibid.
[49] Dear (2004).
[50] Farreras (2016).
[51] Álvarez (2011a).

SYMBOLISM

I argued before that the hijab is not a meaningless abstract symbol. First and foremost, it is a religious requirement, a religious sign with definite criteria on gender relations and women's sexuality in the public sphere. Accordingly, I will use THE HIJAB IS A SIGN metaphor as a leading metaphor for this part of the analysis.

The HIJAB IS A SIGN is a shared metaphor by the two European contexts in both dominant and minority discourse. Yet, each European context or social variety attributes different meanings to that SIGN. The colonial and stereotypical framings convert the hijab to a SYMBOL because they attribute to the hijab SIGN meanings that are not related to its original significance.

SIGN OF IDENTITY-SYMBOL OF IDENTITY

The HIJAB IS A SIGN OF RELIGIOUS IDENTITY metaphor is used by British hijab-wearers. Some of the linguistic triggers are direct and clear, e.g., "it is a symbol of their faith"[52] and "a sign of religious identity."[53] Some hijab-wearers uses indirect linguistic triggers, e.g., "I liked the idea of being a Muslim woman and being recognized as one,"[54] "Muslim women who adopt the veil in Europe may simultaneously be seeking to affirm their religious identity,"[55] and "I want to be identified as a hijab-wearing Muslim woman. I love wearing the hijab because I like the idea that anyone who sees me will identify me as a Muslim."[56] The linguistic expressions "recognized as," "affirm," and "be identified as" are indirect triggers of the SIGN OF RELIGIOUS IDENTITY.

The British dominant discourse uses THE VEIL IS A SIGN OF RELIGIOUS IDENTITY metaphor in the French ban-law debate. In the justification of the ban law, the British dominant discourse refers that the hijab is UNDESIRABLE RELIGIOUS IDENTITY in the French public sphere. The same metaphor is used in the Spanish dominant discourse. But it does not refer to the French public sphere but the Spanish one. The linguistic triggers are those which announce its banning, e.g., the need to "specific regulation" on the hijab at school,[57] the need to "normalize the use of the veil,"[58] *"no se admite"* (it is not allowed), *"quitarlo o cambiar el centro"* (to take it off or to change the center), *"prohibir el velo"* (prohibit the veil), etc. The HIJAB IS A RELIGIOUS SIGN metaphor is used by the lawyer Ivan Jimenez Aybar who defended the students in the hijab exclusion cases, e.g., *"el 'hiyab' no es sólo un*

---

[52] Khan (2015).
[53] Aly (2015).
[54] Akbar (2010d).
[55] Malik (2006).
[56] Perves (2013).
[57] Belaza (2010).
[58] Montero (2010).

pañuelo sino que se trata de un símbolo religioso" (The hijab is not a simple veil. It is a religious symbol).[59]

THE HIJAB IS A SIGN OF RELIGIOUS IDENTITY metaphor de-attach the practice from foreign cultural identities. On the contrary, the Spanish dominant discourse uses the HIJAB IS A SYMBOL OF CULTURAL IDENTITY metaphor. I use the source "SYMBOL" instead of "SIGN" because it is not part of the original meaning of the hijab.[60] The linguistic triggers are direct and repetitive, e.g., *"sim-bolo de la identidad"* "sign of identity," *"el velo es un símbolo de identidad. Lo es para las féminas que viven en Países occidentales, que lo utilizan como una manera de permanecer fieles a sus orígenes, lejos de su tierra"*[61] (the veil is a symbol of identity. It is for women who live in Western countries, who use it as a way to remain faithful to their origins, far from their land) and *"el velo ha cobrado fuerza en los últimos años como símbolo de identidad. Si Occidente no las quiere, ellas le vuelven la espalda y se aferran a las tradiciones"*[62] (the veil has gained strength in recent years as a symbol of identity. If the West does not want them (Muslim women), they turn their backs and cling to traditions).

Although the dominant Spanish discourse uses the HIJAB IS A SYMBOL OF CULTURAL IDENTITY, it also uses the HIJAB IS A SIGN OF RELIGIOUS IDEN-TITY. The latter is used to link the hijab to extremism; HIJAB IS A SYMBOL OF EXTREMISM. The British dominant discourse also uses this metaphor to justify the hijab rejection in the British multicultural public sphere, the CONTAINER, e.g., "Has this woman gone mad? [...] in donning the hijab, she is kow-to-wing to the very fundamentalism"[63] and "One friend joked that I was officially a fundamentalist."[64]

SYMBOL OF OPPRESSION/IGNORANCE/DISCRIMINATION/DISORIENTATION

THE HIJAB IS A SYMBOL OF IGNORANCE, THE HIJAB IS A SYMBOL OF OPPRESSION, THE HIJAB IS A SYMBOL OF DISCRIMINATION, and THE HIJAB IS A SYMBOL OF DISORIENTATION are shared metaphors in the Spanish and British dominant discourse. The linguistic triggers are direct on the hijab or its practitioners. These metaphors correlate with the mental frames which activate

[59]Figueras (2011b).

[60]I doubt if I can call HIJAB IS A SIGN OF RELIGIOUS IDENTITY a metaphor. Because it is part of the hijab meaning and I do not see it as a metaphorical structure. However, I mantian this structure as metaphorical in this section to provide you with an overall view of the findings. But still, I hope to discuss this point in detail with someone experts in metaphors and signs.

[61]Meneses (2010).

[62]Carbajos (2008).

[63]Burchill (2011).

[64]Takolia (2010).

them, e.g., in the Spanish dominant discourse: *"sumision"* (submission), *"la pres-sion de los novios"*[65] (the pressure of the boyfriends), *"impondría"* (impose), and *"no sabe qué opinar"*[66] (she does not know what to opine), *"disorientada"* (disoriented), *"no conocen otra cosa"* (they do not know another way). In the British dominant discourse: "I can't think of a more dramatic visual symbol of oppression,"[67] "Voge-lenzang's 54-year-old wife said Tazi's Islamic dress represented oppression and was a form of bondage,"[68] "The practice of covering women is a human rights issue in two senses, not just as a symbol of inequality,"[69] "A symbol of oppression and inequality between the sexes."[70]

The British hijab-wearing women argue against these metaphors imposed on the practice and them, e.g., "When we talk about headscarves, the first thing that comes into a lot of people's heads is 'oppressed woman,'[71] "In short, the perception of the hijab as a symbol of Islam's backwardness,"[72] "while others disdain it as a symbol of oppression.".[73] In the Spanish context, hijab-wearers use the simple negation of these metaphors, as we have seen in the previous chapters.

SIGN OF LIBERATION

THE VEIL IS A SIGN OF LIBERATION metaphor is only used by the British hijab-wearers. The linguistic expressions used to indicate this metaphor is direct "sign of liberation," e.g., "It's hard for some people to accept that it's a sign of liberation. You don't always have to conform to a certain stereotype or fashion statement"[74] and "with some viewing it as a feminist symbol of liberation."[75] According to these women, the hijab practice liberates them from being sexually objectified in the public sphere.

---

[65] Montero (2010).
[66] Carranco (2010).
[67] Smith (2006a).
[68] Carter (2009).
[69] Smith (2006a).
[70] Dhumieres (2013).
[71] Akbar (2010d).
[72] Khan (2015).
[73] Aly (2015).
[74] Akbar (2010d).
[75] Aly (2015).

TOOL

TOOLS metaphors express mental mappings between an instrument and a purpose achieved by it. THE HIJAB IS A TOOL is a shared metaphor in the European contexts and across them. It indicates that the hijab is not limited to religious practice; it is a tool used to achieve particular purposes in the public sphere, the CONTAINER. In both European contexts, the triggers of this embodied understanding of the hijab are the repetitive linguistic trigger: "use" in English and Spanish ("*usar*" y "*utilizar*").

Mappings of THE HIJAB IS A TOOL metaphor differs across the European contexts. For example, the Spanish dominant press discourse refers to the practice as a "used veil" without further determining the utility of this usage. It is left to the reader's mind to interpret the practice's utility according to his/her social or political orientation. It is also based on the rooted mental frames he/she maintains on the hijab visibility in the public sphere (cultural identity assertion, radicalism, extremism, submission to the male partner, breaking the law of the school, etc.) On the contrary, the British TOOL metaphor is followed by the utility of the practice in the public sphere, CONTAINER. For example, the British dominant discourse indicates that "the use of Islamic dress has helped women to carve out legitimate public space for themselves […] a possible entrance into modernity"[76] and "The use of the veil is a modern response, with which women are taking up a position against staying indoors. Young women who don a headscarf and come out of their closed societies to develop themselves".[77] Both usages of the Islamic dress in the British contexts carry stereotypical framing of women's role in their Muslim community and enforce the "Oppression" mental frames of the hijab and the hijab-wearing women.

Another difference in THE HIJAB IS A TOOL across the Spanish and British contexts is that, in the British press discourse, hijab-wearers used this metaphor to highlight its utility; expressing the religious identity, e.g., "We used a hijab because it's become what we automatically associate with Muslims"[78] and "The hijab has long been an object that many people use to identify with Muslims."[79] Hijab-wearers also indicate that the hijab is turned to be a TOOL by media to impose stereotypes on Muslim women: "it is insulting to think that the Daily Mail is using the hijab as a litmus test to state that by not wearing it in the professional arena it somehow excuses your choice of religion."[80]

The HIJAB IS A TOOL metaphor is a shared metaphor between and among social varieties, as I mentioned before. But the usage of this TOOL differs as we will see ahead.

---

[76] Walter (2004).

[77] Abbasi (2004).

[78] Sanghani (2015).

[79] Perves (2013).

[80] Ibid.

THE HIJAB IS A PROTECTIVE TOOL

Both social diversities use this entailment of TOOL metaphor in Spanish and British contexts. The linguistic triggers are: "protect," "instrument," and "tool." Yet, the "protected from" is mapped differently. In the Spanish context, only the German convert, Oballe, uses this metaphor. She says, *"me siento mas protegida y más respetuosa con Dios"*[81] (I feel more protected and more respected by God). According to her words, the hijab is a TOOL that provides her with God's protection and respect. She does not specify "the protected from" nor how. In the British minority discourse, this metaphor is more elaborated. British hijab-wearers specify the "protected from." It is essential to highlight that this is not a contribution of a Spanish hijab-wearer.

The HIJAB IS A PROTECTIVE TOOL entailment is used more frequently by the British hijab-wearers. They indicate the "protected from": the social judgment on the physical appearance and the sexual exploitation of women's bodies, e.g., "Now I feel completely protected in my headscarf. People treat you with a new level of respect; they judge you by your words and your deeds, not how you look."[82] Such kind of protection transforms the hijab into a contributor to gender equality; THE VEIL IS A TOOL OF GENDER EQUALITY, e.g., "To address the question of sexual equality: from my point of view as a Muslim woman, it is the veil which affords that equality."[83] The hijab criteria that are understood to afford the equality of sexual visibility in the public sphere; the CONTAINER.

The Spanish and British dominant discourse reduced the "protected from" to "male' lust." The Spanish dominant discourse puts it straight forward, e.g., *"la protege de individuos frívolos e inmorales [...]instrumento de liberación o protección ante el frenesí masculine"*[84] (it protects her from frivolous and immoral individuals [...] it is an instrument of liberation or protection from male's frenzy). The "protected from" in the British dominant discourse is "lust and violence" in Muslim ghettos, e.g., (forced veil) "girls are being pressurized to wear it, as much to protect themselves from the casual violence of the ghetto"[85]; and (free-choice veil) "The claim that veils protect women from lasciviousness and disrespect carries an element of self-deception."[86]

The "protected from" in both Spanish and British social varieties is the same wickedness: the sexual exploitation of women's bodies in the public sphere. Although several western feminist campaigns fight against such objectifying of women's bodies, the dominant discourse, by women who consider themselves defenders of women's rights, stigmatizes the "protected from" as a restricted feature to the Muslim community. It is introduced as an archaic practice by Muslim men in Muslim ghettos,

---

[81]Carbajos (2008).

[82]Marrison (2011).

[83]Mursaleen (2010).

[84]Carbajos (2008).

[85]Wyatt (2003).

[86]Alibhai-Brown (2015).

putting away the European social reality from this gender-discriminatory practice against women in the European public sphere.

THE HIJAB IS A HARMING TOOL

The Spanish dominant discourse uses the HIJAB IS A HARMING TOOL entailment as follows: *"(hijab) es una moda que arrasa"*[87] (it is a fashion that sweeps) and *"si se pone el pañuelo le perjudicará en su trabajo"*[88] (if she wears the veil, it will harm her job). This metaphor appears only in the Spanish dominant discourse and indicates that the hijab does harm its practitioners.

TTHE VEIL IS AN OPPRESSIVE/PROBLEMATIC TOOL

The British dominant discourse uses this metaphor in the hijab debate. The hijab is "a tool of oppression,"[89] and "(it) something that is used to oppress women." THE VEIL IS AN OPPRESSIVE TOOL entailment is also found in the BBC articles that justified the ban law in the French context.

The dominant Spanish discourse uses the HIJAB IS A PROBLEMATIC TOOL entailment, e.g., *"genera alarma e intranquilidad"*[90] (it generates alarm and unease) and THE HIJAB IS A PROVOCATIVE TOOL, e.g., Every time it is used, a conflict outbreaks *"estalla un conflicto"*[91] (a conflict breaks out).

THE VEIL IS AN EMPOWERING/LIBERATING TOOL

British hijab-wearers exclusively use these two entailments. It is somehow related to the PROTECTIVE TOOL entailment I explained before. THE HIJAB IS A PROTEC-TIVE TOOL indicates that the hijab practice is an instrument that affords equality and protects women from being reduced to a sex object in the public sphere, the CONTAINER. Through this protection, they feel empowered and liberated in social interaction.

The linguistic triggers of THE VEIL IS AN EMPOWERMENT TOOL, and THE VEIL IS A LIBERATING TOOL are direct and repetitive in the British minority discourse. Mostly followed by an explanation on that metaphor, e.g., "Many consider

---

[87]Carbajos (2008).

[88]Sahuquillo (2008).

[89]Alibhai-Brown (2015).

[90]Gallego-Díaz (2010).

[91]Obelleiro (2011).

it a symbol of their faith and find it empowering and liberating,"[92] "I wear it because I know it forces people to listen to my words and to look beyond my aesthetics. I know this from experience"[93] and "The head veil with or without the face veil (which incidentally is not a religious requirement) is, in fact, a liberating and an empowering force rather than an oppressive one."[94] Another hijab-wearer, Nadiya Takolia, explain the embodied experience of this metaphor in detail as follows:

> "But in a society where a woman's value seems focused on her sexual charms, some wear it explicitly as a feminist statement asserting an alternative mode of women empowerment. Politics, not religion, is the motivator here. I am one of these women. It is me telling the world that my femininity is not available for public consumption. I am taking control of it, and I don't want to be part of a system that reduces and demeans women".[95]

According to these hijab-wearers, the hijab is AN EMPOWERING TOOL and a LIBERATING TOOL that provides them with the strength to say "no" the unconditional access to their sexuality. It provides them with total command over their sexuality in the public sphere, the CONTAINER, where unconditional access to women's sexuality is guaranteed. They are liberated from the social patterns that impose the perfect image of women's visibility in the public sphere, e.g., "I don't feel trapped or restricted by the hijab; I feel liberated from worry about hair, clothing, and makeup"[96] and "The hijab has liberated me from society's expectations of women."[97] The HIJAB IS A PROTECTIVE TOOL entailment is not related to the WAR metaphor we will go through below.

ENTITY

ENTITY metaphor means to understand signs or experiences as objects and substances. This cognitive process allows us to pick out parts of the abstract concepts and treat them as discrete entities or substances of a uniform kind. Once we identify these abstract concepts, we can refer to them, categorize them, and, more importantly, reason about them (Lakoff and Johnson 1980).

THE HIJAB IS AN ENTITY metaphor amplifies the hijab's meaning to more than a piece of cloth. For example, in the British dominant discourse, the journalist announces, "Hijab hit the news following the decision of the French government to introduce a law to stop Muslim schoolgirls wearing headscarves (or veils) in school."[98] the linguistic trigger "hit" picture the hijab as an ENTITY that strike and leaves marks (debates, conflicts, etc.).

---

[92] Khan (2015).

[93] Perves (2013).

[94] Mursaleen (2010).

[95] Takolia (2010).

[96] Cllr Khan (2006).

[97] Takolia (2010).

[98] Marin (2004).

THE HIJAB IS ENTITY and IDENTITY IS ENTITY

THE VEIL IS AN ENTITY metaphor is used together with IDENTITY IS AN ENTITY in the Spanish and British minority discourse. In the Spanish contexts, it was the lawyer Jimenez Aybar who argues that the hijab is an inseparable part of the "official" identity, e.g., *"el velo algo que forma parte de la identidad de la persona, la autoridad de un centro docente no puede prohibirlo"*[99] (The veil forms part of the person's identity. The education center authority cannot ban it). The lawyer repeated this argument in almost all of his contributions to the exclusion cases. Spanish hijab-wearers do not elaborate on this metaphor as the British hijab-wearers do. They consider both hijab and identity interrelated ENTITIES. The linguistic trigger is "part of," e.g., "There first time I did so (don hijab) was when I went to university at Oxford, in 1992, where people didn't know me, and the scarf was just part of who I was,"[100] "It's part of who I am. It's not just some bit of fabric on my head. It's everything,"[101] and "Here was a country which wants to ban a form of dress that for many Muslim women forms an integral part of their identity."[102] In the minority British discourse, the hijab is not part of the "official" identity; it is part of their being.

THE HIJAB IS AN ENTITY/BODY PART

The BODY PART entailment of the ENTITY metaphor is used by young Spanish students who refused to quit the hijab practice. THE HIJAB IS A BODY PART metaphor indicates the inseparability of the hijab and their bodily appearance, e.g., *"Renunciar al velo sería como quitarme la piel"*[103] (giving up the veil is like taking off my skin) and *"si me obligan a quitarlo es como arrancarme la piel"*[104] (if they force me to remove it, it's like ripping my skin off).

Mapping the hijab as a BODY PART/SKIN explains how these women understand their practice, e.g., self-confidence with healthy skin, sense of belonging with colored skin, the skin protects the body as much as the hijab provides the girls a sense of protection, the skin is a sense organ like the hijab is an identity organ, etc.

---

[99] Figueras (2011c).

[100] Akbar (2010c).

[101] Jones (2005).

[102] Akbar (2010b).

[103] Álvarez (2011c).

[104] Bohorquez (2016).

JOURNEY

VEILING IS A JOURNEY metaphor is used exclusively by the British hijab-wearers' discourse. Hijab-wearers use this metaphor when they narrate their hijab decision experience. The linguistic triggers of this metaphor are the following: "journey," "go down the path," "meeting the rules," and "guidelines." For example, "My journey has been a long, long journey, it was a very difficult decision to wear these clothes,"[105] "My journey towards hijab began when I finally moved past all my agnostic swinging of, "Yes I believe," "No I don't" and then back again,"[106] and "For others still hijab is a complicated journey, one with twists and turns where veils are briefly discarded on the ground or taken up with willing fervor."[107]

The JOURNEY path starts with searching for religious principles, e.g., "they go down the path, trying to find out more about their religion."[108] The JOURNEY is not compulsory or haphazard. It has a guideline and an objective to be accomplished, e.g., "there are simple guidelines, but ultimately it is up to individual women to decide what they feel comfortable wearing,"[109] "I realize there is criteria I have to meet. Your ears, neck, and bosom have to be covered"[110] and "sometimes you can meet the rules, but they don't conform to the spirit."[111]

WAR

WAR metaphor is used by Spanish and British dominant and minority discourse to talk about cultural integration; CULTURAL INTEGRATION IS A WAR. The repetition of this metaphor is relatively high in both European press discourse. In this WAR, several components of the CONTAINER are involved, e.g., diverse cultures, (European) hijab-wearing women, the hijab, the ban law, European non-Muslim women, Islamophobia, and stereotypes. Linguistic triggers of this metaphor in the Spanish press are many, e.g., *"atacar"* (attack), *"cession"* (surrender), *"conflicto"* (conflict), *"defender"* (defend), *"vícitmas"* (victims), *"batalla"* (battle), etc. In the British press, similar triggers are used, e.g., "attack," "battle," "affronting," "defend," "victims," "revolution," "fight," "victory," (Islamic extremists) "take over the debate,"[112] and president Chirac "refuses to back down in the face of demonstrations,"[113]

---

[105]Carter (2009).

[106]Aslam (2014).

[107]Akbar (2010a).

[108]Akbar (2010b).

[109]Cllr Khan (2006).

[110]Akbar (2010d).

[111]Akbar (2010c).

[112]Marin (2004).

[113]Smith (2004).

The CULTURAL INTEGRATION IS WAR metaphor has complex mappings because each social group understands the components role in the WAR differently. However, mappings are more complex in British discourse because of the participants' diversity in the national hijab debate.

The ENEMY

The enemy in the CULTURAL INTEGRATION IS WAR metaphor is not fixed. It varies across the dominant and minority discourse in both contexts.

ISLAM IS THE ENEMY

The British dominant discourse defines the ENEMY of the French Republic in order to justify the 2004 ban law for the British reader. Along with this justification, Islamization is defined as the Republic's enemy, e.g., "the problem is not Islam as such, but the obsessive feeling of being besieged, the dread Islamization."[114] In the same article, Marie Dhumieres describes the street prayers as "occupation." The Spanish dominant discourse announces the hijab as AN EXTREMIST MILITARY SIGN. The hijab is linked to extremism, violence, and militant ideologies, e.g., *"ultranza de hiyab"* "outrage of hijab,"[115] "a sign of violence,"[116] *"extrema derecha"* "right extremism," and "a uniform of a concrete militant ideology."[117]

In the British context, both Islam and Christian religions are set to be the ENEMY. RELIGIONS AT SCHOOL ARE THE ENEMY. Joan Smith in the Independent uses the same Spanish AN EXTREMIST MILITARY SIGN entailment; she states "a struggle between militant forms of different religions over the final say on sexual relationships, crime and punishment, education and foreign policy,"[118] "it has been left to the House of Lords to act, halting a dangerous process under which fundamentalists seek to extend their influence on state education Under a government that is recklessly expanding the number of faith schools, religious extremists have spotted an opportunity."[119] She points out that the theory of Samuel Huntington's "clash of civilizations" has been projected into the British CONTAINER; "This is a beginning version of Samuel Huntington's 'clash of civilizations' theory which divides the world into two camps, Western and Islamic, and assumes that their values are different, if not mutually hostile."[120]

---

[114]Dhumieres (2013).

[115]Montero (2010).

[116]Farreras (2016).

[117]Gallego-Díaz (2010).

[118]Smith (2004).

[119]Smith (2006b).

[120]Smith (2004).

HIJAB-WEARERS ARE THE ENEMY

As the dominant discourse understands the hijab through THE HIJAB IS AN EXTREMIST MILITARY SIGN metaphor; hijab-wearers are mapped as recruits of that ENEMY; Isalm. For example, British hijab-wearing women use this metaphor when they narrate how they are treated in the public sphere. The linguistic triggers as "mistrusted," e.g., "(we are) viewed with mistrust and suspicion, and many feel that they have to make more of an effort being nice than those who don't wear a hijab."[121] Merryl Wyn Davies and Katy Guest criticized Hazel Blears' declarations that "people of "Islamic appearance" must accept being stopped and searched "disproportionately—in the interest of public safety," they continue "Coming soon after Tony Blair talked of "several hundred" people in the United Kingdom intent on terrorism, Ms. Blears' comments have again raised the spectra of all Muslims being regarded as potential terrorists."[122] Such political discourse categorizes Muslims, especially hijab-wearers, as THE ENEMY.

British hijab-wearers criticize being treated as THE ENEMY, e.g., "Most Muslim women who don the hijab aren't doing so in a quest to combat western hegemonies, or because they are contemptuous of progressive values. Many consider it a symbol of their faith."[123] Such negation repeals the ENEMY mappings of the hijab-wearers and creates an alternative mapping to the hijab practice; THE HIJAB IS A RELIGIOUS SIGN.

Spanish hijab-wearers consider themselves WORRIERS in the CULTURE INTEGRATION IS WAR. They are not Islamist militants' worriers but Spanish citizens who fight for their rights in the public sphere, the CONTAINER. Their fight *"lucha"* is to combine their religious rights and their rights to education and work. Their enemy is not the mainstream culture as the dominant discourse claims.

THE BAN LAW IS THE ENEMY

This entailment is found in the British and Spanish minority discourse. Spanish and British hijab-wearers consider the ban law as the ENEMY in the cultural integration WAR. In the Spanish context, Muslim women set themselves as WORRIERS who fight against this discriminatory law; HIJAB WEARERS ARE WORRIERS and THE BAN LAW IS THE ENEMY. For example, *"cree que la lucha ha merecido la pena 'sobre todo para las niñas que vengan detrás de mi'"* (She believes that the fight has been worth it "especially for the girls who come after me.")[124]

In the British context, hijab-wearers did not use the linguistic expression "fight," maybe because they do not go through work or school hijab exclusion. Yet, the French ban law generates anxiety and inquietude in the British Muslim community;

---

[121]Perves (2013).

[122]Guest and Davies (2005).

[123]Khan (2015).

[124]Figueras (2011c).

THE FRENCH BAN LAW IS THE ENEMY, e.g., "That move was a very scary development because although it is a different country, it is just across the water from us."[125] The linguistic expression "fight" is mentioned in the British dominant discourse to describe the French hijab-wearing student struggle with the ban law; FRENCH HIJAB WEARERS ARE WORRIERS, e.g., "to discuss their strategy to fight a strict interpretation of the law at their school;" they are looking for a "compromise."[126]

THE HIJAB IS THE ENEMY

This entailment is only used in the British dominant discourse that justifies the French 2004 ban law. The ENEMY is not Islam nor Muslim women; it is the discriminatory meaning of the practice in the French Republic, e.g., "what is targeted is not a specific religion, but the 'expression of a sexist practice of religion'"[127] and "everyone here knows that the ruling isn't really about the wearing of a small cross on a chain or even the Jewish skullcap. It is about the headscarf".[128] As the hijab stands against the French national values; it is "targeted" as an ENEMY.[129]

STEREOTYPES ARE THE ENEMY

This entailment is found in the minority Spanish discourse. Stereotypes motivate social discrimination and marginalization. Spanish hijab-wearers are WORRIERS fight against the stereotypes, e.g., *"Ella tiene sus pequeñas luchas cotidianas contra los estereotipos"*[130] (She has her little everyday fights with stereotypes).

ETHNOCENTRIC FEMINISM ARE THE ENEMY

It refers to the one-sided exclusive approach of feminism, which imposes false interpretations on women's diversity and "other's" social realities. This approach underestimates the Muslim women's choices. They take over women's self-sovereignty and announce themselves as spokeswomen on their behalf.

This entailment is used in the Spanish minority discourse. Amanda Figueras states: "Su lucha también es contra otras tendencias feministas que consideran que las

---

[125]Akbar (2010b).

[126]Jones (2005).

[127]Dhumieres (2013).

[128]Wyatt (2003).

[129]HE HIJAB IS AN ENEMY is not an entailment of the PERSONIFICATION of the hijab because the ENEMY is not understood in a sense of a HUMAN ENEMY. It is mapped as an abstract ENEMY, just like a SIGN.

[130]Juárez (2015).

musulmanas somos incapaces de hablar por nosotras mismas y sienten la necesidad de liberarnos"[131] (Her fight is also against feminist tendencies that consider that Muslim women are incapable of speaking for ourselves and feel the need to liberate us).

THE THREATENED

The dominant discourse in both European contexts uses the same mappings for the under-threat elements in the WAR metaphor. It is OUR POSSESSED CULTURE that is being attacked in OUR CONTAINER. After all, it is the "us" and "other" positionality in the public sphere which motivates such entailments. Such positionality frames the ENEMY and the THREATENED metaphors.

OUR CULTURE IS UNDER-THREAT

The linguistic triggers are not direct in this entailment. It is detected from the context. In the Spanish contexts, the OUR CULTURE IS UNDER-THREAT entailment consists of rich mappings: the attacker, the attacking tools, the defense tools, and the solution (all will be discussed below), e.g., *"es un pulso al modelo social y debemos definir y defender ese modelo"*[132] (it (the veil) is a pulse (strike) on the social model, and we have to define and defend this model).

In the dominant British discourse, we have seen above that the threatening ENEMY is Islam and/or the hijab (Smith, 2004), (Wyatt, 2004) and (Marin, 2004). In the British national debate on the French ban law, the THREATENED is the French *Laïcité*. In the debate on the national hijab, the dominant discourse uses the BRITISH VALUES ARE THREATENED entailment. Therefore, there are calls to draw a line for tolerance, for example:

> "in British culture where we are beginning to be inclined to draw the line of tolerance. We are beginning to feel, after years of misguided multiculturalist propaganda about diversity, that what we must emphasize is similarity. There is a growing feeling that the host culture should stand up for itself as the common culture and be less tolerant of the intolerant."[133]

Islam visibility in the British public sphere, the CONTAINER, is seen as a threat to British values; ISLAM IS THREATENING OUR VALUES. In this entailment, both Islam and British values are framed as entities that attack or are under attack, ISLAM IS THE ENEMY, and OUR BRITISH CULTURE IS THREATENED.

---

[131] Figueras (2015).
[132] Montero (2010).
[133] Marin (2004).

HIJAB-WEARING WOMEN ARE UNDER-THREAT

The British minority discourse maps hijab-wearers as THREATENED in the WAR metaphor. This embodied experience of being targeted increases by the terrorist attacks that occur in the West. The linguistic trigger is direct: "under threat." For example, Faiza, the radio show presenter, states that "after the London bombings on 7 July, she said she felt "really vulnerable" wearing the hijab."[134] In the same article, Dr. Zaki Badawi advises that "Muslim women should feel free to take off their scarf if they felt threatened." Shelina Zahra JanMohamaed narrates that after 9/11, there are "discussions around the removal of headscarves for women who felt under threat."[135] Some hijab-wearing women describe the insecurity that takes over their life and question how politicians ask for their loyalty after terrorizing them, e.g., "the Government is basically saying, 'We have a right to terrorize you.' We feel under more threat than ever. How are we supposed to feel allegiance to this country?"[136]

THE VICTIMS

In both dominant European discourses, the hijab-wearing women are mapped as the VICTIMS in THE CULTURAL INTEGRATION IS WAR metaphor. Yet, some of these mappings are shared across the two European contexts, and others are not.

HIJAB-WEARERS ARE IGNORANT VICTIMS

For example, in the Spanish context, the "Ignorance" mental frame imposed on the hijab-wearers reveals the entailment of HIJAB-WEARING WOMEN ARE IGNO-RANT VICTIMS in the WAR metaphor. This recycled image schema justifies contemporary Muslim women's discrimination. It provides the WAR metaphor with a legitimate cause, liberating these VICTIMS. The linguistic triggers of this entailment are not direct but repetitive, e.g., "*no sabe que opinar*"[137] (she does not know what to opine (to say)), "*le han comido la cabeza*",[138] "*no vas a estudiar carrera*"[139] (you are not going to have a career). These two expressions were told to hijab-wearers in their social interaction. The IGNORANT VICTIMS mapping indirectly extends to include the non-Muslim voices who defend the women's right to hijab. They are accused that they, mistakenly, support extreme political ideologies, e.g., "[I]ntellectual Europeans

---

[134]Byrne (2005).

[135]Akbar (2010b).

[136]Smith (2006a).

[137]Carranco (2010).

[138]Figueras (2015).

[139]Juárez (2015).

who defend the use of burqa or niqab in their countries. There is no way to make them understand that they are not defending a right *[derecho]*, but (they defend) the extreme right *[derecho]* political ideology."[140]

HIJAB WEARERS ARE IGNORANT VICTIMS entailments explain the cognitive structure that the hijab opposers have. From this cognitive structure, Spanish journalists of dominant discourse analyze the hijab practice motivation and fight against it to provide hijab-wearers with enlightenment and liberation. The hijab-wearing visibility criticizes this mapping in the 2015/2016 discourse, e.g., Figueras[141] and El-Akil.[142]

HIJAB-WEARERS ARE VICTIMS OF PATRIARCHY

In the Dominant British and Spanish discourse, hijab-wearers are mainly mapped as VICTIMS OF PATRIARCHY. In Spanish dominant discourse, some of the linguistic triggers are direct. Still, not all: "(the father of Hasna Isslal) sacrifices his daughter, so ships get winds,"[143] "gender discrimination and patriarchy,"[144] "(the hijab) its victims are affected,"[145] "(because of the ban law) we convict her to the ignorance to get married at a young age."[146] These narrations activate the VICTIMS OF PATRIARCHY mappings of Spanish hijab-wearing women.

In the British dominant discourse, the triggers of the HIJAB-WEARERS ARE VICTIMS OF PATRIARCHY entailment are similar to the Spanish ones, e.g., "Some go further, arguing that women should not be allowed to mix with men at work, and should stay at home as much as possible"[147] and "The children are pawns in a larger battle, and who can say that girls of eight or nine are able to make an informed choice about wearing the veil?"[148] Although these are no direct linguistic triggers, the entire statements stand for VICTIMS OF PATRIARCHY entailment. It is a robust metaphorical entailment that becomes a social reality that controls the European cognition on the hijab. Muslim girls are accused of accepting being a victim. For example, the winner of Great British Bake Off indicates that when she adopted the hijab, she has been told by a friend that she "was bending to male enslavement."

---

[140]Gallego-Díaz (2010).

[141]Figueras (2015).

[142]Juárez (2015).

[143]Álvarez (2011c).

[144]Del Barrio (2008), Sotero and Bécares (2010a) and Montero (2010).

[145]Farreras (2016).

[146]Galarraga (2010).

[147]Smith (2006b).

[148]Smith (2004).

HIJAB WEARERS ARE VICTIMS OF THE BAN LAW

This mapping of the VICTIMS in the WAR metaphor appears in the Spanish contexts due to the recurrent exclusion cases. The mapping includes the school staff's abusive treatment; which is mentioned mainly in El Mundo, e.g., "(the decision of the transferring) causes harm to the right of Najwa," "they humiliated me," "she grabbed me from my hand," "she closed the door at my face," "the harm they are causing to the girl is irrecoverable," "she suffers from anxiety," "they obliged her to take it off," etc.

Hijab-wearers consider the ban law as the DISCRIMINATIVE TOOL, and they fight against it. Curiously, when the Spanish hijab-wearing women announce the ban law's discriminative aspect and application in the public sphere, they are accused of playing the victim's role. For example, In the Usera case, covered in EL Mundo, the minor states that the teacher accused her of faking the abusive treatment: "they say that I invented the whole thing and I am playing the victim."[149]

HIJAB-WEARERS ARE VICTIM Of DISCRIMINATION

This mapping of the VICTIM entailment in the WAR metaphor is found in the British minority discourse. The linguistic trigger is not direct. The DISCRIMINATION TOOL is not the ban law. It includes all aspects of Islamophobic treatments and stereotypes which the Muslim community suffers from. For example:

> "Discrimination, in some form or another, has become a daily part of the lives of millions of Muslims in Britain. We are being stopped and searched, arrested randomly, and held in custody without charge. All in the name of the prevention of "terror." Many of us are spat at, verbally abused, vilified, criminalized, and demonized."[150]

Hijab-wearing women specify that they are more victimized in the public sphere due to religious visibility, e.g., "I am not playing the victim card here. Hijab-wearers are often the first victims of backlashes in the wake of terror attacks; they are stereotyped as being oppressed."[151] and "being judged by others based on prejudices about Muslim women (because now I would look like one) before they even got a chance to know me."[152]

WESTERN WOMEN ARE VICTIMS

British hijab-wearers reverse the VICTIM entailment in the WAR metaphor imposed on them and maps western women as VICTIMS TO LIBERAL VALUES in the CONTAINER. The victimizer is "the liberal culture" of "uncovering,"[153] e.g.,

---

[149]Figueras (2011b).

[150]Chowdhury (2005).

[151]Perves (2013).

[152]Ibid..

[153]Takolia (2010).

"People say that it's the women who wear the veil that are submissive… but I think it is those women who are submissive because it is what men want, women half-naked."[154]

TOOLS

The TOOLS mappings explain many aspects of the WAR metaphor. The TOOL in the WAR is more complicated in the Spanish contexts, as we will see below. In the British context, minority discourse elaborates on the TOOL metaphor more than the dominant discourse. The linguistic trigger of the TOOL entailment is the repetitive vocabulary "use" of the hijab instead of wearing the hijab or practicing the hijab.

OTHER'S CULTURE IS AN ATTACKING TOOL

In the Spanish dominant discourse, the OUR POSSESSED CULTURE IS UNDER-THREAT entailment is used. But what is threatening the Spanish culture? It is Islam's visibility in the public sphere. It is essential to highlight the relationship between Islam's visibility and the historical frame of La Conquista, in which Islam was seen as the enemy of the peninsula. The "we" and "they" positionality plays an essential trigger in mapping this metaphor. The Spanish culture is defined as democratic and anti-discriminatory in opposition to the "other's" culture, e.g., "we have to be very careful that these cultural traditions do not attack liberty… or attack human rights."[155] Accordingly, the abstract concepts of equality and liberty are understood in terms of entities; LIBERTY AND EQUALITY ARE ENTITIES in OUR CONTAINER. They are "attacked" by other's religion.

THE BAN LAW IS A PROTECTIVE TOOL/WEAPON

The BAN LAW IS PROTECTIVE TOOL mapping is also used in the British debate on the French ban. Through the use of this metaphor, the dominant discourse justifies the French ban to the British reader, e.g., "This law is here to protect those girls who are compelled to do things they don't want to do,"[156] "We have to work with our teachers, we have to work with the students, the families, we have to explain to them that this is a law for their own protection,"[157] and "and I have a visceral sympathy

[154] Jones (2005).

[155] Del Barrio (2008) and Carbajos (2008)..

[156] Jones (2005).

[157] Wyatt (2004).

with those women in France and elsewhere who argue that such a law will protect women."[158]

THE BAN LAW IS A DESTRUCTIVE (OPPRESSIVE) TOOL/WEAPON

The Spanish minority discourse understands the national BAN LAW as a DESTRUC-TIVE TOOL or an OPPRESSIVE TOOL. THE BAN LAW IS AN OPPRESSIVE TOOL mapping that appears in the exclusion cases. The linguistic triggers are those vocabularies that indicate destruction: attack, destroy, threat, provoke, e.g., *"Todo lo que hemos construido a favor de la convivencia lo están destruyendo"*[159] (Everything we have built in favor of coexistence is being destroyed.)

Religious rights and coexistence are understood as ENTITIES in the Spanish CONTAINER. The ban law is a DESTRUCTIVE TOOL/WEAPON of these ENTI-TIES. The ban law is "attentive" against religious rights. The ban law violates the rights to education and religious liberty (*"vulnera"* and "contraviene").[160] It gener-ates restlessness, e.g., *"se transmite la 'inquietud y malestar' ante el quebrantamiento de los derechos de la joven a la educación y a la libertad religiosa"*[161] (It transmits restlessness and the discomfort about the violation of the young woman's right to education and religious freedom). These perceptions of the ban law generate the need to fight against it. From this embodied experience, hijab-wearers use WORRIERS metaphor to narrate their struggle of being part of the Spanish diversity.

This entailment is not used in the British national debate on the hijab. Perhaps, the British hijab-wearers do not go through an explicit exclusion from the public sphere as the Spanish women do. Yet, in the British debate on the French ban law, it is seen as a DIVISIVE TOOL in the French CONTAINER, e.g., "this new measure will divide it more than ever."[162]

THE HIJAB IS A DESTRUCTIVE TOOL/WEAPON

This mapping is shared across the British and the Spanish contexts. In the British context, the hijab-wearing writers use THE HIJAB IS AN ATTACKING TOOL/WEAPON metaphor. They state that the dominant discourse uses the hijab to attack Muslims, e.g., "(the veil) often used by misinformed critics to attack Muslims and the traditions of Islam."[163] In the Spanish context, the dominant discourse uses the HIJAB IS ATTACKING TOOL/WEAPON metaphor. It is used to attack OUR

---

[158]Walter (2004).
[159]Del Barrio (2010b.
[160]Ibid..
[161]Galafate (2010).
[162]Wyatt (2004).
[163]Perves (2013).

POSSESSED ENTITY, our culture, and our values, e.g., *"El ataque a la igualdad"*[164] ("the hijab is" the attack to equality). The hijab is a THREATENING TOOL, e.g., "our democratic values are strong enough that neither a bonnet nor a hijab threatens it."[165] The hijab is a PROVOCATIVE TOOL that causes the social disorder, e.g., every time a girl "uses" it *"estalló la polemica."* As the hijab is mapped as a DESTRUC-TIVE TOOL, there are demands to "regulate its use"[166] the same way weapons are controlled.

THE CONSTITUTIONAL LAW IS A PROTECTIVE TOOL/WEAPON

This entailment in the WAR metaphor is used in the Spanish discourse by both social varieties. The lawyer Jiménez Aybar indicates that the Constitutional law is an empowering and a PROTECTIVE TOOL, e.g., *"esta garantizado por una regla superior (la Constitución)"*[167] ([the right to hijab] is guaranteed by a superior regulation (the Constitution)" and "The law protects the use of the veil."[168]

The dominant discourse does not seem happy about the lawyer's statements. They use the metaphor to indicates the Muslim's use of the Constitutional law, e.g., *"Los musulmanes en España han empezado a movilizarse. [...]el que aseguran tener 'con la ley en la mano,'"*[169] (Spanish Muslims have started to mobilize [...] they make sure to have 'the law in hand') and *"amparándose en la Constitución artículo 18"*[170] (protected by/based on the Constitution, article 18).

THE BATTLE

The Battle of the CULTURE INTEGRATION IS WAR metaphor occurs on the women's body as the dominant Spanish discourse indicates: *"Las mujeres se han convertido en el campo de batalla entre Oriente y Occidente tras el 11-S"*[171] (Women have become the battlefield between East and West after 9/11).

In the Spanish context, the hijab-wearers map themselves as WORRIERS who fight the ban law, stereotypes, and ethnocentric feminism. The fight in the British WAR is for a general cause that includes all the diverse components in the CONTAINER, e.g., "whether we are atheist or agnostic, white or black, butcher

---

[164]Carbajos (2008).

[165]Espinosa (2010).

[166]Montero (2010).

[167]Figueras (2011c).

[168]De Ganuza (2008). and Figueras and Piantadosi (2011a).

[169]Figueras and Piantadosi (2011a).

[170]Galafate (2010).

[171]Carbajos (2008).

or baker, we are, and should be, striving to be part of—brace yourselves—a diverse, multi-faceted, thriving society."[172]

The VICTORY in the WAR across these two European contexts is not the same. The Spanish dominant discourse considers the ban of the hijab practice in the exclusion cases as a VICTORY. When the school accepted the hijab practice in the Arteixo case, Mariano Rajoy criticized the Catalan government, which, according to him, renounced in front of a childish whim "*el chantaje*" and he asserted the need to "specify to the maximum these Spanish costumes and principles."[173] In contrast, In Usera Case, where the school permitted the practice, the Spanish minority discourse negated the VICTORY entailments of the dominant discourse. Jimenez Aybar asserted that the agreement on wearing the hijab is based on Rights, and it is not a renouncement, e.g., "the center has not given up to a whim of a Muslim. It has acted according to the Right."[174]

For the hijab-wearers, the RENOUNCEMENT in the WAR is to quit the hijab practice, e.g., the massive support to Najwa called for Najwa's right to education "without renouncing her Islamic veil"[175] and "In this way, the 16-year old who has been unable to attend class since last week will have to make a decision. Thus, she could change to a center 300 meters from her current 'IES' or give up wearing the Islamic 'hijab' and stay in her current class with her classmates."[176] Some hijab-wearers understand this RENOUNCMENT as a deadly end: "to renounce the hijab is to take off her skin"[177] and "To oblige me to take off my veil is to tear off my own skin."[178] To take off the skin of a WORRIER in the BATTLE implies a certain death in the WAR.

In the Spanish and British minority discourse, there is no winner in the exclusion or stigmatization cases. In the Spanish context, the lawyer indicates that allowing the hijab practice in the public school does not imply a victory for one social diversity over others. The VICTORY is the respect of the Constitutional Law; he states: "There are no winners or losers, in these cases. What wins out is respect for the Law and the best interests of the minor."[179] However, Amanda Figueras states that, in her personal experience as a convert Muslim, "stereotypes win" in her BATLLE.[180] In the British context, hijab-wearers indicate that in the "confrontations" on the dress code, "no one wins" and "a great deal of damage" is done.[181] Even though the

---

[172] Aly and Remona (2015).

[173] De Ganuza (2008).

[174] Figueras (2011c).

[175] Galafate (2010).

[176] Belvar and Blasco (2010).

[177] Álvarez (2011c).

[178] Bohorquez (2016).

[179] Figueras (2011c).

[180] Figueras (2015).

[181] Elkin (2013).

dominant British discourse stigmatizes Shabina's jilbab case by the "victory" of extremist ideologies,[182] the British Muslim community did not receive it as such.[183]

The British hijab-wearing public figures in 2015, Nadiya Hussain (who later made the birthday cake for the Queen 90th birthday in 2016[184]) and Mariah Idrissi, are seen as a revolution on stereotypes and an act to be celebrated because it overcomes divisive ideologies in the British public sphere, the CONTAINER. Sajda Khan referred to their appearance in the public arena as follow:

> "Is this the beginning of a revolution? […] (It is) a celebration of the religious and individual freedom David Cameron spoke about on Wednesday. It defeats those who want to fracture our multi-faceted society and brings the rest of us closer together. We need to keep upholding our core value of respecting diversity, which means showing respect for and being tolerant of different faiths and cultures."[185]

Remona Aly wrote on those hijab-wearing public figure:

> "It's a celebration of the diversity of the United Kingdom and good news for ordinary Muslims. The hijab may have been dressed up by some as being "at odds with society," but the fact that it is entering popular culture is in itself a celebration of the religious freedoms and universal values that Britain prides itself on."[186]

Both writers consider the hijab-wearing women's visibility as British culture and values representatives, as a VICTORY celebrated in the Muslim community.

Conclusion

The PUBLIC SPHERE IS A CONTAINER metaphor explains how dominant discourse in both countries legitimates their ownership of the public sphere as much as their sovereignty over the visible diversities. Within the CONTAINER metaphor, the WAR over the POSSESSED ENTITY (the mainstream culture) is raging to impose a homogenous symmetric public sphere or homogenous diverse public sphere.

In the dominant discourse, conquering women's bodies and sexuality are the victory factor. Women who conceal their bodies in the CONTAINER are undesirable ("Concealment" mental frame). The item used to conceal their body, the hijab, is understood as a SIGN OF IGNORANCE, OPPRESSION, DISCRIMINATION, and above all, EXTREMIST MILITANCY ("Submission," "Discrimination," and "Extremist" "Religiosity" frames). For the dominant discourse, the hijab is a TOOL in the WAR to impose others' ideologies and customs in OUR CONTAINER ("Othering" frame). The "mirror effect" achieves homogeneity in the CONTAINER in the

---

[182] Cassidy (2005).

[183] Chowdhury (2005).

[184] See: http://www.independent.co.uk/news/people/queens−birthday−gbbo−winner−nadiya −hussain−will−make−cake−for−monarchs−90th−a6986271.html.

[185] Khan (2015).

[186] Aly (2015).

Spanish dominant discourse, whereas in the dominant British discourse, diversity is allowed as long as it is not a religious one, specifically an Islamic one. The hijab is a SOLID BARRIER between the women practitioners and the belonging to the CONTAINER. These cognitive structures are consistent with the stereotypical mental frames revealed in the previous chapters on the hijab and hijab-wearing women.

In the Spanish and British minority discourse, the CONTAINER is possessed by all the diverse participants who work hard for coexistence (de-activating the "Othering" frame). The limited participation of Spanish Muslim women reveals their understanding of diversity as MOSAIC ENTITIES in the CONTAINER (Activating the "Religiosity" frame). The ban law is a DESTRUCTIVE TOOL to these colorful ENTITIES. In both contexts, Muslim women consider that STEREOTYPES ARE BARRIERS to a fully homogenous sphere. The control over their bodies, what to cover and what to reveal, belongs to them first and foremost. Therefore, the hijab is an EMPOWERING TOOL to take control over the exposition of their body in the public sphere ("Empowering" and "Concealment" frame).

This chapter showed that the analysis of Conceptual Metaphors Theory is helpful in the Cognitive Critical Discourse Analysis (CCDA). The conceptual metaphors analysis reveals the cognitive structure beneath the linguistic forms. Specifically, it exposes how the underlying mental frames in the press debate on hijab are built.

References

Lakoff, G., & Johnson, M. (1980). *Metaphors we live by*. Chicago: Chicago University Press.
Lakoff, G., & Johnson, M. (1999). *Philosophy in the flesh: The embodied mind and its challenge to western thought*. Basic books.

Annex 1

Spanish Articles
Álvarez, P. (2011a). *A clase con el velo*. http://sociedad.elpais.com/sociedad/2011/10/18/actualidad/1318888806_850215.html. 18 October 2011.
Álvarez, P. (2011b). *Renunciar al velo islámico sería como quitarme la piel.*. http://elpais.com/diario/2011/10/23/sociedad/1319320802_850215.html. 23 October 2011.
Álvarez, P. (2011c). *Renunciar al velo islámico sería como quitarme la piel*. http://elpais.com/diario/2011/10/23/sociedad/1319320802_850215.html. 23 October 2011.
Álvarez, P., & Cembrero, I. (2010). *Mi hija seguirá en el mismo instituto y con el 'hiyab.'* http://elpais.com/diario/2010/04/23/sociedad/1271973603_850215.html. 23 April 2010.
Ayuso, B. (2016). *De María a Maryam: así se convirtió al islam una española de 29 años*. http://politica.elpais.com/politica/2016/06/23/actualidad/1466664764_761081.html. 16 July 2016.
Barik Edidi, Z. (2009). *Encuentro*. http://www.elmundo.es/encuentros/invitados/2009/11/3898/index.html. 11 November 2009.
Belaza, M. C. (2010). *El Supremo decidirá sobre el uso del "hiyab" en los juicios.*" El País. http://elpais.com/diario/2010/01/15/sociedad/1263510007_850215.html. 15 January 2010.
Belvar, M., & Blasco, P. (2010). *El instituto de Pozuelo no modifica sus normas e impide a Najwa ir con veil*. http://www.elmundo.es/elmundo/2010/04/20/madrid/1271786689.html. 21 April 2010.

Bohorquez, L. (2016). *Que me obliguen a quitarme el velo es como arrancarme mi propia piel.* http://politica.elpais.com/politica/2016/12/20/actualidad/1482237712_030858.html. 20 December 2016.

Carbajos, A. (2008). Más musulmanas con velo. ¿Porque quieren?" http://www.elpais.com/articulo/sociedad/musulmanas/velo/quieren/elpepisoc/20080628elpepisoc_1/Tes. 28 June 2008.

Carranco, R. (2010). No me quito el 'hiyab' porque no quiero. http://elpais.com/diario/2010/04/22/sociedad/1271887206_850215.html. 22 April 2010.

De Ganuza, C. R. (2008). El Partido Popular propondrá prohibir el uso del velo en todas las escuelas. http://www.elmundo.es/elmundo/2008/02/08/espana/1202448607.html. 8 February 2008.

Del Barrio, A. (2008). De la Vega desautoriza a Aído y dice que el Gobierno respeta la tradición del velo islámico. http://www.elmundo.es/elmundo/2008/06/26/espana/1214475820.html. 27 June 2008.

Del Barrio, A. (2010a). *El velo no me limita para trabajar, que no te limita a ti para contratarme..* http://www.elmundo.es/elmundo/2010/12/21/espana/1292933868.html. 22 December 2010.

Del Barrio, A. (2010b). *Los musulmanes anuncian acciones legales contra el colegio de Pozuelo.* http://www.elmundo.es/elmundo/2010/04/21/madrid/1271852171.html. 21 April 2010.

Espinosa, A. (2010). *En mi clase había una monja.* http://elpais.com/diario/2010/04/23/sociedad/1271973602_850215.html. 23 April 2010.

Farreras, C. (2016). Los Nuevos Significados del velo. http://www.lavanguardia.com/vida/20160717/403268947566/universitarias-musulmanas-velo-hiyab-expresion-religion.html. 18 July 2016.

Figueras, A. (2011a). *La menor expulsada de un examen por el 'hiyab': 'Dicen que me lo invento y me hago la víctima.* http://www.elmundo.es/elmundo/2011/10/04/madrid/1317750847.html. 06 October 2011.

Figueras, A. (2011b). *El instituto que echó a una niña por llevar 'hiyab' acepta que pueda seguir utilizándolo.* http://www.elmundo.es/elmundo/2011/10/17/madrid/1318888325.html. 19 October 2011.

Figueras, A. (2011c). *El director que prohibió ir con el velo a clase podría ser acusado de prevaricación.* http://www.elmundo.es/elmundo/2011/10/27/castillayleon/1319714393.html. 27 October 2011.

Figueras, A. (2012). *La angustia de decir que eres musulmán..* http://www.elmundo.es/elmundo/2012/04/27/espana/1335521507.html. 29 April 2012.

Figueras, A. (2015). *¿Por qué se me cuestiona por abrazar esta fe? El islam no es el velo ni el IS ni ningún tipo de terrorismo'.* http://www.elmundo.es/espana/2015/06/24/55797914ca4741a6268b457d.html. 30 June 2015.

Figueras, A., & Piantadosi, G. (2011). *Me echaron de un examen y del instituto por llevar el 'hiyab'.* http://www.elmundo.es/elmundo/2011/09/30/madrid/1317407926.html. 03 October 2011.

Galafate, C. (2010). *Crean un grupo en Facebook para apoyar a Najwa.* http://www.elmundo.es/elmundo/2010/04/23/madrid/1272044565.html. 23 April 2010.

Galarraga, N. (2010). *¿Velo de sumisión o de rebeldía?* http://elpais.com/diario/2010/04/23/sociedad/1271973601_850215.html. 23 April 2010.

Gallego-Díaz, S. (2010). *El velo no merece una ley.* http://elpais.com/diario/2010/04/25/domingo/1272166236_850215.html. 25 April 2010.

Iglesias, N. (2007). *La Generalitat obliga a admitir en clase a una menor con 'hiyab'.* http://elpais.com/diario/2007/10/02/sociedad/1191276010_850215.html. 10 February 2007.

Juárez, A. S. (2015). *Musulmanas y tan españolas como vosotras.* http://www.elmundo.es/yodona/2015/02/28/54ef5340ca4741216d8b4578.html. 28 February 2015.

Meneses, R. (2010). *Cual es el significado y el origen del Hiyab.* http://www.elmundo.es/elmundo/2010/04/21/madrid/1271853528.html. 22 April 2010.

Montero, R. (2010). *Ahí le duele.* http://elpais.com/diario/2010/04/27/ultima/1272319201_850215.html. 27 April 2010.

Obelleiro, P. (2011). *El director del colegio de Arteixo impide a la niña del 'hiyab' entrar a recoger las notas.* http://elpais.com/diario/2011/06/23/galicia/1308824289_850215.html. 23 June 2011.

Quelart, R. (2011). *He conocido a mujeres muy felices detrás del velo.* http://www.lavang uardia.com/salud/20111212/54239960536/beatriz-goyoaga-entrevista-meditacion-velo.html. 12 December 2011.

Sahuquillo, M. R. (2008). *Integración, si, asimilación, no.* http://www.elpais.com/articulo/sociedad/ Integracion/asimilacion/elpepisoc/20080216elpepisoc_1/Tes. 16 February 2008.

Sotero, P. D. (2010). *Gabilondo alerta de que la polémica del velo puede terminar en 'segregación.* http://www.elmundo.es/elmundo/2010/04/27/espana/1272367212.html. 27 April 2010.

Sotero, P. D., & Bécares, R. (2010). El Ministerio de Educación apela a respetar las creencias de los alumnos. http://www.elmundo.es/elmundo/2010/04/16/madrid/1271434711.html. 16 April 2010.

Annex 2

English Articles

Abbasi, H. (2004). *Trapped or liberated by the hijab?"* https://www.theguardian.com/world/2004/ jan/21/gender.religion. 21 January 2004.

Akbar, A. (2010a). *The many faces behind the veil.* Introduction. http://www.independent.co.uk/ news/uk/this-britain/the-many-faces-behind-the-veil-1865772.html. 13 January 2010.

Akbar, A. (2010b). *The many faces behind the veil.* with Rajnaara Akhtar. http://www.independent. co.uk/news/uk/this-britain/the-many-faces-behind-the-veil-1865772.html. 13 January 2010.

Akbar, A. (2010c). *The many faces behind the veil.* with Shelina Zahra JanMohamaed. http:// www.independent.co.uk/news/uk/this-britain/the-many-faces-behind-the-veil-1865772.html. 13 January 2010.

Akbar, A. (2010d). *The many faces behind the veil.* with Soha Sheikh. http://www.independent.co. uk/news/uk/this-britain/the-many-faces-behind-the-veil-1865772.html. 13 January 2010.

Alam, F. (2005). *We must move beyond the hijab.* https://www.theguardian.com/education/2005/ nov/29/highereducation.uk. 29 November 2005.

Alibhai-Brown, Y. (2015). *As a Muslim woman, I see the veil as a rejection of progressive values.* https://www.theguardian.com/commentisfree/2015/mar/20/muslim-woman-veil-hijab. 20 March 2015.

Aly, R. (2015). *How the hijab-and H&M- are reshaping mainstream British culture.* http://www. theguardian.com/commentisfree/2015/sep/28/hijab-h-and-m-mainstream-culture-great-british-bake-off-diversity. 30 September 2015.

Aslam, S. (2014). *To hijab or not to hijab—A Muslim businesswoman's view.* http://www.the guardian.com/uk/the-northerner/2012/dec/10/hijab-muslims-women-islam-business-bradford-niqab-burka. 21 May 2014.

Bennett, C. (2004). *Why should we defend the veil?* http://www.theguardian.com/world/2004/jan/ 22/gender.schoolsworldwide. 22 January 2004.

Bentham, M., & Davis, A. (2007). *Hairdresser sued in row about headscarf.* http://www.standard. co.uk/news/hairdresser-sued-in-row-about-headscarf-6657648.html. 08 November 2007.

Burchill, J. (2011). *Carla Bruni is standing up to the stoners. Lauren Booth just covers up for them.* http://www.independent.co.uk/voices/columnists/julie-burchill/julie-burchill-carla-bruni-is-sta nding-up-to-the-stoners-lauren-booth-just-covers-up-for-them-2067119.html. 04 April 2011.

Byrne, C. (2005). *Heard the one about the Mickey Mouse hijab?"* http://www.independent.co.uk/ news/media/heard-the-one-about-the-mickey-mouse-hijab-320202.html. 17 October 2005.

Carter, H. (2009). *Guest asked whether her hijab meant she was a terrorist, court told.* https://www. theguardian.com/uk/2009/dec/08/hijab-hotel-alleged-abuse-trial. 08 December 2009.

Cassidy, S. (2005). *Schoolgirl banned from wearing Muslim dress wins appeal.* http://www.indepe ndent.co.uk/news/education/education-news/schoolgirl-banned-from-wearing-muslim-dress-wins-appeal-527023.html. 03 March 2005.

Chowdhury, S. (2005). *We have more urgent issues to fight for than dress codes.* http://www. independent.co.uk/voices/commentators/shamim-chowdhury-we-have-more-urgent-issues-to-fight-for-than-dress-codes-4576.html. 04 March 2005.

Cllr Khan, R. (2006). *The hijab does not restrict it-it liberates.* https://www.theguardian.com/lifean dstyle/2009/apr/07/letters-hijab-islam-women. 07 April 2009.

Dear, P. (2004). *Women vow to protect Muslim hijab.* http://news.bbc.co.uk/2/hi/uk_news/380573 3.stm. 14 June 2004.

Dhumieres, M. (2013). *Why is the right of Muslim women to wear the veil still so controversial in France?* http://www.independent.co.uk/voices/comment/why-is-the-right-of-muslim-women-to-wear-the-veil-still-so-controversial-in-france-8575052.html. 16 April 2013.

Elkin, S. (2013). *Common sense and respect for children in hijabs, please.* http://www.independent.co.uk/voices/comment/common-sense-and-respect-for-children-in-hijabs-please-8437433.html. 03 January 2013.

Guest, K., & Davies, M. W. (2005). *The Muslims next door.* http://www.independent.co.uk/news/uk/this-britain/focus-the-muslims-next-door-527359.html. 06 March 2005.

Jones, E. C. (2005). *Muslim girls unveil their fears.* http://news.bbc.co.uk/2/hi/programmes/this_w orld/4352171.stm. 28 March 2005.

Khan, S. (2015). *It is not the hijab which holds women back, but prejudice.* http://www.telegr aph.co.uk/culture/tvandradio/great-british-bake-off/11919553/Its-not-the-hijab-which-holds-women-back-but-intolerance-and-prejudice.html. 08 October 2015.

Malik, M. (2006). *This veil fixation is doing Muslim women no favors.* https://www.theguardian.com/commentisfree/2006/oct/19/religion.immigration. 19 October 2006.

Marin, M. (2004). *Cry freedom and accept the Muslim headscarf.* https://www.thetimes.co.uk/art icle/comment-minette-marrin-cry-freedom-and-accept-the-muslim-headscarf-tcxvm85lhqd. 01 February 2004.

Marrison, S. (2011). *The Islamification of Britain: Record numbers embrace Muslim faith.* http://www.independent.co.uk/news/uk/home-news/the-islamification-of-britain-record-numbers-emb race-muslim-faith-2175178.html. 04 January 2011.

Mortimer, C. (2015). *Mariah Idrissi: H&M's first hijab-wearing model says her work 'isn't immodest'.* http://www.independent.co.uk/news/uk/home-news/mariah-idrissi-hms-first-hijab-wearing-model-says-her-work-isnt-immodest-a6673901.html. 30 September 2015.

Mursaleen, S. (2010). *The power behind the veil.* https://www.theguardian.com/commentisfree/bel ief/2010/jan/25/burqa-ban-veil-sarkozy-ukip. 25 January 2010.

Orr, D. (2005). *Blairism is simply Thatcherism administered by do-gooders.* http://www.indepe ndent.co.uk/voices/commentators/deborah-orr/blairism-is-simply-thatcherism-administered-by-do-gooders-527246.html. 05 March 2005.

Perves, S. (2013). *Mishal Husain and the veil: What the daily mail was really trying to say.* https://www.theguardian.com/uk-news/the-northerner/2013/oct/08/mishal-husain-veil-daily-mail. 8 October 2013.

Sanghani, R. (2015). *Armistice day: Great British Bake off winner Nadiya Hussain wears 'poppy hijab'.* http://www.telegraph.co.uk/women/womens-life/11988184/Armistice-Day-2015-Great-British-Bake-Off-winner-Nadiya-Hussain-wears-poppy-hijab.html. 11 November 2015.

Smith, J. (2004). *What lies beneath the veil.* http://www.independent.co.uk/voices/commentators/joan-smith/what-lies-beneath-the-veil-8833948.html. 25 January 2004.

Smith, J. (2006a). *The veil is a feminist issue.* http://www.independent.co.uk/voices/commentators/joan-smith/joan-smith-the-veil-is-a-feminist-issue-419119.html. 08 October 2006.

Smith, J. (2006b). *Our schools are no place for Jilbab. Or for Creationists.* http://www.indepe ndent.co.uk/voices/commentators/joan-smith/joan-smith-our-schools-are-no-place-for-the-jil bab-or-for-the-creationists-6105619.html. 26 March 2006.

Takolia, N. (2010). *The hijab has liberated me from society expectations of women.* https://www.theguardian.com/commentisfree/2012/may/28/hijab-society-women-religious-political. 28 May 2012.

Walter, N. (2004). *When the veil means freedom.* https://www.theguardian.com/world/2004/jan/20/france.schoolsworldwide1. 20 January 2004.

Wyatt, C. (2003). *Liberty, equality and the headscarf.* http://news.bbc.co.uk/2/hi/programmes/from_our_own_correspondent/3334881.stm. 20 December 2003.

Wyatt, C. (2004). *French headscarf ban opens rifts.* http://news.bbc.co.uk/2/hi/europe/3478895.stm.

Conclusion

Conclusions

Using the Critical Discourse Analysis to detect the mental frames on the national hijab and hijab-wearers women exposes social inclusion and exclusion of each context. Conceptual metaphor analysis discloses the curtain on how minorities and majorities understand the abstract process of social integration and diversity. Human social experiences are embodied practices in thought and body; that is why they are called embodied experiences. The conceptual metaphors found in this analysis show how the physical (bodily) experiences are framed in mind. Simultaneously, the innovative Cognitive Critical Discourse Analysis (CCDA) methodology proves its capability to uncover the cognitive structures that shape the Spanish and British hijab debate and expose the social inequalities and injustices that manifest in the public discourse.

This book shows that the hijab-opposers understand the hijab as an abstract symbol that embodies negative references. They frame the hijab through the "Discrimination," "Submission," "Compulsivity," "Concealment," "Religiosity," and "Othering" frames. Hijab-wearing women are framed through the "Ignorance," "Oppression," "Othering," and "Indiscipline" frames. These frames are significant because they do not represent individual framings of the hijab and hijab-wearing women. These activated framings, particularly in the Spanish context, reflect how readers, who are part of a linguistic community, in historical and social contexts, frame the hijab and its wearers. In the British context, the de-activation of these stereotypical frames by national hijab-wearers is perceived as part of the collective national discourse built on diversity and multiculturalism values. In contrast, in the absence of alternative contra-arguments, these frames are more intense, direct, and rooted in the Spanish press.

The analysis of conceptual metaphors reveals the contributors' cognitive preferences in the national hijab debate in each context. Conceptual metaphors on the abstract concepts "public sphere," "French ban law," "the hijab sign," and "social integration" disclose the national values in the hijab debate and uncover the underground behind the found mental frames.

In the introduction of this book, I argued that the 2004 ban significantly impacted the hijab national debate in the British and Spanish national press. The British national

© Springer Nature Singapore Pte Ltd. 2021   259
G. Khir-Allah, *Framing Hijab in the European Mind*,
https://doi.org/10.1007/978-981-16-1653-2_9

press debated the French ban in 2003 and 2004 when it is announced and implemented in France. On the contrary, Spanish women journalists were not interested in the neighbor's ban law in 2004. In 2007, a hijab exclusion case ignited the debate on the use of the hijab in the Spanish public sphere. However, a serious hijab debate in the Spanish press appeared only in 2010. In 2010, the French full-veil ban law was the trigger for several hijab exclusion cases at school and the workplace as much as for a massive debate on hijab visibility in the national public sphere. Women journalists went back to 2004 to revive the French arguments on the hijab ban. They imported them into the Spanish social context as if what applies to France could be applied to Spain and ignoring all the historical and demographical differences between the two social structures.

The British debate of the French ban differentiates between the British multicultural "we" in opposition to the French intolerant "others." British journalists show awareness of the British diverse social structure, even when they oppose the hijab. In contrast, the Spanish debate on the French ban marks the Spanish in-danger "we," who need to follow the French wise steps. Spanish journalists are unable to make a difference between laïcité and secularism, between the Spanish State's relationship with the Church and the French one, and between the Spanish social peculiarity and the French one. The French social anti-hijab movements were introduced as heroic.

Women journalist's authority in the hijab debate differs across the two social contexts. British national press demonstrates inclusive debate in which hijab-wearers, non-hijab-wearers, non-Muslim (against or for the practice) journalists and activists participate. Several hijab-opposer journalists interview hijab-wearing women without taking over the Muslim women's agency. The national hijab debate is diverse, and every woman participant is allowed to express her beliefs and arguments. Colonial framing of the hijab and hijab-wearing women are activated and re-activated by the hijab opposers. However, Muslim (hijab-wearing) women de-activate these stereotypical frames by potent arguments and activate alternative mental frames on the use of hijab. Accordingly, British readers are offered mental freedom, the possibility to read through perspectives against and in favor of hijab and decide which they opt to follow.

Contrary to the British inclusive and diverse debate, the Spanish debate is exclusive, restricted, and controlled by hijab-opposer journalists. The Spanish press, especially El País, is an ethnocentric and politicized platform. The Spanish press discourse represents the newspaper's voice rather than the journalists' voice. Both women journalists and contributors in the hijab debate activate the stereotypical frames on hijab-wearing women. Before 2015, the visibility of national hijab-wearers is close to zero. Hijab-wearing participants and hijab supporters are anonymous; their contributions are insignificant, or their participation is used by the journalist to assert some stereotypical frames. In 2015/2016, national hijab-wearers' contribution is controlled by the journalists who conduct the interviews. Only one article is written by a Muslim hijab-wearer, an ex-journalist in El Mundo who converted to Islam. It is to say, national hijab-wearing women are invisiblized and excluded from the national hijab debate. Spanish hijab-opposers journalists announce themselves as spokeswomen on behalf of the ignorant, oppressed, and discriminated hijab-wearing women. They use the national hijab-exclusion cases as evidence of the incompatibility of the hijab with the national values, although the Spanish constitution guarantees these women's religious rights.

The biased hijab debate in the Spanish national press re-activates the neo-colonial frames of the hijab and the hijab-wearing women without balancing the arguments in favor and against it. Hijab-wearers do not have the opportunity to de-activate these stereotypical frames imposed on them. Their limited engagement reinforces the stereotypical colonial frame in the debate and increases their stigmatization in everyday life. Accordingly, Spanish readers do not enjoy a balanced debate in which they decide how to frame the hijab and hijab-wearing women. They lack the instruments to think of the hijab visibility in the public sphere critically. Depriving Spanish readers of this mental freedom is the journalists' responsibility. Their discourse on Muslim minority women is based on their personal preferences and biases in understanding Muslim heritage, instead of impartially documenting the value attributed to the practice by hijab-wearing women.

The hijab needs to be understood as a universal, transnational religious practice that aims to reduce women's body exposure in the public sphere. However, body concealment is considered offensive in the British hijab-opposers discourse and empowering in the British hijab-wearers discourse. In the Spanish context, body concealment led to the concealment of women who refuse to provide open access to their bodies in the public sphere. They are invisibilized; their voice and agency are also concealed. They are referred to as objects. Othering the hijab and the hijab-wearing women exist in both contexts, yet it is more direct and intense in the Spanish context. Othering, the hijab and hijab-wearers, is a strategy to create a gap between hijab-wearing women and the Spanish national identity, driving the attention away from the integration crisis that occurs in Spanish public schools. The hijab display in the public sphere is considered a threat to Spanish national values. In 2015/2016, the Spanish discourse included few hijab-wearers' limited contributions, whereas the British press covers an ascending number of Islamophobic attacks on hijab-wearing women in the public sphere. Due to the constant social change, the research on the national discourse framing of the hijab and hijab-wearing women needs to be analyzed.

The methodology proposed in this book can be adopted in future studies to re-open the debate on diversity within feminism, to analyze the national identity and secularism in the European public or political discourse, to study the visibility of religious signs in the European public sphere, to research the European identity construction of Muslim minorities, and to explore the level of diversity in European social structures. This contribution is the first step forward.

Bibliography

Abbas, T. (2004). After 9/11: British south Asian Muslims, islamophobia, multiculturalism, and the state. *American Journal of Islamic Social Sciences, 21*(3), 26–38.

Abu-Baker, O. (2001). Islamic feminism: What is in a name? *Middle East Women's Studies Review, 15*(4).

Adelkhah F. (1999). Family restructuring and affirmation of individual in Muslim countries: The case of Iran. In G. M. Munoz (Ed.), *Islam, modernism and the West: Cultural and political relations at the end of the millennium*. IB Tauris.

Adida, C. L., Laitin, D. D., & Valfort, M. A. (2010). Identifying barriers to Muslim integration in France. *Proceedings of the National Academy of Sciences, 107*(52), 22384–22390.

Aixelá, Y. (2006). Islam and women; Europe and Islam: Mirror play. Transfer. *Journal of Contemporary Culture, 1*, 67–76.

Aixelá, Y., & Planet, A. I. (2004, jun). Mujer y política en el mundo árabe. Un estado de la cuestión. Feminismo/s, n. 3, 149–159.

Al-Ali, N. (2000). *Secularism, gender and the state in the Middle East: The Egyptian women's movement* (Vol. 14). Cambridge University Press.

Alcoff, L. (2006). *Visible identities: Race, gender, and the self* (Vol. 10). Oxford University Press.

al-Hibri, A. (1994). Who defines women's rights? A third world woman's response. *Human Rights Brief, 2*(1), 13.

Al-Hibri, A. (1997). *Islam, law and custom: Redefining Muslim women's rights*.

Al-Hibri, A. (2001). Muslim women's rights in the global village: Challenges and opportunities. *Journal of Law and Religion, 15*, 37–66.

Ali, N., & Whitham, B. (2018). The unbearable anxiety of being: Ideological fantasies of British Muslims beyond the politics of security. *Security Dialogue, 49*(5), 400–417.

Allan, K. (2012). *Contemporary social and sociological theory: Visualizing social worlds*. Sage publications.

Al-Saji, A. (2010). The racialization of Muslim veils: A philosophical analysis. *Philosophy & Social Criticism, 36*(8), 875–902.

Amghar, S., Boubekeur, A., & Emerson, M. (2007). *European islam: Challenges for public policy and society*. CEPS.

Anthias, F. (2002). Where do I belong? Narrating collective identity and translocational positionality. *Ethnicities, 2*(4), 491–514.

Arbatli, E., & Rosenberg, D. (Eds.). (2017). *Non-western social movements and participatory democracy: Protest in the age of transnationalism*. Springer.

Arkoun, M. (1999), History of legitimation: A comparative Approach in Islamic and European Context. In G. M. Munoz (Ed.), *Islam, modernism and the West: cultural and political relations at the end of the millennium*. IB Tauris.

Asad, M. (2005). *The message of Quran*. The Book Foundation.

© Springer Nature Singapore Pte Ltd. 2021
G. Khir-Allah, *Framing Hijab in the European Mind*,
https://doi.org/10.1007/978-981-16-1653-2

Aubarell, G., Zapata-Barrero, R., & Allievi, S. (2004). *Inmigración y procesos de cambio: Europa y el Mediterráneo en el contexto global* (Vol. 199). Icaria Editorial.

Badran, M. (2006). Islamic feminism revisited. *Al-Ahram Weekly On-Line, 781*, 9–15.

Bajekal N. (2015). Why thousands of migrants are risking their lives at Calais. *Time*. Retrieved September 26, 2016 from http://time.com/3980758/calais-migrant-eurotunnel-deaths/.

Bakr, O. A. (2001). Islamic feminism: What is in a name? *Middle East Women's Studies Review*.

Balibar, E. (2004). Dissonances dans la laïcité. *Mouvements* (3), 148–161.

Bañón, A. M. (1996). *Racismo, discurso periodístico y didáctica de la lengua*. Universidad de Almería.

Bañón, A. M. (2002). *Discurso e inmigración: propuestas para el análisis de un debate social*. Editum.

Bañón, A. M. (2006). La asociación discursiva de terrorismo e inmigración. Un ejemplo de incomunicación intercultural. *Revista Internacional de Comunicación Audiovisual, Publicidad y Literatura, 1*(4), 259–277.

Barcelona, A. (2003). The cognitive theory of metaphor and metonymy. In A. Barcelona (Ed.) *Metaphor and metonymy at the crossroad* (pp. 1–31). Walter de Gruyter.

Barlas, A. (2019). *Believing women in Islam: Unreading patriarchal interpretations of the Qur'an*. University of Texas Press. https://www.researchgate.net/profile/Adis_Duderija/publication/477 39324_Believing_Women_in_Islam/links/5456f2690cf26d5090a968fb.pdf.

Barry, B. (2001). *Culture and equality: An Egalitarian critique of multiculturalism*. Harvard University Press.

Beary, D. (2014). Pro wrestling is fake, but its race problem isn't. *The Atlantic, Atlantic*.

Beck, G. (2015). *It is About Islam: Exposing the Truth About ISIS, Al Qaeda, Iran, and the Caliphate* (Vol. 3). Simon and Schuster.

Bhagwati, J. (2003). Borders beyond control. *Foreign Affairs, 82*, 98.

Bisin, A., Patacchini, E., Verdier, T., & Zenou, Y. (2016). Bend it like Beckham: Ethnic identity and integration. *European Economic Review, 90*, 146–164.

Borrmans M. (1999). Cultural dialogue and "Islamic Specificity". In G. M. Munoz (Ed.), *Islam, modernism and the West: Cultural and political relations at the end of the millennium*. IB Tauris.

Brah, A. (2005). *Cartographies of diaspora: Contesting identities*. Routledge.

Brah, A., & Phoenix, A. (2004). Ain't IA woman? Revisiting intersectionality. *Journal of international women's studies, 5*(3), 75–86.

Brake, M., & Bailey, R. V. (1980). *Radical social work and practice*. Sage.

Bucar, E. M. (2012). *The Islamic veil: A beginner's guide*. One world Publications.

Bull, P. (2000). New labour, new rhetoric? An analysis of the rhetoric of Tony Blair. Beyond public speech and symbols: Explorations in the rhetoric of politicians and the media, p. 1.

Bullock, K. (2002). *Rethinking Muslim women and the veil: Challenging historical & modern stereotypes*. IIIT.

Casanova, J. (2011). *Public religions in the modern world*. University of Chicago Press.

Césaire, A. (2006). *Discursos sobre el colonialismo* (Vol. 39). Ediciones Akal.

Cesarani, D., & Fulbrook, M. (1996). *Citizenship, nationality, and migration in Europe*. Psychology Press.

Contractor, S. (2012). *Muslim women in Britain: De-mystifying the Muslimah*. Routledge.

Cooke, M. (2002). Islamic feminism before and after September 11th. *Duke J. Gender L. & Pol'y, 9*, 227.

Corfixen, K. (2015). Flygtninge drejer af: Den sønderjyske motorvej er nu genåbnet. *Politiken*. Retrieved September 26, 2016 from http://politiken.dk/udland/fokus_int/Flygtningestroem/ECE 2834738/flygtninge-drejer-af-den-soenderjyske-motorvej-er-nu-genaabnet/.

Crenshaw, K. (1989). Demarginalizing the intersection of race and sex: A black feminist critique of antidiscrimination doctrine, feminist theory and antiracist politics University of Chicago Legal Forum, pp. 139–167.

Darvishpour, M. (2003). *Islamic feminism: Compromise or challenge to feminism*. University, Sociologiska institutionen.

Del Olmo, M. (2000). Los conversos españoles al Islam: de mayoría a minoría por la llamada de Dios. In *Anales del Museo Nacional de Antropología* (No. 7, pp. 13–40). Dirección General de Bellas Artes y de Conservación y Restauración de Bienes Culturales.

Del Olmo, M. (2002). *La utopía en el exilio* (Vol. 38). Editorial CSIC-CSIC Press.

Diem, R. A., & Berson, M. J. (2010). *Technology in retrospect: Social studies in the information age, 1984-2009.* IAP.

Dietz, M. G. (2003). Current controversies in feminist theory. *Annual Review of Political Science, 6*(1), 399–431.

Dijk, T. A. (1993). *Discourse and cognition in society.*

Dumont l. (1992). *Essays on individualism: Modern ideology in anthropological perspective.* Chicago: University of Chicago Press.

Düvell, F. (2006). The irregular migration dilemma: Keeping control, out of control or regaining control?. In *Illegal Immigration in Europe* (pp. 3–13). Palgrave Macmillan UK.

El-Madkouri. (1992) *Mujeres Árabe y Prensa Española: Representaciones de un Colectivo Migrante.* Asparkia (No. 1). Universitat Jaume I.

Engbersen, G., Guiraudon, V., & Joppke, C. (2001). The unanticipated consequences of Panopticon Europe. *Guiraudon V. et Joppke C., Controlling a new migration world, op. cit,* pp. 222–246.

Erickson, J. (2009). *Islam and postcolonial narrative.* Cambridge University Press.

Esposito, J. L. (1999). Clash of civilization? Contemporary images of Islam in the west. In G. M. Munoz (Ed.), *Islam, modernism and the West: cultural and political relations at the end of the millennium.* IB Tauris.

EU Commission. (2015). *Immigration in the EU.* Retrieved September 26, 2016 from http://ec.eur opa.eu/dgs/home-affairs/e-library/docs/infographics/immigration/migration-in-eu-infographic_ en.pdf.

Fassmann, H., Haller, M., & Lane, D. S. (Eds.). (2009). *Migration and mobility in Europe: Trends, patterns and control.* Edward Elgar Publishing.

Fauconnier, G., & Turner, M. (1998). Conceptual integration networks. *Cognitive Science, 22*(2), 133–187.

Fekete, L., & Sivanandan, A. (2009). *A suitable enemy: Racism, migration and Islamophobia in Europe.* Pluto Press.

Fernandez, J. W. (1986). *Persuasion and performance: The play of trops in culture.* Indiana University Press.

Fetzer, J. S., & Soper, J. C. (2005). *Muslims and the state in Britain, France, and Germany.* Cambridge University Press

Feyaerts, K. (2000). Refining the Inheritance Hypothesis: Interaction between metaphoric and metonymic hierarchies. In *Metaphor and metonymy at the crossroads. A cognitive perspective* (pp. 59–78).

Fischer, C. S. (1982). *To dwell among friends: Personal networks in town and city.* University of Chicago Press.

Forte, J. A. (2014). *An introduction to using theory in social work practice.* Routledge.

Forum, B. (No. 44, pp. 235–301). Međunarodni forum Bosna.

Freedman, J. (2007). Women, Islam and rights in Europe: Beyond a universalist/culturalist dichotomy. *Review of International Studies, 33*(01), 29–44.

García, B. L., & López, F. B. (2008). Visiones del Islam y la inmigración musulmana: Un intento de clasificación. In *La inmigración en la sociedad española: una radiografía multidisciplinar* (pp. 811–832). Ediciones Bellaterrra.

Givón, T. (2005). *Context as other minds: The pragmatics of sociality, cognition and communication.* John Benjamins Publishing.

Gordon, A. A. (1996). *Transforming capitalism and patriarchy: Gender and development in Africa.* Lynne Rienner Publishers.

Gottschalk, P., & Greenberg, G. (2008). *Islamophobia: Making Muslims the enemy.* Rowman & Littlefield.

Gunn, T. J. (2004). Religious freedom and Laïcité: A comparison of the United States and France. *Brigham Young University Law Review*, 419.

Haller, M., & Richter, R. (1994). *Toward a European nation. Political Trends in Europe-East and West, Centre and Periphery*. Armonk, NY.

Hammer, J. (2012). *American Muslim women, religious authority, and activism: More than a prayer*. University of Texas Press.

Härpe, J. (1995). Islamisk feminism. *Kvinnor och fundamentalism* (10), 26–28.

Harris, A. (1990). Race and essentialism in feminist legal theory. *Stanford Law Review, 42*, 581–616.

Hart, C. (2011). Moving beyond metaphor in the cognitive linguistic approach to CDA. *Critical discourse studies in context and cognition, 43*, 171–192.

Haser, V. (2003). *Metaphor in semantic change. Metaphor and metonymy at the crossroads* (pp. 171–194). Mouton de Gruyter.

Hassan, M. H. (2005). Localising political Islam for minority muslims (Vol. 5, p. 47) (CSRC Discussion Paper).

Henkel, H. (2009). Are Muslim women in Europe threatening the secular public sphere? *Social Anthropology, 17*(4), 471–473.

Heron, L. (2014). *Truth, Dare or Promise: girls growing up in the fifties*. Virago.

Hill, C. P. (1990). *Black feminist thought. Knowledge, consciousness, and the politics of empowerment*. Routledge.

Hirschmann, N. J. (2009). *The subject of liberty: Toward a feminist theory of freedom*. Princeton University Press.

Hollander, J. A., & Howard, J. A. (2000). Social psychological theories on social inequalities. *Social Psychology Quarterly*, 338–351.

Hooks, B. (1989). *Feminist theory: From margin to the center*. South End Press.

Jacobson, J. (2006). *Islam in transition: Religion and identity among British Pakistani youth*. Routledge.

Jakel, O. (1995). The metaphorical concept of mind: "Mental activities are manipulation.". In J. R. Taylor & R. MacLaury (Eds.), *Language and the cognitive construal of the world* (pp. 197–229). Mouton de Gruyter.

Jelen, T. G., Rozell, M. J., & Shally-Jensen, M. (Eds.). (2015). *American political culture: An encyclopedia [3 volumes]*. ABC-CLIO.

Johnson, T. M., & Zurlo G. A. (2014). The world by religion. In B. J. Grim, T. M. Johnson, V. Skirbekk, & G. A. Zurlo (Eds.), *Yearbook of international religious demography 2014*. Brill.

Joppke, C. (1999). How immigration is changing citizenship: A comparative view. *Ethnic and Racial Studies, 22*(4), 629–652.

Kalantry, S., & Pradhan, M. (2017). *Veil Bans in the European Court of Human Rights*. American Society of International Law.

Karamer, G. (1999). Techniques and values: Contemporary Muslim debates on Islam and democracy. In G. M. Munoz (Ed.), *Islam, modernism and the West: Cultural and political relations at the end of the millennium*. IB Tauris

Keddie, A. (2016). School autonomy as 'the way of the future' Issues of equity, public purpose and moral leadership. *Educational Management Administration & Leadership, 44*(5), 713–727.

Keddie, A. (2016): Disrupting (gendered) Islamophobia: The practice of feminist ijtihad to support the agency of young Muslim women. *Journal of Gender Studies*. https://doi.org/10.1080/095 89236.2016.1243047.

Kertzer, D. I. (1989). *Ritual, politics, and power*. Yale University Press.

Khader B. (1999). The Euro-mediterranean partnership: A singular approach to a plural mediterranean. In G. M. Munoz (Ed.), *Islam, modernism and the West: Cultural and political relations at the end of the millennium*. IB Tauris.

Khir Allah, G. (2010). Metaphor within-culture variation metaphors of "The Islamic Veil". "Female's Body" and "Cultural Integration" among the mainstream.

King, R. (2002). Towards a new map of European migration. *International Journal of Population Geography, 8*(2), 89–106.

Knauss, P. R. (1987). *The persistence of patriarchy: Class, gender, and ideology in twentieth century Algeria.* Greenwood Publishing Group.

Kogan, I. (2011). New immigrants—old disadvantage patterns? Labour market integration of recent immigrants into Germany. *International Migration, 49*(1), 91–117.

Kovecses, Z. (2015). *Where metaphors come from: Reconsidering context in metaphor.* Oxford University Press.

Krämer, G. (1999). Techniques and values: Contemporary Muslim debates on Islam and democracy. In *Modernism and the West: Cultural and political relations at the end of the millennium* (pp. 174–190).

La Barbera, M. C. (2012). Intersectional-gender and the Locationality of Women in Transit. In G. Bonifacio (Ed.), *Feminism and migration: Cross-cultural engagements* (pp. 17–31). Springer.

La Barbera, MC. (2015). Identity and migration: An introduction. In M. C. La Barbera (Ed.), *Identity and migration in Europe: Multidisciplinary perspectives* (pp. 1–13). Springer.

La Barbera, M. C. (2017). Interseccionalidad. *Eunomía: Revista en Cultura de la Legalidad, 12,* 91–198.

La Barbera, M. (2017). Intersectionality and its journeys: From counterhegemonic feminist theories to law of European multilevel democracy. *Investigationes Feministas, 8*(1), 131–149.

Lakoff, G. (1993). The contemporary theory of metaphor. In A. Ortony (Ed.), *Metaphor and thought* (2nd ed., pp. 202–251). Cambridge University Press.

Lakoff, G. (2004). *Don't think of an elephant! Know your values and frame the debate.* The Essential Guide for Progressives, Including Post-Election Updates.

Lakoff, G. (2014). *The all new don't think of an elephant! Know your values and frame the debate.* Chelsea Green Publishing.

Lakoff, G., Espenson, J., & Schwartz, A. (1991). *Master metaphor list.* Cognitive Linguistics Group.

Lane, J. E., Redissi, H., & Ṣaydāwī, R. (2009). *Religion and politics: Islam and Muslim civilization.* Ashgate Publishing, Ltd.

Lazreg, M. (2009). *Questioning the veil: Open letters to Muslim women.* Princeton University Press.

Leiken, R. S. (2005). Europe's angry Muslims. *Foreign Affairs,* 120–135.

Lewis, G. (1985). From deepest Kilburn. In L. Heron (Ed.), *Truth, dare or promise.*

Lewis, G. (2000) *Race, gender, social welfare.* Polity

López García, B., Bravo López, F., García Ortiz, P., Planet Contreras, A. I., & Ramírez Fernández, Á. (2004). Desarrollo y pervivencia de las redes de origen en la inmigración marroquí en España. *Hacia la actualización del "Atlas de la inmigración magrebí en España", Madrid, Observatorio Permanente de la Inmigración, Ministerio de Trabajo y Asuntos Sociales.*

Lugones, M. (2012). Subjetividad esclava, colonialidad de género, marginalidad y opresiones múltiples. In P. Montes (Ed.), *Pensando los feminismos en Bolivia* (pp. 129–139). Conexión Fondos de Emancipación.

Maataoui, M. E. M. (2006). El Otro entre Nosotros: el musulmán en la prensa. Medios de comunicación e inmigración, 97.

Magone, J. M. (2008). *Contemporary Spanish politics.* Routledge.

Mahmood, M. (2004). *Good Muslim, bad Muslim: America, the Cold War, and the roots of terror.* Pantheon.

Mahmood, S. (2001). Feminist theory, embodiment, and the docile agent: Some reflections on the Egyptian Islamic revival. *Cultural Anthropology, 16*(2), 202–236.

Malik, F. M. (2008). *What is Islam Who are the Muslims?* The Institution of Islamic Knowledge.

Mammo, T. (1999). *The paradox of Africas poverty: The role of indigenous knowledge, traditional practices and local institutions—The case of Ethiopia.* The Red Sea Press.

Médecins Sans Frontières. (2016). *Migration: European policies dramatically worsened the so-called 2015 "refugee crisis".* Retrieve September 26, 2016 from http://www.msf.org/article/migration-european-policies-dramatically-worsened-so-called-2015-"refugee-crisis".

Mernissi, F. (1985). *Beyond the veil: Male-female dynamics in Muslim society* (rev. ed.). London: Al Saqi.

268

Bibliography

Mernissi, F. (1987). *Beyond the veil: Male-female dynamics in modern Muslim society* (Vol. 423). Indiana University Press.

Mernissi, F. (1994). *Dreams of trespass: Tales of a harem girlhood*. Basic Books.

Meyer, J., Boli, J., Thomas, G., & Ramirez, F. (1997). World society and the Nation-State. *American Journal of Sociology, 103*(1), 144–181. Retrieved from http://www.jstor.org/stable/10.1086/231174.

Mohanty, C. T. (1988). Under Western eyes: Feminist scholarship and colonial discourses. *Feminist Review* (30), 61–88.

Mojab, S. (1995). Islamic feminism: Alternative or Contradiction. *Fireweed*, no. 47

Moors, A. (2009). The Dutch and the face-veil: The politics of discomfort. *Social Anthropology, 17*(4), 393–408.

Morgan, K. W. (1987). *Islam, the straight path: Islam interpreted by Muslims*. Motilal Banarsidass.

Muñoz, M. G., & Grosfoguel, R. (2012) (Eds.). *La islamofobia a debate: La genealogía del miedo al Islam y la construcción de los discursos antiislámicos*. Casa Arabe.

Norris, P., & Ronald, F. I. (2012). Muslim integration into Western cultures: Between origins and destinations. *Political Studies, 60*(2), 228–251.

Öberg, S. (1996). Spatial and economic factors in future South-North migration. In W. Lutz (Ed.), *The future population of the world: What can we assume today?* (pp. 336–357). Earthscan.

Okin, S. M. (1999). Is multiculturalism bad for women?" In J. Cohen, M. Howard, & M. C. Nussbaum (Eds.), *Is Multiculturalism Bad for Women?* (pp. 9–24). Princeton University Press.

Peters, R. (2014). *Islam and colonialism: The doctrine of jihad in modern history*. Walter de Gruyter GmbH & Co KG (original book published 1980).

Poptcheva, E. M. (2015). *EU legal framework on asylum and irregular immigration 'on arrival'* (PDF). European Parliamentary Research Service. Retrieved September 26, 2016 from http://www.europarl.europa.eu/RegData/etudes/BRIE/2015/551333/EPRS_BRI%282015%29551333_EN.pdf.

Rabasa, A., & Benard, C. (2014). *Eurojihad*. Cambridge University Press.

Ramadan, T. (1998). *Immigration, integration and cooperation policies: Europe's Muslims find a place for themselves* (pp. 3–4). Le Monde Diplomatique.

Read, G. (2007). The politics of veiling in comparative perspective. *The Official Journal of Sociology of Religion, A Quarterly Review, 68*(3), v–ix.

Reese, S. D. (2007). The framing project: A bridging model for media research revisited. *Journal of Communication, 57*(1), 148–154.

Ritcher, D. (2007). Religious garments at public schools. In W. Brugger, M. Karayanni, & M. M. Karayanni (Eds.), *Separation systems: France and the United States of America. "Religion in the public sphere: a comparative analysis of German, Israeli, American and International Law"* (Vol. 190). Springer.

Riyad, N. (2004). *Calling Muslim to support the ban on Hijab; "Intellectual" sophistry or ignorant "philosophy"?* http://www.occri.org.uk/Articles/callingMuslims.pdf.

Roy, O. (2004). *Globalized Islam: The search for a new ummah*. Columbia University Press.

Sabbati, G., Poptcheva, A. M., & Saliba S. (2015). *Asylum in the EU: Facts and figures* (PDF). European Parliamentary Research Service. Retrieved September 26, 2016 from http://www.europarl.europa.eu/RegData/etudes/BRIE/2015/551332/EPRS_BRI%282015%29551332_EN.pdf.

Said, E. W. (2002). *Orientalismo*. 1990 (M. L. Fuentes, Trans.). Debate.

Salas, A. (2012). *Aportaciones del feminismo islámico como feminismo poscolonial para la emancipación de las mujeres musulmanas*. Revisión bibliográfica de fuentes. Trabajo de fin de Máster, Máster universitario en estudios feministas.

Salt J. (2000, November 10–11), Europe's migration field, Workshop on demographic and cultural specificity and integration of migrants organized by the Network for Integrated European Population Studies. Bingen.

Sandikcioglu, E. (2000). More metaphorical warfare in the Gulf: Orientalist frames in news coverage. *Metaphor and Metonymy at the Crossroads: A Cognitive Perspective, 30*, 299.

Saussure, F. D. (1983). *Course in general linguistics* (R. Harris, Trans.). Duckworth.

Scheherazade, B. (2015). *Amnesty international calls for Spain to Cease cooperation with Morocco on migration policy.* Morocco World News. Retrieved September 26, 2016 from http://www.moroccoworldnews.com/2015/11/172878/amnesty-international-calls-on-spain-to-cease-cooperation-with-morocco-on-migration-policy/.

Schiffauer, W. (2004). *Civil enculturation: Nation-state, schools and ethnic difference in four European countries.* Berghahn Books.

Schönwälder, K. (1996). *Migration, refugees and ethnic plurality as issues of public and political debates in (West) Germany.* na. In Cesarani and fulbrook 1996.

Scott, J. W. (2005). Symptomatic politics: The banning of Islamic head scarves in French public schools. *French Politics, Culture & Society, 23*(3), 106–127.

Sibai, S. A. (2010b). 'Sometimes I am Spanish and sometimes not': A study of the identity and integration of Spanish Muslim women. *Research in Comparative and International Education, 5*(2), 185–204.

Sibai, S. A. (2015). Narratives of Spanish Muslim women on the hijab as a Tool to assert identity. In *Identity and migration in Europe: Multidisciplinary perspectives* (pp. 251–268). Springer International Publishing.

Steven, M. (2010). *Christianity and party politics: Keeping the faith.* Routledge.

Strauss, C., & N. Quinn (1997). *A cognitive theory of Cultural Meaning.* Cambridge University Press.

Suad, J., & Afsaneh, N. (2005). *Encyclopedia of women & Islamic cultures: Family, body, sexuality and health* (Vol. 3, p. 174). Netherlands.

Tannen, D. (1994). *Gender and discourse.* Oxford University Press.

The Economist. (2016). *Europe's migrants crisis: Forming an orderly queue.* Retrieved September 26, 2016 from http://www.economist.com/news/briefing/21690066-europe-desperately-needs-control-wave-migrants-breaking-over-its-borders-how.

Thomassen, L. (2012). *The politics of the hijab at the European Court of Human Rights.* APSA 2012 Annual Meeting Paper.

Thompson, W. C. (2015). *Western Europe 2015-2016.* Rowman & Littlefield.

Tilley, C. Y. (1999). *Metaphor and material culture.* Blackwell Publisher Inc.

Townson, D. (1990). *La España musulmana* (Vol. 19). Ediciones AKAL.

Townson, N. (2015). Anticlericalism and secularization: A European exception? In N. Townson (Ed.), *Is Spain different? A comparative look at the 19th and 20th centuries.* Sussex Academic PressTozy Mohamed. Islamism and some of its perception of the west. In Muñoz, G. M. (Ed.). (1999). *Islam, modernism and the West: Cultural and political relations at the end of the millennium.* IB Tauris.

Vakulenko, A. (2007). Islamic headscarves' and the European convention on human rights: An intersectional perspective. *Social & Legal Studies, 16*(2), 183–199.

Van Dijk, T. (2007). El racismo y la prensa en España. *Discursos periodísticos y procesos migratorios, San Sebastián, España: Gakoa Liburuak.*

Van Dijk, T. (2008). *Discourse and power.* Palgrave Macmillan.

Wadud, A. (2006). *Inside the gender Jihad: Women's reform in Islam.* Oneworld.

Waliño, D., & Innerarity, C. (2013). *Las actitudes de los españoles hacia el islam y su reproducción en la prensa escrita.* XI Congreso Español de Sociología, Madrid, Sociología de las Migraciones.

Walker, T. (2016). *Shariᶜa councils and Muslim women in Britain: Rethinking the role of power and authority.* Brill.

Werbner, P. (2005). Islamophobia: Incitement to religious hatred–legislating for a new fear? *Anthropology Today, 21*(1), 5–9.

Williams, R. H., & Vashi, G. (2007). Hijab and American Muslim women: Creating the space for autonomous selves. *Sociology of Religion, 68*(3), 269–287.

Wodak, R. (2006). Mediation between discourse and society: Assessing cognitive approaches in CDA. *Discourse Studies, 8*(1), 179–190.

Yegenoglu, M. (1998). *Colonial fantasies: Towards a feminist reading of Orientalism.* Cambridge University Press.

Yurdakul, G. (2015). What is veiling? *Sociology of Religion, 76*(4), 482–484.
Zettle, R. D., Hayes, S. C., Barnes-Holmes, D., & Biglan, A. (2016). *The Wiley handbook of contextual behavioral science*. Wiley.

Annex 1

Spanish Articles

Abad, R. (2007a). *A la Asamblea con el 'hiyab'*. http://elpais.com/diario/2007/06/17/espana/118 2031209_850215.html. 17 June 2007.

Abad, R. (2007b). *"Este velo es para siempre" Vuelven a clase las alumnas del colegio ceutí obligado por Educación a aceptar el 'hiyab'*. http://elpais.com/diario/2007/10/11/sociedad/119 2053613_850215.html. 11 October 2007.

Álvarez, P. (2011a). *A clase con el velo*. http://sociedad.elpais.com/sociedad/2011/10/18/actualidad/ 1318888806_850215.html. 18 October 2011.

Álvarez, P. (2011b). *Mi velo sí entra en clase*. http://elpais.com/diario/2011/10/19/madrid/131902 3459_850215.html. 19 October 2011.

Álvarez, P. (2011c). *Renunciar al velo islámico sería como quitarme la piel*. http://elpais.com/dia rio/2011/10/23/sociedad/1319320802_850215.html. 23 October 2011.

Álvarez, P. (2013). *El Tribunal Superior avala Al centro que veto a una Alumna por llevar el velo*. http://ccaa.elpais.com/ccaa/2013/04/02/madrid/1364932389_921756.html. 2 April 2013.

Álvarez, P., & Cembrero, I. (2010a). *Estalla el debate sobre legislar el uso del pañuelo islámico en clase*. http://elpais.com/diario/2010/04/22/sociedad/1271887203_850215.html. 22 April 2010.

Álvarez, P., & Cembrero, I. (2010b). *Mi hija seguira en el mismo instituto y con hijab* http://www.elpais.com/articulo/sociedad/hija/seguira/mismo/instituto/hiyab/elpepu soc/20100423elpepisoc_3/Tes. 23 April 2010.

Álvarez, P., & Garriga, J. (2010c). *Aguirre ficha de asesor al director del centro que vetó el velo de Najwa*. http://elpais.com/diario/2010/05/25/sociedad/1274738410_850215.html. 25 May 2010.

Álvarez, P., & Cembrero, I. (2010d). *La justicia examinará la expulsión de Najwa de un colegio por llevar 'hiyab'*. http://elpais.com/diario/2010/09/03/sociedad/1283464807_850215.html. 3 September 2010.

Ayuso, B. (2016). *De María a Maryam: así se convirtió al islam una española de 29 años*. http:// politica.elpais.com/politica/2016/06/23/actualidad/1466664764_761081.html. 16 July 2016.

Barik Edidi, Z. (2009). *Encuentro*. http://www.elmundo.es/encuentros/invitados/2009/11/3898/ index.html. 11 November 2009.

Belaza, M. C. (2010). *El Supremo decidirá sobre el uso del "hiyab" en los juicios*. http://elpais. com/diario/2010/01/15/sociedad/1263510007_850215.html. 15 January 2010.

Belvar, M., & Blasco, P. (2010). *El instituto de Pozuelo no modifica sus normas e impide a Najwa ir con veil*. http://www.elmundo.es/elmundo/2010/04/20/madrid/1271786689.html. 21 April 2010.

Bohorquez, L. (2016). *Que me obliguen a quitarme el velo es como arrancarme mi propia piel*. http://politica.elpais.com/politica/2016/12/20/actualidad/1482237712_030858.html. 20 December 2016.

Caballero, C. (2010). *Un velo y una toca*. http://www.elpais.com/articulo/andalucia/velo/toca/elp epiespand/20100424elpand_10/Tes. 24 April 2010.

Carbajos, A. (2008). *Más musulmanas con velo. ¿Porque quieren?* http://www.elpais.com/articulo/ sociedad/musulmanas/velo/quieren/elpepisoc/20080628elpepisoc_1/Tes. 28 June 2008.

Carranco, R. (2010). *No me quito el 'hiyab' porque no quiero*. http://elpais.com/diario/2010/04/22/ sociedad/1271887206_850215.html. 22 April 2010.

De Ganuza, C. R. (2008). *El Partido Popular propondrá prohibir el uso del velo en todas las escuelas*. http://www.elmundo.es/elmundo/2008/02/08/espana/1202448607.html. 8 February 2008.

Del Barrio, A. (2008). *De la Vega desautoriza a Aído y dice que el Gobierno respeta la tradición del velo islámico.* http://www.elmundo.es/elmundo/2008/06/26/espana/1214475820.html. 27 June 2008.

Del Barrio, A. (2010a). *Los marroquíes exigen la intervención de la Comunidad en el caso de Najwa.* http://www.elmundo.es/elmundo/2010/04/16/madrid/1271421715.html. 16 April 2010.

Del Barrio, A. (2010b). *El velo no me limita para trabajar, que no te limita a ti para contratarme.* http://www.elmundo.es/elmundo/2010/12/21/espana/1292933868.html. 22 December 2010.

Del Barrio, A. (2010c). *Los musulmanes anuncian acciones legales contra el colegio de Pozuelo.* http://www.elmundo.es/elmundo/2010/04/21/madrid/1271852171.html. 21 April 2010.

Espinosa, A. (2010). *En mi clase había una monja.* http://elpais.com/diario/2010/04/23/sociedad/1271973602_850215.html. 23 April 2010.

Etxenike, L. (2004). *Tirar de la manta.* http://elpais.com/diario/2004/02/08/paisvasco/1076272805_850215.html. 8 February 2004.

Farreras, C. (2016). *Los Nuevos Significados del velo.* http://www.lavanguardia.com/vida/20160717/403268947566/universitarias-musulmanas-velo-hiyab-expresion-religion.html. 18 July 2016.

Figueras, A., & Piantadosi, G. (2011a). *Me echaron de un examen y del instituto por llevar el 'hiyab'.* http://www.elmundo.es/elmundo/2011/09/30/madrid/1317407926.html. 3 October 2011.

Figueras, A. (2011b). *La menor expulsada de un examen por el 'hiyab': 'Dicen que me lo invento y me hago la víctima.* http://www.elmundo.es/elmundo/2011/10/04/madrid/1317750847.html. 6 October 2011.

Figueras, A. (2011c). *El instituto que echó a una niña por llevar 'hiyab' acepta que pueda seguir utilizándolo.* http://www.elmundo.es/elmundo/2011/10/17/madrid/1318888325.html. 19 October 2011.

Figueras, A. (2011d). *El director que prohibió ir con el velo a clase podría ser acusado de prevaricación.* http://www.elmundo.es/elmundo/2011/10/27/castillayleon/1319714393.html. 27 October 2011.

Figueras, A. (2012). *La angustia de decir que eres Musulmán.* http://www.elmundo.es/elmundo/2012/04/27/espana/1335521507.html. 29 April 2012.

Figueras, A. (2015). *'¿Por qué se me cuestiona por abrazar esta fe? El islam no es el velo ni el IS ni ningún tipo de terrorismo'.* http://www.elmundo.es/espana/2015/06/24/55797914ca4741a6268b457d.html. 30 June 2015.

Galafate, C. (2010). *Crean un grupo en Facebook para apoyar a Najwa.* http://www.elmundo.es/elmundo/2010/04/23/madrid/1272044565.html. 23 April 2010.

Galarraga, N. (2010). *¿Velo de sumisión o de rebeldía?* http://elpais.com/diario/2010/04/23/sociedad/1271973601_850215.html. 23 April 2010.

Gallego-Díaz, S. (2010). *El velo no merece una ley.* http://elpais.com/diario/2010/04/25/domingo/1272166236_850215.html. 25 April 2010.

Iglesias, N. (2007). *La Generalitat obliga a admitir en clase a una menor con 'hiyab'.* http://elpais.com/diario/2007/10/02/sociedad/1191276010_850215.html. 10 February 2007.

Juárez, A. S. (2015). *Musulmanas y tan españolas como vosotras.* http://www.elmundo.es/yodona/2015/02/28/54ef5340ca4741216d8b4578.html. 28 February 2015.

Lidón, I. (2016). *Vetada en el instituto por su hiyab: Me dijeron: o te lo quitas o te das baja.* http://www.elmundo.es/comunidad-valenciana/2016/09/16/57dc38c2ca4741b51d8b4676.html 18 September 2016.

Meneses, R. (2010). *Cual es el significado y el origen del Hiyab.* http://www.elmundo.es/elmundo/2010/04/21/madrid/1271853528.html. 22 April 2010.

Moliner, E. (2004). *A favor y en contra.* http://elpais.com/diario/2004/09/12/domingo/1094957850_850215.html. 12 September 2004.

Montero, R. (2010). *Ahí le duele.* http://elpais.com/diario/2010/04/27/ultima/1272319201_850215.html. 27 April 2010.

Muñoz, G. M. (2010). *Esto alimenta a la derecha islamófoba.* http://elpais.com/diario/2010/04/22/sociedad/1271887205_850215.html. 22 April 2010.

Obelleiro, P. (2011a). *La familia de la niña de Arteixo invoca una norma estatal que permite el velo.* http://elpais.com/diario/2011/02/26/galicia/1298719096_850215.html. 26 February 2011.

Obelleiro, P. (2011b). *Educación avala la prohibición del velo en clase a una niña.* http://elpais.com/diario/2011/02/25/galicia/1298632692_850215.html. 25 February 2011.

Obelleiro, P. (2011c). *La Xunta anula la sanción a la niña del velo por un defecto formal.* http://elpais.com/diario/2011/03/11/sociedad/1299798012_850215.html. 11 March 2011.

Obelleiro, P. (2011d). *La 'niña del velo', excluida de la fiesta de fin de curso.* http://elpais.com/diario/2011/06/23/sociedad/1308780009_850215.html 23 June 2011.

Obelleiro, P. (2011e). *El director del colegio de Arteixo impide a la niña del 'hiyab' entrar a recoger las notas.* http://elpais.com/diario/2011/06/23/galicia/1308824289_850215.html. 23 June 2011.

Obelleiro, P. (2012). *Declara ante el juez el director que prohibió el velo islámico.* http://elpais.com/diario/2011/06/23/galicia/1308824289_850215.html. 13 January 2012.

Peral, M. (2010). *Permitir el 'hiyab', facultad de cada juez.* http://www.elmundo.es/elmundo/2010/02/09/espana/1265687043.html. 9 February 2010.

Quelart, R. (2011). *He conocido a mujeres muy felices detrás del velo.* http://www.lavanguardia.com/salud/20111212/54239960536/beatriz-goyoaga-entrevista-meditacion-velo.html. 12 December 2011.

Sahuquillo, M. R. (2008). *Integración, si, asimilación, no.* http://www.elpais.com/articulo/sociedad/Integracion/asimilacion/elpepisoc/20080216elpepisoc_1/Tes. 16 February 2008.

Sotero, P. D. (2010). *Gabilondo alerta de que la polémica del velo puede terminar en 'segregación'.* http://www.elmundo.es/elmundo/2010/04/27/espana/1272367212.html. 27 April 2010.

Sotero, P. D., & Bécares, R. (2010a). *El Ministerio de Educación apela a respetar las creencias de los alumnos.* http://www.elmundo.es/elmundo/2010/04/16/madrid/1271434711.html. 16 April 2010.

Velasco, I. (2016). *Tengo el derecho a trabajar con velo.* http://www.elmundo.es/sociedad/2016/06/10/5756a1bd468aeb14228b45b8.html. 10 June 2016.

Annex 2

English Articles

Abbasi, H. (2004). *Trapped or liberated by the hijab?* https://www.theguardian.com/world/2004/jan/21/gender.religion. 21 January 2004.

Akbar, A. (2010a). *The many faces behind the veil* (Introduction). http://www.independent.co.uk/news/uk/this-britain/the-many-faces-behind-the-veil-1865772.html. 13 January 2010.

Akbar, A. (2010b). *The many faces behind the veil* with Nursat Husain. http://www.independent.co.uk/news/uk/this-britain/the-many-faces-behind-the-veil-1865772.html. 13 January 2010.

Akbar, A. (2010c). *The many faces behind the veil* with Rajnaara Akhtar. http://www.independent.co.uk/news/uk/this-britain/the-many-faces-behind-the-veil-1865772.html. 13 January 2010.

Akbar, A. (2010d). *The many faces behind the veil* with Shelina Zahra JanMohamaed. http://www.independent.co.uk/news/uk/this-britain/the-many-faces-behind-the-veil-1865772.html. 13 January 2010.

Akbar, A. (2010e). *The many faces behind the veil* with Soha Sheikh. http://www.independent.co.uk/news/uk/this-britain/the-many-faces-behind-the-veil-1865772.html. 13 January 2010.

Akhtar, R. (2004). *Britain for me is a safe place.* https://www.theguardian.com/uk/2004/nov/30/islamandbritain1. 30 November 2004.

Alam, F. (2005). *We must move beyond the hijab.* https://www.theguardian.com/education/2005/nov/29/highereducation.uk. 29 Novenber 2005.

Alibhai-Brown, Y. (2015). *As a Muslim woman, I see the veil as a rejection of progressive values.* https://www.theguardian.com/commentisfree/2015/mar/20/muslim-woman-veil-hijab. 20 March 2015.

Aly, R. (2010). *Hijab-wearing women rock!* http://www.theguardian.com/world/2010/feb/14/why-muslim-women-like-hard-rock. 14 February 2010.

Aly, R. (2015). *How the hijab-and H&M- are reshaping mainstream British culture.* http://www.theguardian.com/commentisfree/2015/sep/28/hijab-h-and-m-mainstream-culture-great-british-bake-off-diversity. 30 September 2015.

Aslam, S. (2014). *To hijab or not to hijab- A Muslim businesswoman's view.* http://www.theguardian.com/uk/the-northerner/2012/dec/10/hijab-muslims-women-islam-business-bradford-niqab-burka. 21 May 2014.

Aziz, S. (2014). *Laugh, not at my hijab please.* http://www.theguardian.com/theobserver/she-said/2014/apr/01/laugh-not-at-my-hijab-please. 1 April 2014.

Bennett, C. (2004). *Why should we defend the veil?* http://www.theguardian.com/world/2004/jan/22/gender.schoolsworldwide. 22 January 2004.

Bentham, M., & Davis, A. (2007). *Hairdresser sued in row about headscarf* http://www.standard.co.uk/news/hairdresser-sued-in-row-about-headscarf-6657648.html. 8 November 2007.

Bunglawala, I. (2007). *Has the veil been banned?* http://www.theguardian.com/commentisfree/2007/mar/20/hastheveilbeenbanned. 20 March 2007.

Burchill, J. (2011). *Carla Bruni is standing up to the stoners. Lauren Booth just covers up for them.* http://www.independent.co.uk/voices/columnists/julie-burchill/julie-burchill-carla-bruni-is-standing-up-to-the-stoners-lauren-booth-just-covers-up-for-them-2067119.html. 4 April 2011.

Byrne, C. (2005). *Heard the one about the Mickey Mouse hijab?* http://www.independent.co.uk/news/media/heard-the-one-about-the-mickey-mouse-hijab-320202.html. 17 October 2005.

Carter, H. (2009). *Guest asked whether her hijab meant she was a terrorist, court told.* https://www.theguardian.com/uk/2009/dec/08/hijab-hotel-alleged-abuse-trial. 8 December 2009.

Cassidy, S. (2004). *Teacher in headscarf case cleared of racial assault on Muslim Girl.* http://www.independent.co.uk/news/education/education-news/teacher-in-headscarf-case-cleared-of-racial-assault-on-muslim-girl-63962.html. 12 March 2004.

Cassidy, S. (2005). *Schoolgirl banned from wearing Muslim dress wins appeal.* http://www.independent.co.uk/news/education/education-news/schoolgirl-banned-from-wearing-muslim-dress-wins-appeal-527023.html. 3 March 2005.

Chowdhury, S. (2005). *We have more urgent issues to fight for than dress codes.* http://www.independent.co.uk/voices/commentators/shamim-chowdhury-we-have-more-urgent-issues-to-fight-for-than-dress-codes-4576.html. 4 March 2005.

Cllr Khan, R. (2006). *The hijab does not restrict it-it liberates.* https://www.theguardian.com/lifeandstyle/2009/apr/07/letters-hijab-islam-women. 7 April 2009.

Dear, P. (2004). *Women vow to protect Muslim hijab.* http://news.bbc.co.uk/2/hi/uk_news/3805733.stm. 14 June 2004.

Dhumieres, M. (2013). *Why is the right of Muslim women to wear the veil still so controversial in France?* http://www.independent.co.uk/voices/comment/why-is-the-right-of-muslim-women-to-wear-the-veil-still-so-controversial-in-france-8575052.html. 16 April 2013.

Elkin, S. (2013). *Common sense and respect for children in hijabs, please.* http://www.independent.co.uk/voices/comment/common-sense-and-respect-for-children-in-hijabs-please-8437433.html. 03 January 2013.

England, C. (2016, October 18). Muslim women in hijab are assaulted by man who tried to pull off headscarf in central London. *The Independent.* http://www.independent.co.uk/news/uk/home-news/muslim-woman-attacked-london-oxford-street-hate-crime-hijab-assault-a7367696.html.

Guest, K., & Davies, M. W. (2005). *The Muslims next door.* http://www.independent.co.uk/news/uk/this-britain/focus-the-muslims-next-door-527359.html. 6 March 2005.

Jones, E. C. (2005). *Muslim girls unveil their fears.* http://news.bbc.co.uk/2/hi/programmes/this_world/4352171.stm. 28 March 2005.

Kaleeli, H. (2012). *Sports hijabs help Muslim women to Olympic success.* https://www.theguardian.com/sport/the-womens-blog-with-jane-martinson/2012/jul/23/sports-hijabs-muslim-women-olympics. 23 July 2012.

Khaleeli, H. (2008). *The hijab goes high-fashion.* https://www.theguardian.com/lifeandstyle/2008/jul/28/fashion.women. 28 July 2008.

Khan, S. (2015). *It is not the hijab which holds women back, but prejudice.* http://www.telegraph.co.uk/culture/tvandradio/great-british-bake-off/11919553/Its-not-the-hijab-which-holds-women-back-but-intolerance-and-prejudice.html. 8 October 2015.

Kossaibati, J. (2009). *It is a wrap!* https://www.theguardian.com/lifeandstyle/2009/mar/30/fashion-hijab-muslim-women. 30 March 2009.

Lacey, H. (2004). *Dressed to impress.* http://www.independent.co.uk/news/education/education-news/dressed-to-impress-51309.html. 12 August 2004. (BH33) (Lacey 2004).

Malik, M. (2006). *This veil fixation is doing Muslim women no favors.* https://www.theguardian.com/commentisfree/2006/oct/19/religion.immigration. 19 October 2006.

Marin, M. (2004). *Cry freedom and accept the Muslim headscarf.* https://www.thetimes.co.uk/article/comment-minette-marrin-cry-freedom-and-accept-the-muslim-headscarf-tcxvm85lhqd. 1 February 2004.

Marrison, S. (2011). *The Islamification of Britain: Record numbers embrace Muslim faith.* http://www.independent.co.uk/news/uk/home-news/the-islamification-of-britain-record-numbers-embrace-muslim-faith-2175178.html. 4 January 2011.

Melville, K. (2009). *Muslim patriarchy served well by hijab.* https://www.theguardian.com/world/2009/apr/04/hijab-niqab-islam-muslims. 4 April 2009.

Mortimer, C. (2015). *Mariah Idrissi: H&M's first hijab-wearing model says her work 'isn't immodest'.* http://www.independent.co.uk/news/uk/home-news/mariah-idrissi-hms-first-hijab-wearing-model-says-her-work-isnt-immodest-a6673901.html. 30 September 2015.

Mursaleen, S. (2010). *The power behind the veil.* https://www.theguardian.com/commentisfree/belief/2010/jan/25/burqa-ban-veil-sarkozy-ukip. 25 January 2010.

Orr, D. (2005). *Blairism is simply Thatcherism administered by do-gooders.* http://www.independent.co.uk/voices/commentators/deborah-orr/blairism-is-simply-thatcherism-administered-by-do-gooders-527246.html. 5 March 2005.

Penketh, A. (2013). *Call for headscarf ban at universities to reignite Islamic debate in France.* http://www.independent.co.uk/news/world/europe/call-for-headscarf-ban-at-universities-to-reignite-islamic-debate-in-france-8748950.html. 6 August 2013.

Perves, S. (2013). *Mishal Husain and the Veil: What the Daily Mail was really trying to say.* https://www.theguardian.com/uk-news/the-northerner/2013/oct/08/mishal-husain-veil-daily-mail. 8 October 2013.

Riddell, M. (2003). *Veiled threats.* https://www.theguardian.com/world/2003/dec/14/religion.britishidentity. 4 December 2003.

Sanghani, R. (2015a). *H&M advert features first Muslim Model in a hijab (finally).* http://www.telegraph.co.uk/women/womens-life/11898632/HandM-advert-features-first-Muslim-model-in-a-hijab-finally.html. 29 September 2015.

Sanghani, R. (2015b). *Armistice Day: Great British Bake off winner Nadiya Hussain wears 'poppy hijab'.* http://www.telegraph.co.uk/women/womens-life/11988184/Armistice-Day-2015-Great-British-Bake-Off-winner-Nadiya-Hussain-wears-poppy-hijab.html. 11 November 2015.

Smith, J. (2004). *What lies beneath the veil.* http://www.independent.co.uk/voices/commentators/joan-smith/what-lies-beneath-the-veil-8833948.html. 25 January 2004.

Smith, J. (2006a). *The veil is a feminist issue.* http://www.independent.co.uk/voices/commentators/joan-smith/joan-smith-the-veil-is-a-feminist-issue-419119.html. 8 October 2006.

Smith, J. (2006b). Our schools are no place for jilbab. Or for Creationists. http://www.independent.co.uk/voices/commentators/joan-smith/joan-smith-our-schools-are-no-place-for-the-jilbab-or-for-the-creationists-6105619.html. 26 March 2006.

Takolia, N. (2010). *The hijab has liberated me from society expectations of women.* https://www.theguardian.com/commentisfree/2012/may/28/hijab-society-women-religious-political. 28 May 2012.

Walter, N. (2004). *When the veil means freedom.* https://www.theguardian.com/world/2004/jan/20/france.schoolsworldwide1. 20 January 2004.

Ware, J. (2015). *Muslim nursery worker loses appeal to wear jilbab gown at work because it is a 'tripping hazard'*. http://www.independent.co.uk/news/uk/home-news/muslim-nursery-worker-loses-appeal-to-wear-jilbab-at-work-because-it-is-a-tripping-hazard-10317739.html. 13 June 2015.

Wyatt, C. (2003). *Liberty, equality and the headscarf*. http://news.bbc.co.uk/2/hi/programmes/from_our_own_correspondent/3334881.stm. 20 December 2003.

Wyatt, C. (2004). *French headscarf ban opens rifts*. http://news.bbc.co.uk/2/hi/europe/3478895.stm. 11 February 2004.

Printed in Great Britain
by Amazon

44346120R00163